# REPORTING NUCLEAR PAKISTAN
## Security Perceptions and the Indian Press

# REPORTING NUCLEAR PAKISTAN

## Security Perceptions and the Indian Press

**Teresa Joseph**

Reference Press

4831/24, Ansari Road, Darya Ganj,
New Delhi-110002
Tel. : 23260807, 41563444
Fax : 011-41563334
E-mail: info@essessreference.com
url:http://www.essessreference.com

**Reference Press**
4831/24, Ansari Road,
Darya Ganj,
New Delhi-110 002.

Tel.: 23260807, 41563444
Fax: 41563334
E-mail: info@essessreference.com
www.essessreference.com



**Rs.1100/-**



**First Published - 2009**

ISBN: 978-81-8405-044-8

*Cover Design by Patch Creative Unit*

Published By Reference Press and printed at Salasar Imaging Systems

PRINTED IN INDIA

# Contents

# Preface

The mass media have long been recognised as a major instrument of social and political change. In an age of information revolution the role of the media is indisputable. It is primarily through the media that information is disseminated, images are projected and opinions are shaped. This has obvious implications for all aspects of social life, particularly in the context of state policies. Policy-makers turn to the media for information and opinion, as well as for support to legitimise their own policies. Although the mass media form an integral part of the democratic processes of any society, the quality of information being disseminated by the media often determines the behaviour of social and political structures. This is particularly relevant in the context of the media's role in shaping perceptions of security/insecurity. The media even set the parameters of security in some countries.

Traditionally, 'security' has been viewed solely from the perspective of the State and military-strategic threats. As such, military-strategic means were advanced to achieve security. However, there is a growing realisation today that security needs to be viewed from a larger societal perspective, focusing on economic, social, political and environmental concerns. In so far as the approaches to the concept of security are vast and varied, the manner in which threats are perceived and projected is of crucial significance. Herein comes the role of the media. The projection of images of security/insecurity could have serious implications for the formulation or justification of policies in the realms of security and defence. The manner in which issues are framed by the media could help to either reinforce and legitimise the policies of the government or bring about change in existing policies.

This book is a result of several years of my observation and study of the Indian press. During a study on human rights violations in Kashmir, I found that while human rights organisations at the national and international level documented, in detail, instances of human rights violations by militants as well as security forces in Kashmir, the Indian press, by and large, tended to reinforce a state security perspective. The press seemed to project the government's position that most reports of violations were the result of propaganda by Pakistan and the militants of Kashmir. There was an underlying projection of Pakistan as a major threat, especially in the reporting of its defence and foreign policies. There was a reflection of government perspectives – both in times of conflict and peace building. These observations were substantiated by my content analysis of the coverage of Pakistan by the Indian print media (Joseph, 1993), as well as my study on the Indian press coverage of human rights violations in Kashmir (Joseph, 2000).

A major persisting concern that has kept me engaged all these years, has been the 'security problematique' – what constitutes security, how threat perceptions are formulated and sustained, and what role the mass media tend to play in the realm of security. This book is the culmination of my research into these questions relating to the Indian press. It essentially examines the concept of security and the interrelationship between threat perceptions and the mass media, taking the South Asian conflict scenario as a case in point.

A persistent trend in the relations between India and Pakistan has been the enduring nature of their threat perceptions. Threat perceptions and militarisation in the region have reinforced each other, thus forming major obstacles to peace and development in the subcontinent. The adversarial relations between the two countries are sustained by the images they have of each other. Despite the emergence of new generations on both sides of the border, these images continue to persist, albeit at varying levels of intensity. Evidently, perceptions and mindsets of the people are an underlying factor in the relations between India and Pakistan, and are fundamental to an understanding of bilateral relations. Decades of mutual hostility has resulted in the tendency for each side to take for granted the aggressive designs of the 'other'. The mass media have, in turn, over the years played an important role in sustaining and reinforcing these images, and in exacerbating the perception of threat from each other.

This study analyses the nature of the security discourse in the Indian press focusing on the coverage of Pakistan and its nuclear programme. It provides insights into the role of the Indian print media in securitising or shaping threat perceptions of Pakistan. In this process it throws light on the role of the press with regard to official government policy towards Pakistan as well as in sustaining India's own nuclear policy.

The book is divided into five chapters. The first

chapter provides a theoretical background to the study, contextualising security perceptions and the mass media. It examines the various approaches to the concept of security and securitisation, and the role of the mass media. The second chapter surveys the discourses on security in South Asia, the nature of the mainstream Indian press and its underlying security perceptions, particularly with regard to the coverage of Pakistan. Indian perspectives on Pakistan's nuclear programme are examined in the third chapter. It focuses particularly on that of the government, political parties and the strategic community, which together constitute the dominant discourse on the issue. An insight into the voices of dissent on the issue is also provided. This sets the contextual background to understanding media coverage of the issue. The fourth chapter provides a historical review of Indian press coverage of Pakistan's nuclear programme. This review is interspersed with the approach of the press to nuclear weapons in general as well as India's nuclear policy over the years as this is essential for an understanding of the issue in perspective. Juxtaposed against the perspectives of the dominant discourse, the chapter provides clear indications of the role of the Indian press in the process of securitisation vis-à-vis Pakistan, and in sustaining India's own policy. The findings of the study are brought together in the fifth and concluding chapter, which provides an analysis of the study in its entirety, interlinking the theoretical questions with empirical evidence.

The study is based on the historical-analytical and content-analysis methods, utilising both primary as well as secondary sources. Content-analysis enables a systematic study of the content of communication. It helps to identify the ideological framework of the mass media, and to evaluate the values, motives and attitudes of identified texts. It is quantitative when it deals with the frequency of coverage, space devoted, sources of news and the trend of coverage, and is qualitative when it focuses on the actual matter spoken or printed and the nature of the content. This study emphasises a qualitative analysis, which is supplemented by quantitative data.

Studies have shown that English language dailies occupy a significant place in India, not only among the decision-makers, but also as opinion setters among the Indian language newspapers where issues of defence and foreign policy are concerned. The content-analysis in the fourth chapter initially makes a random survey of English language Indian newspapers up to May 1998. In order to facilitate a detailed quantitative as well as qualitative analysis, a study of three English language newspapers – *The Hindu, The Indian Express* and *The Times of India,* during a three month period from 1 May to 31 July 1998 was then undertaken. The selected newspapers were the largest circulated multi-edition dailies during this period, which was witness to an invigorated debate on threat perceptions and nuclear issues in the context of the nuclear tests in the subcontinent. The Thiruvananthapuram, Kochi and Mumbai editions respectively of these newspapers were selected for the study. Differences among the various editions of these newspapers are basically related to local news, which is adapted according to the particular region they serve, differences in national and international news coverage being marginal. The chapter further proceeds with a random survey of English language dailies throwing light on the basic trends in reporting Pakistan's nuclear programme in the years following the 1998 nuclear tests. The study attempts to systematically explore the linkages between the mass media and threat perceptions, providing insights into the role of the mass media in the process of securitisation.

This book would not have been possible without the help and support of a number of persons and institutions. Dr. K.M.Seethi, Director, School of International Relations and Politics, Mahatma Gandhi University, Kottayam has been a constant source of inspiration and encouragement and I am extremely indebted to him. This book has certainly been enriched by his guidance. I also thank other members of the faculty of the School of International Relations and Politics - Dr. G.P.Ramachandra, Dr. Raju K.Thadikaran, Dr. A.K.Ramakrishnan and Mr. Babu Jose. I am particularly grateful to Dr. M.V.Ramana of the Centre for Interdisciplinary Studies in Environment and Development, Bangalore, for all his help and encouragement. I acknowledge my gratitude to Dr. Pervaiz Iqbal Cheema of the Islamabad Policy Research Institute, Dr. Pervez Hoodbhoy and Dr. Syed Rifat Hussain of Quaid-e-Azam University, Islamabad; and Dr. Lawrence Prabhakar, Madras Christian College, Chennai for their various insights into this study. I thank the Regional Centre for Strategic Studies, Colombo, for the opportunity to participate in a workshop in Sri Lanka, on cooperative security in South Asia, which facilitated interaction with a number of scholars working in this realm. I also thank Rev. Sr. Jais, Principal of Alphonsa College, Pala and all my colleagues at Alphonsa College, especially those in the Department of Political Science. I express my gratitude to Shima, Shirley, Mini and Elizabeth for all their help and support.

I am also deeply indebted to my parents and other

members of the family. I particularly thank Thomas for his constant support and encouragement, but for which this work would not have been possible, and my little son Mathew for those welcome interventions. I owe a very special word of appreciation to my daughter Annie, whose contribution to the completion of this work has been invaluable.

*Teresa Joseph*

# List of Tables

# Abbreviations

| | |
|---|---|
| AEC | Atomic Energy Commission |
| AICC | All India Congress Committee |
| BJP | Bharatiya Janata Party |
| BJS | Bharatiya Jan Sangh |
| CBMs | Confidence Building Measures |
| CPI | Communist Party of India |
| CPI (M) | Communist Party of India (Marxist) |
| CTBT | Comprehensive Test Ban Treaty |
| DAE | Department of Atomic Energy |
| DND | Draft Nuclear Doctrine |
| DRDO | Defence Research and Development Organization |
| FMCT | Fissile Material Cut-off Treaty |
| HDR | Human Development Report |
| IAEA | International Atomic Energy Agency |
| IDSA | Institute for Defence Studies and Analyses |
| IIMC | Indian Institute of Mass Communication |
| INC | Indian National Congress |
| ISI | Inter Services Intelligence |
| MEA | Ministry of External Affairs |
| MHA | Ministry of Home Affairs |
| MoD | Ministry of Defence |

| | |
|---|---|
| MTCR | Missile Technology Control Regime |
| NPT | Nuclear Non-Proliferation Treaty |
| NSAB | National Security Advisory Board |
| NWFZ | Nuclear-Weapon-Free Zone |
| PAEC | Pakistan Atomic Energy Commission |
| PML | Pakistan Muslim League |
| PPP | Pakistan People's Party |
| POK | Pakistan Occupied Kashmir |
| RAW | Research and Analysis Wing |
| RSS | Rashtriya Swayamsevak Sangh |

# 1
# Contextualising Security and the Mass Media

The mass media play a critical role in society as a major source of information as well as a channel for articulating the views of different sections of society. Attitudes and opinions of people as well as their collective identity are largely shaped by the media. The media are clearly of crucial importance to the policy-makers of any society. This is particularly true in the context of issues relating to security/insecurity. The mass media play an important role in defining security and shaping threat perceptions. This has serious implications for formulating or sustaining policies relating to security in the national as well as international context. The ramifications of this become explicit when we take into account the changing trends in the security scenario. Recent years have witnessed the emergence of new ways of approaching the concept of security. While traditionally security was viewed from a state centric, military-strategic perspective, there are changing perceptions regarding the referent object of security and the manner in which security can be attained. There are calls to include economic, social, political and environmental concerns within its ambit. It is in this context that the role of the mass media in shaping perceptions of threat and security gains significance. The conceptual framework for this study necessitates an analysis of the concept of security and the role of the mass media in shaping perceptions of security.

## PROBLEMATISING SECURITY

Traditionally, security has been defined in relation to threats and most often in relation to threats to the state. But, because of its widespread use the term is inherently ambiguous. In the usage 'national security', its meaning is both taken for granted and imprecise, and this ambiguity is often considered a virtue. Michael Dillon points out that security "saturates the language of modern politics. Our political vocabularies reek of it and our political imagination is confined by it."[1] According to Arnold Wolfers, "security, in an objective sense, measures the absence of threats to acquired values, in a subjective sense, the absence of fear that such values will be attacked."[2] To Raimo Vayrynen, the idea of security can be viewed either as freedom from threats, or as a social construct. As a freedom from threats, it is the 'objective' specification of the types, sources, and intensity of threats, and the kinds of responses that are needed. As a social construct, it is seen as being defined by people in the process of their interactions. It is based on the definition of threats by an individual or a group, which could be either real or imagined. Social reality is therefore constructed by the identification of threats, and responses to them.[3] Security and insecurity clearly have their roots in one's perception of vulnerabilities and threats. Dominant forces of society usually influence the security discourse, and this may later be translated into policy. The processes of securitisation, through which narratives about security and insecurity are created, are thus complex and ever changing.

Although the concept of security was historically understood in terms of threats to state sovereignty and territory, alternative explanations of security have emerged since the 1980s. This has resulted in a virtual redefinition of the concept. The varying approaches to the concept of security are influenced by ideology, the unit of analysis identified, the time frame being addressed, etc. An overview of the plethora of approaches to security would be essential to contextualise the perceptions of security in South Asia.

## REALIST AND NEOREALIST APPROACHES

Traditionally, the concept of security has been viewed in the realist paradigm, which has had tremendous influence on most studies of international security. Within the conventional realist approach, definitions of security usually refer to defence of a state's territorial boundaries and the protection of its core values. The meaning of security is placed within the concept of power. This conception of security is based on the assumption that threats to a state's security arise mainly from outside its borders. These threats are primarily, if not exclusively, military in nature and usually necessitate a military response if the security of the state is to be preserved. This focus on a state-centric definition of security emerged from realist notions of a distinct boundary between domestic 'order' and international 'anarchy' - a 'state of nature' where war is a constant possibility. Security is represented in geopolitical terms as the spatial exclusion of threats and is explained primarily in terms of war, the survival of the state, and the role of military power in settling international disputes. In the absence of an international sovereign authority, states depend solely on their own military capabilities for security. This often leads to a 'security dilemma', as one state's military build-up is likely to be perceived as a security threat by other states. This often gives rise to an arms race among states, threatening the overall security of the entire system. To realists, what brings stability and security to the system is the balance of power.[4] Security is also synonymous with nuclear deterrence as nuclear wars are considered too dangerous to be fought.

The justification for the focus on nation-states is that in the anarchic world polity, individuals must ultimately rely on the power and authority of their respective national governments in order to secure their basic needs. Since states are the primary providers of security, an individual achieves his/her security by virtue of being a member of the national community. This approach seeks to justify the attention paid to military capabilities and resources. Foreign policy, from this perspective, is essentially national security policy, which, in turn, is predominantly military policy.[5]

Doctrines of national security are therefore an integral part of the realist and neorealist theories. Security is seen as the need to ensure the survival of the nation-state. National security is seen to be the basis of foreign policy and international relations, and as being interrelated with military power. This military-strategic view of national security, presumes that diplomatic or political responses to threats to the integrity of a country are inadequate, and prefers military responses to such threats. However, critics point out that this traditional approach to security fails to identify the most urgent concerns of many people in the world's poorer states whose real security dilemma is how to survive. In the realist tradition the security of individuals tends to be overwhelmed by the security of the state. Militarisation itself has become one of the greatest threats to security today. The military security of the state is becoming synonymous with the insecurity of individuals in the era of nuclear deterrence.

The neorealist debate which emerged with Kenneth Waltz's book *Theory of International Politics* published in 1979[6] saw an emphasis on the international system as the unit of analysis. Neorealists focus on the importance of structures and the systemic forces that states are subject to. Concern with questions of power and security remain crucial. According to Waltz, states are primarily concerned with security, as the pursuit of other goals becomes meaningful only if survival is assured. States will be able to ensure their own security only if they provide for it themselves. The international system is therefore a 'self-help' system. In view of the anarchical nature of the international system, states are forced to rely on 'self-help', resulting in the build-up of their state power. As existence requires balancing by units, the concept of balance of power is reshaped by neorealists as part of this structural analysis. According to Kenneth Waltz, nuclear weapons were a crucial source of international stability after the Second World War. He argues that the controlled spread of nuclear weapons to other societies could have a stabilising effect. Therefore nuclear proliferation is to be encouraged. Being certain that ultimately losses would outweigh the gains of fighting, nuclear powers would refrain from waging war with each other.[7]

An important re-examination of the concept of security is found in the works of Barry Buzan, who reintroduced important realist points.[8] Buzan broadens the traditional definition of security to include freedom from political, societal, economic and environmental threats. Examining security from the perspective of the individual, the state, as well as the international system, he contends that the most important and effective provider of security is likely to remain the sovereign state. Buzan distinguishes between weak and strong states depending on the level of socio-political cohesion between civil society and institutions of government. The stronger states will tend to find most threats emerging from outside their borders. This distinction between states with serious domestic security problems and those, whose primary security concerns are external, is seen to be crucial to the understanding of national security. The weaker a state is, the more ambiguous the concept of national security becomes in relation to it. Weak states tend to make more use of the term for domestic political purposes. Factional interests attain legitimacy, and the security of governments becomes confused with the security of states. Governments are tempted to invoke national security in their own defence, by identifying domestic political opposition with the policies of some foreign state. This is particularly true of governments that are not strong in their domestic environment and face much opposition. Consequently, Buzan argues, the evolution towards 'strong states', which is more typical of the West, will result in a greater degree of security for individuals. Buzan also defines a group of states whose primary security concerns are linked together so closely that their national securities cannot be realistically considered separate from each other as a security complex. This Classical Security Complex Theory acknowledges the existence of regional subsystems as objects of security analysis.[9]

Although Buzan addresses the problem of both individual as well as national (i.e., state) security, his approach retains the traditional emphasis on the state and the international system. The analysis remains almost entirely preoccupied with the security of states. As R.B.J.Walker points out "proclaimed intentions to the contrary, (Buzan) does not address the concerns of those worried by, for example, ecological breakdown, unequal development within and between states or the manner in which states continue to be the primary threat to people's security in many places."[10]

Critics also point out that the claim that strong states can successfully provide security could be challenged by marginalised groups, such as women and minorities, whose economic or social security is often sidelined when military security is given priority. It is usually political and military elites who define the national interest and frame national security policies. Hence, even strong states implement policies that are not necessarily formulated democratically. Despite Buzan's broadening of the analysis of security, it remains rooted in a framework in which the North is the guarantor of global security. Buzan envisages a decline in military conflict as the system progresses towards mature anarchy, increase in economic well being, and the world economy becomes more interdependent. However, the South perceives security threats to be the result of Northern build-up of high-technology weapons for wars of intervention, its control of the unequal world economy, and the over consumption of natural resources which are leading to negative consequences for the global environment. Buzan's critics disagree with his liberal assumption that the benefits of progress can be available to all. Structural constraints and the uneven development of the world capitalist economy hinder the achievement of security for the poorest states and individuals. In essence, critics argue that Buzan's work favours liberal capitalism, territorial states, and the willingness to use force to maintain international order. This reformed realism continues to equate security with an international system dominated by the great powers and to privilege the security of the state, although less explicitly than traditional realism.[11]

Buzan's 'classical' version of the security complex theory was however, later reformulated to take into account the widening of the security agenda (from the strictly military one to non-military ones, and the opening up of security studies to referent objects other than the state), as well as the move towards a more constructivist understanding of security dynamics. A security complex was therefore redefined to represent a set of units whose major processes of securitisation, desecuritisation or both are so interlinked that their national security problems cannot be analysed or resolved separately.[12]

Responding to criticism from peace groups, feminists, people's movements and others, realists and neorealists acknowledge that security is a multifaceted concept. Military build-up that is meant to ensure the security of one state might fuel fears in others, heighten threat perceptions and escalate the arms race. Military budgets create a negative impact in terms of social and economic development and constitute a source of insecurity to the people. However, in both the realist and neorealist discourses, the methods to guarantee security remain militaristic and nationalist. While realists consider the idea that security can be guaranteed through disarmament, development, or upholding human rights, as utopian; neorealists are more receptive to these critiques.[13] Approaches that are critical of realist and neorealist perspectives attempt to reconceptualise 'security' towards a more comprehensive, less state-centric orientation.

## REDEFINING SECURITY

In the context of global interdependence as well as the fragmentation of the state into competing ethnic and social groups, the traditional emphasis on state security has been faced with severe challenges. Military-centred notions of national security are proving to be ineffective in an interdependent world facing multidimensional threats. In the case of Third World societies particularly, given the distinct socio-economic and political dynamics of security facing the people of these postcolonial societies, the traditional approaches to security with their state-centric external orientation are problematic. Security threats often arise from the failure to integrate diverse social groups into the political process rather than from outside aggression. Mohammed Ayoob points out that contrary to the external orientation of traditional security discourse, and despite the rhetoric of many of the leaders of the Third World, the sense of insecurity from which these states suffer emanates to a substantial degree from sources within their boundaries rather than from outside. This does not mean that external threats do not exist. But it does imply that where external threats do exist, they often gain importance primarily because of the insecurities and conflicts that exist within the states. These internal conflicts and insecurities frequently get transformed into inter-state conflicts because of their impact on neighbouring states that often suffer from similar domestic insecurities.[14] These internal security problems are therefore enhanced by the impact of international forces, whether military, political, or economic. Third World states do not conform to the idea of homogeneous political units.

One cannot speak of national security in the Third World where often nations and states do not coincide. While these states are marked by diversity, they are often characterised by a lack of internal legitimacy, which has serious implications for security - domestically, regionally and globally.[15] They are extremely vulnerable due to their economic weaknesses or their dependence on a single commodity. Their dependence on advanced capitalist countries for technology, financial resources and markets also has its impact on their definition of insecurity. The onset of globalisation has raised further questions for the security problematique in the Third World.

The traditional definition of national security was also criticised by liberal-institutional scholars who maintained that this approach was outmoded as a result of cross-territorial movements. They argued that since states are ultimately concerned with protecting national security and maintaining economic growth, they may be incapable of adequately addressing certain non-political, though fundamental issues, which may give rise to international security problems. Preserving international safety requires going beyond the realist paradigm and re-thinking security interests in terms of the global territory.[16]

Reflecting an emerging international opinion that it was no longer adequate to look at the management of national and international security in narrow realist terms, recent decades witnessed various attempts at redefining the concept of security. The new approaches to security acknowledge that security is not an objective concept. Security provided by states need not necessarily reflect the needs of the population. What is secured could be only a political order or a particular political identity. The redefinition of security therefore also implies a notion of security from the perspective of the marginalised sections of society.

The reconceptualisation of security is largely based on three core arguments. The first is an understanding of *whose security is at stake*. The answer includes individuals and other groups (minorities, ethnic groups, indigenous peoples) below the state; humanity at large above the state; and also the biosphere on which human survival depends, as the referent objects of security. The second is the question of *what security itself involves*. This incorporates a much wider range of threats, including threats from environmental destruction, economic vulnerability and the breakdown of social cohesion. The concept of security is, in other words, broadened to include a variety of threats normally excluded from a strategic studies analysis. The third argument is that *responsibility for the provision of security rests not just on the state but also on international institutions and on non-governmental organizations (NGO) and civil society*. There is also a stress on the need to break down artificial distinctions between security and development.[17] These arguments strike at the very core of the traditional security discourse, as governments usually refer to national security as the highest value of their state's existence. These questions therefore challenge the basic premise that states provide protection and safety to their citizens. A change in the referent object of security results in changes in the perceptions of the source and nature of threats to that security. This also alters notions regarding the manner by which security can be achieved.

Calls for a reconceptualisation of security had been made prior to the end of the cold war itself, by noted world leaders including Olaf Palme of Sweden and Willy Brandt of West Germany. These were carried forward in reports of well known international commissions that were chaired by Gro Harlem Brundtland of Norway, Julius Nyerere of Tanzania, Ingvar Carlsson of Sweden, and others.[18] These international commissions provided suggestions to improve international relations and to strengthen international institutions. They argued that better representation and accountability at the global level could enable better management of economic, military and environmental problems, which cannot be handled separately by each state. In particular, these commissions introduced the important concepts of common security, human security and comprehensive security for the formulation of future world security policies.

The end of the cold war facilitated this trend towards redefining the concept of security and reshaping the security discourse. There emerged a growing alternative security discourse centred on the concepts of common security, human security and comprehensive security. Although these concepts were not concerned with radical reconstruction, but with problem-solving within the framework of the dominant paradigm, they were nevertheless an improvement on traditional approaches to security that simply privileged the 'state'.[19]

Focusing on the insecurities of contemporary societies in the context of advancing technological warfare, the concept of common security calls on states to abandon their own military measures. 'Common security' generates a vision of a world where defence and security would be pursued in collaboration with potential adversaries and not by generating insecurity for others. This line of thinking, reflected in the Palme

Commission Report of 1982 is based on the realisation that there are global dangers that threaten the entire system and that security can be achieved today only if it is held in common with other countries. In the nuclear age, no state can find security by itself. As Willy Brandt points out: "In the long run, security for *one* side cannot be achieved by armaments which reduce the security of the *other* side."[20]

The correlated concepts of human security, comprehensive security, global security, democratic security, etc. emphasise the importance of human beings and their complex socio-political and economic relations rather than states. The human security orientation was initially emphasised in the 1994 United Nations' *Human Development Report* (HDR), in the chapter entitled "New Dimensions of Human Security." The report offered a model that incorporated seven broad categories of security – economic, environmental, personal, community, health, political and food. It also adopted a key postulate that, if applied, could have major implications for security politics: a 'secure state' untroubled by contested territorial boundaries could still be inhabited by insecure people. The Report clearly implied that international security politics must widen its focus and include not only "the security of borders (but) also ... the security of peoples' lives."[21] The report of the Commission on Human Security, *Human Security Now: Protecting and Empowering People* emphasises both the protection of people from critical and pervasive threats and their empowerment. It calls on both nation states and international organisations to meet the requirements of this protection through rule of law, accountable and transparent institutions, and democratic governance structures. The report stresses the importance of economic, social and cultural rights, and argues that a human security framework must complement human rights and human development frameworks.[22] The term 'human security' has come to be used at the United Nations, in academia and in the foreign policies of a number of countries, as a possible alternative to the traditional approach to security.

There are various standpoints on the concept of human security, including the neorealist postures of the Canadian and Norwegian governments.[23] The concept of human security was in fact originally promoted by these two governments as a new *leitmotif* in foreign policy as it evoked 'progressive values' that were integral to the foreign policy identity of both countries, and were useful to them at that particular point of time. Canada was then a new member on the United Nations Security Council (UNSC) and the Norwegian government was lobbying for a seat on the UNSC for the 2001-2003 period.[24]

However, to some scholars, the concept of human security differs fundamentally from neoliberal notions of 'security of the individual', of competitive and possessive individualism. Rather, human security describes a condition of existence in which basic material needs are met, and in which human dignity, including meaningful participation in the life of the community is ensured. Human security is oriented towards a notion of democracy that ensures the opportunity for all to participate in the decisions that affect their lives. Therefore, it is engaged directly with democracy at all levels, from the local to the global.[25]

Writing along similar lines, Robert C. Johansen states that 'democratic security', is based on the assumption that all people are entitled to participate in and to determine together those decisions that profoundly affect their lives. Democratic security policies emphasise that security is for people – all people – not for abstractions like the state or concrete realities like particular governments, governing elites, and their immediate supporters.[26] Similarly, the International Commission on Global Governance brought to focus that global security must be broadened from its traditional focus on the security of states to include the security of the people and the planet. It is clearly pointed out that "too often in the past, however, preserving the security of the state has been used as an excuse for policies that undermined the security of people."[27] Particularly since the events of 9/11, there is an increasing fear among human security advocates that human rights and democracy may be threatened in the name of security.

Redefinitions of security, which shifted the emphasis from the security of the state to the security of people was based on the economic and political developments of the late twentieth century that included the political economy of liberalisation and privatisation. The ideological shift to a human security framework was generated by the insecurities that emerged with these developments. There was "a pervasive fear that impoverished people will threaten the institutions of neoliberal global governance."[28] The recent emphasis on broader conceptions of human security is therefore seen by Saba Gul Khattak to be a consequence of capitalist expansion, especially when viewed from the perspective of Third World countries experiencing the consequences of 'development'. He illustrates that the Structural Adjustment Programmes devised by the International Monetary Fund (IMF) and the World Bank, to recover their loans, imposed harsh and stringent conditions upon recipient countries. These included market liberalisation and privatisation of the economy, elimination of subsidies and the devaluation of currency. These programmes resulted in increased impoverishment for the poor, as subsidies continued to be lifted from essential commodities, prices were raised to world market levels and wages were much lower than in the advanced capitalist world.

> Poverty-alleviation schemes were thus introduced to deal with the 'social consequences' of structural adjustment, and the World Bank and other donors began to emphasize notions of 'human security', even while maintaining the structural adjustment programs that made so many people even more vulnerable.... The purpose of these programs, as well as those aimed at poverty alleviation, is to create 'market players' who would be consumers as well as the providers of labour. In this context, discourses about 'human security' play a key role in mystifying the consequences of capitalist expansion as well as in the creation of new markets in capital-poor countries. Much the same can be said of the broader accounts of security emerging from the most powerful countries. Having established itself as the sole superpower in the world, for example, the United States can now afford to promote its role in the struggle for democracy, freedom, and cooperative security throughout the world. While such a stance is promoted uniformly at the rhetorical level, many US policies in fact promote militarisation abroad.[29]

Khattak elaborates that the United States government has promoted the expanded meaning of security over recent years - exerting pressure on Third World states to invest more in the social sectors, trying to promote peace through dialogues and initiating confidence-building measures (CBMs). As the United States has made human security issues (at least at the discursive level) a priority, the United Nations and the World Bank to which the US contributes substantially, also now encourage governments to make people the focus of state policies. Khattak argues that despite the link between foreign policy and development issues, in the context of human security, donors usually attribute the lack of development to the selfish policies of particular governments, rather than to international structures. Hence, human security issues are promoted based on the premise that governments have failed and the issue at hand is governance rather than the wider constraints of the concerned governments.[30]

At the same time there are arguments that the human security discourse that has emerged in recent years could be a potential solution to the global socio-political and economic impasse, since the objective of human security is that of general human well-being. The concept of human security provides an alternative framework for thinking about security that views peace, security, equality, human rights and development as interrelated. Since the mid nineteen nineties there have been attempts to establish a 'human security' discourse at the United Nations, in academia and in the foreign policies of several countries. But it has not been aggressively promoted by the United Nations or widely accepted by the international community. There have however, been increased pressures to strengthen state security to counteract terrorism. To some observers a human security outlook appeals only to the middle powers. Countries with large military budgets do not adhere to this perspective, given its implications for a shift away from reliance on military security. Countries with border conflicts or internal ethnic problems are also unlikely to adopt this framework as it gives a lower priority to military expenditure. Similarly countries like the United States are also well aware that globalisation relies to some extent on the powerful military industrial complex for its continued success.[31]

More recently there has been an increasing realisation that the existing approaches to security are unable to address the issue adequately. More radical reformulations of the concept of security have been advanced from varying perspectives. In the neo-materialist perspective, security issues are seen to be defined by the positions and perceptions of the particular class or faction in power, which claims to articulate national security concerns but, in fact, advances factional, if not individual, interests. Security in reality was seen to be 'state' or 'regime' or 'presidential' rather than 'national' security. As the conventional discourse on security centres around states as the providers of security, radically rethinking security inevitably focuses on the role of the states. Scholars adopting structural perspectives argue that global structures place economic and other constraints on the autonomy of national decision makers. Accordingly, the ideal manner in which to understand conflict is to focus on the single global system with its interrelated levels and dimensions of analysis.

Feminist thinkers have also added to the traditional critiques of security doctrines through a gender perspective. Gender studies have questioned the basic values that are generally taken for granted in security studies. Analysing security by using the identity of gender, the traditional notions of security are deconstructed and redefined as it is understood by individuals in general and women in particular. Arguing that military and national security functions of the state have always been viewed from a masculine perspective, the feminist approach has favoured defining security in multidimensional terms. Feminist theorists examine how oppressive gender hierarchies, which decrease the security of individuals, are constructed and maintained. Often those living beyond the boundaries of one's own state are projected as feminised, less rational, and more unpredictable than those on the inside.[32] According to some, the modern notion of 'human security' has evolved from the comprehensive approach adopted by peace researchers, particularly those who identify themselves as feminist peace researchers. Women's movements, it is argued, have been a major influence on current trends towards the redefinition of security and the conception that real human security lies in the meeting of basic needs, the fulfilment of human rights and a healthy natural environment capable of sustaining life.[33]

Postmodernists and poststructuralists also argue against the traditional theories and approaches to security. By 'deconstructing' these theories, postmodernists attempt to show how they produce a highly selective and biased view of the world in which certain features are emphasised (eg. states, sovereignty, power) and other features are ignored (eg. humanity, community, gender, ecology). The sovereign state is often seen as a vehicle of oppression and a barrier to change. Postmodernism thus talks of overcoming that barrier, first in theory and then in practice.[34]

Scholars have also begun to link security to

identity, in order to explain how or why actors behave as they do in a security context. Identity is therefore important in understanding threat perceptions. Identity exists at various levels ranging from the individual to the systemic. Collective identity is most important as far as the impact on national security is concerned. The creation of a collective identity occurs within a specific social sphere and is often felt when contrasted to other external identities. Critical Security Studies scholars argue that states and other actors cannot be understood without examining their identities as well as the identities they attribute to others. Critical Security Studies adopt a constructivist approach whereby security is not viewed as an objective condition. On the other hand, the nature and sources of threats are considered to be constructed. These scholars therefore focus on how threats are defined, constructed and mobilised against. The language in which security is framed is seen to be one of division and exclusion. In criticising the language of division associated with realist thinking, R.B.J.Walker points out that assumptions that security can be provided only within states work in the interest of elites and reinforce boundary distinctions between inside and outside, self and other, friend and foe, citizen and foreigner. This sets up barriers that inhibit the achievement of world security. Walker argues that not until people, rather than citizens, are the primary subjects of security can a truly comprehensive security be achieved.[35] Security needs to be viewed from a holistic perspective rather than as privileging the state and its military power.

## ON SECURITISATION

The concept of securitisation introduced by the Copenhagen School[36] in the early 1990s is of particular relevance in understanding the security scenario in South Asia, as well as the role of the mass media. Securitisation involves the interpretation of security as a social construct and as an effect of mobilisation. It is the process of raising security issues above politics so that they are made unquestionable. Accordingly, security is defined not as an objective condition, but as the outcome of a specific social process. An important aspect of this concept as enunciated by the Copenhagen School is to create an awareness of the arbitrary nature of 'threats', to stimulate the thought that the foundation of any national security policy is not given by 'nature' but chosen by politicians and decision-makers who have an interest in defining it in just that way.[37] Dominant sections of society identify and create the enemies of the state through the process of discourse by labelling them as enemies, or as threats to national security, etc. Like these main actors in security policy-making, traditional security studies speak of threats as existing objectively, and evaluate options and strategies. However, unlike even the 'critical' or 'human security' studies, the Copenhagen School does not regard security as something unquestionable – to be maximised and achieved as much as possible by states or other entities. On the contrary, the crucial question is whether or not an issue should be treated as a security issue.

The theory of securitisation examines the manner in which some object is projected as being threatened. Securitisation is not merely a question of representation or a symbolic act. It has clear political implications. Identifying something as a security issue is not an innocent practice. It changes the legitimate modes of engagement with a particular problem. Hence securitisation can be seen as a powerful strategy that shapes and maintains the unity of a political community. As such securitisation can become an important political act determining not only the boundaries of political communities but also how to deal with those on the outside.[38] The process of securitisation can therefore be seen as a 'speech act' through which certain phenomena, actors or events are designated as threats to the status and security of the state. Statesmen representing the state and uttering security in the name of the state are the privileged agents in the securitising process. As Saba Gul Khattak points out

> References to *national security* suggest a broad and very powerful repertoire of meanings through which to convince a population both that its being and unity are threatened and that collective protection can be ensured... . Nation can be associated with civilization, culture, community, and family, all of which are framed as essential values that can be preserved despite a threatening external environment. The negative qualities of aggression, threat, and consequent danger can then be attributed to the Other, to the realm of the foreign, the outside, to the arena of international politics.[39]

Such demarcations of internal community in antithesis to external threats, is fundamental to how security is constructed. It is essentially about creating the political identity of the domestic community. Articulation of external threats is often used to shape the identity of a state. In the process of creating external 'others' as threats, a domestic 'self' is constructed in terms of security. As Simon Dalby posits, identity, the intangible and often contested social construction of who 'we' are is very much the subject of state discourse on security. In order to secure the boundaries of the statist identity, the construction of 'danger' on the outside is used. The state requires this discourse of danger to secure its identity and legitimation.[40]

Khattak argues that the discourse of nuclear security is one example that explains how insecurity is carefully crafted and constantly reproduced in fairly traditional terms. Strategies that range from appeals for protection of the motherland, to representations of the enemy as dangerous, threatening the very existence of the nation are made use of in this process. What is important to the discourse is the construction of the enemy, which can be both inside and outside. Such strategies help to reinforce insecurity together with the idea that the state is the ultimate source of hope in any context.[41]

Thus, as Ken Booth points out the issue of identity that "makes us believe we are the same and them different" is inseparable from security and is central to the conception of security.[42] Security depends on how identity and interests are chosen. Bill McSweeney discusses two ways of practising or 'doing' security. One is the traditional approach based on the perception of external threat and the organisation of resources to remedy any perceived vulnerabilities. Military defence is, however, only one aspect of security policy. Relying wholly on this could in fact exacerbate the problem. The second way of doing security, while not excluding the essentially material orientation of the first, focuses primarily on addressing the long-term security problem of regional relationships through the management of identity and interests.[43]

Security utterances are often manipulated by the state elite to realise their own objectives. "By uttering 'security', a state-representative moves a particular development into a specific area, and thereby claims a special right to use whatever means are necessary to block it."[44] The speech act of security thus becomes a means to an end. It is by labelling something a security issue that it becomes one. Barry Buzan and Ole Waever define securitisation as "the discursive process through which an intersubjective understanding is constructed within a political community to treat something as an existential threat to a valued referent object and to enable and call for urgent and exceptional measures to deal with the threat."[45] Securitisation can be a powerful political strategy and has clear political implications as a result of its impact on policy formulation, public debate and stimulation of conflict. Securitising actors may be the state, international organisations, non-governmental organisations, the mass media, etc.

The concept of desecuritisation naturally follows from the securitisation approach. Desecuritisation is the long-range option to move issues out of the threat-defence scenario into the ordinary public sphere. Desecuritisation is identified as the process by which a political community "downgrades or ceases to treat something as an existential threat to a valued referent object and reduces or stops calling for urgent and exceptional measures to deal with the threat."[46] This process is often indirect, where sometimes a shift of focus towards other issues reduces the attention given to the previously securitised issue.

However, in a social-constructivist perspective, not all utterances have an equal capacity to 'securitise'. It depends on the position from which the utterance is made and on how it is constructed. In other words, some security utterances have a higher capacity to mobilise security dispositions than others. There are specific positions that have a privileged capacity to securitise issues because they are producers of professional security knowledge. Language also plays a crucial role in this process. The mobilisation of security relies heavily on the use of security language. This is particularly true of the security knowledge produced by police agencies and the military, the articulation of danger by the media, etc.[47] For instance, matters relating to defence and nuclear weapons are the subjects of discourses by experts who often use obscure technical jargon. As a result the layman is excluded from participation. This limits the content and quality of discussions. In the process, security discourse is limited to a small group of security experts. They see their task to be that of planning the security of their states. Thus articulating security is not as innocent or neutral as it would seem to be. Security language may be used with the intention of securitising an area. The need for security is inculcated through a culture of nationalism and patriotism that is perpetuated through various rituals, including patriotic songs and programmes and the designation and observance of national days, etc. The security narrative provides a continuity of meaning by emphasising certain events, while ignoring others that contradict "the meaning-making exercise."[48] As Pasha argues, security "as the drive to homogenise and silence difference – has been a crucial aspect of nation-building."[49]

It is often pointed out that the best way of preserving a state, and guaranteeing it against rebellion and civil war is to keep the subjects in amity with one another, and to find a common enemy against whom they can unite. Very negative images of external enemies are often promoted towards this end. The adversary is dehumanised and demonised as being unreasonable and obstructive, who is not open to persuasion but responds only to the threat of force. In defining the national security paradigm a key factor is the readiness to classify the adversary as 'enemy'. 'Naming' identifies an object and gives it a value/ characteristic. Names and their meanings form part of the cultural systems that structure and nuance the way we see, understand and imagine the world.[50] Thus such names are more than simple reflections of reality. But the name given will not always reflect all its characteristics. It will emphasise certain characteristics while neglecting other important ones. Naming fulfils two main functions – to get supporters by projecting a discourse of belonging and opposition, and to justify action through such labelling. With the break up of concepts such as East and West after the Cold War, new mental geographical divisions have emerged, differentiating the virtue, moderation and reasonableness of the West and the fanaticism and lack of reason of the East. The naming of people, territory and phenomena are all part of this attempt to recruit and identify allies and opponents, and to demarcate similarity from difference.[51] Recent examples include President George Bush's rhetoric of 'good versus evil', 'with us or against us', 'just war', 'war on terror', Operation Just Cause, Operation Provide Comfort, Operation Restore Hope, Operation Uphold Democracy, Operation Enduring Freedom, etc. Such representation also helps to legitimise violence and justify intervention. It is particularly during conflicts that one assigns virtue to one's own identity and decisions, and identifies negative characteristics to the opponent.

The mass media are an important channel through which names and narratives are transmitted to the public. The processes of securitisation are carried out by various actors including the state, political parties, non-governmental organisations, and most importantly the mass media.

## MEDIA AND SOCIETY

The mass media play a critical role in projecting images and moulding perceptions. It is primarily through the media that information is received, perceptions shaped and policies articulated. The media operate within society by acting as agents of change or as agents to reinforce the dominant values of society. They may provide interpretations, confer status by approval or disapproval, offer models for identification, define problems, suggest remedies, and so on. Although the influence of the media varies according to time, place and circumstances, it is undoubtedly a significant factor in society. Precisely what influence the mass media have on its audience, and the nature and extent to which media shape rather than reflect public opinion is the subject of much academic discussion.[52]

Policy-makers turn to the media for information and agenda, as well as for analyses and evaluations of developments and proposals. How events and opinions are reported affects policy-makers. To some analysts, the nature of reporting may narrow the policy choices available to public officials, enable governmental action when no action might have taken place otherwise, or force ongoing or projected policies to be stopped. At the same time, the media also often play a reinforcing or legitimising role vis-à-vis the policy-maker. The media are the primary means by which governments communicate with their public. Despite the fact that there may have been occasions where the media have appeared to perform a dramatic role in social or political change, generally, in most societies, the media perform a reinforcing function vis-à-vis existing values. This policy-making - media relationship is therefore symbiotic. It has also been pointed out that there is a large body of evidence to indicate that what appears in the media has a substantial impact not only upon 'how citizens think' but also 'what they think about'. This 'agenda-setting' is seen to be another important function or sphere of influence of the media.

At the same time, the performance of the media cannot be overly generalised. As the media are situated in specific social, political, historical and institutional contexts, they need to be analysed within this larger context. The performance of the mass media reflects to a large extent, the political, economic and socio-cultural institutions of a given country. Thus the media cannot be seen in isolation. It should be seen as one of these social institutions, interacting with the others within the wider social system. What any medium can do on its own may be limited. The crucial question, therefore, is not about "what the media do to people, or what they could do to people, but what will people, variously located in society, with different experiences, opportunities, skills, competencies and needs make of what the media and other sources provide, and which are available to them. This is really at the heart of the problem."[53]

In the case of democratic societies, the traditional concept of democracy is based on the idea that it is the people who, directly or indirectly, make decisions, and that the media provide the factual information for them to make these decisions. Democratic politics as a collective activity is closely linked to the existence and survival of the public sphere. Among the institutions that contribute to the constitution of the public sphere in society, it is perhaps the media that performs the most critical function. Media are seen to be the principal source of information and access to public debate, and the key to informed, participating, self-governing citizens. Media are viewed as the principal means through which citizens and their elected representatives communicate with each other in their reciprocal efforts to inform and influence.[54] The mass media have a significant role in facilitating the construction of the public sphere and democratic politics, by helping to shape people's orientations, beliefs and attitudes.

The media are part of the democratic processes because of their role in the dissemination of information and opinion. As such the quality of that information and opinion is of vital concern. Democracy requires a media system that provides people with a wide range of opinion and analyses. Debates on important issues should reflect the diversity of citizens, and promote public accountability. Therefore in an ideal democracy the media must foster deliberation and diversity, and ensure accountability. If there is no coverage of dissent in the press, there can be no true democracy. However, as far as the mainstream media is concerned, the reality is often different.

It has been pointed out that the actual agenda setting of the media is, in fact, done by the media's primary sources. The overall implication of agenda-setting is often to legitimise and reinforce the status quo. The media can shape agenda by means of placement, tone, repetition, and more importantly by the frames of analysis and facts, which it chooses and excludes. A frame refers to the way media organise and present the issues and events that they cover, and the way audiences interpret what they are provided. It is through this process of framing that those elements which make the strongest case for one's position are selected and highlighted. It is the basic method by which the media shape public opinion. Identifying media frames is therefore essential to understanding the media and how public opinion is shaped. News frames determine what is selected, what is excluded and what is emphasised. Frames give a different meaning than would be the case had the subject not been placed within such a frame.

Clearly, news does not happen but is constructed, with various considerations including economic and political, or a country's specific national interests exerting pressure on the selection and presentation of themes in the mass media. Edward Herman and Noam Chomsky maintain that the mass media serve to mobilise support for the dominant interests of the state and private activity. The choices, emphases and omissions of the media can thus be understood by analysing them in such terms. Their 'propaganda model' suggests that the 'societal purpose' of the media is to inculcate and defend the economic, social, and political agenda of privileged groups that dominate the society and state. Through the selection of topics, filtering of information, framing of issues, emphasis, placement and tone, and keeping debate within the bounds of acceptable premises, the media serve this purpose. The propaganda model traces the manner in which money and power can filter out news, marginalise dissent, and permit the government and dominant private interests to publicise their messages.[55]

In fact, media objectivity is increasingly being

recognised to be a myth. News essentially entails a selective production process leading to the presentation of a version of reality, which is also governed by professional values and occupational routines. The process of news gathering predisposes reporters to certain concepts and views. In the very selection of facts and in their presentation there is an interpretative framework, which shows bias. Although complete absence of bias may not be possible it is essential to understand that not all biases are equal. In order to maintain the image of objectivity and to protect themselves from criticisms of bias and threats of libel suits, the media look for material that can be portrayed as accurate. This so-called objectivity favours the use of sources, particularly official sources that are considered to be credible by the public. The question of sourcing is of particular importance in the context of the present study. Communications research has revealed that government officials serve as the chief sources of political news and tend to constrain the range of debate found in the media. This view supports the hegemony theory of the media according to which the media largely pass along official propaganda, particularly in the context of foreign affairs. This suggests that perspectives in the media may reflect whatever political forces are dominant in society as a whole. [56]

The mass media are drawn into a special relationship with powerful sources of information due to economic necessity as well as reciprocity of interest. The media need a steady and reliable flow of information. Consequently, they rely heavily upon news provided by corporate and government sources, which have well developed bureaucratic structures to provide this material to the media. In effect, these bureaucracies subsidise the media and the media are careful not to antagonise such important suppliers. Furthermore, these corporate and government sources are recognisable and credible by their status and prestige. Anti-elite sources, on the other hand, are regarded with suspicion.

In order to consolidate their pre-eminent position as sources, government and business-news promoters take serious efforts to make things easy for the news organizations. They provide all required facilities, including advance copies of speeches and forthcoming reports; scheduling press conferences according to news deadlines; and writing press releases in usable language. Powerful sources may also use their leverage to deny critics access to the media.

The relation between power and sourcing also extends to influencing the supply of 'experts'. The dominance of official sources can be weakened by the existence of highly respectable unofficial sources that give dissident views with great authority. "This problem is alleviated by 'co-opting the experts' – i.e., putting them on the payroll as consultants, funding their research, and organizing think–tanks that will hire them directly and help disseminate their messages.... This process of creating the needed body of experts has been carried out on a deliberate basis and a massive scale."[57] Thus, the media often provide 'experts' who regularly echo the official view. By giving them plenty of exposure, the media confer them status and make them the obvious candidates for opinion and analysis. Deliberate government leaks are also common in most countries. The media willingly accept and print information 'off the record' from 'sources close to the government'. While dissent from the mainstream is given little coverage, governments and big business gain easy access to the public.

Media contribution to 'consensus' therefore occurs in various ways. It is particularly when there is little or no elite dissent from government policy that facts that tend to undermine government perspectives are found on the back pages of newspapers. The attention given to a fact, its placement, tone, and the framework of analysis within which it is presented, and the related facts that accompany it are all of importance in this context. A dominant frame is created and alternate frames are ignored. Sources that tend to look at the issue alternatively are often excluded from the media and facts that fit the dominant frame are selected. A form of self censorship occurs where dissenting information is removed. Such information is filtered out by either conditioned reporters in the field or as a result of narrative frames. As Herman and Chomsky point out, most biased choices in the media arise from the selection of right-thinking people, internalised preconceptions, and the adaptation of personnel to the constraints of ownership, organization, market, and political power. Censorship is largely self-censorship, by reporters and people at higher levels within media organizations who have usually internalised the constraints imposed by proprietary and other market and governmental centres of power. In most cases, however, media leaders do similar things because they see the world through the same lenses, are subject to similar constraints and incentives, and thus feature stories or maintain silence together.[58]

Robert W. McChesney argues that the structure of media systems, with the wealthy and powerful few making the most important media decisions, draws attention to the severe contradiction between a privately held media system and the needs of a democratic society. It is one thing to argue that a commercial media system works for democracy when there are numerous newspapers in a community, when barriers to entry are relatively low, and when immigrant and dissident media proliferate widely. For newspapers to be partisan in such circumstances is not so problematic as there are alternative viewpoints available. It is quite another thing to make such a claim when there are only one or two newspapers, usually owned by chains or very wealthy and powerful individuals. As such, the overall impact of media as political actors may depend largely on how political perspectives are distributed among them. The public is thus denied the tools it needs to participate as informed citizens.[59] Certain sections of the media in democracies do discover facts and fearlessly expose governments' efforts to misinform the public. However, this is not the case with regard to reporting foreign and security policies.

## MEDIA AND SECURITY

The dominance of official perspectives in the mainstream media is particularly evident in the security sphere. The media, both electronic as well as print, help define the parameters of security and serve to mediate assessments of threat. It is primarily through the media that information is gleaned, perceptions shaped and policies articulated on such issues. The media play a critical role in projecting images and moulding perceptions in the realm of foreign and defence policies. Public opinion on such issues is therefore closely related to the media's role in creating perceptions of national and international insecurity. The Media Conference of the Non-Aligned Movement, in its Declaration of 1983, states: "...the battle for freedom and justice, like that for peace, has to be fought and won in the minds of men. In this battle the role of the media is of crucial importance. It can hardly be overemphasised."[60] Similarly, Article III of the Mass Media Declaration of UNESCO states: "The mass media have an important contribution to make to the strengthening of peace and international understanding and in countering racialism, apartheid and incitement to war."[61]

Barry Buzan, in his seminal work on security, pointed out that the security policy of any state is not arrived at through a detached and rational formula. Various competing interests, including the mass media intervene in the policy process. These factors may however, have other interests which influence their security perspectives in various ways. The media are constrained in what they report by their need to sell their product to readers and advertisers, often resulting in sensational reporting. As a result, "the media distort the public view of what is important in national security, focusing attention on short term issues and military means, while largely ignoring longer-range and more abstract issues."[62]

The role played by the media is not only important but can also be fundamental to the process of conflict resolution. The media can play a critical role in the promotion of peace by emphasising the benefits that peace can bring, raising the legitimacy of groups or leaders working for peace, and transforming images of the enemy. The media, however, can also serve as destructive agents in the process by emphasising the risks and dangers associated with compromise, raising the legitimacy of those opposed to concessions, and reinforcing negative stereotypes of the enemy. Foreign news journalism without enemy images could in fact be analytically oriented journalism, placing events in a historical context and basing the use of sources, the angling and the perspective of articles on well-accepted criteria from international law, human rights, etc,[63] thereby facilitating peace and cooperation.

In the specific context of foreign policy, scholars have maintained that the media have an increasing influence, with policy-makers paying close attention to news stories, watching for events that might have escaped normal diplomatic observations as well as for the opinion-shaping images that might be conveyed.[64] CNN's coverage of the 1991 Gulf War and other international conflicts during the following years led to advocates of the 'CNN effect' arguing that the media play an important role in determining foreign policy action, particularly with regard to 'humanitarian intervention'. The understanding is that the media set the agenda, and when they focus on an issue, political action follows. CNN's role in the United States intervention in Somalia is shown as the best example. However, a study of CNN's coverage revealed that it was initially the government that manipulated the press. This then changed to the press manipulating the government.[65] More recent studies, particularly those relating to the impact of media coverage on decisions to intervene during humanitarian crises, have shown that media influence usually occurs when official policy towards the crisis is uncertain and media coverage is framed so as to empathise with suffering people. On the other hand, when policy is certain, media influence is unlikely to occur. Media coverage of the conflict may be framed so as to empathise with suffering people, for example by identifying them as 'victims'; or so as to maintain an emotional distance, for example by classifying suffering people as warring 'tribes'.[66]

In his study on the media coverage of military interventions of the United States in the post-Vietnam era (i.e. in Grenada and Panama, bombing of Libya, build up to the Gulf War, the war itself and interventions in Somalia and Haiti), Jonathan Mermin points out that when official sources are in consensus, the media play a relatively passive role and tend to reinforce the official management of public opinion. His study revealed that the 'spectrum of debate' in Washington determined the spectrum of debate in the news. The impact of the media is to reinforce the spectrum of debate produced by government policies, and to exclude from the public sphere, perspectives that do not have political support inside the government.[67] According to this 'indexing hypotheses', the spectrum of debate in the news reflects the spectrum of debate in official circles. The increasingly market driven media largely ignores dissenting voices to favour the corporate sector/government, especially where foreign policy/security issues are concerned. It is only in cases where consensus begins to disappear that the media is forced to reflect public debate.

So while on the one hand media have influence in foreign policy-making through processes of agenda setting and framing; on the other hand it is often manipulated by the policy-maker. This is particularly true in the case of the coverage of security matters. Various studies have shown that in the sphere of security the mass media, have generally promoted and legitimised, rather than contested, the policies of their governments.[68] This is especially the case if events are placed in the 'national security' frame by the political elite.

In determining 'news' the mainstream mass media tend to give priority to issues framed within a national security state-centric paradigm reflecting official perspectives, than to issues emerging from a notion of the security of the people. There is little space for democratic struggles, human rights concerns and other issues relating to the majority of the population. The emphasis of the media on conflict tends to highlight issues of threat and generate hostility. With the market as a major criterion for the selection of 'news', the social nature and significance of events are sometimes ignored. There is a natural discrimination against those events, which cannot be 'sold'. While concentrating on the topical and dramatic; important economic, social, cultural and political developments are not perceived as news. The very concept of news generally refers to the sensational and extraordinary rather than normal processes.[69] The media may therefore distort the public perception of security issues. Rita Manchanda points out that conflicts revolving around socio-economic issues are downplayed or depoliticised as 'law and order' or 'ethnic' conflicts.

> There is a politics of the media's coverage of social and political conflicts or the lack of coverage of certain conflicts, particularly those arising from denial of social justice.... The decoupling of social and political conflicts has a critical impact on the way the event of armed struggle or war is covered, but not its root causes. It makes conflict appear normal and inevitable and irresolvable.... This decoupling of social issues from the outbreak of conflict is ... part and parcel of the trend to delegitimise as 'newsworthy' struggles for social justice against an unjust and unresponsive system of governance. The media is implicated in

this hierarchisation of conflict and the discrediting of social struggles as law and disorder events.[70]

Locating an issue in its historical, social, economic and political context is of critical importance. Tapan Bose points out that there is often a reductionist construction of conflict as a territorial dispute or as a border conflict. The outbreak of conflict is located as an 'event' without situating it within its larger context. There is a clear priority for national security conflicts, with a misleading categorisation of struggles for justice, political assertion and legitimate power sharing, as posing a threat to national security. It is a knowledge categorisation, which the media reproduces without questioning.[71] In times of international crises particularly, there is a presumption that the media must serve the "national interest." Khattak points out that references to national security suggest a broad and very powerful range of meanings through which to convince a population that its being and unity are threatened and that collective protection can be ensured. Such rhetorical manoeuvres can be effected in a variety of ways, especially through the mass media.[72]

In its conceptualisation of security the media clearly tend to stress issues of national or state security, even if it is at the cost of human security or the human rights concerns of the people. This reflects the traditional state-centric approach to security which emphasises military security against external threats. This should be seen in contrast to the more recent recognition of the need for wider notions of security to emphasise questions of human rights and social justice. The realist frame in the media is characterised by its state centeredness. International conflicts in this frame are defined in terms of a power struggle between states. As such these frames provide justifications for war that are based on perceptions of hostility by one state against another.[73] The performance of the media in conflict situations is evidently more an issue of internalisation of myths and mindsets rather than one of overt censorship. This is sometimes enhanced by the competing pulls of the "democratic imperative embedded in the traditional culture of the media which impel it to responsibly inform the citizen, and the patriotic imperatives which pushes the media to become an adjunct of the government/state propaganda machine of war and demonisation."[74] The coverage of conflict is also interrelated to the intensity of conflict, location, who the participants are, strategic implications, etc. The performance and role of the mass media particularly during international conflicts therefore need to be understood in this context.

Where the media are controlled by the state there will be a more explicit bias towards securitisation of the 'enemy' and the official interpretations of events. The media are needed not only to report from the battlefield, but also to justify or legitimise war. The United States attack of Iraq in 1991 and other US interventions in Somalia, Haiti, Bosnia, Kosovo and Afghanistan were all presented by the western media within a humanitarian framework. Similarly, the US invasion of Iraq since 2003 has been framed as part of the 'war on terror'. The media in both the United Kingdom and the United States securitised Iraq and supported the policy of going to war. The western media played a major role in the securitisation of Iraq by projecting stories of the existence of weapons of mass destruction in the country. However, changes in the spectrum of debate in Washington saw changes in media coverage.

Over the years, the media have clearly become the battleground for wars – the means through which societies experience war. The media of a particular country generally propagate official versions of conflict as was evident in the 'War on Terror', the war against the Taliban in Afghanistan, etc. It has been argued that historically the media have helped the prosecution of national wars during this century far more than they have ever hindered them.[75] This has been possible through the process of securitisation carried out by the media. Drawing from the examples of Libya, Iraq, Vietnam, Grenada, etc., Barry L. Gan points out that many of the wars fought by the United States were possible only because the mass media misinformed the public and depicted opponents as evil. This helped to generate popular support for previously unpopular or unknown causes. One such recent example being the misinformation that led to the invasion of Iraq. Similar reporting contributed to the Gulf War, bombings of Libya, invasion of Grenada, the Vietnam War, etc. Gan argues that if the media had refused to report any claims until they could be independently verified, there would have been fewer wars and fewer deaths of innocent people.[76] Examples of government manipulation of the media to bolster its own policy issues are numerous. Throughout the Vietnam War the American media were given a misleading impression that the United States was winning the war. Henry Kissinger, then Secretary of State, deliberately misled the media to conceal the bombing of Cambodia. In 1983, prior to the Argentinean invasion of Falkland Islands, the British Ministry of Defence circulated rumours that the nuclear submarine *HMS Superb* had been sent to the South Atlantic. During the 1991 Gulf

War American military supplied the media with impressive videos claiming to show Patriot missiles shooting down Iraqi Scud missiles. Officially the Patriot was claimed to be ninety four percent effective. In fact it was largely ineffective.[77]

Since 9/11 a new euphemism emerged – 'embedded journalism', which referred to reporters accompanying troops in the battlefield. The freedom to report on any aspect is partially surrendered for access to the battlefield. Often reporting is only through a military censor. Even otherwise, through daily briefings, press conferences, interviews, etc. one often joins common cause with the unit and accepts their values. Often reporters accompanying troops tend to succumb to a language of identification with the soldiers whose experiences they are sharing. This results in the use of a military language that defines the opposition as 'other' and dehumanises the experiences of those outside.[78] While over 155 journalists were said to have been embedded during the first Gulf War, over 2700 journalists accompanied NATO forces in Kosovo.

Thussu and Freedman point out that the mainstream media accept and reproduce dominant definitions of concepts such as 'terrorism' (what others do to us) and 'self defence' (what we do to others) in order to mobilise popular consent for military action against 'rogue states'. This results in the securitisation of 'enemy countries'.[79] Other similar usages include 'just war', 'war on terror', 'collateral damage', 'axis of evil', etc. On 11 September 2001 CNN broke the news with the headlines 'America under Attack'. This news frame soon changed to 'America Strikes Back'. The distinction between official accounts and reports of the media were difficult to discern. The Anglo-American forces in the invasion of Iraq in 2003 were referred to by the media as 'allies' or 'coalition forces' which were involved in a 'liberation mission'. A study of television coverage of the Israeli-Palestine conflict by the Glasgow University Media Group, found major differences in the manner in which Palestinians and Israelis were described in news reports. Words such as 'murder', 'atrocity', 'lynching' and 'savage, cold blooded killing' were used only to describe Israeli deaths but not those of Palestinians.[80] Again CNN's coverage of the 1991 Gulf War, the first war in which there was live TV coverage, was a clear example of how news is framed.

In justifying strategic geopolitical policies and corporate interests around the world, the demonisation of opponents is considered useful or even essential. The media play an important role in this process of securitisation. How it frames and presents threats, as well as the amount of attention that is paid to such issues will influence the threat perceptions and responses of the audience. Enemy images are used in propaganda and war preparation by both sides in a conflict and the mass media are often willing participants in this process of demonisation. Adversaries are seen to be of interest only as threats. Thus news stories about them essentially focus on the level of danger that they pose. An important element of war reporting is to 'demonise' the enemy. This has been evident in the western media during the post cold war era when radical Islam has been projected as the main threat to western interests. Enemy images can thus be linked to the journalistic process itself. Whatever be the orientation of editorials and opinion pieces, the angling of articles through headlines, illustrations and cartoons may reveal the attitudes of news desks as to who the 'enemy' is, even when the text itself may be written in 'neutral' prose. Herman and Chomsky posit that a "propaganda system will consistently portray people abused in enemy states as *worthy* victims, whereas those treated with equal or greater severity by its own government or clients will be *unworthy.*"[81] Worthy victims will be reported prominently and dramatically. They will be humanised and their victimisation will get detailed coverage, generating reader interest and sympathy. In contrast, unworthy victims will get only minor coverage with minimal humanisation. At the same time the media also tend to modify enemy images when attitudes among the political elites change.

Given these circumstances, censorship is sometimes considered a natural process of state building, which in turn is seen to be the responsibility of all, including the media. Censorship thus results both from the security management efforts of the state's institutions as well as from the media's own notion of what security should be.[82] According to Cynthia Boaz, the reason why Americans were persuaded to support the invasion of Iraq when citizens elsewhere were not, was because the United States' press coverage in the days leading up to the war portrayed protest as unpatriotic and arguments against war as irrelevant. But the case for deliberation and caution against rushing to war was given much more legitimacy by the European press.[83]

Western media reporting of the Vietnam War was also significant for what it excluded or chose not to reveal. More recently, the world was kept largely ignorant of the impact of the United States invasion of 2003 on the ordinary citizens of Iraq, or the shockingly large number of over half a million children who died in Iraq as a result of sanctions against the country.

The suffering of ordinary people, particularly of the Third World often goes unreported, unless the West has its own interests in the region. The media language of the 2003 Iraq invasion dehumanised the entire conflict situation. The media oversimplified the conflict between United States and Iraq and created the feeling that war was the only solution to the conflict. The condition of the thousands of displaced persons, and the hospitals overcrowded with victims of 'precision bombing' or 'collateral damage' was ignored. Such reporting clearly obscures the terrible reality of war and its human costs. Analysing western media coverage of Sierra Leone and Congo, Hans-Henrik Helm argues that humanitarian crises in failing states are often forgotten by the media and political leaders. This is because of the dominance of national foreign policy in framing the agenda of the news media.[84]

Such selective reporting, the sidelining of dissent, and censorship – whether it be imposed or self motivated, all have very serious implications. Jean Dreze points out that the temptation to suppress dissent on grounds of 'national interest' in a conflict situation, although understandable, precludes informed public discussion of the situation and fosters a jingoistic climate where alternative means of conflict resolution receive little consideration. Furthermore, disinformation can lead to dangerous misperceptions among the protagonists about each other's intentions, which could have devastating consequences.[85]

Evidently, although security debates in academia over recent years have witnessed the emergence of wider and more comprehensive levels of analysis in contrast to the traditional realist state-centric approach, the security perceptions in the mainstream mass media generally continue to reflect traditional perspectives. The mainstream media tend to give priority to issues framed within a national security paradigm than to issues emerging from a notion of the security of the people. Enemy images are used in propaganda by both sides in a conflict and the mass media are often willing participants in this process of demonisation. Adversaries are usually of interest only as sources of threat. Thus news stories about them essentially focus on the level of danger that they pose. Through the nature of selection and presentation of news, the use of sources, the process of framing, etc., the mainstream media clearly reflect the dominant security discourse in society and play a crucial role in the process of securitisation.

## NOTES AND REFERENCES

1 Michael Dillon, *Politics of Security: Towards a Political Philosophy of Continental Thought* (London: Routledge, 1996), p.12.

2 Arnold Wolfers, *Discord and Collaboration* (Baltimore: Johns Hopkins University Press, 1962), p.150.

3 Raimo Vayrynen, "Environmental Security and Conflicts: Concepts and Policies," *International Studies*, Vol.35, No.1, January-March 1998, p.3.

4 Kenneth N. Waltz, *Theory of International Politics* (Reading, Mass.: Addison-Wesley, 1979), p.102.

5 Seyom Brown, "World Interests and the Changing Dimensions of Security," in Michael T. Klare and Yogesh Chandrani (eds.), *World Security: Challenges for a New Century* (New York: St. Martin's Press, 1998), pp.1-2.

6 Kenneth N. Waltz, n.4; also refer Kenneth N. Waltz, "Realist Thought and Neorealist Theory," *Journal of International Affairs*, Vol.44, No.1, 1991, pp.21-32; Robert Keohane (ed.), *Neorealism and its Critics* (New York: Columbia University Press, 1986).

7 See Kenneth N.Waltz, n.4, p.126; Kenneth N. Waltz, "The Spread of Nuclear Weapons: More May be Better," *Adelphi Papers*, No.171, Autumn 1981; Kenneth N.Waltz, *Man, the*

*State and War* (New York: Columbia University Press, 1959); Kenneth N. Waltz, "The Origin of War in Neorealist Theory," *Journal of Interdisciplinary History*, No.18, 1988, pp.624-627.

8 For a defence of realism, see Barry Buzan, Charles Jones and Richard Little, *The Logic of Anarchy: Neorealism to Structural Realism* (New York: Columbia University Press, 1993); Barry Buzan, "The Timeless Wisdom of Realism," in Steve Smith, Ken Booth and Marysia Zalewski (eds.), *International Theory: Positivism and Beyond* (Cambridge: Cambridge University Press, 1996), pp.47-65.

9 Barry Buzan, *People, States and Fear: The National Security Problem in International Relations* (New Delhi: Transasia, 1987), p.106; also see Barry Buzan, "New Patterns of Global Security in the Twenty First Century," *International Affairs*, Vol.67, No.3, July 1991, pp. 432-433.

10 R. B. J.Walker, *Inside/Outside: International Relations as Political Theory* (New York: Cambridge University Press, 1993), p.139.

11 J.Ann Tickner, "Re-visioning Security," in Ken Booth and Steve Smith (eds.), *International Relations Theory Today* (University Park: The Pennsylvania State University Press, 1995), pp.186-187.

12 Barry Buzan, "South Asia Moving Towards Transformation: Emergence of India as a Great Power," *International Studies*, Vol. 39. No.1, January-March 2002, pp.1-2.

13 Anuradha M. Chenoy, "Bringing Gender into National Security and International Relations," *International Studies*, Vol.37, No.1, January-March 2000, pp.26-27.

14 Mohammad Ayoob, "The Security Problematic of the Third World," *World Politics*, Vol. 43, No.2, January 1991, p.263.

15 See Caroline Thomas, "Third World Security," in Roger Carey and Trevor C.Salmon (eds.), *International Security in the Modern World* (Basingstoke: Macmillan, 1996), pp.94-105.

16 See Runa Das, "Broadening the Security Paradigm: A Note on the Tension between the Realist and Anti-Proliferation Lobbies in India," *The Indian Journal of Political Science*, Vol.62, No.2, June 2001, p.260.

17 Andrew Hurrell, "Security in Latin America," *International Affairs*, Vol. 74, No.3, July 1998, p.542; also see R.B.J.Walker, "Security, Sovereignty, and the Challenge of World Politics," *Alternatives*, Vol. 15. No.1, Winter 4.

18 See Report of the Independent Commission on International Development Issues, *North-South: A Programme for Survival* (London: Pan Books, 1980); Report of the Independent Commission on Disarmament and Security Issues, *Common Security: A Programme for Disarmament* (London: Pan Books, 1982); The Brandt Commission, *Common Crisis: North-South: Cooperation for World Recovery* (London: Pan Books, 1983); World Commission on Environment and Development, *Our Common Future* (Oxford: Oxford University Press, 1987); The Report of the South Commission, *The Challenge to the South* (Oxford: Oxford University Press, 1990).

19 Larry A. Swatuk and Peter Vale, "Why Democracy is Not Enough: Southern Africa and Human Security in the Twenty-First Century," *Alternatives*, Vol.24, No. 3, July-September 1999, p.369.

20 Willy Brandt, World *Armament and World Hunger: A Call for Action* (London: Victor Gollancz, 1986), pp.37-38. Also see Independent Commission on Disarmament and Security Issues, n.18.

21 United Nations Development Programme, *Human Development Report: New Dimensions of Human Security* (Oxford: Oxford University Press, 1994), pp.22-46.

22 See Commission on Human Security, *Human Security Now: Protecting and Empowering People* (New York: UN, 2003).

23 For details see *Human Security: Safety for People in a Changing World* (Ottawa: Department of Foreign Affairs and International Trends, 1999), www.yorku.ca; also see Sverre Lodgaard, *Human Security: Concept and Operationalization*, www.hsph.harvard.edu.

24 Astri Suhrke, "Human Security and the Interests of States," *Security Dialogue*, Vol.30, No.3, September 1999, pp.265-268.

25 Caroline Thomas, "Global Governance, Development and Human Security: Exploring the Links," *Third World Quarterly*, Vol.22, No.2, April 2001, pp.161-162.

26 Robert C. Johansen, "Real Security is Democratic Security," *Alternatives*, Vol.16, No.2, Spring 1991, pp.211-214; Robert Johansen, "Building World Security: The Need for Strengthened International Institutions," in Michael T. Klare and Yogesh Chandrani (eds.), n.5, p.388.

27 *Our Global Neighbourhood: The Report of the Commission on*

*Global Governance* (Oxford: Oxford University Press, 1995), pp.78-81.

28 Peter Wilkin, "Global Poverty and Orthodox Security," *Third World Quarterly,* Vol.23, No.4, August 2002, p.633.

29 Saba Gul Khattak, "Security Discourses and the State in Pakistan," *Alternatives,* Vol.21, No.3, July-September 1996, pp.342-343.

30 Ibid., p.354.

31 Kristen Timothy, "Human Security Discourse at the UN," *Peace Review,* Vol.16, No.1, March 2004, pp. 21-22.

32 J.Ann Tickner, "Feminist Responses to International Security Studies," *Peace Review,* Vol.16, No.1, March 2004, pp.46-47.

33 Rita Manchanda, "Redefining and Feminising Security," *Economic and Political Weekly,* Vol. 36, No.22, 2 June 2001, pp.1956-1968; also see J. Ann Tickner, n.11, pp.175-197; Anuradha M.Chenoy, n.13, p.24; Gunheild Hoogensen and Svein Vigeland Rotten, "Gender, Identity and the Subject of Security," *Security Dialogue,* Vol. 35, No.2, June 2004, p.155.

34 Georg Sorensen, "Individual Security and National Security: The State Remains the Principal Problem," *Security Dialogue,* Vol.27, No.4, December 1996, p. 371.

35 R.B.J.Walker, *One World, Many Worlds: Struggles for a Just World Peace* (Boulder: Lynne Reinner, 1988); and R.B.J.Walker, n.17, pp.3-27; also see Keith Krause, "Critical Theory and Security Studies," *YCISS Occasional Paper 33,* 1996, p.16.

36 The name Copenghagen School was coined by Bill McSweeny in "Identity and Security: Buzan and the Copenhagen School," *Review of International Studies,* Vol.22, No.1, 1996, pp.81-94. The Copenhagen School focuses on the three main aspects of securitisation, sectors and regional security complexes. Sectors refer to the distinction between political, economic, environmental, military and societal security. The concept of security complexes emphasise the regional level in security analysis.

37 Olav F.Knudsen, "Post-Copenhagen Security Studies: Desecuritizing Securitization," *Security Dialogue,* Vol.32, No.3, September 2001, p.359.

38 Rita Abrahamsen, "Blair's Africa: The Politics of Securitisation

and Fear," *Alternatives*, Vol.30, No.1, January-March 2005, pp.59-70.

39 Saba Gul Khattak, n.29, pp.341-342.

40 Simon Dalby, "Security, Modernity, Ecology: The Dilemmas of Post-Cold War Security Discourse," *Alternatives*, Vol.17, No.1, Winter 1992, p.107; also see David Campbell, *Writing Security: United States Foreign Policy and the Politics of Identity* (Minneapolis: University of Minnesota Press, 1992), cited in J.Ann Tickner, n.11, p.189.

41 Saba Gul Khattak, n.29, p.35.

42 Ken Booth, "Security and Self: Reflections of a Fallen Realist," in Keith Krause and Michael C. Williams (eds.), *Critical Security Studies: Concepts and Case* (London: UCL Press, 1997), p.6.

43 Bill McSweeney, *Security, Identity and Interests: A Sociology of International Relations* (Cambridge: Cambridge University Press, 1999), pp.101, 176.

44 Ole Waever, "Securitization and Desecuritization," in Ronnie Lipschutz (ed.), *On Security* (New York: Columbia University Press, 1995), pp. 54-55.

45 Barry Buzan and Ole Waever, *Regions and Powers: The Structure of International Security* (Cambridge: Cambridge University Press, 2003), p.491.

46 Ibid., p.489.

47 Jef Huysmans, "Defining Social Constructivism in Security Studies: The Normative Dilemma of Writing Security," *Alternatives*, Vol.27, No.1, January-March 2002, pp.44-58.

48 Saba Gul Khattak, n. 29, pp. 346-347.

49 Mustapha Kamal Pasha, "Security as Hegemony," *Alternatives*, Vol.21, No.3, July-September 1996, pp.288-289.

50 Julie Peteet, "Words as Interventions: Naming in the Palestine-Israel Conflict", *Third World Quarterly*, Vol.26, No.1, 2006, p.153.

51 Michael V. Bhatia, "Fighting Words: Naming Terrorists, Bandits, Rebels and other Violent Actors," *Third World Quarterly*, Vol.26, No.1, 2006, p.12.

52 Research on the influence of the mass media on public opinion has a long and contentious history. Arguments range from the earlier claim that the media have a very limited

influence (see Joseph T.Klapper, *The Effects of Mass Communication* (New York: Free Press, 1960)) to the more recent studies that cite the mass media as a powerful tool, capable of moulding perceptions. (See Edward S.Herman and Noam Chomsky, *Manufacturing Consent: The Political Economy of the Mass Media* (New York: Pantheon, 1988); M.A.Lee, *Unreliable Sources: A Guide to Detecting Bias in Mass Media* (New York: Carol Publishing Group, 1990)).

53 James D. Halloran, "Mass Communication Research: Asking the Right Questions," in Anders Hansen, Simon Cottle, Ralph Negrine and Chris Newbold (eds.), *Mass Communication Research Methods* (Basingstoke: Macmillan, 1998), pp.18-19; also see John B. Thompson, "Mass Communication and Modern Culture: Contribution to a Critical Theory of Ideology," in Oliver Boyd–Barrett and Chris Newbold (eds.), *Approaches to Media: A Reader* (London: Arnold, 1995), p.64; Sripada K.S.Raju, S.K.Jagadeswari and Wimal Dissanayake, "Treating the Indo-Pakistan Conflict: The Role of Indian Newspapers and Magazines," in Andrew Arno and Wimal Dissanayake (eds.), *The News Media in National and International Conflict* (Boulder: Westview, 1984), p.101.

54 Anthony Mughan and Richard Gunther, "The Media in Democratic and Nondemocratic Regimes: A Multilevel Perspective," in Richard Gunther and Anthony Mughan (eds.), *Democracy and the Media: A Comparative Perspective* (Cambridge: Cambridge University Press, 2000), p.1.

55 Edward S. Herman and Noam Chomsky, n.52, p.2. *Manufacturing Consent* was written in 1988 in the context of the American media, which reflects particularly on the fifth filter.

56 Benjamin I. Page, "The Mass Media as Political Actors," *Political Science and Politics*, March 1996, p. 22.

57 Edward S. Herman and Noam Chomsky, n.52, pp.18-23.

58 Ibid., pp.xii, 112-113.

59 Robert W. McChesney, "Journalism, Democracy, ... and Class Struggle," *Monthly Review*, Vol.52, No.6, November 2000, pp.1-15; also see Benjamin I. Page, n.56, p.23.

60 NAMEDIA, *Media Conference of the Non-Aligned Movement, New Delhi: 9-12 December 1983: Final Report and Documents* (New Delhi: NAMEDIA, 1984), p.15.

61 Article III of Annexure XII of "Declaration on Fundamental

Principles Concerning the Contribution of the Mass Media to Strengthening Peace and International Understanding to the Promotion of Human Rights and to Countering Racialism, Apartheid and Incitement to War," Document 20c/20Rev, Adopted on 22 November 1978 at the Twentieth Session of the General Conference of UNESCO, Paris, in UNESCO, *New Communication Order-9: Historical Background of the Mass Media Declaration* (Paris, 1978), p.128.

62 Barry Buzan, n.9, p.233.

63 Rune Ottosen, "Enemy Images and the Journalistic Process," *Journal of Peace Research*, Vol.32, No.1, 1995, pp. 97-99.

64 Keith Hindell, "The Influence of the Media on Foreign Policy," *International Relations*, Vol.12, No.4, April 1995, pp.73-74; Benjamin I. Page, n.56, pp.20-21; also see Bernard C. Cohen, "Foreign Policy-Makers and the Press," in Andrew Scott and Raymond Dawson (eds.), *Readings on the Making of American Foreign Policy* (New York: Macmillan, 1966), p.137; Philip M. Taylor, *Global Communications, International Affairs and Media Since 1945* (London: Routledge, 1997), p.29.

65 Hans-Henrik Helm, "Failing Failed States: Who Forgets the Forgotten?" *Security Dialogue*, Vol. 33, No.4, December 2002, p.461.

66 See Piers Robinson, "The Policy-Media Interaction Model: Measuring Media Power During Humanitarian Crisis," *Journal of Peace Research*, Vol.37, No.5, September 2000, pp.613-633.

67 Jonathan Mermin, *Debating War and Peace: Media Coverage of US Intervention in the Post-Vietnam Era* (Princeton: Princeton University Press, 1999), pp.8, 145, 151-152.

68 See for example, Edward S. Herman and Noam Chomsky, n.52; Jonathan Mermin, n. 67; N. Bhaskara Rao, *Indo-Pak Conflict: Controlled Mass Communication in Inter-State Relations* (New Delhi: S.Chand, 1971); J.V.Vilanilam, *Reporting A Revolution: The Iranian Revolution and the NIICO Debate* (New Delhi: Sage, 1989); Andrew Rojecki, *Silencing the Opposition: Antinuclear Movements and the Media in the Cold War* (Urbana: University of Illinois Press, 1999), p.5.

69 Juan Somavia, "The Transnational Power Structure and International Information: Elements of a Third World Policy for Transnational News Agencies," *Development Dialogue*, No.2, 1976, p.16; Doudou Diene, "UNESCO and

Communications in the Modern World," *Journal of International Affairs,* Vol.35, No.1, Spring/Summer 1981, p.222; Anthony Smith, *The Geopolitics of Information: How Western Culture Dominates the World* (London: Faber and Faber, 1980), pp.98-99.

70 Rita Manchanda, *Reporting Conflict: A Radical Critique of the Mass Media, SAFHR Paper Series 9,* May 2001, www.safhr.org.

71 Tapan Bose, in ibid.

72 Saba Gul Khattak, n.29, pp.341-347.

73 Cynthia Boaz, "War and Foreign Policy Framing in International Media," *Peace Review,* Vol.17, No.4, October-December 2005, p.349.

74 Rita Manchanda, n.70.

75 Philip M. Taylor, n.64, p.105.

76 Barry L.Gan, "Pressed into War," *Peace Review,* Vol.17, No.4, 2005, p.341.

77 Keith Hindell, n.64, pp.74-75.

78 Peter Beaumon, "Bartering Freedom?" *The Hindu,* 26 November 2004.

79 Daya Kishan Thussu and Des Freedman, "Introduction," in Daya Kishan Thussu and Des Freedman (eds.), *War and the Media : Reporting Conflict 24/7* ((New Delhi: Vistaar Publications, 2003), p.8.

80 Glasgow University Media Group, "The Israeli Palestinian Conflict: TV News and Public Understanding," in Daya Kishan Thussu and Des Freedman (eds.), ibid., p.144.

81 Edward S. Herman and Noam Chomsky, n.52, pp.35-37.

82 Afsan Chowdhury in Rita Manchanda, n.70.

83 Cynthia Boaz, n.73, p. 349.

84 Hans-Henrik Helm, n.65, pp.45-48.

85 Jean Dreze, "Militarism, Development and Democracy," *Economic and Political Weekly,* Vol. 35, No. 14, 1 April 2000, P. 1177.

# 2
# Security Discourses in South Asia and the Indian Press

In studying the role of the mass media in the context of security, the South Asian scenario is a particularly interesting case in point. Given the multifaceted dimensions of security in the region, it is crucial to understand the South Asian experience in the light of the insights derived from the emerging traditions of security analyses. In view of the fact that threat perceptions and identity formations are constructed within societal discourses, this chapter initially examines the discourses on security in South Asia. This provides an insight into the broad contours of securitisation in the subcontinent, as well as the contextual background to the study of the role of the press. Although the press coverage of each other by both India and Pakistan are mutually reflective, the present chapter focuses on the role of the press in India, taking into consideration the larger context of the study. It provides an analyses of the nature of coverage of issues relating to security by the Indian press, with a historical overview of Indian press reporting of Pakistan. It examines how Pakistan is framed and represented in the mainstream Indian press.

Given the specific socio-political context of South Asia, perceptions of security and their translation into policies are of significance. This is particularly so in the context of India and Pakistan. Traditionally, the nature of the struggle for independence and the circumstances of partition, including the conflict between the Muslim League and the Indian National Congress, the demand for partition and the ensuing competition for princely states, the dispute over boundaries, division of assets, evacuee property, sharing of river waters and, most importantly, the conflict over Kashmir, are perceived to have played an important role in defining the security/insecurity narratives in the subcontinent.

Barry Buzan maintains that South Asia is an example of an important middle level security complex, the heart of which is the rivalry between India and Pakistan. Their insecurities are so deeply intertwined that their national securities, particularly in terms of political and military security, cannot be separated. Bangladesh, Bhutan, Nepal, Sri Lanka and Maldives are bound into the complex for geographical reasons. Regional issues and relations define the national security priorities of these states, binding the South Asian security complex together. Buzan argues that none of the South Asian states is strong as a state. As a result most of them face substantial security threats arising from within their own boundaries. Religious, national and historical factors cut across state boundaries, making domestic problems inseparable from relations among states. It is these rivalries and hostilities, particularly between India and Pakistan, which not only define the South Asian security complex, but also its relations with the larger complexes which surround it.[1]

The process of securitisation between India and Pakistan has been based on varying claims to territory, balance of power issues, mutual accusation of interference in each other's domestic affairs, and the nature of their constitutions - given their rival principles of legitimacy. While India's secular, federal constitution was perceived to threaten Pakistan with reabsorption, the principle of Pakistan's ideology as a homeland for Muslims was viewed as threatening India's ethnic and religious groups with dismemberment. Buzan contends that this constitutional tension provided fertile ground for the securitisation of national identities on both sides, and governments found it convenient to cultivate threat perceptions of the other for their own domestic political purposes. This rivalry led to four wars and generated several major crises. It is a common practice on the part of each government to accuse the other of fomenting domestic political violence across the border. This helps to sustain an arms build-up, which from the 1970s onwards acquired a nuclear dimension.[2] In the context of the present study, it would be relevant to examine the security/insecurity narratives of the dominant discourse in Pakistan and India, focusing particularly on the latter, given the nature of the thrust of the study.

## SECURITY/INSECURITY NARRATIVES IN PAKISTAN

In the case of Pakistan, the basic events that constitute the insecurity narrative in the dominant discourse include the struggle for Pakistan, which involved the partitioning of India, opposed by the Hindu community; the 1948 and 1965 conflicts with India over Kashmir; India's role in the break-up of Pakistan in 1971, and India's 1974 nuclear explosion, which was interpreted in Pakistan as a direct threat to its survival. These events are reinforced by such instances as India's military exercise Operation Brasstacks in

1986-87, the belief that Pakistan and India were on the brink of nuclear war over Kashmir in 1990[3] and the major crises in 1999 and 2002. The problems emanating from the partition process and India's stance on many of those issues resulted in strengthening Pakistan's conviction, at the time, that India had not really accepted the division of the subcontinent and would do its utmost to undo the same. The prevalent notion in Pakistan reflected the perceptions of Zulfikar Ali Bhutto that Indians accepted partition "as a matter of bitter expediency, in the hope and expectation that the new State would not be viable and would collapse under pressure from its larger and more powerful neighbour."[4] Consequently, India's take-over of Junagadh and Hyderabad, the curtailment of irrigation waters in the Punjab, the withholding of funds and military equipment, New Delhi's acceptance of accession by the Maharaja of Kashmir and the sending of troops into the state, compounded by the numerous statements of Indian leaders promising to undo the partition were also viewed as part of the insecurity narrative.[5]

Leaders like Acharya Kripalani, President of the Indian National Congress, were quoted as having said that "neither Congress nor the nation has given up its claim of a United India," while Sardar Patel, Home Minister, stated that "sooner than later, we shall again be united in common allegiance to our country."[6] Other Indian leaders foresaw a 'short-lived partition' and maintained "Pakistan was not viable and could not last."[7] The All India Congress Committee Resolution of 14 June 1947, accepting partition, spoke in terms of the essential unity of India:

> Geography and the mountains and seas fashioned India as she is, and no human

> agency can change that shape or come in the way of her final destiny.... The AICC earnestly trusts that when the present passions have subsided, India's problems will be viewed in their proper perspective and the false doctrine of two nations in India will be discredited and discarded by all.[8]

Shyama Prasad Mookerjee, former President of the erstwhile Bharatiya Jana Sangh, stated that "the vision of India in the short term was 'Akhand Bharat', undoing the partition of the subcontinent and reuniting Pakistan with India, and in the long-term, establishment of Dharma Rajya, revival of the ancient Hindu civilisation and glory of its empire."[9] Acharya D.P.Ghosh, another former President of the party claimed that the only permanent solution to the India-Pakistan problem was the "annulment of Pakistan," "if Pakistan cannot be mended, it must be ended."[10]

Reflecting the tenor of his numerous speeches, Zulfikar Ali Bhutto wrote in 1969 :

> Pakistan achieved equality with India in the struggle for independence. The Indian Congress Party resisted the partition of the country, but failed to prevent the establishment of Pakistan. It is thus natural that some Indian leaders should continue to nurture grievances against Pakistan.... In the light of these historical and psychological factors which govern the Indian attitude towards Pakistan, it is clear that Indian leaders have come to tolerate Pakistan, because they do not have the power to destroy her. If they could forge this power, as they are endeavouring to do by the augmentation of their military forces, they

> would end partition and reabsorb Pakistan into the India of their dreams.... Every conceivable situation in our internal affairs continues to be exploited by India with the aim of aggravating our difficulties and weakening our national integrity.... From time immemorial the exponents of Greater Bharat have maintained that its political, cultural, and economic hegemony should extend from the Hindukush to the Mekong. Throughout Indian history political philosophers have propounded this theme at such length and with such frequency that it has become a part of the tradition which modern India has inherited.... As a first step towards its realisation, Pakistan must be neutralised, but ultimately the semi-religious concept of *Akhand Bharat* demands the end of Pakistan itself.[11]

The leader of opposition in the Pakistan National Assembly, Mohammad Aslam Khattak observed that it was a fact that India had not reconciled itself to the partition of the subcontinent. It cherished the dream that partition could be undone.[12] Similarly, former Ambassador of Pakistan in India, Sajjad Hyder wrote:

> To us in Pakistan the reason for this malaise is our perception that beneath a thin veneer, the Indian leadership and a sizable segment of its following continue to regard the formation of Pakistan as an historical error forced on India, that given the opportunity they would like in some way to redress the situation and that in their mind, the 1971 War supported this presumption.[13]

Compounding the above was the fear of a

subordinate power status being thrust on Pakistan vis-à-vis India. This was a reflection of the transformation of the struggle for parity between the Muslim League and the Indian National Congress, and the resultant Pakistani search for parity with India. The United States-British military support to India during the Sino-Indian war of 1962, and its increased defence expenditure, further enhanced Pakistan's threat perceptions. United States' supply of arms to the 'enemy', as well as the Indian military build up, were perceived as threats to its position in the subcontinent. Pakistan was also concerned at the declining prospects for resolving the Kashmir dispute in its favour. It maintained that India was extracting maximum advantage from the issue so as to unite the country, which was falling apart, as well as to obtain massive military assistance.[14] Bhutto wrote in 1969: "By herself she is a menace to the security of Pakistan and, aided by powerful external forces she will be a greater menace."[15]

Twenty-four years after partition, many Pakistanis saw the Indian role in the 'dismemberment' of Pakistan in the 1971 war as the 'ultimate proof' of India's continued 'intentions' and 'unwavered determination'. The separation of East Pakistan, which became Bangladesh, was perceived to have destroyed some of the fundamental and ideological arguments that had justified Pakistan's existence as an independent state.[16] Patterns of alignment remained the same since 1971; although the growth of nuclear rivalry between the two countries, the Soviet intervention in Afghanistan[17] the post-11 September 2001 attacks on Afghanistan, India's ten month troop deployment along the border during 2001-2002, India's improving relations with the United States, all had their impact on the dominant discourse on security in Pakistan. According to Sajjad Hyder, "the first determinant of our foreign policy is safeguarding Pakistan from India."[18] Reflective of the dominant discourse in Pakistan, Pervaiz Iqbal Cheema points out that almost all Pakistanis perceive a threat from India. Apart from a few patches of peace, abnormality of relations between India and Pakistan have become an accepted norm. Almost all governments in Pakistan have justified periodic increase in allocation of resources for defence by using arguments revolving around the existing geo-political realities.[19]

Since the early 1990s certain elements of a broader, more positive conception of security began to emerge. Khattak points out that this was a consequence of the changes in donor discourses and international perceptions in the context of the impact of capitalist expansion in the Third World. However, in state-sponsored security discourses, the collapse of the Soviet Union and its security system were framed as the key event to convince policy-makers that arms races are destructive and that old ways of speaking about security are inadequate. No mention was made of other factors, including the impact of structural adjustment on the people from the mid-1980s onwards. The United States foreign policy emphasis on human security was publicised widely, as the United Nations Development Programme, the World Bank and the IMF projected similar ideas. Pakistani governments, anxious to obtain foreign aid, began to integrate positive security issues into their public policy formulations. Attempts to involve the private sector in these ventures were also initiated. The Pakistan government's Social Action Programme which called for greater emphasis on people's development was a case in point. This was in line with the new thinking as twenty five per cent of the funding was provided by donor agencies, including UNDP, International Development Agency (IDA), Asian Development Bank (ADB), and the government of the Netherlands. Consequently, what the UNDP and the United States considered as priorities were given prominence. However, what is of significance here is the fact that the human security discourse has not replaced the mainstream security discourses but is only being given greater importance than before.[20]

## SECURITY/INSECURITY NARRATIVES IN INDIA

In the context of India, the insecurity narratives largely referred to the wars with Pakistan, the defeat by China in 1962, the nuclear explosions by China in 1964 and later by Pakistan in 1998, the US support to Pakistan from time to time, the 'aiding and abetting of insurgency' and the attempts at 'balkanisation' of India by Pakistan over the years. The dominant security discourse in India maintained that the main threat to the country was from 'external enemies', who 'fomented trouble within the country' so as to achieve their objectives. As such, internal dissent was to a large extent seen as the work of some 'foreign hand'. Pakistan emerged as 'the most dangerous of all threats' as it sought to 'Balkanise' India.[21] Several publications of the Ministry of External Affairs including *Pakistan's War Propaganda Against India* reproduced inciting statements by Pakistan's leaders, political organisations and the mass media which were aimed at arousing enmity towards India.[22] The Annual Reports of the Ministry of Home Affairs have also over the years highlighted the threat from Pakistan. For instance, the *Annual Report 2001-02* of the Ministry, stated:

Pakistan has consistently used terrorism

> and covert action as an instrument of State policy against India. It has recruited, trained, financed, armed and infiltrated terrorists into India. It has provided sanctuary to known anti-Indian elements, and those declared as fugitives from the law in India. It has also sought to promote disaffection among the Indian people towards the State, with a view to destabilize (sic) the country.[23]

Prior to partition, Nehru had stated that the conception of Pakistan "is not only dangerous to the unity of India, but it is dangerous to the Muslims themselves."[24] In 1949 Nehru proclaimed: "Pakistan has this slogan: 'First Kashmir, then Patiala and then on to Delhi'. This shall not happen.... Pakistan appears to be afflicted with some mental disorder which makes her often talk against India and undertake things which are really suicidal."[25] Over the years, political leaders of the country, political parties and the Defence and External Affairs establishments stressed the threat to India from Pakistan's aggressive designs.[26] Speaking in the Lok Sabha, Balraj Madhok, Secretary of the Bharatiya Jan Sangh (BJS) party, pointed out that Pakistan was born out of hostility towards India and it lived on hostility for India. "Let us realise that so long as Pakistan exists, it will remain an enemy of India, whatever we may do to appease it and to befriend it. Only a policy of reciprocity can solve the problems. We must have tooth for tooth and eye for eye. That may be a barbaric principle but that is the only language that Pakistan understands".[27] In 1963 itself the BJS had pointed out:

> It has been the considered view of the Bharatiya Jana Sangh that Pakistan by its

> very genesis and nature is destined to treat India as its enemy No.1, so long as it exists. Hostility to India and Hindus is the only prop which keeps going this artificial State of two parts separated by a thousand miles of Indian territory. Its continual adventures against India, the continuous anti-India and anti-Hindu outbursts of its rulers and press and the constant harassment of its Hindu population... are manifestations of a set policy of keeping at the highest pitch the anti-India and anti-Hindu frenzy in Pakistan at all times.[28]

India perceived Pakistan's membership of Western–sponsored defence alliances and its drive for security as a dangerous trend aimed at attaining parity with India and challenging the natural power-hierarchy in the sub-continent.[29] Although Pakistan's relationship with the United States was often problematic, particularly over nuclear proliferation issues from the 1970s onwards, it regained US support during the 1980s as an ally against the Soviet presence in Afghanistan. The Indian perception of the threat from Pakistan has, therefore, been inextricably related to the Indian assessment of the extent of support Pakistan could obtain from the United States at any particular point in time. As such, the Chinese and American factors are not viewed as entirely distinct from the Pakistani factor in the formulation of Indian foreign policy. After its defeat in the Sino-Indian war of 1962, India became increasingly concerned at the prospect of a two-front attack by China and Pakistan, particularly as a strong military partnership had developed between the two countries.[30]

Indian military preponderance in South Asia,

according to Raju G. C. Thomas, is precisely the goal of Indian defence policy and is considered to be the desirable state of affairs to maintain peace and stability in the region. However, from the Pakistani perspective Indian demands for military superiority in proportion to its size and perceived security requirements are unacceptable. Pakistan has consequently sought parity with India in the distribution of forces. Indian and Pakistani defence programmes have therefore tended to be mirror images of each other. Proponents of the Indian military build-up argue that this kind of comparison with Pakistan is not only misleading but also irrelevant as India's security problems are much wider than expressed by the Indo-Pakistani military balance.[31] India does not accept that her security problems are entirely linked to Pakistan. It has also strongly opposed Pakistan's enhancement of defence capabilities on grounds that there is no real threat to Pakistan.

Despite the exigencies, no attempt was made to formally articulate India's security policies. The evaluation of the security environment by the Ministry of Defence (MoD) in about two or three pages in its annual reports was the closest available document. The first chapter of these annual reports entitled 'National Security Environment' laid out the threat perceptions. After commenting on the international security situation, evaluations of the security threat from China and Pakistan, and then from other countries in the region were made. The evidence of the Defence Secretary before the Estimates Committee of Parliament has also over the years affirmed that India's defence policy "has been basically a policy to defend our territory, our sovereignty and our freedom and no more than that."[32]

Although matters relating to internal security come under the Ministry of Home Affairs (MHA), Gautam Navlakha argues that no reasons were cited for the emergence of militancy nor mention made of their political demands, the only refrain being the 'evil designs of Pakistan'. The Union Home Minister often voiced the opinion that the biggest challenge is the threat posed by the activities of the Inter Services Intelligence (ISI). It seemed fruitful to demonise opponents and highlight security risks posed by them. This could be utilised to justify allocation of resources for building up the security forces.[33]

In its report of 20 August 1992, the Estimates Committee had recommended that the country should have a formal national security doctrine. But it was only with the *Annual Report 1997-1998* that the MoD spelt out India's national security objectives. In its opening chapter entitled "National Security Environment," the report stated that India's national security objectives are served by: defending the country's borders as defined by law and enshrined in the Constitution and protecting the lives and property of its citizens against terrorism and insurgencies; promoting further co-operation and understanding with neighbouring countries and implementing mutually agreed confidence-building measures; working with countries of the Non-Aligned Movement to address key challenges before the international community and engaging in co-operative security initiatives such as the ASEAN Regional Forum (ARF); pursuing security and strategic dialogues with major powers and key partners; and following a consistent and principled policy on disarmament and international security issues based on universality, non-discrimination and equal security for all.[34] Later years witnessed a gradual widening of the security discourse. Speaking at the United Service Institute of India in 1997, I.K.Gujral, the then Minister of External Affairs, observed:

> In this period of significant change, where we are trying to transform the politico-economic face of our region, the concept of security has to be viewed afresh. Security can no longer be visualised in narrow military terms. Today, it calls for interdependence among all the countries of the world, to tackle non-conventional and non-military threats arising out of international terrorism, narcotics, ethnic conflicts, fundamentalism, environmental pollution, natural disasters, etc., all of which impinge upon overall security of nations....[35]

Given this situation he called for a cooperative approach rather than a conflictual one. The 'Gujral Doctrine', as it came to be called, sought a new framework of relations in South Asia based on non-reciprocity with small powers, non-intervention, and peaceful bilateral negotiations for resolution of disputes. In his first statement to the national press, K.C.Pant, who played an important role in the creation of India's National Security Council noted: "The concept of security should be holistic and not confined to military aspects. Since India is a nuclear weapon state now, it is even more urgent that the country advance rapidly in the economic sphere."[36] The problem of internal security came to be perceived as a "security policy issue" in India during the 1980s. The Ministry of External Affairs (MEA) in its *Annual Report 1998-99* stated that the country's foreign policy was viewed as an integral part of the larger effort of building the nation's capabilities: through economic development, strengthening social well-being and the quality of life and of protecting India's sovereignty, territorial integrity and security, not only in its defence and economic aspects, but in the widest strategic sense of the term.[37]

At the same time however, the securitisation of Pakistan continues unabated in official security discourse and documents. The web page relating to the Indian Armed Forces on the website of the Ministry of Defence states that

> ... the single greatest threat to peace and stability in the region is posed by the combination of terrorism nurtured in and by Pakistan for its strategic objectives, and the ingrained adventurism of the Pakistani military motivated by its obsessive and compulsive hostility towards India. Virtually every terrorist act anywhere in the world today has a Pakistani fingerprint somewhere. It is the root and epicentre of international terrorism in the region and beyond.[38]

The *Annual Report, 2006-2007* of the Ministry of Defence also highlights the threat from terrorist groups based in Pakistan. Similarly, the Ministry of Home Affairs in its *Annual Report, 2005-2006,* states that the terrorist outfits operating and indulging in acts of terror in India continue to be based in Pakistan/PoK. The focus of these Pakistan sponsored terrorist outfits is also to promote disaffection and communal disharmony among the Indian people towards the State in order to destabilise the country. It also points out that one of the main features of the ISI strategy in India is to intensify the low cost and proxy war operations in a wide area extending from Jammu and Kashmir to the hinterland.[39] The *Annual Report 2006-2007* as well as speeches and statements of government officials, also read along the same lines.[40] Although the government seems to have acknowledged that national security has larger dimensions beyond the traditional perception of military security and that there is a need to proceed beyond the historical concerns of national security in the security debate in India, the concern with Pakistan clearly continues in policy-making circles.

Another characteristic feature of the security discourse in South Asia is its state-centric and inward-looking approach based on certain assumptions relating to domestic political processes. These include the assumptions that the state as a territorial entity encapsulates the society and the nation, which have no existence without it; that there is a separation of the 'domestic' sphere from the 'international'; that the state is an integrated unit which has the capability to act effectively in different policy areas and faces the outside world as a unitary actor; and the reliance on military power as a strategic resource.[41] Ranabir Samadar argues that territoriality is the core of the politics of security in the subcontinent. The interlinked existence of the ideology of territoriality and the national security state in postcolonial South Asia needs to be emphasised. India secured her independence through partition, communities were segregated on the basis of dimensions of territoriality, and frontiers changed into borders, transforming the flexible existence of communities in the outlying regions into a rigid one.[42] The defence of the territorial integrity of the country has formed the crux of the dominant security discourse.

Security policies in both India and Pakistan continue to prioritise military power with threat perceptions relating to military balances and imbalances being given highest priority. Normal military exercises lead to dangerous spiralling of tensions and misperceptions. The consequent militarisation of the economy, the civil society, and international relations exacerbate tensions both within and between these countries.[43] Evidently, in both India and Pakistan security perspectives continue to be entrenched in traditional cold war concepts. Albeit changes in security discourses to accommodate the emerging conceptualisations of security, the human security discourse has not replaced the traditional state centric discourse in South Asia.

## NATION BUILDING, IDENTITY AND IMAGES

The security dilemma in South Asia is not restricted to the state but is an integral part of civil society itself. Mustapha Kamal Pasha maintains that civil society is no longer an escape from the security dilemma in South Asia than the state is. Civil society is inseparable from the state and the national security project in India and Pakistan. The crux of the security discourse in both India and Pakistan is linked to a particular articulation of the idea of the modern nation. This idea is not restricted to state practices but draws support in civil society. Competing conceptions of national identity are interlinked with security in India and Pakistan. According to Pasha:

> the 'national' project serves quite different purposes for India and Pakistan: in India's case, providing a basis for building a regional hegemonic order; in the case of Pakistan, providing a basic raison d'etre for that country as a separate homeland. Given these two meanings, 'national' security is

> correlated with different articulations of political space in the region.... In question here are not only different conceptions of security but also those of national identity.[44]

Rita Manchanda also posits that the nation-state building project of the postcolonial states of South Asia has focused on forming nationalist identities based on the politics of exclusion, "walling in people in a confrontationist security agenda, with implications for minorities within the state and for external relations."[45] National security in South Asia is perceived as the legitimate expression of state interests, closely linked to the idea of nation building. National security has been invoked to justify the process of nation-building. Consequently, the notion of national security has often been used to evoke feelings of hostility toward an imagined 'other'.

In the case of Pakistan, the regime's search for legitimacy has been reflected in the militarisation of politics that led to the continuous emphasis on threat and conflict from external factors. The security imperative was raised to the status of an ideology fundamental to the survival of the state. The Pakistani military's vested interests in its own expansion and strength also kept alive the hostility towards India. Thus, according to the dominant security discourse, the primary threat to Pakistan arises from external sources. India is the nearest and the most dangerous of them, followed by Israel and the West. The threatened community is that of a Muslim Pakistan whose Islamic identity is endangered by external enemies and their local collaborators. Faced with this situation, Nizamani points out that traditionally the key objectives of Pakistan's security policy are the strengthening of an independent Islamic identity, bringing Kashmir into the fold of Pakistan to complete the unfinished agenda of Partition and, finally, building the solid foundations of an Islamic *Ummah* (community) in world politics.[46]

In the case of India, the dominant security discourse envisages the idea of regional dominance, consistent with India's perceived self-image as both the legitimate successor to the British Raj and the civilising power in the subcontinent. Indian civil society generally supports the idea of equating security with domination. According to the dominant discourse, India is a secular democracy, which has a special responsibility to ensure peace and stability in South Asia. In view of its size, population and history, India ought to be respected by the neighbouring countries and treated as a major power by the international community. The dominant security discourse maintains that external enemies foment troubles within India to achieve their objectives. Therefore, internal dissent is only the extension of some foreign hand. Pakistan emerges as the most dangerous of all threats because it strives to Balkanise India.[47] Rita Manchanda points out that part of the intellectual framing of what can be termed as the Hindutva agenda is "a nostalgic re-visioning of a powerful (Hindu) India which calls upon (Hindu) India to shake off the slough of weakness and unmanliness and reclaim the fear and awe due to her, especially from neighbours."[48] It is largely the rhetoric of 'national unity and integrity', 'patriotism', 'secularism' and 'democracy' 'fighting fundamentalism and terrorism' etc. that constitute the discourse of power and the legitimating ideology of the state in India.[49]

The need for security is inculcated through a culture of nationalism and patriotism and is perpetuated through various rituals and programmes.

Partisan history being taught on both sides of the border often engenders visions of the 'other', with the average school children of both countries being taught that the 'other country' is their enemy.[50] The dominant security discourse of post-partition generations have been based on the powerful adversary images each country created for itself on partition and which continues to be sustained.

## OF COUNTER-NARRATIVES

Counter-narratives, which attempt to offer alternative views on security, do exist in both India and Pakistan. These counter-narratives generally identify threats to be at the internal level, in the form of social, economic, political and gender inequalities, which are exacerbated by external factors. The search for military security is seen to have only made the people of South Asia more insecure, militarising their polities and undermining democratic institutions. Rita Manchanda asks "whose security is being guarded by these weapons? Ask the millions of the poor and disadvantaged, the majority of whom are women – how do they define 'dangerous'?"[51]

The quest for military security ignores the 'latent threats', which Verghese Koithara describes as an enfeebled people, a fragmented society, economic and technological mismanagement, jeopardisation of vital security areas such as food and energy, environment degradation, alienation of citizens and disputes.[52] The challenges to human security are evident from the dismal statistics relating to illiteracy, population growth, infant mortality, and women's empowerment in South Asia. They highlight the people's lack of access to food, shelter, clean drinking water, basic health and educational facilities. Although the Human

Development Report for South Asia has over the years reported that South Asia is fast emerging as the poorest, the most illiterate, the most malnourished, the least gender-sensitive, and the most deprived region in the world, the region continues to make more investment in arms than in the education and health of its people.[53] Analysing India's defence budget for 2006-2007, Gautam Navlakha points out that "it is intriguing that concerns of the sovereign people do not matter although issues of national sovereignty are supposedly the main focus of national security and therefore the budgetary exercise. It is this disconnect that needs addressing."[54]

Counter-narratives in Pakistan argue that the dominant notions of national security are created by the ruling classes to sustain higher military spending and legitimacy for military rule. Dissident voices seek a Pakistan, which would have friendly relations with India through drastic cuts in defence spending – including renouncement of the nuclear programme – and moderation in Islam-based rhetoric.[55]

Lt. Gen. V.R.Raghavan (retd.) of India argues that ruling parties have allowed the state to become a tool in the hands of those threatening national security. Taking into account the military strength and economic power of India in the region, it is not under threat of military invasion or defeat from any of its neighbours. However, the citizen's well being is seriously undermined by social and political violence. The much-vaunted power of the state is seen to be incapable of defending the citizen or protecting his well-being. Indian citizens are insecure behind secure borders thereby mocking the power of the state.[56]

The dominant discourse's perception of internal security problems as being linked to external sources of threat ignores the causes of militancy and the consequences of adopting a militaristic approach. As a result the root causes of problems remain unaddressed. On the other hand, the search for political solutions relies on military success against insurgents. In this process, atrocities, civilian casualties, destruction of democratic institutions, etc. become unavoidable collateral damage. Imaginary or exaggerated threats can be used to arm the government with weapons and laws. The counter-narrative therefore argues that an examination of the official assessment of threats to security is of vital importance. A change in the political approach in favour of diplomacy, dialogue, and economic cooperation can enable a cutback in military build-up and the nuclear weapons programme, which could help save scarce resources. However, Gautam Navlakha points out that given the size of the border and coastline as well as armed militancy, military expenditure cannot be wished away. The point is whether it should carry on along the present lines. "Were the Indian government to pursue a policy of enlightened self-interest it would be possible to maintain a credible military strength for external defence by substantial reduction of the military budget."[57]

Analysing the reports of the Ministry of Home Affairs over the years, Navlakha points out that "there is a subjective bias in all these threat assessments. Only those conflicts are elevated to the rank of an internal security threat, where the presence of a foreign hand can be shown, unmindful of how and what caused them."[58]

Counter-narratives in India question the basis of the dominant discourse by not considering the 'others' of this discourse, as a manifestation of evil. Rather than viewing Pakistan as the main source of India's troubles, they consider most of India's problems to be an outcome of unresolved aspects of the question of Indian identity, poor governance and international economic factors. Similarly, rather than viewing India as a custodian of regional order, these counter-narratives would like the government to abandon policies that are construed by smaller neighbours as having hegemonic designs. Where the dominant discourse dismisses the demands for separate identities and decentralisation as the handiwork of a few insurgents acting upon external instructions, there is an assertion by the counter-narrative, of India as a genuinely democratic, secular and federal society. Counter-narratives view the demands of various identity-based movements with sympathy, holding New Delhi responsible for mishandling the contending demands of various groups. Alleged external enemies are not blamed for instigating trouble in India. Thereby the entire premises of the dominant discourse are brought into question.[59] The Pakistan factor is viewed as being conveniently used to cover all domestic dissent as a result of external subversion. National security is used by the state to unleash repression. As is found in the use of the anti-terrorist and disturbed areas acts against political dissidents, Rajni Kothari points out that what the state sees as 'internal disturbances' are often people's genuine struggles to preserve their rights and sources of survival, to protect their resources and their livelihoods.[60] Pasha argues that as the 'security dilemma' in South Asia is not confined to the state but is a generative feature of civil society itself, attempts either to rethink national security or to set up confidence-building measures remain pious aspirations without substantive content. A key implication here is the necessity of recovering civil society from the national security project of the state.[61]

As Feroz Hassan Khan points out, politics in South Asia lurches from fears of mutual annihilation to euphoria of the beginning of an era of historic peace and prosperity. This trend has been more evident since the 1998 nuclear tests. For instance, the historic peace summit in Lahore in 1999 was followed by the Kargil crisis. Two years later another high profile summit was held in Agra, which was again followed by a massive troop deployment at the border following the 13 December terrorist attacks on the Indian Parliament. Another summit was held in early 2004 and the ensuing process of dialogue continues – with summits as well as other methods of transport and cricket diplomacy, and Track-II initiatives. But relations continue to be fragile. Despite the desire for peace among sections of civil society, there continues to exist "a persistent belief in India that any crazy event either in India or Kashmir ... could trigger a war with Pakistan."[62]

It is clear that despite the reconceptualisation of security over recent years, the dominant security discourse in South Asia continues to be based on the realist paradigm of state-centric, military security focused on external threats, or internal threats compounded by external forces. Counter-narratives perceive the basic threats to security to be due to domestic socio-economic and political problems, international economic factors, and the militarisation of the subcontinent, which need to be reversed, together with improved relations between nations. Both narratives are executed through various channels, the most important being the mass media.

Suneet Vir Singh, in his content analysis of the

print media of South Asia, reveals the low level of interest about neighbouring countries in the national dailies of each country. In reporting political events and developments, the press in each country is guided more by the passions and prejudices of its own elite and by the state of bilateral relations with the other country. Communication among the countries of South Asia has not encouraged an orientation towards cooperation. The media have not seriously attempted to weaken or remove barriers, but have strengthened them by feeding adversary perceptions.[63] The mainstream mass media of the region approach the issue of security from a traditional/realist perspective, with demonic representations of the 'other'. The India-Pakistan scenario is a particular case in point. Although the situation as viewed from both India and Pakistan has been mutually reflective,[64] the present focus is on the role of the press in India, taking into consideration the larger context of the study.

## PRESS IN INDIA

The mass media play a critical role in the construction of the public sphere in India. The press in India is an important forum of debate on vital issues of public policy. On the one hand, it is the voice of the establishment and the expression of the dominant elite group and its ideology. On the other hand, it has also been an agency of communication, information dissemination and public debate. Newspapers have contributed significantly to raising general awareness on a range of issues, from changing social values, to policy and programme failures. The ability of the print media to influence the perceptions of both ordinary readers as well as policy-makers cannot be underestimated. It has been an integral part of the political process of Indian democracy.[65] Media reports have often been quoted in parliament while raising issues or substantiating arguments. Prime Minister Jawaharlal Nehru stressed the importance of the press in shaping perceptions when he stated:

> ...it plays a very important part in our lives; it moulds people's minds and thoughts and thus affects policies of Government, if not always directly. Therefore when we have to deal with any major problem it is important that the press should – if I may say so with all humility – give the right lead.... the press gives the lead which gradually sinks into people's minds. A person forms his opinion about distant occurrences by the news he gets from the press. Very few individuals are competent enough to know the facts or form an opinion independently. They are naturally guided by what the press says.[66]

Newspapers in India are largely owned by individuals, societies and associations, joint stock companies, or firms and partnerships. Although there are also newspapers run by political parties, trusts and co-operative societies, these are exceptions to the rule and have relatively small circulations. Many of the big newspaper groups are owned and controlled by industrial and commercial enterprises. Over the years, the Indian press has developed strong monopolistic tendencies with a few large business houses owning a major share of the market, establishing chains and groups, and dominating circulation and advertising revenue. Press ownership in India has to a large extent been concentrated in the hands of a few industrialist families who have significant economic stakes or interests outside the newspaper business. Newspapers such as *The Times of India, The Hindustan Times, The Statesman* and *The Indian Express* are connected with huge industrial concerns such as Tatas, Birlas, Goenkas and others. Directors of large cement, jute, steel and rubber companies have guided the destinies of some of these newspapers.[67] Of late, they have also made forays into the electronic media.

The two Press Commissions appointed by the Government of India traced the major problems in the Indian press, to imbalances in its ownership structure. The Report of the Press Commission of India of 1954 stated that it was inevitable that newspapers owned by businessmen or industrialists should adopt editorial policies, which advanced directly or indirectly the interests or commitments of the proprietors. The Press Commission also held that the bulk of the persons who own and publish newspapers encouraged the expression of views and news which favour the continuance of the present order, while discouraging and blacking out contrary views.[68] The Second Press Commission Report of 1982 pointed out that when newspapers were controlled by other big business, they became vehicles of expression of the ideology of their owners, and the selection, presentation and display of news in such papers could be dictated by their ideology.[69] The business houses have in their newspapers a potent weapon to fight change and maintain the status quo. These newspapers need not have any responsibility to the people or society. The Mahalanobis Report on the Concentration of Economic Power pointed out that economic power could also be exercised through control over the mass media. This link between industry and newspapers, which has existed in India, to a much larger extent than in most other democratic countries of the world, is of significance.[70]

The Indian press today also works in a highly competitive environment. With revolutionary changes in technology, communication and printing taking place, the cost of various inputs for publication of newspapers is increasing. This has had a severe impact on the circulation, quality and financial viability of newspapers. To maintain their existing economic status, with expectation of growth at a reasonable rate, newspapers have adopted the most modern technology in printing, requiring huge investments. This factor, among others also helped the increased concentration of the ownership of newspapers in the hands of some big business houses or trading interests.[71] Over the recent years, while media content has become more market-driven, much control has shifted, although indirectly, to "foreign corporates." Advertising and market research, which have an important role in determining the scope of media, are in the hands of companies largely controlled by foreign corporates.[72] The expansion of television over the 1990s eroded the advertising share of newspapers. A more recent trend has seen newspapers charging fees for publishing news, publicity notes and pictures. N.Ram points out that "in the name of the omnipotent market, a new kind of demand is made for manipulating news, analysis, and opinion to suit the owners' financial and political interests - and for tailoring the editorial product to subserve marketing goals."[73]

Analysing the impact of globalisation on the Indian media, Praful Bidwai argues that the likely effect will be extremely harmful and could severely restrict the fundamental right to inform and be informed, while strengthening right wing political forces in the country. Corporate intrusion into, and the takeover of, the vital functions of the media could undermine the public-oriented role of the media, and enlarge the conservative pro-establishment role. This could either be through the actual entry of foreign publishers, or through Indian publishers emulating global or Western models. It involves the destruction of the media as a responsible institution that disseminates information and promotes debate. It means obliterating the distinction between the editorial and business functions in a publication. Serious analytical writing is at a discount. Left-wing views, criticism of the post–1991 neoliberal economic policies and any questioning of jingoistic ideas about national security are increasingly hard to come across.[74]

Besides the above-mentioned problems arising from concentrated ownership and rules of the market in determining news content, the other constraints on the freedom of the press in India include the Official Secrets Act, the Parliamentary Privileges, and the Contempt of Court Act. The Indian press faced its worst crisis during 1975-76 with the declaration of national emergency, when censorship was imposed on the press. However, obstacles to news flow go beyond specific government regulations, laws and statutes. There have been instances of extra-legal methods of coercion employed by governments to silence or coerce unfriendly sections of the press. Government is a major advertiser and a large number of complaints pertaining to discriminatory release of advertising voiced during evidence before the Press Commission, as well as those recorded in the Annual Reports of the Press Council were related to pressure exerted by the State and Central governments as advertisers. There has also been criticism of the manner in which accreditation facilities are conferred or withheld as reward or punishment, especially by the state governments, stoppage of subscription to newspapers and electricity supply being cut off in retaliation to editorial policy, the selection of correspondents to accompany the Prime Minister on foreign trips and for radio and television assignments, etc.[75]

More importantly, editors and journalists have been co-opted into governmental—advisory positions, as in India's National Security Advisory Council. Sevanti Ninan points out that as more and more newspaper owners become Members of Parliament, more sensitivities have entered the newsroom. Self-censorship in India includes that imposed by the market, by political correctness, by militancy and extremism, by political connections of editors/owners, by the inability to substantiate, and generally on account of laziness accompanied by fear of libel.[76] Clearly there is often a blurring of the dividing line between the media and the institutions of government.

Another basic weakness of the press has been the minimum amount of resources usually spent on news-gathering. Even the more affluent newspapers often do not have full time staff reporters covering development issues, nor are they posted in the major capital cities of the world. Newspapers are also reluctant to share correspondents with others while at the same time generous use is made of government handouts. The First Press Commission Report states: "Our impression is that while Government is big news, newspapers are publishing far too many handouts obviously because material is made available to them in ready form at no cost."[77] In fact, many newspapers in India still substantially rely on government handouts and news services. A main feature common to all news agencies of South Asia is that they depend heavily on government patronage and government funding. Hence there is a definite inclination on the part of the news agencies not to embarrass the government. There is also a great deal of emphasis on official statements and governmental activity.

As is the case with the media in general, sensationalism and focus on immediate events and disasters rather than on long-term developmental processes with concerns for human security has been evident in the press in India also. Although there have been exceptions to the contrary, particularly among news magazines/journals, this study focuses on English language daily newspapers. Most Indian newspapers being run on corporate lines, profits and advertising are apparently not seen to correlate with socially relevant news. There has been a dearth of news on socio-economic processes in South Asia, while news concerning violence, disasters, and statements and escapades of political leaders often find their way into the front pages. P. Sainath points out that over recent years, the Indian press has been obsessed with the most trivial topics. The press has "no link at all to what hundreds of millions of Indians are thinking. This growing disconnect of the 'mass' media from mass reality is getting worse."[78] This is reflected in the 'beats' (or portfolios) of journalists within newspapers. For instance, from the mid-1990s, evidence of farmers committing suicide in large numbers began to pour in from several states, particularly Andhra Pradesh in the south. By the end of 2000, it was clear India was facing its most serious agricultural crisis in over two decades. Not a single national newspaper assigned a full-time correspondent to report on this crucial development, despite the fact that millions of people in India still depend on agriculture for a living. The Indian press covers far more than the basic politics, sports and commerce stories it concentrated on a decade ago, with full-time correspondents for fashion, glamour, design, even eating out! Beats related to covering the lives of ordinary people are vanishing at a rapid rate, the media proving to be increasingly inept at covering development issues. According to Jean Dreze, "(lack) of media concern for hunger and related issues makes it that much easier for the state to get away with doing nothing."[79]

Historically, the press in India was more zealous in covering the issues it today tends to ignore. Indian journalism was interlinked with the nation's freedom struggle. Mahatma Gandhi, Jawaharlal Nehru and a host of other freedom fighters were also journalists or publishers bringing out their own newspapers. The struggle for independence witnessed the importance of the press, particularly of newspapers like Lokmanya Tilak's *Kesari,* Mahatma Gandhi's *Young India, Harijan,* etc. Despite being very ill equipped, they reflected much wider concerns than newspapers do today. This historical role of the press and the journalistic efforts of those who led the crusade for freedom represented an adversarial role for the fourth estate in relation to the foreign ruler. Independence brought a turning point in the history of the Indian press, bringing to an end the era of journalism as a mission. The media was left free to become an industry. However, the crusading anti-British nationalist press assumed a largely supportive attitude towards the state in independent India. With Jawaharlal Nehru as the Prime Minister, and a democratic base established, the press found itself in a situation where a militant approach seemed inappropriate. The press apparently found it improper and unfair to be very critical of the new fledgling state, particularly given the strong tide of nationalism and anti-colonialism.[80] This was compounded by Nehru's cordial relations with the Indian business community, which controlled some of the large newspaper groups in India. Many of the norms set by this early relationship between the press and the state continued to govern the nature of journalism in the years to follow. There was a tendency to accept whatever represented the 'national interest' – particularly, with regard to the concerns of security.

## FRAMING NATIONAL SECURITY

The dominant security discourse in India, centred on the realist national security paradigm, found its reflection in the Indian press. The press has reflected a state-centric perspective rooted in military security against external threats. The major source of threat to the country has been projected as that arising from outside its borders. These threats often call for military responses, by way of enhanced capabilities. In the process, given the historical circumstances of the region, Pakistan has been projected as the major source of threat to the country in terms of both external aggression as well as inciting trouble within. Reflecting government perspectives, this is particularly evident in the media projection of the role of the Inter Services Intelligence (ISI) of Pakistan. The cause of numerous problems within the country is ascribed to the ISI, often without any substantive evidence. It has been observed that the selective leaking of unverifiable data through an obliging media is meant to fuel threat perceptions, which can be exploited for electoral gains.[81] Speaking about the role of the press in India-Pakistan relations, Prime Minister Jawaharlal Nehru pointed out:

I have been watching the press and I have

> seen what passions have been aroused through it. It is understandable. I am prepared to admit that there has been provocation. I am not comparing the Pakistan press with the Indian press but the fact is that the press has carried headlines and banner headlines which have excited the people. I am not saying that the facts should not be published but it is a question of how they are published.[82]

Rita Manchanda argues that in conflicts between India and Pakistan the mass media has functioned as an adjunct of the national security apparatus of the state. In representing India-Pakistan conflicts and interpreting internal conflicts like in North East India or Sind in Pakistan, the media in both countries have "internalised the national security psyche of the dominant elite and consequentially treat organised political violence as law and order-disorder."[83]

In the context of Kashmir particularly, the press in India has, over the years, reflected state-centric national security perspectives, continuing to repeat the official Indian version of the conflict. Persistent and simplified propaganda has built up an image of the Kashmir problem which ignores its complexities. It is characterised as a dispute over real estate between India and Pakistan, and a matter of national prestige. Human rights organisations, national as well as international, and also other media sources have documented in detail gross human rights violations in Kashmir by both the militants as well as the security forces. However, such a picture is not reflected in the Indian press, which, on the other hand, has portrayed the issue from a state-centric approach. The Indian press has tended to project the government's position that the reports of human rights violations in the Valley were merely the result of propaganda by Pakistan and the militants of Kashmir. Even the condemnation of human rights violations in Kashmir, by other countries and their calls for the respect of the rights of the people of Kashmir, including the right of self-determination have most often been blacked out. A survey of the sources of news on Kashmir is even more revealing. A study of the coverage of Kashmir, in three English language newspapers over a period of three months revealed that seventy eight per cent of the reports had as their sources - Indian Government officials and leaders of mainstream Indian political parties. Only seven per cent were based on Kashmiri sources, eight per cent on Pakistani sources and seven per cent on other sources including that of officials from other countries.[84]

The extent of near-jingoism on the issue in the Indian press becomes evident when one considers its staunch criticism of reports of human rights' violations in India, while at the same time quoting verbatim reports of violations in Pakistan. For instance, Subhash Kirpekar, a correspondent of *The Times of India,* published three articles (one of them in three instalments), strongly criticising the Asia Watch and Amnesty International reports of 1991 on India and Kashmir respectively, as being biased against India. He contended that the reports took a one sided view of the situation and were an 'intrinsic part of Pakistan's propaganda offensive against India'. Kirpekar's reports in *The Times of India* projected a nexus between Pakistan and the two Human Rights organisations. He strongly asserted that allegations of violations were mere propaganda by Pakistan and the militants, and the few such cases had been punished. However, the same writer, in the very same newspaper during the same period quoted almost verbatim the United States' Department of State's 1991 'Human Rights Report' which strongly criticises the situation in Pakistan.[85]

In the context of the Kargil conflict, Rita Manchanda points out that security became military security, at whose territorial altar was sacrificed the notion of human security. Although the Kargil crisis was also related to territorial security, it concerned the deeper issue of the people of Kashmir. The Vajpayee government delinked Kargil from Kashmir for political reasons, but the media, by uncritically endorsing that perspective reinforced the public perception of an essential antagonism between India and Pakistan. In covering the conflict, the mass media unquestioningly projected the official militarist framing of the conflict.[86] Such was the jingoistic coverage that in response to calls for restraint, *The Times of India* retaliated: "it is like advocating restraint equally to rapist and rape victim."[87] Due to various compulsions ranging from electoral-political to commercial, the India media served the cause of the state, which tends to project the military solution as the best possible solution. The media came to the state's assistance during the 'war' by framing news in such a way that the distinction between military achievements and patriotism became blurred.[88]

In a study of the coverage of Pakistan in the Indian press, based on a content analysis of select English language Indian newspapers over a period of three months, from 1 December 1991 to 29 February 1992, this author found that in reporting Pakistan's foreign policy, the major concern of the Indian press was with reports referring to its alliances with other countries, arms acquisitions and nuclear dimensions. Seventy per cent of the foreign policy coverage of Pakistan during the period of the study were related to nuclear/ defence aspects, thirty two per cent of which appeared on the front pages. The nuclear contract with China, the defence treaty with France, United States' Senator Larry Pressler's comments on Pakistan's nuclear programme, and Pakistan's own admission to having the capability to explode at least one nuclear device were the major foreign policy events highlighted by the Indian press during this period. Most reports sought to build up and reiterate the perception of a threat from Sino-Pak collusion – a factor that has been much highlighted by Indian leaders. Moreover, most of these reports placed much importance on giving detailed inventories of Pakistan's arms purchases and their capability against Indian offensive and defensive systems, thereby exacerbating such notions. Reports, which facilitated the increase of threat perceptions of the Indian reader, were highlighted, with provocative headlines. There was a persistent attempt to highlight the threat of aggression faced by the country from Pakistan, and the bogey of the 'Pakistani hand' in the efforts to destabilise the country. There were frequent front-page reports of highly inflammatory speeches alluding that Pakistan was seeking to annex India. More than the reports per se, it was their headlines and prominent display on the front pages, which served to instil such threat perceptions.[89] Headlines often ferret out something or the other negative of Pakistan from the article, no matter what the actual thrust of the article may have been. This nature of coverage has continued over the years with varying intensity.

In her study of the press in India and Pakistan for a period of one month starting from 15 January 2006, Subarno Chattarji states that there is "a lingering crossborder neurosis about the other country's interference.... The cycles of accusations and counter-accusations thus remained intact."[90] An impetus to the arms build-up in the region is thereby provided by the 'enemy' image shaped by the media. Analysing militarisation in South Asia, Paul Bracken points out that what puts arms races into overdrive is the appearance of falling behind. This creates an overwhelming impulse to catch up, even if no catching up needs to be done. Imaginary missile gaps, created and exaggerated in the Asian mass media have its impact on nations with histories of mutual hatred and long-standing feelings of inferiority. Sensational distortions or charges of 'falling behind' could incite public hysteria, raising tensions throughout the region.[91]

Editorials and opinion pieces often called for increased budget allocations for defence and arms build-up, the following editorial of *The Hindu* being a case in point:

> Modernisation of the defence forces with state-of-the-art weapons system and infrastructure is vital to safeguard the nation's security interests. Supply of M-11 missiles by China – which can carry an 800 kg. payload for a 290 km. range – to Pakistan and developments in the field of nuclear weapons across the borders pose serious threats to India's security. While there is little justification for an exaggerated reaction by the Centre, any complacency will be disastrous in defence preparedness.... If the targets set for the next five years are to be achieved, budgetary allocations for defence production have to be stepped up.[92]

The Indian press also inculcated a need for national security through a culture of militaristic nationalism and patriotism. This was particularly evident in times of conflict. Historically, whenever there was a conflict between India and Pakistan, the politicians of the two countries, in order to achieve as much legitimacy as possible, would contribute to the war hysteria by branding the 'other' as the aggressor and creating 'patriotic paranoia'. The mainstream media in both countries acted as catalysts in this process. In times of crisis, the media inevitably succumbed to patriotism at the expense of objectivity, resulting in jingoistic reporting and reinforcing stereotyped images and prejudices. Every conflict was an occasion for whipping up patriotism and sidelining dissent. The Indian media coverage of the Kargil conflict witnessed "the glamorisation of war and martyrdom," and a jingoistic hysteria of a "militarised patriotism." During the conflict, the media defined nationalism as patriotic flag waving, dangerously intolerant, and demonising all Pakistanis. The dominant media images of the war were the ceremonially draped coffins and ritualistic public mourning of heroic martyrs, which "constructed a martyrdom that defined a patriotic nationalist discourse of self sacrificing macho heroes who died valiantly...."[93] The 'valour of death on the battle-field', the 'celebration' of the 'martyrdom' of the officer or soldier, the readiness of others to 'give up' more youth for the country were the common themes running through news reports. Another interesting aspect was the fund-raising projects for Kargil organised by most newspapers.

The threat to India from Pakistan sponsored terrorism has been a consistent theme in the Indian press. For instance, V.K.Grover wrote in *The Asian Age* that "the greatest threat to our national security comes from Pakistan abetted terrorism and Jihad fanned by fundamentalists in Pakistan and Afghanistan."[94] Editorialising in 2001 on the activities of the ISI in India, *The Pioneer* pointed out that there were about 35,000 ISI agents in India whose objective was to bleed and exhaust India to such an extent that it has no longer any will to fight and is prepared even to surrender Kashmir for peace. Their other objective is to balkanise India by continuing with cross border terrorism and exploiting its ethnic, linguistic and religious diversity to stoke secessionist forces.[95] The post 9 September 2001 coverage of Pakistan saw an increased projection of threat from Pakistan sponsored terrorism. Shekar Gupta writes that the fundamental truth is that the "Pakistani establishment is driven by a hatred of India, bitter moral outrage over Kashmir and the overwhelming desire not merely to avenge 1971 but to win at least one war against India."[96]

## MEDIATING THE 'OTHER'

The language in which security has been framed in the Indian press is one of division and exclusion with negative qualities of aggression, threat and consequent danger being attributed to the external 'other'/Pakistan. On the contrary, the 'self'/India has been depicted as an icon of virtue. The explicit demonisation of "the enemy," sometimes becomes more implicit depending on the political circumstances. The press tends to highlight the detrimental aspects of Pakistani politics and society, giving extensive coverage to, and sensationalising issues relating to human rights violations, separatist movements, terrorism, voices of dissent, etc.[97] News which depict Pakistan in negative light tend to appear on the front pages, or get prominent coverage; whereas those which depict it positively appear, if at all, as tiny reports in some obscure corner. In other words, reports that reinforce old stereotypes are given prominence, while others ignored. It is not uncommon to find editorials decrying "Pak dominated by mullahs and Generals steeped in drug trafficking, money laundering and international terrorism."[98] Pakistan has often been projected as a failed state, a dangerous and aggressive country, with an obsessive hatred for India. Consequently, the perceptions of a threat from that country are exacerbated. Numerous reports appear in the Indian press on various aspects of the India-Pakistan dialogue. The common trend noticed is the positive projection of India as being ready for a dialogue and settlement of issues, while Pakistan is depicted as attempting to stall any such process. The message that comes through is that while India has been keenly striving to improve bilateral relations, Pakistan has sought to obstruct all efforts for peace.[99]

The internalisation of the 'other' as enemy is not restricted to times of conflict, but has also been reflected in peacetime interaction. The reporting on India-Pakistan cricket matches is a case in point. For instance, a headline of *The Indian Express* of 8 June 1999 reads, "India, Pakistan to 'fight' it out today," while *Asian Age* of 9 June 1999 declares, "Reborn India kill Pak." Metaphorical use of headlines has long been a part of reporting the game and is still very much in evidence, depending on the overall political climate of India-Pakistan relations. A typical headline reads: "Let the battle begin: Can Saurav and his men fulfil every Indian's ultimate dream?" The article opens thus:

> When Ian Botham stated that Pakistan is the place to send your mother-in-law for an all expenses-paid holiday, he was not

> kidding. It is that sort of a place.... Ball tampering, reverse swing, match-fixing, terrorist strikes, bomb blasts, boycotts, threats, anything goes in Pakistan. For a booming, shining India, Pakistan is wilder than the Wild West.[100]

This is merely a reflection of the nature of reporting which has been very much evident over the years. Depictions of the 'other' as a failed state and an Islamic fundamentalist terrorism sponsoring country are also evident. An editorial in *The Pioneer* reads: "Every new army ruler frames or amends the Constitution according to his personal desire or requirement.... Pakistan is a strange country where an army General, who is, after all, a government servant, suddenly comes out of his barracks, usurps power and rules the country without any hindrance or hesitation."[101] Bhaskara Rao states that the press in both countries depict a similar view of each other's country: "they are the aggressors," "their government encourages internal dissent and revolt," "their government uses aid equipment," "their army first used the American supplied arms," "their leaders cannot be trusted," etc.[102] Another feature of framing is what Dipankar Sinha calls the *pan-Indian syndrome* – a dissemination of information implying that the whole of India thinks and acts alike when it comes to teaching Pakistan a lesson.[103] In times of conflict, such framing becomes inevitable, the coverage of Pakistan during the Kargil conflict being a case in point. The media depiction of Pakistan as the monstrous 'other', was clearly evidenced in reporting on the return of the mutilated bodies of Indian soldiers during the crisis. Reports were full of value-loaded expressions such as 'martyr' and 'enemy', 'hero' and 'mercenary', 'laid life' and 'killed', and, 'our' and 'their'.[104]

The United States collaboration with Pakistan in its 'war against terror', in the context of the 9/11 tragedy found the Indian dailies vying with each other to highlight Pakistan's connections with terrorists and terrorist activities – particularly the Taliban and Al Qaeda. An article in *The Times of India* stated that it was Pakistan's former Interior Minister Major General (Retd.) Nasirulla Babbar who is credited with the creation of the Taliban and Pakistan has been supporting it financially in a big way from the payment of salary to the purchase of arms.[105] Similarly, Brahma Chellaney wrote in *The Hindustan Times*:

> Dictator Pervez Musharraf's smooth talk no longer is able to hide from global view Pakistan's position as the main sanctuary of Al Qaeda, the Taliban, Kashmiri and other transnational terrorists. After all, no other nation today has more deadly transnational terrorists on its territory. With the West constantly worrying about terrorists possibly acquiring weapons of mass destruction, it cannot fail to see that Pakistan has both State-supported terrorists and nuclear weapons controlled by Islamist generals.[106]

Another article in *The Pioneer* read: "King Abdullah should know better than most others the dangers that the Saudi-Pakistan nexus poses to moderate Islamic regimes and secular, pluralistic societies like India."[107] An editorial in the same newspaper states: "Political leaders should turn their attention to the clear and present danger to the nation's security persistently emanating from Islamabad despite international pressure. The Government should be prepared for the worst."[108]

## CONSTRUCTING CONSENSUS ON INDIA-PAKISTAN RELATIONS

There is a general perception that the Indian press is a liberal, vibrant institution carrying dissident views. However, while there is sharp criticism of government policies on domestic matters, when it comes to defence and foreign policy issues, the press largely avoids going openly against government perspectives. Reporting on defence and foreign affairs continues to be considered almost sacrosanct. The press has generally accepted without questioning, whatever the state maintained regarding territorial security and 'national interests'. There have evidently been certain limits to the space available for independent reporting on security matters. The Ministry of External Affairs (MEA) plays a major role in the projection of government policy in the international sphere. It continues to dominate not only the policies in relation to foreign countries, but also over what the media need to be told. Mani Shankar Aiyar writes of the efforts by the External Publicity Division of the MEA in disseminating anti-Pakistan information.[109]

According to the Second Press Commission Report, on every occasion when the country was involved in hostilities, not of its seeking, with other countries, the press stood behind the government and mobilised public opinion for the defence effort, irrespective of differences on domestic policies.[110] Subir Bhaumik contends that with the Indian press displaying absolute nationalist credentials, the army has no problems in a conflict with a foreign enemy. The problem is when it fights internal insurgencies. This may explain why the Indian establishment is so keen to project insurgencies as 'proxy wars' fought by Pakistan through 'other means'. The army has been quite successful in managing the mainstream national press. The press has shied away from reporting human rights violations, corruption, and even incompetence in the Indian military establishment, except for the occasional leak from disgruntled officials regarding defence deals which often end up as major exposes.[111] The propaganda of the two governments aided by the media made conflict between the two states seem to be an inevitable legacy of Partition. On the basis of his personal experience as the Islamabad correspondent of *The Hindu*, B. Muralidhar Reddy exclaims at the extent to which the Indian media has come to reflect the government line at least vis-à-vis Pakistan. Barring rare exceptions, he notes the complete resonance between the government's Pakistan policy and that of the media.[112]

At the time of the invasion of Kashmir by Pathan tribesmen from the Northwestern frontier, supported by Pakistan in 1947 the Indian occupation of Hyderabad and Junagadh during 1947-48, and the conflict between India and Pakistan over Kashmir in 1947, the press in both India and Pakistan failed to look at the issues objectively and supported in jingoistic language the viewpoints of their own governments. The Indian press almost unanimously supported the takeover of Hyderabad and Junagadh as being a manifestation of the democratic right of the people, the majority of whom were Hindus with a Muslim ruler. However, in the case of Kashmir, a Muslim majority area ruled by Maharaja Hari Singh, a Dogra, the Indian press went volte-face on their arguments about 'democratic rights'.[113] Sisir Gupta writes that in 1954 "a climate of conflict was created by a relentless press campaign in the two countries."[114] Russell Brines, a veteran war correspondent, who covered the 1965 war, describes the constant cries of 'aggression' evident in the press of the countries involved as having been designed primarily for propaganda.[115] In his study of the press coverage in both India and Pakistan of the 1965 war, Bhaskara Rao concludes that editorials in both countries repeated official versions of the conflict and served to further deepen in public opinion the sense of injury over their strained relationships.[116] During this period, press campaigns were so intense that it became an important preoccupation for the negotiators of the Tashkent Declaration of 1966. The *Annual Report 1965-1966* of the Ministry of External Affairs stated that Pakistan's hostile propaganda against India had reached unprecedented depths, which merely served to further poison the already bitter atmosphere between the two countries. According to the Tashkent Declaration of 1966, both countries agreed to "discourage any propaganda directed against the other country" and to "encourage propaganda which promotes the development of friendly relations."[117]

The 1971 Bangladesh war also illustrated the role of the media and its relationship with the state construction process and censorship. During the war, the government of India "enjoyed steadfast support of the press.... This 'national interest bias' was further underlined by the pronouncedly anti-Pakistan sentiment expressed in the editorials."[118] The United States aid packages to Pakistan have always been viewed with anxiety in the media. During Indira Gandhi's tenure this assumed near-hysterical proportions in the press. Indira Gandhi was the beneficiary of articles and editorials praising her courage and determination under the circumstances. The press gave unqualified support to the Prime Minister.[119]

After the Gulf War of 1991, the Indian army sought to emulate the United States model of 'Media-Military Cooperation', whereby CNN and other American networks had played 'force multipliers'. Since 1991-92, the Indian army initiated a series of 'Army-Media seminars'. A wide cross section of journalists and editors were invited to these seminars at which were present officers from the newly created PSYOPS (Psychological Operations) cell of the Military Intelligence (MI) Directorate. During the course of these programmes the MI officials picked up 'potential assets' who could be used as 'force multipliers' (nomenclature for favoured journalists who would accept favours in cash and kind, and plant pro-army or anti-insurgent stories). A list of "friends, acquaintances, pliables, toughnuts and hostiles" was drawn up.[120]

In the context of the Kargil conflict, it has been observed that as the official institutions developed their ability to control the information environment, the media became less critical, and more dependent on official versions. Winning the 'information war' was clearly seen as an important strategic objective. A study by the Indian Institute of Mass Communication (IIMC) on the role of the mass media during the Kargil conflict concluded that the Indian newspapers reflected only the official Indian viewpoint throughout the conflict.[121] In its findings on Media Relations and Information, the Kargil Review Committee Report categorically states:

> If the media served the country well, much of the credit goes to the initiative it itself took and to some individuals within the Government and the Armed Forces. Information is power, especially in this Information Age. The media moulds national

> and international opinion and can be a potent force multiplier. This was evident at Kargil, India's first television war. All things considered, coverage by the print and electronic media was by and large satisfactory.[122]

Barkha Dutt, who was noted for her reporting from the battlefront of Kargil for NDTV, later revealed: "It is true though, that we reported the war as Indian journalists, not because we were writing an anthem for the State, but because our own responses had been blurred by the situation we found ourselves in...."[123]

The 13 December 2001 terrorist attack on the Indian parliament and the subsequent troop deployment or Operation Parakram, by India along the border, also witnessed media coverage strongly supportive of the Government. While A.G.Noorani points out that the media was particularly uncritical on Operation Parakram, Rita Manchanda argues that the "media provided the context for fostering a jingoistic public opinion that backed the BJP government deploying 800,000 troops in a tense eyeball to eyeball military standoff along the border."[124] The website of the Media Foundation has a section entitled: 'Indo-Pak Monitoring Series'. As part of this series, Mannika Chopra, in her monitoring of newspapers between 15 July 2004 and 15 August 2004 discovered that it was "very rare to find a pro-Pakistan line in an Indian newspaper or vice versa."[125] Another survey by Subarno Chattarji during 15 January 2006 to 15 February 2006 revealed a consensus on issues relating to Kashmir, Baluchistan and the peace process. "Generally, there was a mirroring of suspicion and stereotypes of the 'other in most reportage'."[126]

In the context of confidence building measures

(CBMs), attitudes towards CBMs in the English language press often paralleled the perspectives of their leaders. Support for CBMs in the press was directly related to the commitment of national leaders toward the dialogue process.[127] All the India-Pakistan summits of the recent years, particularly since Agra in 2001, saw a hyped up media blitzkrieg. This was as true of the Lahore, New York and Delhi summits, as of the mediated celebration of the Agra summit. Such media hype was also evident during the government sponsored cricket diplomacy during 2004 and 2005. In March 2004, the Pakistan Government relaxed its visa restrictions on Indian journalists for the series of one-day matches and three test matches between the two countries in Pakistan. The deluge of Indian journalists in Pakistan was again reflected in the explosion of news on all aspects of Pakistan society, polity and culture. Coverage of such CBMs clearly mirrored government perspectives at that particular point of time.

## ON DISSENT

In the process of this consensus building, events and reports that reinforced establishment perspectives were selected and emphasised while those that contradicted it were often ignored. In both India and Pakistan, the media has tended to marginalise voices of dissent. While reports within the dominant frame require little corroboration, a dissenting approach calls for strong substantiation. This could become a time consuming exercise in a profession where time is crucial. Speaking on the role of the media in national security, George Fernandes asserted that dissent "is the essence of a democratic polity. But when it comes to matters of national security, it is the unity of purpose and action of entire people alone which will see us through."[128] In the context of Kargil, the military establishment also made no secret of its satisfaction with the media, with the defence minister himself praising the media for its 'morale boosting' role during the war. As the conflict deepened, the demand grew for suspension of critical comments on the inadequacies and failures that led to the crisis. After the initial criticism on the gross intelligence failure, the media soon fell in line.[129] The real issues regarding the pros and cons of the war, the impact on the people and economy, and so on, were conspicuous by their absence. The tragedy and futility of war, the waste of lives and the loss to families, and other such sentiments were rarely reflected in news reports. While numerous reports mentioned the government version of the torture and mutilation of six Indian soldiers, basic questions such as the motivation of Pakistan to return mutilated bodies, whether all or only one body was mutilated (as later reports) or the possibility of natural decomposition went unanswered.[130]

According to Jean Dreze, the interest of the Indian military establishment in 'media management' is not confined to periods of active conflict. Even at other times, a steady stream of propaganda seeps through the media. Much of this arises from 'experts' based in organisations such as the Institute for Defence Studies and Analyses (IDSA), the Defence Research and Development Organisation (DRDO), and the Research and Analysis Wing (RAW). Although propagating establishment views is not an explicit part of their brief, these experts are unlikely to display much independence of thought, given that they are on the payroll of the military establishment. He quotes P.R.Chari, former member of the Joint Intelligence

Committee and former director of IDSA, that DRDO is definitely a sinister organisation, which bribes both journalists and academics to press hard-line causes in the media, while RAW would have to reduce its staff and budget by one-third if the threat from Pakistan and China was allowed to fade. Dreze lists the affiliations of the thirty-five authors who wrote opinion articles on defence-related matters in *The Times of India* between April 1998 and March 1999 (before the Kargil crisis). Excluding professional journalists and editors, a majority of authors are members of strategic think tanks, retired army personnel or retired civil servants. Dreze concludes that there is "a deep asymmetry of resources, and influence between the 'doves' and the 'hawks' with the latter enjoying ample infrastructural resources and media access. The result is a pronounced militaristic bias in the Indian media." [131]

While acknowledging the scope of the media as an ideal bridge to overcome obstacles in India-Pakistan relations, constraints of the media have also been pointed out by journalists themselves.[132] At the same time hopes for a change in media perspectives through the efforts of a younger generation of journalists have also been perceived. They have begun to aggressively question the 'conventional wisdom' prescribed by the bureaucrats of New Delhi. C.K. Lal points out that Barkha Dutt questioning the handling of Kargil, even if retrospectively, was so different from the usual practice of veteran Indian journalists merely accepting official interpretations of apparently controversial decisions. The so-called Defencegate Scam exposed by the investigative team of Tehelka.com took India by storm precisely because it was in complete contrast to the way 'official secrets' have been handled before by the mainstream media.[133]

Similarly, publications such as *Himal South Asian* and organisations like South Asia Free Media Association, South Asia Forum for Human Rights and Panos South Asia have all organised conferences on media related issues of the region. Maintaining that a solution to the imbroglio between India and Pakistan requires a holistic vision, involving mainstream forces, powerful stakeholders and respective civil societies, political leaders as well as journalists have been invited to several of these conferences.[134] The comparatively restrained and responsible writing in publications such as *Frontline, Economic and Political Weekly*, etc. also provide some relief.

Evidently, notwithstanding the emergence of wider and more comprehensive levels of analysis in security debates over recent years, the dominant security discourse in South Asia continues to be based on the realist paradigm of state-centric, military security focused on external threats, or internal threats compounded by external forces. The dominant security discourses in both India and Pakistan are based upon the portrayal of the 'other' as evil, dangerous and inferior, while considering the 'self' as an icon of virtue. Decades of hostile relations have engendered a degree of rigidity, in which each side takes for granted the aggressive designs of the other. This creates a situation in which the general public in each country is seen to be peaceful and generous, while the negative qualities of the other nation are the cause of conflict. Historical factors clearly played an important role in defining the security/insecurity narrative in the region, with competing conceptions of national identity being interlinked to perceptions of security. Despite changes in security discourses to accommodate the changing concept of security, the human security discourse has not replaced the traditional security discourse. Such thinking/writing is cultivated through the educational system and the mass media of both countries, which play a crucial role in perpetuating these narratives and sustaining the process of securitisation. The dominant security discourse of post-partition generations have been based on the powerful adversary images each country created for itself on partition and which continues to be sustained. The securitisation of India and Pakistan by each other continues unhindered, particularly in policy-making circles and official documents. However, counter-narratives do exist in both countries. These counter-narratives perceive the basic threats to security to be due to domestic socio-economic and political problems, international economic factors, and the militarisation of the subcontinent, which need to be reversed, together with improved relations between nations. Both narratives are executed through various channels, the most important being the mass media.

Situated as it is within the historical circumstances of the subcontinent, news in the region is constructed, with political, economic, and socio-cultural interests exerting pressure on the selection and presentation of news. While being critical of domestic affairs, the press has seldom encouraged positive reporting of 'hostile' neighbours, or comments that are critical of government policies vis-a-vis such countries. There has been a focus on the traditional state-centric approach to security centred on the national security paradigm. The language in which security has been articulated is one of division and exclusion, reinforcing distinctions between 'self' and 'other'. Negative qualities of aggression and threat have been attributed to the 'other'. This is especially noticeable in the selection and presentation of news, use of news frames, headlines, etc. In this process, Pakistan is projected as a major threat. This is evident in the coverage of Pakistan's defence and foreign policy, and of issues relating to India-Pakistan relations, Kashmir, and the projection of the ISI bogey in the innumerable issues and conflicts within the country. Enemy images of Pakistan have been projected through the language of exclusion and the demonisation and dehumanisation of the country. This explicit demonisation of 'the enemy', sometimes becomes less explicit depending on the political circumstances. Threat perceptions of Pakistan are evidently mediated according to government perspectives, be it in times of conflict or of peace building. The governmental process of securitisation as well as desecuritisation of Pakistan in India has to a large extent had the unwavering support of the mainstream Indian press.

## NOTES AND REFERENCES

1 Barry Buzan, *People, States and Fear: The National Security Problem in International Relations* (New Delhi: Transasia, 1987), pp.108-109.

2 Barry Buzan, "South Asia Moving Towards Transformation: Emergence of India as a Great Power," *International Studies*, Vol. 39. No.1, January-March 2002, p.3.

3 Saba Gul Khattak, "Security Discourses and the State in Pakistan," *Alternatives*, Vol.21, No.3, July-September 1996, pp. 344-345.

4 Zulfikar Ali Bhutto, *The Myth of Independence* (London: Oxford University Press, 1969), p.170.

5 For example, see statements of V.K.Krishna Menon quoted in Zulfikar Ali Bhutto, *The Quest for Peace: Selections from Speeches and Writings 1963-65* (Karachi: Pakistan Institute of International Affairs, 1966), p.42; also see Liaquat Ali Khan, *Pakistan: The Heart of Asia: Speeches in the United States and Canada, May and June 1950, by the Prime Minister of Pakistan* (Karachi: National Book Foundation, 1976),

pp.15-47; Mohammad Ayub Khan, *Pakistan Perspective: A Collection of Important Articles and Excerpts from Major Addresses* (Washington DC: Embassy of Pakistan, n.d.), pp.71-72; Zulfikar Ali Bhutto, *Foreign Policy of Pakistan: A Compendium of Speeches made in the National Assembly of Pakistan, 1962-64* (Karachi: Pakistan Institute of International Affairs, 1964), pp.34-35; Pakistan, National Assembly, *Debates,* Vol.2 No.2, 22 November 1962, pp.4-5; also see Pervaiz Iqbal Cheema, *Pakistan's Defence Policy, 1947-1958* (Houndmills: Macmillan, 1990), pp.23-66.

6 Mohammad Ayub Khan, *Friends, Not Masters: A Political Autobiography* (London: Oxford University Press, 1967), pp.115-116.

7 William J.Barnds, *India, Pakistan, and the Great Powers* (London: Pall Mall, 1972), p.72; also see "Speech at Lucknow," 6 January 1948, India, Ministry of Information and Broadcasting, *For a United India: Speeches of Sardar Patel: 1947-1950* (New Delhi: Publications Division, 1982), pp.51-52.

8 The Resolution on the Statement of 3 June, All India Congress Committee, 14-15 June 1947, A.M.Zaidi and S.G.Zaidi (eds.), *India Wins Freedom: The Encyclopaedia of the I.N.C. Vol.13: 1946-1950* (New Delhi: S.Chand, 1981), p.111.

9 Khalid Mahmud, *Indian Political Scene, 1989: Main Contenders for Power* (Islamabad: Institute of Regional Studies, 1989), pp.130-31.

10 K.Raman Pillai, "Jana Sangh: A Rightist Opposition," in Verinder Grover (ed.), *Political System in India,* Vol.V (New Delhi: Deep and Deep, 1989), p.227.

11 Zulfikar Ali Bhutto, *The Myth of Independence* (London: Oxford University Press, 1969), pp.163-175.

12 Pakistan, National Assembly, *Debates,* Vol.3, Part-11, 21 August 1964, p.1213.

13 Sajjad Hyder, *Foreign Policy of Pakistan: Reflections of an Ambassador* (Lahore: Progressive Publishers, 1987), pp.74-75.

14 See Zulfikar Ali Bhutto, 1964, n. 5, pp.37-40, 69-74; Pakistan, National Assembly, *Debates,* Vol.2, No.4, 24 November 1962, pp.135-143; Pakistan, National Assembly, *Debates,* Vol.2, No.4, 26 November 1962, pp.79-86; also see Barry Buzan, n.1, p. 109.

15 Zulfikar Ali Bhutto, n.11, p.185.

16 See speeches in Pakistan, National Assembly, *Debates,* 14 April 1972; Pervaiz Iqbal Cheema, *Defence Expenditure in Pakistan, RCSS Policy Studies,* No.10, March 2000, www.rcss.org.

17 In 1988, Agha Shahi, who had been the President's Adviser on foreign affairs and leader of the Pakistan delegation to the UN General Assembly wrote that "an armed attack by India could be instigated, encouraged or supported by the Soviet Union should the Afghanistan situation remain unresolved." See Agha Shahi, *Pakistan's Security and Foreign Policy* (Lahore: Progressive Publications, 1988), p.180; also see Sajjad Hyder, n. 13, pp.127-147.

18 Sajjad Hyder, n.13, p.75; also see *Speeches and Statements by Field Marshal Ayub Khan, Vol.IV, July 1961-June 1962* (Karachi: Pakistan Publications, n.d.), pp.86-87; Bhutto, 1964, n.5, pp.15-46; Pakistan, National Assembly, *Debates,* Vol.3, no.2, 21 August 1964, pp.1208-1266.

19 Pervaiz Iqbal Cheema, n.16.

20 Sabha Gul Khattak, n.3, pp.342–357; also see World Bank, *Staff Appraisal Report: Islamic Republic of Pakistan: Social Action Program Project* (Washington D.C: World Bank, 8 March 1994), p.28.

21 Haider K.Nizamani, "Limits of Dissent: A Comparative Study of Dissident Voices in the Nuclear Discourse of Pakistan and India," *Contemporary South Asia,* Vol.7, No.3, November 1998, pp. 323-330.

22 India, Ministry of External Affairs, *Pakistan's War Propaganda Against India: September 1950-June 1951* (New Delhi, n.d.); India, Ministry of External Affairs, *Pakistan's War Propaganda Against India: 1 July 1951-15 August 1951* (New Delhi, n.d); India, Information Service of India, *Pakistan's War Propaganda* (New Delhi, n.d.).

23 India, Ministry of Home Affairs, *Annual Report, 2001-02* (New Delhi, 2002), www.mha.nic.in; also see India, Ministry of Defence, *Annual Report, 1988-89* (New Delhi, 1989), pp.1-2; India, Ministry of Defence, *Annual Report, 1993-94* (New Delhi, 1994), pp.2-3; India, Ministry of External Affairs, *Annual Report, 2001-02* (New Delhi, 2002), pp.9-10.

24 Speech at Delhi, 3 November 1945 in S.Gopal (ed.), *Selected Works of Jawaharlal Nehru* (New Delhi: Orient Longman,

1981), Vol.14, p.196.

25 Address at a Public Meeting, Ferozepur, 17 September 1949 in S.Gopal (ed.), *Selected Works of Jawaharlal Nehru* (New Delhi: Jawaharlal Nehru Memorial Fund, 1992), Second Series, Vol. 13, pp.249-250.

26 For instance, see among others, Speech in Lok Sabha, 28 April 1965, India, Ministry of Information and Broadcasting, *Selected Speeches of Lal Bahadur Shastri: 11 June 1964 to 10 January 1966* (New Delhi: Publications Division, 1974), pp.5-6; India, Ministry of Defence, *Annual Report, 1971-72* (New Delhi, 1972), p.1; India, Ministry of Defence, *Annual Report, 1991-92* (New Delhi, 1992), p.4; Address at National Defence College, New Delhi, 8 October 1985 in India, Ministry of Information and Broadcasting, *Rajiv Gandhi: Selected Speeches and Writings: 31 October 1984 to 31 December 1985, Vol.I* (New Delhi: Publications Division, 1987), p.54; V.P.Singh, "Developments in Relationship with Neighbours, Letters to MPs, New Delhi, 5 July 1990" in India, Ministry of Information and Broadcasting, *V.P.Singh, Selected Speeches and Writings, 1989-1990* (New Delhi: Publications Division, 1993), pp.274-275.

27 India, Lok Sabha, *Debates*, Vol.59, 29 November 1961, cols.2153-2158.

28 "Reappraisal of India's Pakistan Policy," 30 December 1963, Ahmedabad, XI AIS, in *Bharatiya Jana Sangh, Party Documents: Vol.3: Resolutions on Defence and External Affairs* (New Delhi: Bharatiya Jana Sangh, 1973), p.99; also see "Annul Partition and Liberate Pakistan," 1 March 1964, Delhi CWC, in *ibid.*, pp.104-107; Resolutions of the All India Congress Committee 1985 in A.M.Zaidi (ed.), *The Annual Register of Indian Political Parties: Proceedings and Fundamental Texts: 1985* (New Delhi: Indian Institute of Applied Political Research, 1987), pp.120, 181-182; also see Resolutions of the Central Committee of the CPI(M), 1984 in ibid., p.354.

29 See Nehru's Speech in the Lok Sabha, 22 February 1954 in India, Ministry of Information and Broadcasting, *Jawaharlal Nehru's Speeches: March 1953 to August 1957* (New Delhi: Publications Division, 1983), Vol III, p. 344; India, Lok Sabha, *Debates*, Vol.28, No.45, 22 April 1968, pp.246-266; K.Raman Pillai, *India's Foreign Policy* (Meerut: Meenakshi Prakasan, 1969), pp.53-60; India, Ministry of Defence, *Annual Report*

*1969-70* (New Delhi, 1971), pp.1-2; India, Ministry of Defence, *Annual Report 1970-71* (New Delhi, 1971), p.3; Statement by Sardar Swaran Singh, Minister of External Affairs, Lok Sabha, 28 June 1971 in India, Ministry of External Affairs, *Foreign Affairs Record*, Vol.17, No.6, June 1971, p.97; Statement by P.V.Narasimha Rao, Minister of External Affairs, Lok Sabha, 23 January 1980 in India, Ministry of External Affairs, *Foreign Affairs Record*, Vol.26, No.1, January 1980, pp.19-20.

30 See India, Ministry of Defence, *Annual Report 1963-64* (New Delhi, 1964), pp.2-3; India, Ministry of External Affairs, *Annual Report 1963-64* (New Delhi, 1964), p.26; Statement in Lok Sabha, 14 November 1962 in India, Ministry of Information and Broadcasting, *Jawaharlal Nehru's Speeches: September 1957 – April 1963* (New Delhi: Publications Division, 1983), Vol. IV, pp.243-44; Statement by Dinesh Singh, Minister of External Affairs, Lok Sabha, 22 July 1969, *Foreign Affairs Record*, Vol.15, No.7, July 1969, p.142; also see Raju G.C.Thomas, *The Defence of India: A Budgetary Perspective of Strategy and Politics* (Delhi: Macmillan, 1978), p.106; Lorne J. Kavic, *India's Quest for Security: Defence Policies 1947-1965* (Berkeley: University of California Press, 1967), pp.192-195.

31 Raju G.C.Thomas, "The Growth of Indian Military Power: From Sufficient Defence to Nuclear Deterrence," in Ross Babbage and Sandy Gordon (eds.), *India's Strategic Future: Regional State or Global Power?* (Delhi: Oxford University Press, 1992), pp.47-51.

32 See, for instance, India, Lok Sabha Secretariat, Estimates Committee, 1992-93, Nineteenth Report, *Defence Force Levels, Manpower Management and Policy*, Presented to the Lok Sabha on 20 August 1992 (New Delhi: Lok Sabha Secretariat, 1992), p.3.

33 Gautam Navlakha, "Whither People's Security," *Economic and Political Weekly*, Vol.36, No.23, 9 June 2001, pp.2038-2043.

34 India, Ministry of Defence, *Annual Report, 1997-98* (New Delhi, 1998), pp.2-8.

35 Speech by External Affairs Minister, I.K.Gujral, at the United Service Institute of India, 23 January 1997 (New Delhi: External Publicity Division, 1997), p.6, cited in Shrikant Paranjpe, "India's Security Policy: An Evaluation After Fifty

Years," *International Studies*, Vol.35, No.2, April-June 1998, p.164.

36 "Need to integrate national security with planning: Pant", *Indian Express* (New Delhi), 6 February 1999.

37 India, Ministry of External Affairs, *Annual Report 1998-99* (New Delhi, 1999), p.1.

38 India, Ministry of Defence, www.mod.nic.in.

39 India, Ministry of Home Affairs, *Annual Report 2005-2006*, p.30, www.mha.gov.in

40 See ibid; also see for eg. Address by Pranab Mukherjee, Defence Minister on India's strategic Perspective at Harvard University, 29 September 2006, www.indianembassy.org/newsite.

41 Sushil Kumar, "Rethinking Security in South Asia," *International Studies*, Vol. 36, No.2, April-June 1999, pp.95-100.

42 Ranabir Samaddar, "The Failed Dialectic of Territoriality and Security, and the Imperatives of Dialogue," *International Studies*, Vol.35, No.1, January-March 1998, p.108.

43 See ibid., pp.107-108; and Sushil Kumar, n.41, p. 103.

44 Mustapha Kamal Pasha, "Security as Hegemony," *Alternatives*, Vol.21, No.3, July-September 1996, pp.284-287.

45 Rita Manchanda, "Media Wages Info War," *Himal South Asian*, January 2000, www.himalmag.com.

46 Haider K.Nizamani, n. 21, pp.321-322.

47 Ibid., p.333; Haider K. Nizamani, *Roots of Rhetoric: Politics of Nuclear Weapons in India and Pakistan* (New Delhi: India Research Press, 2001), p.26. See K.Subrahmanyam, *Indian Security Perspectives* (New Delhi: ABC Publishing House, 1982); Devin T. Hagerty cites three cases in which the Indian security doctrine appears to have been operative: 1.India's efforts between 1983 and 1990 to end the Sri Lankan civil war through political and military pressure, including direct military intervention; 2. India's 1988 military intervention to prevent the coup d'etat in the Maldives; and 3. India's 1989 to 1990 trade dispute with Nepal. Several others could also be included to this list. See Devin T.Hagerty, "India's Regional Security Doctrine," *Asian Survey*, Vol. 31, No.4, April 1991, pp.352-372.

48 Rita Manchanda, "Dialects on Power: New Recipe for Border Security in South Asia," *Economic and Political Weekly,* Vol.36, No.31, 4 August 2001, p.2982.

49 Sumantra Bose, *The Challenge in Kashmir: Democracy, Self-determination and a Just Peace* (New Delhi: Sage, 1997), p.108.

50 See Saba Gul Khattak, n.3, p.345; Irfan Ahmad, "India-Pakistan: Friendship as Enmity," *Economic and Political Weekly,* Vol.38, No.3, 2 August 2003, pp.3231-3233; M.V.Ramana, "Subverting education," *The Daily Times,* 14 August 2003.

51 Rita Manchanda, "Redefining and Feminising Security: Making a Difference in Security Policies," *Economic and Political Weekly,* Vol. 36, No.43, 27 October 2001, p. 4100.

52 For details, see Varghese Koithara, *Society and State: The Indian Experience* (New Delhi: Sage, 1999).

53 Mahbub ul Haq, *Human Development in South Asia, 1997* (New Delhi: Oxford University Press, 1997), p.2; also refer World Bank, *World Development Report 2000-01: Attacking Poverty* (Oxford: Oxford University Press, 2001).

54 Gautam Navlakha, "Shrinking Horizon of an Expanding Enemy: India's Military Spending," *Economic and Political Weekly,* 8 April 2006, p.1340, www.epw.org.

55 Haider K.Nizamani, n.21, p.332.

56 V.R.Raghavan, "Insecure citizens within secure borders," *The Hindu,* 15 March 2002.

57 Gautam Navlakha, "Downsizing 'National' Security," *Economic and Political Weekly,* Vol.35, No.20, 13 May 2000, p.1713; also see Gautam Navlakha, "Reinforcing Insecurity," *Economic and Political Weekly,* Vol. 34, No.39, 25 September 1999, pp. 2782-83; Gautam Navlakha, n.33, pp.2038-2043.

58 Gautam Navlakha, "Securing India: Treating Unlikely as Likely," *Economic and Political Weekly,* 18 September 2004, www.epw.org; also see Gautam Navlakha, "Security Policy: Enemy of Democracy," *Economic and Political Weekly,* 17 August 2002, www.epw.org.

59 Haider K.Nizamani, n.21, pp.330-334.

60 Rajni Kothari, *State Against Democracy: In Search of Humane Governance* (New Delhi: Ajanta, 1988), p.80.

61 Mustapha Kamal Pasha, n.44, pp.288-289.

62 Feroz Hassan Khan, "Nuclear Command and Control in South Asia During Peace, Crisis and War," *Contemporary South Asia*, Vol.14, No.2, June 2005, pp.164-172.

63 Suneet Vir Singh, "A Regional Communication Policy for South Asia," in Bhabani Sen Gupta (ed.), *Regional Cooperation and Development in South Asia* (New Delhi: South Asian Publishers, 1986), pp.71-81.

64 See, for instance, Zubeida Mustafa, "Pakistan-India Relations: The Media in Pakistan," *Pakistan Horizon*, Vol.57, No.3, July 2004, pp.55-66; Nadeem ul Haque and Arif Sheikh, "Concerns of Intelligentsia in Pakistan: Content Analysis of Newspapers," *Economic and Political Weekly*, Vol.29, No.24, 11 June 1994, pp.1182-1186; P.Ghosh-Dastidar, "Pakistani Reporting on India," *Foreign Affairs Reports*, Vol.12, No.11, November 1963, pp.93-100.

65 Praful Bidwai, "Whose Truth: Indian Media in the Global Village," *Humanscape*, December 1996, www.indiawatch.org.

66 Address at the joint session of the Pakistan and India Newspaper Editors' Conference, New Delhi, 4 May 1950, India, Ministry of Information and Broadcasting, *Jawaharlal Nehru's Speeches, 1949-1953: Vol. II* (New Delhi: Publications Division, 1983), pp.441-443.

67 For details, see India, Ministry of Information and Broadcasting, *Report of the Fact Finding Committee on Newspaper Economics* (New Delhi, 1975); S.K.Goyal and M. Challapathi Rao, *Ownership and Control Structure of the Indian Press* (New Delhi: Indian Institute of Public Administration, 1981); S.K.Aggarwal, *Press at the Crossroads in India* (New Delhi: UDH Publishing House, 1988), pp.109-110; P.N.Malhan, *Communication Media: Yesterday, Today and Tomorrow* (New Delhi: Government of India, Ministry of Information and Broadcasting, 1985), pp.27, 90.

68 India, *Report of the Press Commission: Part I* (New Delhi: Government of India Press, 1954), pp.328-330.

69 India, *Report of the Second Press Commission, Vol.I* (New Delhi: Government of India Press, 1982), pp.11, 125-128.

70 See S.K.Aggarwal, n.67, p.110.

71 Press Council of India, *13th Annual Report: 1 April 1991-31 March 1992* (New Delhi, 1992), pp.7-8.

72 According to Bhaskara Rao, the share of advertising in total revenue of media increased from 25-30 per cent some decades ago to 45-55 per cent. In the case of television channels, advertising has largely determined the priorities and preoccupations. Even in the case of some big newspapers, revenue from advertising constitutes as much as 60 per cent of total revenue. See N. Bhaskara Rao, "Foreign Participation in Media," *Economic and Political Weekly*, Vol, 37, No.2, 12 January 2002, p.105.

73 N.Ram, "Yesterday, today, tomorrow," *The Hindu*, 13 September 2003.

74 Praful Bidwai, n.65.

75 Report of the Second Press Commission, n.69, pp. 65-66; also see Report of the Press Commission, n.68, p.320.

76 Sevanti Ninan, "Not Telling it like it is," *The Hindu*, 8 December 2002.

77 Report of the Press Commission, n.68, pp.164-165.

78 P. Sainath, *Everybody Loves A Good Drought* (New Delhi: Penguin, 1996), p.424.

79 "Hunger, Malnutrition and the Media," interview with Jean Dreze, www.thehoot.org.

80 Som Benegal, "The Media in India," in *NAMEDIA, Media Conference of the Non-Aligned Movement, New Delhi: 9-12 December 1983: Final Report and Documents* (New Delhi: NAMEDIA, 1984), p.118; also see Sharad Kharkanis, *Indian Politics and the Role of the Press* (New Delhi: Vikas, 1981), p.191.

81 Gautam Navlakha, "ISI: The Ubiquitous Enemy," *Economic and Political Weekly*, Vol.34, No.51, 18 December 1999, p.3570; See, for instance, the editorial, "Subversion as policy," *The Hindu*, 26 November 1994.

82 Speech in Parliament, 17 March 1950, India, Ministry of Information and Broadcasting, *Jawaharlal Nehru's Speeches* (New Delhi: Publications Division, 1983), Vol.2, pp. 235-236.

83 Rita Manchanda, *Reporting Conflict: A Radical Critique of the Mass Media, SAFHR Paper Series 9*, May 2001, www.safhr.org.

84 For a detailed content analysis of the issue, see Teresa Joseph, "Kashmir, Human Rights and the Indian Press," *Contemporary South Asia*, Vol. 9, No.1, March 2000, pp.41-

55; also see Sumanta Banerjee, "Mid-Summer Madness over Human Rights," *Economic and Political Weekly*, Vol.25, No.22, 2 June 1990, pp.1193-1195; Tavleen Singh, *Kashmir: A Tragedy of Errors* (New Delhi: Penguin Books, 1996).

85 See "Human rights I: Amnesty, Asia Watch biased," 28 January 1992; "Human rights II: dubious role of activists," 29 January 1992; "Human rights III: "Human rights panel stressed by Chavan," 30 January 1992; "Asia Watch report pro-militant," 10 February 1992; "Pakistani women get raw deal," 14 February 1992; all by Subhash Kirpekar in *The Times of India* (Bombay). Also see Teresa Joseph, ibid., p.49.

86 Rita Manchanda, n.83.

87 Editorial, "Us and Them," *The Times of India*, 18 June 1999.

88 Dipankar Sinha, "Kargil Episode in Bengali Print Media," *Economic and Political Weekly*, Vol.37, No.27, 6 July 2002, www.epw.org.

89 Teresa Joseph, *Perceptions of Pakistan in India: A Study of the Coverage of Pakistan in the Indian Press* (Unpublished M.Phil. dissertation submitted to the Mahatma Gandhi University, Kottayam, 1993), pp. 52-71, 132-133.

90 Subarno Chattarji, "Blurry Reflections: Differing Media Accounts of Balochistan," *Himal Southasian*, Vol.9, No.3, May-June 2006, pp.13-16.

91 Paul Bracken, "Asia's Militaries and the New Nuclear Age," *Current History*, Vol.98, No.632, December 1999, pp.420-421.

92 Editorial, "Budgetary outlay for defence," *The Hindu*, 11 March 1997.

93 Rita Manchanda, n.83; For instance, a report on the funeral of a soldier concludes: "...and all that we Indians can do is to thank God for those brave soldiers who sacrifice their todays for the sake of our tomorrows." "Son of India," *Asian Age*, 4 July 1999.

94 V.K.Grover, "Clear and present danger," *The Asian Age*, 5 May 2001.

95 Editorial, "Living with terror," *The Pioneer*, 2 January 2001.

96 Shekar Gupta, "Pakistan's blood-feud psychosis," *The Indian Express*, 22 September 2001.

97 For details see Teresa Joseph, n.89, pp.28-68. During the period of this study, the press sensationalised events like a

strike by the PPP, the separatist movement in Sind, an alleged sexual assault on Farhana Hayat for political goals, and other human rights violations, and the travails of the Bhutto family. At the same time it completely overlooked significant development issues – particularly regarding the state of its economy, etc.

98 Editorial, "Us and them," *The Times of India*, 18 June 1999; also see, "Pakistan in world's top 10 failed states, the region in top 25," *The Indian Express*, 3 February 2006, www.indianexpress.com; Vladimir Radyuhin, "Pakistan a source of terrorists," *The Hindu*, 26 June 2005; "Terror training camps active in Pakistan," *The Times of India*, 18 April 2006.

99 Teresa Joseph, n.89, pp. 73-76.

100 *The New Indian Express*, 29 February 2004; also see "Pakistan greets Indian 'invaders' with warmth," *The Hindu*, 21 March 2004.

101 Editorial, "Pakistan's fictive democracy," *The Pioneer*, 25 July 2002; also see, Paula R.Newberg, "A nation stuck in the past," *The Asian Age*, 20 August 2002; Editorial, "Musharraf's brand of democracy," *The Tribune*, 9 July 2002; Editorial, "A failed state," *The Hindustan Times*, 22 February 2003.

102 N.Bhaskara Rao *Indo-Pak Conflict: Controlled Mass Communication in Inter-State Relations* (New Delhi: S.Chand, 1971), p.169.

103 Dipankar Sinha, n.88.

104 Spartacus, "Manufacturing Jingoisim: Kargil and Media," www.indianmediareview.com. Also see Geeta Seshu, "Media and Kargil: Information Blitz with Dummy Missiles," *Economic and Political Weekly*, Vol.34, No.41, 9 October 1999, p.2917; "Barbarians: Pak army gouged Indian soldiers eyes, chopped off ears, genitals," *The Pioneer*, 11 June 1999.

105 Mohna Chatterjee, "Pakistan a big brother to Taliban," *The Times of India*, 8 October 2001; also see Editorial, "Terror factory's new Trojan horse," *The Pioneer*, 24 July 2002; B.Raman, "Al Qaida empire flourishes in Pakistan," *The Tribune*, 8 January 2003; Wilson John, "9/11: The Pakistan connection," *The Pioneer*, 6 August 2003; Editorial, "Terrorist sanctuaries in Pakistan," *The Economic Times*, 15 January 2003.

106 Brahma Chellaney, "Pakistan as problemistan," *The*

*Hindustan Times*, 8 July 2002.

107 G.Parthasarathy, "Saudi trail to Pakistan," *The Pioneer*, 25 September 2003.

108 Editorial, "A serious threat," *The Pioneer*, 25 September 2002.

109 Mani Shankar Aiyar, "Censorship, Information and Understanding," *Himal South Asian*, June 2002, www.himalmag.com.

110 *Report of the Second Press Commission*, n.69, p.23.

111 Subir Bhaumik in Rita Manchanda, n.83.

112 B.Muralidhar Reddy, "Indian Media: Toeing the Government Line on Pakistan?," www.thehoot.org.

113 See Ikram Sehgal, "Regional Conflicts and the Media," paper presented at the South Asian Media Conference, Islamabad, 1-2 July 2000, www.jang-group.com.

114 Sisir Gupta, *Kashmir: A Study in India-Pakistan Relations* (New Delhi: Asia Publishing House, 1966), p.282.

115 Russell Brines, *India-Pakistan Conflict* (London: Pall Mall Press, 1968), p.12.

116 N.Bhaskara Rao, n.102, p.152.

117 India, Ministry of External Affairs, *Annual Report, 1965-1966* (New Delhi, 1966), p.21; also see Lal Bahadur Shastri's statement on foreign affairs in the Lok Sabha, India, Ministry of External Affairs, *Foreign Affairs Record*, Vol.10, No.2 February 1964, pp.57-58.

118 Partha Pratim Basu, *The Press and Foreign Policy in India* (New Delhi: Lancer's Books, 2003), p.192.

119 Sharad Kharkanis, n.80, p.131.

120 Subir Bhaumik, in Rita Manchanda, n.83.

121 Indian Institute of Mass Communication, *The Media and Kargil: Information War: Media a Victim or a Tool* (1999), www.thehoot.org.

122 The Kargil Review Committee Report, *From Surprise to Reckoning* (New Delhi: Sage, 2000), p.248.

123 Bharka Dutt further elaborates: "I think the time has come to accept that every story we do is shaped by our own set of perceptions, and thus prejudices as well. National identity is just one of the many factors that add up to make the sum total of who we are and what we write or report. It sneaks up on us when we least suspect it, sometimes without us even

being aware of it; it weaves its way into our subconscious, often mangled and confused, but still there, determining what we see and how we see it. And, when I speak of national identity I don't mean chest-thumping, flag-waving nationhood. I mean years of accumulated baggage, what we read in school, how our history was handed down to us, the villains and heroes in our popular cinema, in fact the entire process of socialisation. The Media may not be reduced to being a crude tool of the nation state but it will always have to fight with itself to find a space that is honest." See Bharka Dutt, "Media as a Tool of the Nation State," paper presented at the South Asian Media Conference, n.113.

124 A.G.Noorani, "The Media: Politics, Ethics and the Law," *Economic and Political Weekly,* 11 February 2006, www.epw.org; Rita Manchanda, "Militarised Hindu Nationalism and the Mass Media," SAFHR Paper 11 (Kathmandu: SAFHR, May 2002). Also see for example, Brahma Chellaney, "An act of war," *The Hindu,* 18 December, 2001; Raja Mohan, "Act then, India must," *The Hindu,* 20 December 2001; K.Subrahmanyam, "Containing Pakistan," *The Times of India,*" 31 December 2001; K.Subrahmanyam, "Behind the bonhomie," The *Times of India,*" 28 January 2002.

125 Mannika Chopra, "Indo-Pak Monitoring-III: Sticking to the Official Line," www.thehoot.org.

126 Subarno Chattarji, "Munabao-Khokrapar Link: Indo-Pak Monitoring Part IV," www.thehoot.org.

127 Michael Newbill, "English Media Commentary in India and Pakistan on Confidence-Building Measures, 1990-1997," in Michael Krepon, Khurshid Khoja, Michael Newbill and Jenny S.Drezin (eds.), *A Handbook of Confidence-Building Measures for Regional Security* (Washington D.C.: The Henry L. Stimson Center, 1998), pp.151, 188.

128 George Fernandes, "National Security and the Role of the Media," *Mainstream,* Vol.36, No.36, 29 August 1998, p.15.

129 Rita Manchanda, n.83; also see N. Bhaskara Rao, "The media and the Kargil conflict," *The Hindu,* 31 July 1999. See *The Hindustan Times,* 17 December 1999.

130 Geeta Seshu, n.104, p.2919.

131 Jean Dreze "Militarism, Development and Democracy," *Economic and Political Weekly,* Vol.35, No.14, 1 April 2000,

p.1177. According to Dreze, the statement about RAW is attributed by Chari to one of RAW's own former directors.

132 B.Muralidhar Reddy, a correspondent of *The Hindu*, based in Islamabad, elaborates: "there are just two Indian correspondents in Pakistan and one representative from the Pakistani side in India. *The Hindu* and PTI (Press Trust of India) have their correspondents based in Islamabad. The state run Associated Press of Pakistan (APP) has its presence in New Delhi. Everything between India and Pakistan is on a reciprocal basis.... There is no dearth of media organisations in India keen on having their representatives in Pakistan. But alas the Pakistani media just can't afford to post correspondents in India. Thanks to low readership and abysmal advertisement revenues, the Pakistani media is faced with a dire economic situation.... As an Indian correspondent in Pakistan one can forget about `exclusive' reports. While there is no dearth of resources to get information, one can hardly talk about sources. Most of the time or all the time ... you are either dependent on what is being put out through official channels (Press Information Department, Pakistan Television/Radio, spokesperson and press conferences) or leaning on second hand information." See B.Muralidhar Reddy, "Reporting on the 'Enemy'," www.thehoot.org.

133 C.K. Lal, "Conformist Minds of India," *Himal South Asian*, July 2001, www.himalmag.com.

134 See "Holistic vision needed to tackle India-Pakistan issues," *The Hindu*, 27 July 2003; also see *Himal South Asian*, June 2002, www.himalmag.com.; www.safhr.org.

# 3
# Pakistan's Nuclear Programme: Indian Perceptions

The nuclearisation of South Asia has become an integral part of the security discourse in the subcontinent. Although the nuclear issue began to gain prominence since the 1970s, the Pokhran nuclear tests of India in May 1998, followed by Pakistan's Chagai tests, set the stage for an invigorated nuclear debate in the region. With an introductory overview of the nuclear policies of India and Pakistan, this chapter examines Indian perceptions of Pakistan's nuclear programme focusing particularly on the nuclear tests of 1998. In the diverse socio-cultural and political context of India, there can be no monolithic *Indian* perception regarding Pakistan's nuclear programme, or any issue for that matter. So also, the actual perceptions of policy-makers would be difficult to identify. This chapter however, outlines the broad contours of the perceptions on Pakistan's nuclear programme, of governments, political parties and the strategic community as enunciated in their speeches, statements and writings. Together with these sections of society, which have constituted the dominant discourse on the issue within the country, there is also an overview of 'public opinion' and dissenting voices on the issue. The approaches of these sections of society to nuclear weapons in general and India's nuclear policy are also referred to so as to place the issue in perspective. Such a framework is essential to contextualise Indian press coverage of Pakistan's nuclear programme.

## SETTING THE STAGE: INDIA AND THE NUCLEAR QUESTION

Until the mid-1990s, India was a strong critic of the doctrine of nuclear deterrence and rejected the notion that nuclear weapons could be legitimate or essential to the security of any country. It consistently criticised the international nuclear regime dominated by the nuclear powers and perceived its own nuclear capability to be a form of defiance of that order. In all international fora, India advocated the elimination and prohibition of nuclear weapons. In 1995 pleading before the International Court of Justice that nuclear weapons are illegal and incompatible with international law, it sought to ban their use, threat of use, manufacture or possession.[1]

During the Nehru years, the dominant security discourse in India primarily echoed what Nehru postulated to be the country's national interests. Nehru viewed atomic energy as a harbinger of progress for India, while condemning its military use on moral grounds. He called the possession of this 'evil thing' a crime against humanity.[2] In 1957, Nehru stated in the Lok Sabha: "We have declared quite clearly that we are not interested in making atom bombs, even if we have the capacity to do so and that in no event will we use atomic energy for destructive purposes."[3] He also admitted:

> It is true that in the ultimate analysis, a country which has atomic power fully developed can use it for good or evil

> purposes. And no declaration which I can make today will necessarily bind people in future, but I do hope that we shall create an atmosphere in this country which will bind every Government in future not to use this power for evil proposes.[4]

The numerous speeches and writings of Nehru reflect this perspective.[5] The post-Nehruvian Indian nuclear discourse began to witness a subtle shift from the categorical opposition to nuclear weapons. Yet there was a continued government articulation of opposition to deterrence and weaponisation. The Chinese nuclear test of 1964, which came after India's defeat at the hands of China in 1962, generated an increasing public debate on India's nuclear policy. Arguments for keeping the weapons option open began to gain legitimacy. In his speech following China's test, Homi J. Bhabha, the chief architect of India's atomic energy programme, stated that India too could conduct a nuclear test in eighteen months. Although no change was articulated at the policy level, Bhabha's statements appeared to have set the tone for change. Speaking in Parliament a month later, Prime Minister Lal Bahadur Shastri stated that India was willing to consider the use of nuclear tests for peaceful purposes.[6] Changes were reflected in India's role and attitude to the Nuclear Non Proliferation Treaty (NPT) negotiations, in which it had initially played a significant role. In 1968 India refused to sign the NPT stating that the final draft of the treaty did not reflect its demand for a better balance between the obligations placed on the nuclear weapons-states signatories and the non-nuclear weapons-states signatories.

In April 1968, Prime Minister Indira Gandhi stated in Parliament that India's nuclear policy was framed after due consideration of the national interest, specifically with regard to national security and that the events of the last twenty years clearly showed that the possession of nuclear weapons had not given any military advantage in situations of bitter armed conflict.[7] In her replies to questions in Parliament in 1972 and 1973, Mrs. Gandhi denied that there was any schedule fixed for a nuclear explosion. At the same time she made it clear that the Atomic Energy Commission (AEC) was constantly reviewing progress in the technology of underground nuclear explosion from both the theoretical and experimental angles. On 18 May 1974, during a nation-wide railway strike, India conducted its first nuclear test at Pokhran. Indira Gandhi stressed that India's neighbours need have no fear as "this experiment was part of the research and development work which the Atomic Energy Commission has been carrying on in pursuance of our national objective of harnessing atomic energy for peaceful purposes."[8] However, the Stockholm International Peace Research Institute (SIPRI) pointed out that the issue was really one of intention as there is no technical difference between the initial stages of a programme to develop 'peaceful' nuclear devices and one to develop nuclear weapons.[9]

Indian governments, over the years, strongly advocated nuclear disarmament, while at the same time justifying the country's right to keep the nuclear option open. Even during the Janata rule (1977-79), the then Minister for External Affairs, A.B.Vajpayee stated in the United Nations that India was not only against the proliferation of nuclear weapons but "against nuclear weapons themselves"[10] and that the "concept of a security system of which nuclear weapons represent the most dangerous and totally unacceptable component must be abandoned."[11] During the period 1983-93, India rejected several proposals by Pakistan for nuclear restraint and regional disarmament, on the grounds that it would only discuss nuclear disarmament in "global," "multilateral" fora, and in a "non-discriminatory" framework. Nevertheless, in 1986, India joined the Five-Continent Six-Nation Initiative for Nuclear Disarmament. Following the May 1995 NPT Extension Conference, India argued that as the conference did not extract a time-bound commitment towards disarmament from the declared nuclear states, such a commitment should be made in the context of the Comprehensive Test Ban Treaty (CTBT).

The debates over the CTBT were a turning point in India's nuclear policy. India began to contend that the proposed CTBT contained loopholes, and would not help to achieve the goal of complete elimination of nuclear weapons. Until early 1996, the nuclear discourse in India had not been linked to its national security considerations. For instance, in March 1996, India's Foreign Secretary Salman Haidar had stated at the Conference on Disarmament that India does not believe that the acquisition of nuclear weapons is essential for national security. "We are also convinced that the existence of nuclear weapons diminishes international security. We, therefore, seek their complete elimination. These are fundamental precepts that have been an integral basis of India's foreign and national security policy."[12] This reflected the traditional Indian approach of not relying on nuclear weapons for security. The dominant nuclear discourse in India relating to the CTBT saw a gradual change during the weeks preceding the general elections in India in May 1996. It became characterised by populism, with mainstream political parties, sections of the Indian bureaucracy, the Indian press, and security analysts all beginning to oppose the CTBT. On 20 June 1996, India's Foreign Secretary stated at the Conference on Disarmament, that "our national security considerations (have) become a key factor in our decision-making" and that the proposed CTBT was not "in India's national security interest." He also stated that India would not sign it in its "existing form."[13] For the first time, the government officially cited 'national security' considerations for retaining the nuclear option and invoked the relevance of 'deterrence'. The mainstream nuclear discourse in the country thus witnessed a complete change thereafter.

M.V. Ramana succinctly points out that an understanding of India's nuclear programme as distinct from its policy pronouncements is essential for a better understanding of the ease with which it crossed 'the nuclear Rubicon' in 1998. Material activities often suggested a completely different picture from the statements of political leaders at the domestic and international levels.[14] During the period from 1947 to 1974, Indian scientists had developed the technical means to produce nuclear weapons. The first Indian nuclear reactor, Apsara, went critical in 1956, and from the mid-1960s India undertook the construction of nuclear power stations and large research facilities, and the establishment of independent 'unsafeguarded' sources of weapons-grade plutonium. Homi J. Bhabha used his political influence as well as his personal relationship with Nehru to advance the nuclear power programme.[15]

Although, during the years following the 1974 tests, India did not conduct further nuclear tests or build a nuclear arsenal, Indian scientists and engineers continued, often secretly, to develop nuclear weapon and ballistic missile capabilities. It has been argued that due to the inadequacies of the 1974 test, the scientific community increasingly sought approval to resume testing. However, moral and political doubts, domestic turmoil and competing national and international priorities are perceived to have influenced India's leadership to refrain from articulating nuclear policies similar to that of the existing nuclear powers.[16] The Kargil Review Committee Report maintains that the Indian nuclear progamme was weapons-oriented at least since 1983.[17] Claims have also been made of evidence of attempts by various Indian governments to carry out tests in 1981, 1983, 1984 and in 1995. Each time the preparations were brought to a halt, probably because the costs were considered too high for the gains expected at the time. Although a major shift had occurred at the ground level in India's nuclear preparations, there was no corresponding change in official policy pronouncements. India sought to develop its nuclear programme so that it also included progress in the field of delivery systems. Work on space-launchers and rockets had begun in the 1960s, and by the early 1980s the basic technology required for missile systems in solid and liquid propulsion, control and guidance and, precision fabrication had been established.[18] In 1983, India launched the Integrated Guided Missile Development Programme, which aimed to produce five kinds of missiles. By 1998, analysts believed India possessed roughly twenty-five ready-to-assemble fission weapons with several means for delivering them.[19]

In January 1998, elections to the Lok Sabha were announced. The Bharathiya Janata Party's (BJP) manifesto for the elections stated inter alia that if voted to power, the party would "re-evaluate the country's nuclear policy and exercise the option to induct nuclear weapons."[20] The BJP-led government came to power in March 1998 and on 11 May 1998 India tested three nuclear weapons at Pokhran, followed by two additional tests two days later. On the eve of the first test, Indian Defence Minister George Fernandes had raised concerns about Chinese designs and recent weapons deployment within the region.[21] The official Indian press release of the Prime Minister after the nuclear tests stated that these tests "provide reassurance to the people of India that their national security interests are paramount and will be promoted and protected."[22] India thus witnessed a transition from a state that campaigned for nuclear disarmament and practised nuclear abstinence, to one that suddenly embraced the doctrine of nuclear deterrence and tested these weapons of mass destruction.[23]

The three important texts of official policy explanation for Pokhran-II are the Prime Minister's letter of 11 May 1998 to Bill Clinton, the President of the United States,[24] his *suo motu* statement in Parliament of 27 May 1998, together with the paper entitled "Evolution of India's Nuclear Policy"[25] that goes with it, and his "Statement Re: Bilateral Talks With United States," made in the Rajya Sabha on 15 December 1998.[26] Together they comprised the BJP government's case for Pokhran-II and nuclear weaponisation. Although there were common points in these documents, there were also some inconsistencies and contradictions. The identification of China and Pakistan as security threats to India in the 11 May letter contradicts the claim in the 15 December statement that India's concerns relating to disarmament and non proliferation go beyond the

South Asian region. Vajpayee's statement to Parliament in December 1998 also maintained that the tests were "a continuation of a decision taken nearly 25 years earlier."[27] In various interviews to the media, the Prime Minister pointed out that the "one and only reason for undertaking the tests was to ensure our security and to let the people of India and the world know that we have a credible deterrent."[28] The government also claimed that there was a "strong national consensus supporting the Government's decision to authorise these tests to protect India's security."[29] Following the tests, the statements made by the Indian government described a nuclear posture of minimum deterrence on the one hand, and proclaiming support for nuclear restraint and disarmament, on the other hand.

The Draft Nuclear Doctrine (DND) formulated by the National Security Advisory Board (NSAB) and released in August 1999 marked a further hardening of India's nuclear posture since Pokhran-II. Enumerating its objectives, the DND called for an "effective, credible nuclear deterrence and adequate retaliatory capability should deterrence fail."[30] In January 2003 the Cabinet Committee on Security summarised India's nuclear doctrine as to include the building and maintaining of a credible nuclear deterrent; a posture of 'No First Use'; and massive nuclear retaliation to a first strike.[31] The *Annual Report* of the Ministry of Defence for 2005-2006 also states that India's nuclear policy is characterised by a commitment to No First Use, moratorium on nuclear testing, minimum credible nuclear deterrence and rejection of entering into an arms race.[32] Responding to questions raised on the implications of the India-US nuclear deal of July 2005 on India's nuclear policy, Prime Minister, Manmohan Singh stated that it would not affect the country's strategic programme - the integrity of India's nuclear doctrine and India's ability to sustain a minimum credible nuclear deterrent was protected.[33] The *Annual Report 2006-2007* of the Ministry of Defence reiterated that in formulating its nuclear doctrine of credible minimum deterrence, India has demonstrated a defensive posture, restraint and responsibility. India has a declared policy of no-first-use of nuclear weapons and a firm commitment to avoidance of the use of nuclear weapons against non-nuclear weapon states, except in case of a major weapons-of-mass-destruction attack.[34]

The trajectory of India's nuclear policy over the years has thus witnessed a turnaround from the rejection of the use of nuclear weapons for national security to upholding the concept of nuclear deterrence.

## PAKISTAN'S NUCLEAR POLICY

Pakistan's initiative to develop nuclear energy came from the Atoms for Peace proposal of President Eisenhower, which was submitted to the United Nations in September 1954. In 1956, Pakistan established an Atomic Energy Commission (PAEC), which was intended to be a part of a new body for scientific and industrial research in Pakistan. Despite the PAEC's references to India's nuclear development, as well as the regular coverage in the Pakistani press about Indian nuclear plans, Pakistan's political, diplomatic and military elites in the early years did not concern themselves with the Indian dimension of the nuclear issue. Even during the early 1960s, although the threat from India and the construction of a Pakistani identity to counter it were the central themes of the mainstream political discourse, the nuclear option was absent in Pakistan's strategic discourse. This is evident from the writings and speeches of Ayub Khan, who headed the military that ruled Pakistan during 1958 to 1969.[35]

However, public debate in India, especially the calls for a nuclear weapons programme by several members of Parliament following the 1964 Chinese nuclear test appeared to have provided instigation to Pakistani decision-makers to favour the development of nuclear weapons. When India started reprocessing in 1964, PAEC experts saw it as a significant technical event in the subcontinent. Writing in 2000, George Perkovich revealed that a "recently declassified U.S. government cable indicates that in November 1964, Ayub Khan had expressed his deep concern at the prospect of rapidly developing Indian nuclear capability which could be readily converted from peaceful to war-like purposes.[36] In 1965 Zulfikar Ali Bhutto stated in an interview that if India produced nuclear weapons "then we should have to eat grass and get one, or buy one, of our own."[37] Bhutto was associated with atomic energy as Minister for Natural Resources during 1958-63, and Minister for Foreign Affairs during 1963-66. From 1972 to 1977 he was the President and later Prime Minister of Pakistan.

The 1965 war and the United States suspension of military aid to Pakistan appear to have been a turning point in the reorientation of Pakistan's security policy. The start-up of Indian reprocessing was the technical baseline of the Pakistan Foreign Office advocacy of a nuclear option. This was reinforced by the political baseline of Pakistan's defeat in the 1965 war. However, there is no evidence available to suggest that these Foreign Office reactions led to any change in the orientation of Pakistan's nuclear policy. The peaceful character of the nuclear policy remained unchanged at the policy level. The PAEC was instrumental in vetoing the Foreign Office advocacy to develop Pakistan's nuclear option. However, extraneous factors could have favoured rethinking about the nuclear question.[38]

Addressing the UN General Assembly in September 1965, Zulfikar Ali Bhutto described Pakistan's security dilemma by asserting that it was a small country, "facing a great monster, a great aggressor always given to aggression."[39] In December 1966, Bhutto argued that for Pakistan, the nuclear threat was real and immediate. "It is for this reason that as Foreign Minister and Minister in charge of Atomic Energy, I warned the nation some time back that if India acquires nuclear status, Pakistan will have to follow suit even if it entails eating grass."[40]

General Yahya Khan who was President from 1969 to 1971, did not effect any change in the country's nuclear policy. During the 1970s, the nuclear factor emerged to become an integral part of Pakistan's strategic discourse. Bhutto played an important role in bringing about this change through his speeches, writings, and patronage of the PAEC. Nizamani points out that the salience of the nuclear option to counter the Indian threat, and by implication strengthen the Pakistani identity, was one of the hallmarks of Bhutto's politics.[41] The earliest detailed discussion regarding the nuclear option to counter the Indian threat appeared in Bhutto's book *The Myth of Independence,* in 1969. Describing the nature of the threats faced by Pakistan, and the reasons behind them, the nuclear option was introduced as the solution to meet these threats. Bhutto wrote:

> India is unlikely to concede nuclear monopoly to others and, judging from her

> own nuclear programme and her diplomatic activities, especially at Geneva, it appears that she is determined to proceed with her plans to detonate a nuclear bomb. If Pakistan restricts or suspends her nuclear programme, it would not only enable India to blackmail Pakistan with her nuclear advantage, but would impose a crippling limitation on the development of Pakistan's science and technology.... Our problem, in its essence, is how to obtain such a weapon in time before the crisis begins. India, whose progress in nuclear technology is sufficient to make her a nuclear power in the near future, can provoke this at a time of her own choosing. She has already received foreign assistance for her nuclear programme and will continue to receive it. Pakistan must therefore embark on a similar programme, although a nuclear weapon will be neither a real deterrent nor can it be produced in a few years.[42]

Although Bhutto's book did not invoke an international reaction or initiate a debate over the nuclear option within the country, it contained certain basic arguments that would eventually turn into principles of the dominant security discourse. The 1971 war was a significant event in terms of both the identity issue of Pakistan and its inability to deter India. It reinforced Pakistan's sense of insecurity and accelerated its nuclear programme. The issues of identity and security thus came together during this period. The nuclear factor entered into the dominant security discourse of Pakistan and the rhetoric of militant nuclearism also gathered strength.[43] It is generally held that Pakistan's nuclear weapons programme gained momentum thereafter, when Bhutto ordered the development of nuclear weapons at a secret meeting at Multan in 1972. At the same time, however, inaugurating the Karachi Nuclear Power Plant on 28 November 1972, Bhutto pointed out that for the people of Pakistan, atomic energy should become a symbol of hope rather than of fear. "For this reason we would welcome if the entire subcontinent, by the agreement of the countries concerned, could be declared a nuclear free zone and the introduction of nuclear weapons banned."[44]

An important factor pushing Pakistan towards nuclearisation was the perception since the mid 1960s that it would not be able to attain parity with India in conventional weapons. Pakistan's fears about India's superiority in nuclear technology were confirmed by India's 'peaceful' nuclear explosion of 1974.[45] Bhutto declared that it was a "threatening," "fateful development." However, he added that Pakistan was determined not to be intimidated and would never fall prey to "nuclear blackmail" by India.[46] Bhutto again vowed that his people would "eat grass to ensure nuclear parity with India."[47] During the ensuing parliamentary debates nuclear technology became linked to questions of power, status, and national security. Bhutto expressed doubts about India's intentions, accusing it of "hegemonistic designs" in the subcontinent, and of having introduced a qualitative change in the security system of the region.[48] Bhutto criticised previous governments, especially Ayub Khan's, for not paying due attention to the nuclear option. Responding to Indira Gandhi's letter of 22 May, Bhutto denied any distinction between a peaceful and a military nuclear detonation and declared India's new military capability a permanent factor to be reckoned with. Bhutto then cancelled the scheduled talks with India on normalisation of relations, and began to seek a nuclear security guarantee against the Indian nuclear threat. But his efforts were unsuccessful. At the United Nations General Assembly session on 28 October 1974, Bhutto proposed that South Asia be declared a Nuclear-Weapon-Free Zone. However, India opposed the proposal on the grounds that the initiative for the proposal should come from the countries of the region and not the United Nations.

Pakistan announced plans to add up to twenty-four reactors by the year 2000 and acquire proficiency in all facets of the nuclear fuel cycle. It also signed an agreement with a French firm to construct a plutonium-reprocessing plant at Chashma. The key figure in organising this venture was Abdul Qadeer Khan, a metallurgist by profession who has often been referred to as the 'father of the Pakistan bomb'. However, the new determination by the United States and others to block transfers of nuclear technology to non-parties to the NPT had its impact on Pakistan. Its plans to use French nuclear cooperation for technological infrastructure and training were circumvented. In 1976, the United States adopted the first in a series of anti-proliferation laws aimed at "capping, freezing and rolling back" Pakistan's nuclear programme.[49] As a fallout of these non-proliferation measures, Pakistan's nuclear programme became secretive. It focused on producing highly enriched uranium for nuclear weapons instead of plutonium. Pakistan clandestinely acquired the necessary supplies and equipment to build a gas centrifuge uranium enrichment facility at Kahuta.

During the controversial 1977 National Assembly

elections and its aftermath Pakistan's nuclear programme was portrayed as a symbol of resistance by an independent Islamic state against the United States as well as India's hegemonic designs.[50] It was at this time that General Zia ul Haq came to power through a military coup. General Zia imprisoned Bhutto, who was later sentenced to death on charges of crimes committed during the previous election. From his death cell Bhutto wrote:

> When I took charge of Pakistan's Atomic Energy Commission, it was no more than a signboard of an office. It was only a name.... When I assumed charge of atomic energy, Pakistan was about twenty years behind India's programme. When I ceased to be Prime Minister, I believe, that at most, Pakistan was five to six years behind India... We were on the threshold of full nuclear capability when I left the Government to come to this cell. We know that Israel and South Africa have full nuclear capability. The Christian, Jewish and Hindu civilisations have this capability. The Communist powers also possess it. Only the Islamic civilization was without it, but that was about to change.... What difference does my life make now when I can imagine eighty million of my countrymen standing under the nuclear cloud of a defenceless sky?[51]

Although much of the evidence of a link between Pakistan and rich Arab states was often based on conjecture, Pakistani leaders were also responsible for fuelling Western concern, as evidenced in the above statement by Bhutto. Concerns about an 'Islamic bomb' emerged as a result of Western suspicions that

Pakistan's nuclear capabilities could have been financed by wealthy Muslim states in West Asia. This could be in exchange for technical information that would enable them to embark upon their own nuclear weapons programmes.

In its drive for legitimacy, the Zia regime soon capitalised on Bhutto's nationalist stance on foreign policy matters, particularly the nuclear issue. The politics of the nuclear issue was utilised by the dominant discourse to legitimise the military regime and consolidate an Islamic identity for Pakistan to counter domestic and external enemies.[52] In 1979 the effectiveness of the anti-proliferation laws was diluted by cold war imperatives. During the Soviet intervention in Afghanistan the United States abandoned its non-proliferation goals in return for Pakistan's cooperation as a 'front-line' state. Pakistan, however, did not abandon attempts to address its security problem with India through non-nuclear alternatives also. During General Zia's regime, Pakistan offered India a wide range of nuclear arms control proposals such as: the creation of a Nuclear-Weapon-Free Zone (NWFZ) in South Asia; simultaneous signatures to the NPT by India and Pakistan; mutual acceptance of the International Atomic Energy Agency (IAEA) safeguards; bilateral inspection of each other's nuclear facilities; joint declaration to renounce the development of nuclear weapons; and signing of a regional test ban treaty. The NWFZ proposal had been initially put forth by Bhutto while the remaining five originated during Zia's rule. Prime Minister Mohammad Khan Junejo reiterated these proposals in 1986 and 1987, offering to accept binding obligations if India reciprocated. India's rejection of Pakistani proposals for declaring a NWFZ in South Asia, and international inspection of both countries' nuclear installations, further aggravated Pakistani security concerns. However, critics point out that Pakistan's support for the 'stabilisation' of the nuclear arms race in South Asia was a bid to acquire recognition of its nuclear weapons capability. At the same time, its proposals for other steps towards nuclear restraint, such as non-weaponisation and non-deployment of nuclear weapons and missile systems, would also work to its own advantage in view of India's more developed nuclear infrastructure.[53]

China played an important role in building up Pakistan's nuclear capabilities, particularly with regard to missile technology. It was in this context that the United States imposed military sanctions on Pakistan in August 1993, under the terms of the Missile Technology Control Regime (MTCR). It sought to curb the transfer of Chinese technology for the development of Pakistan's medium-range missile programme. These sanctions did not alter relations between China and Pakistan or diminish China's support for Pakistan's nuclear capability.

By the mid-1990s, the terms of Pakistan's engagement with India on nuclear issues had changed. The CTBT had emerged as a major issue. When it became clear in 1996 that India would not sign the treaty, Pakistan followed suit. Former Pakistan Ambassador Sajjad Hyder notes, "Pakistan's policy towards India is mainly reactive. This is as true of the nuclear issue as it is of our bilateral relations in general. Since India is not only our neighbour but is also far larger, it could not be otherwise."[54]

On 6 April 1998, Pakistan tested the Ghauri missile, which it claimed had a possible range of 1500 kilometres with a payload of 700 kilograms. Pakistani leaders depicted the nuclear and missile programmes as "last-resort protection" against the assertions of nuclear weaponisation by BJP leaders. The Ghauri test was also supposedly used to signal to the BJP that it would not be able to achieve Vajpayee's campaign pledge to "take back that part of Kashmir that is under Pakistan's occupation."[55]

After the Indian nuclear tests of 1998, Nawaz Sharif and other Pakistani officials maintained that they were not surprised by the tests, given their assumptions about the BJP. They declared they would take "necessary steps for addressing Pakistan's legitimate security concerns."[56] Although Abdul Qadeer Khan informed the top civilian and military leadership that Pakistan needed three days at the most to carry out its own tests, Pakistan waited for two weeks before responding accordingly. Sharif bought time to consider Pakistan's options and to evaluate the response of the international community and also the political dynamics within his own country.

Initially the government sought political reassurances as well as material help from other countries, particularly the United States. There were several reasons for Islamabad being cautious. It was clear that Pakistan would be subject to economic sanctions and that its economy was far more externally dependent than India's. It could gain international prestige and political sympathy by not following India. It could also hope to launch a collective diplomatic campaign against India and thus broaden its own support for the Kashmir issue. By the end of the week after India's tests, it appeared that Pakistan would refrain from testing its nuclear weapons. However, on 18 May, India's Home Minister, L. K Advani called upon "Islamabad to realise the change in the geo-strategic situation in the region and the world." Pointing out that India subscribed to the principle of 'no first strike', Advani invited Pakistan to "join India in the common pursuit of peace and prosperity in the Indian subcontinent." He also warned Islamabad that any other course would be futile and costly for Pakistan. [57]

The response to this from Pakistan was one of strong nationalist outrage. More inflammatory statements emerged from Indian leaders, including Defence Minister George Fernandes, threatening "hot pursuit" of Pakistani troops and Pakistan-backed guerrillas into its territory. The eventual Pakistani decision to respond with its own tests was therefore determined by a combination of external as well as internal factors. On the external front, Pakistan was disappointed that the opposition to the Indian action was not as strong as it had hoped and that the United States did not declare its willingness to provide a nuclear umbrella to it. Neither did the financial - military package offered to Pakistan by the United States measure up to its expectations. More significant in shaping the final decision, however, were domestic factors. Prime Minister Nawaz Sharif's political support had been steadily falling. His party, the Pakistan Muslim League (PML) was under pressure not only from the opposition Pakistan People's Party (PPP) but also, more seriously, from explicitly fundamentalist, right-wing Islamic forces that had been strengthened by the successes of the Taliban in Afghanistan. Sentiment among the officer corps was also strongly in favour of a similar Pakistani response to the Indian action. Thus, the Sharif government found it difficult to confront such internal pressures for retaliatory tests.[58] On 28 May 1998 Pakistan detonated five nuclear devices and on 30 May exploded a sixth one, which was apparently intended to establish parity with India by taking into account the latter's Peaceful Nuclear Explosion of 1974. Nawaz Sharif contended that immediately after its nuclear tests, India had brazenly raised the demand that Islamabad should realise the change in the geo-strategic situation in the region and threatened that it would deal firmly and strongly with Pakistan. "Our security, and peace and stability of the entire region was thus gravely threatened. As a self-respecting nation we had no choice left to us. Our hand was forced by the present Indian leaderships' reckless actions."[59]

On 2 June, Pakistan's Ambassador to the United Nations, Munir Akram, stated at the Special Session of the Conference on Disarmament that Pakistan had not instigated or initiated the security crisis in South Asia. It was obliged by security and national considerations to respond to India's provocative nuclear tests. Pakistan's decision to test became virtually inevitable because of three factors: the steady escalation in the provocations and threats emanating from India; the weak and partial response of the world community to India's tests and threats; and the realisation, that given the nature of the Indian regime, it could not leave them in any doubt about the credibility of its capability to deter and respond devastatingly to any aggression against Pakistan or pre-emptive strikes against its facilities.[60]

The nuclear discourse in Pakistan following the Chagai tests was a continuation of the debate during the 1990s. Nizamani points out that the street indignation that followed the Indian tests and the jubilation that accompanied the Pakistani tests further consolidated the nuclear hawks' belief in the nuclear option as a symbol of national self-respect. "Issues of national identity, strategic imperatives, and self-respect became dependent upon the immediate conduct of nuclear tests. Euphoria following the nuclear tests signified the success of the dominant discourse in tying the above factors together."[61]

India's test of its 2500 km range Agni-2 missile in April 1999 initiated a new round of the missile race in South Asia. Pakistan tested its Ghauri-2 missile, which it claimed had a range of 2300 km, arguing that the test was necessary to maintain the strategic balance. The following day Pakistan also tested its short-range Shaheen-1 missile. Such tit-for-tat missile testing continues unabated.

In 2003 when IAEA inspected Iran's nuclear facilities, it found centrifuges and traces of highly enriched uranium. It appeared that Pakistan was the source of its crucial technology. Further revelations by Libya and North Korea forced President Musharraf to launch an investigation and to finally concede that there was involvement by persons in their individual capacity. Abdul Qadeer Khan was removed from his post as Senior Advisor to the Prime Minister. In a dramatic television appearance on 4 February 2004 Khan acknowledged that during the past two decades he had secretly provided North Korea, Libya and Iran with crucial technology for making nuclear weapons. He apologised to the people of Pakistan for what he had done and was pardoned by Musharraf. The entire issue however captured international attention and was a major source of embarrassment to President Musharraf and Pakistan's nuclear programme.

Although Pakistan set up its National Command Authority in February 2000 to take decisions on its nuclear programme, in contrast to India's nuclear doctrine, it does not have a document detailing its envisaged nuclear policy. Pakistani leadership made it clear that the country does not abide by a No First Use doctrine, but would "respond with full might," if war occurred. In May 2005, Pakistani Foreign Minister Khurshid M.Kasuri stated that "Pakistan's acquisition of nuclear capability was driven by its security compulsions.... Following Indian nuclear tests of 1998, we were left with no other option but to acquire and sustain minimum credible deterrence against a growing external threat and restore the strategic balance which had been disturbed due to Indian action."[62] He also made it clear that nuclear deterrence now forms an indispensable part of Pakistan's security calculus. Addressing the sixty first United Nations General Assembly session in September 2006, Musharraf stated that a stable security environment is important for peace in the region. He pointed out that Pakistan had proposed the creation of a Strategic Restraint Regime in South Asia, "encompassing minimum nuclear deterrence and a balance of conventional forces. We do not want to enter into an arms race. But we will do whatever is necessary to preserve the credibility of our minimum defensive deterrence level."[63] This perspective has often been reiterated as in his address to the National Defence University in March 2008.[64] Pakistan's nuclear weapons programme over the years has clearly been shaped by and geared towards India and the developments in India's nuclear weapons programme.

## INDIAN PERCEPTIONS OF PAKISTAN'S NUCLEAR PROGRAMME

### Government Perspectives

During the early years after independence, Jawaharlal Nehru had dominated India's foreign policy-making, including nuclear policy. His views and perceptions had a tremendous influence on the general public and policy-making circles. According to Nizamani "Nehru's portrayal of Pakistan as an intimate yet puzzling Other on the one hand, and his depiction of China as a friendly country up until the 1950s have had a lasting impact on India's strategic discourse where Pakistan continues to be the ideal candidate to identify as an enemy in the Indian nukespeak."[65] However, such public identification in the government nuclear discourse began to emerge only in the late 1970s. Responding to a Lok Sabha debate on the Non Proliferation Treaty in 1967, the then Minister for Foreign Affairs, M.C.Chagla had stated that "at present the threat is from China."[66]

In the Lok Sabha in March 1972, the government was asked in writing whether the war with Pakistan "brought out the necessity for India to have more modern weapons" and, if so, "whether Government propose to embark upon the manufacture of nuclear bombs." The Minister of Defence, Jagjivan Ram, answered that army modernisation was an ongoing process and that the government's policy with regard to production of nuclear weapons "is to use nuclear energy for peaceful purposes only." He said, "the defence of our borders can be best ensured by adequate military preparedness based on conventional weapons. In their view the possession of nuclear weapons is no substitute for such military preparedness."[67]

In explaining the nuclear tests in 1974, India did not cite any nuclear threat from Pakistan.[68] Replying to the Lok Sabha debate on the 1974 explosion, K.C.Pant, Minister of Irrigation and Power emphasised that the test was a landmark for development of nuclear technology for peaceful purposes. He further stated:

> ... in 1972 we had talked of an experimental

> angle of the underground explosion. Against this background, it is difficult to appreciate Pakistan's somewhat hysterical reaction to this explosion. We know that Pakistan has its own internal difficulties, but if it wants to divert the attention of its people, we would be grateful if Mr. Bhutto would find something more credible. The way he has over-reacted to our explosion almost suggests that Mr. Bhutto feels that India made all the efforts of exploding a nuclear device underground, with the sole object of impressing him! He seems to be looking around for assurances against threat. But the basic question is, threat from whom? We have already declared categorically that our experiment was for peaceful purposes and our Prime Minister has conveyed this assurance to Mr. Bhutto. Therefore, there is in fact no danger or threat from India to Pakistan. The need to seek assurance or support against a non-existing threat is not there.[69]

However, the government articulation on the nuclear issue began to change by the late 1970s. An increasing emphasis on the Pakistani threat became part of the strategy of keeping the option open. The Charan Singh government, in 1979, declared that India did not want to use nuclear energy for military purposes, "but we may have to reconsider our earlier decision if Pakistan goes ahead with the atom bomb."[70] Indira Gandhi declared in the Lok Sabha in 1981 that Pakistan's development of nuclear weapons would have "grave and irreversible consequences for the subcontinent." She added: "we are fully aware of our responsibilities and the House can be confident that we shall respond in an appropriate way to any development. Our own policy has been to use nuclear energy only for peaceful purposes and we crusade for the total banning of all nuclear weapons."[71] In March 1984, after Abdul Qadeer Khan's statement that Pakistan had the capacity to enrich uranium, the Minister for External Affairs, Narasimha Rao addressed a parliamentary request that the government respond to "the situation arising out of the reported nuclear collaboration between Pakistan and China." Rao referred to reports from the United States that China had transferred sensitive nuclear weapons design information to Pakistan. Rao pointed out that "we cannot but note with concern reports of contacts between Pakistan and China in the nuclear field. I would however like to assure the house that Government have been keeping a constant watch on all developments having a bearing on India's security. Government would continue to do so with utmost vigil."[72]

A few months later, Indira Gandhi told a gathering of Indian Army commanders that Pakistan's nuclear programme had brought about a qualitative change in India's security environment. She added that the United States continued to supply Pakistan with military equipment despite "evidence compiled by Americans themselves about Pakistan's nuclear programme."[73] Tacit American assistance to Pakistan's nuclear programme was continually stressed. In April 1985, Prime Minister Rajiv Gandhi stated in Parliament: "We do not like what we see about their nuclear programme. We have still no indication that they are not making a bomb. We know that they are getting aircraft; they have got aircraft, which have the capability of carrying nuclear weapons."[74] Rajiv Gandhi began to adopt a more rigid posture, as for example, at a meeting of the All India Congress Committee (AICC) on 4 May 1985, he stated: "We feel that they [Pakistan] are developing nuclear weapons... [and] we are looking into various aspects of this question to see what action we should take."[75] In an interview in June 1985, when asked what India would do if Pakistan developed a nuclear weapon, Rajiv Gandhi declared: "Then we would have to really re-think all our policies."[76] In August 1985, the Minister of State for External Affairs, Khurshid Alam Khan stated:

> The non-peaceful dimension of Pakistan's nuclear programme has been a matter of concern for India. Contrary to the claims by Pakistan's leaders, available evidence and public statements by Pakistani scientists suggest that Pakistan has been pursuing the objective of acquiring the wherewithal to manufacture nuclear weapons.... Reports which have appeared from time to time in the international media in this regard, particularly about the clandestine procurement of nuclear equipment and components by Pakistan, have reinforced our apprehensions.... I wish to assure the house that government have been keeping, and will continue to keep, a constant vigil on all developments having a bearing on the country's security....[77]

Although various members of parliament called for a nuclear weapons programme by India, Khurshid Alam Khan maintained that India remained committed to develop nuclear technology for peaceful purposes. India's options were clear but could not be spelt out, as this would not be in the interest/safety of the country.[78] At a press conference in October 1985, Rajiv Gandhi added: "What is even more worrying about Pakistan's programme is that we are fairly sure that at least part of the finances of this programme have come from other countries. Now, what we worry about is that the nuclear weapon when developed will also have to go to these countries."[79] In this context, the reports of India already having made preparations for nuclear tests in 1983, 1984 and 1985 should be kept in mind.

The *Annual Report 1987-1988* of the Ministry of Defence stated that Pakistan's weapon-oriented nuclear programme and its quest for sophisticated weapons like an airborne early warning system, which go far beyond her genuine defence requirements, are a matter of great concern to India.[80] In the aftermath of A.Q.Khan's interview with Kuldip Nayar, in 1987, Defence Minister K.C.Pant told the Lok Sabha, "the emerging nuclear threat to us from Pakistan is forcing us to review our options... I assure the house that our response will be adequate to our perception of the threat."[81] Similarly, in April 1988, Pant stated that India had not allowed a window of vulnerability to develop and that Indian armed forces would not be at a disadvantage in the face of a nuclear attack by Pakistan.[82]

In December 1988 three important bilateral agreements were signed by Rajiv Gandhi and Benazir Bhutto, including the agreement on the prohibition of any attack against each other's nuclear installations and facilities. The Kargil Review Committee Report makes it a point to stress that the agreement was first proposed by Rajiv Gandhi to Zia ul Haq in December 1985 during the latter's brief stop-over in Delhi, and that it was mooted as a confidence building measure to reassure Pakistan that India had no intention of undertaking a pre-emptive strike against its nuclear installations.[83] The statement on nuclear non-proliferation of the Embassy of India, Washington D.C. posted on its website, while asserting that India's nuclear programme is indigenous and entirely peaceful, points out:

> In 1994, Pakistan not only was involved in international plutonium smuggling but it also received from China, with which it has an ongoing military relationship, long-range missiles capable of carrying nuclear warheads. The US press has widely reported on hard evidence that Pakistan has obtained ring magnets, an item used for producing weapons-grade uranium, from China.[84]

This reflected the general trend in government articulation regarding Pakistan's nuclear programme over the years. In the context of the 1998 nuclear tests, important government statements regarding the threat from Pakistan have been mentioned in the previous section. Special emphasis needs to be placed on the Prime Minister's letter to President Clinton identifying China and Pakistan as threats posed to India. The Kargil Review Committee in a single sweeping statement on India's tests posits: "Finally, in 1998, in the wake of Pakistan's Ghauri missile test in April 1998, Prime Minister Vajpayee ordered the nuclear tests."[85]

In response to Pakistan's nuclear tests of May 1998, the official statement of the spokesman for the Indian government read: "Pakistan's nuclear tests have confirmed what has been known all along - that that country has been in possession of nuclear weapons. This event vindicates our assessment and our policy as well as the measures that have been taken. We expect that those who disagreed with us will reassess their stand."[86] The Ministry of External Affairs brief further clarified:

> Another impression which needs to be promptly corrected is that because Pakistan's tests followed ours, it was a reaction to India's action. Again, as the evolution of events makes clear, it was India that was obliged to react to a progressive build up of nuclear weaponry and missiles in our neighbourhood. Pakistan's nuclear weapons programme predated ours and was built after years of clandestine acquisition. While we are mentioning the Pakistan factor, there is no obsession with Pakistan. Our security concerns go far beyond Pakistan and South Asia.... It is also a well-established fact that Pakistan is working systematically to create border tension and LOC/border firing as a proven method, for attracting attention and encouraging the 'flash point' theory.[87]

Another press release of the Ministry of External Affairs stated: "The misleading references in Security Council's Presidential statement obfuscate the nature of Pakistan's nuclear and missile programmes, particularly the well documented fact that they are long established and are based on clandestine acquisitions and transfers."[88] Vajpayee's securitisation of the issue was evident when he stated in the Lok Sabha: "a new situation has arisen.... The house should think about it deeply and seriously. We may have differences in our house, but if the challenge is from the outside, we should give the message that ... the country is together."[89] The government also maintained that

Pakistan's nuclear tests were no match for India's. Referring to Pakistan's tests, the Kargil Review Committee Report makes no mention of the immediately preceding Indian tests, but pointedly questions the number and yield of the tests as claimed by Pakistan. It also emphasises the China connection, insinuating that preparations for the Pakistan tests had already been well under way (before the Indian tests).[90]

The passage of time witnessed more vociferous articulation of threats from Pakistan, as well as the government's capability to protect the country. Two years after the nuclear tests, Vajpayee argued that Pakistan was threatening a nuclear war "...but do they even know what it means? They think that they will drop one bomb and they'll win and we'll lose. This won't happen. We said we wont be the first to use nuclear weapons, but if anyone uses them against us, anyone threatens us, we will not wait for our annihilation.... We are prepared for any eventuality."[91]

Addressing the fifty seventh session of the United Nations General Assembly on 13 September 2002, Vajpayee stated that India faced nuclear blackmail from the South Asian region.[92]

The nuclear threat from Pakistan was constantly highlighted in Parliament. Speaking in the Lok Sabha, Minister of State for External Affairs, Rao Inderjit Singh pointed out that it was well known that for more that three decades Pakistan has actively pursued a clandestine nuclear weapons programme. This problem of clandestine acquisition of nuclear weapons technologies by Pakistan is a matter of deep concern. He stated that the Government carefully monitored all such developments which had a bearing on the country's security and was committed to taking all necessary steps to safeguard the nation's security.[93]

India's Defence Minister Pranab Mukherjee reiterated in September 2006 that "India's nuclear deterrence is a measure of self defence in a hostile and nuclearised environment."[94] Such statements are reflective of the nature of government articulation over the years on Pakistan's nuclear programme. The threat from a nuclear Pakistan, its reckless proliferation and the danger of its nuclear weapons falling into terrorist hands, have been increasingly emphasised, together with US tacit aid and Chinese direct assistance to it. There has been an ongoing vociferous articulation of threats and the capability of the government to protect the country. As T.Jayaraman points out, post Pokhran-II Indian nuclear dogma has maintained that India's nuclear weapons are 'good nukes', the result of decades of self-reliant labour of Indian scientists and engineers, and a symbol of India's scientific and technological capability. In contrast, Pakistan's nuclear weapons were always 'bad'. It was the knee jerk reaction of a technologically weak country to the legitimate ambitions of the regional superpower. Moreover, technologically, Pakistan's bombs were mostly stolen goods, and politically the product of an undemocratic, military-ruled and theocratic state (unlike India's 'democratic' nukes).[95]

## Perceptions and Responses of Political Parties

Prior to 1998, there was a general consensus among the political parties in India regarding the country's nuclear policy. The general focus was on the call for global disarmament, while keeping the nuclear option open and endorsing the government's determination to meet the threat from Pakistan. None of the political parties in India explicitly opposed India's threshold status. The BJP, however, had over the years consistently called on governments to exercise the nuclear option.

The Indian National Congress (INC), in keeping with the Nehruvian tradition, was initially officially opposed to the development of nuclear energy for anything other than peaceful purposes.[96] Having been the party in power for the longest period since independence, its perspective can be seen in consonance with that of the Congress governments, which have already been referred to. Notwithstanding official pronouncements, there were however, conflicting views within the party. Several members including K.C.Pant, Secretary of the Congress Parliamentary Party in 1966 and later to become a Union Minister, urged the government to give up its policy of "nuclear celibacy" and become technologically prepared for making the bomb. AICC sessions of 1964 and 1965 witnessed strong pleas from some delegates for the indigenous production of atom bombs.[97] It may be recalled that it was the Congress governments under Lal Bahadur Shastri and Indira Gandhi, which initiated the policy of ambiguity that ultimately led to the 1974 nuclear tests. Reflecting the differences within the party, in August 1985 (when the Congress was in power), during the Lok Sabha debate regarding Pakistan's attempt to develop a nuclear bomb and the supply of Krypton electronic triggers, P.J.Kurien queried whether "we can afford not to go nuclear in the present context." He contended that any agreement with Pakistan on nuclear weapons would not serve the purpose as it could still conduct explosions, and assemble and store nuclear weapons in secrecy. He argued that a country possessing a nuclear weapon was definitely in a psychologically superior position. In view of the fact that India had to settle so many issues with Pakistan, facing a nuclear armed Pakistan would place India in a psychologically weaker position. The greatest deterrent against nuclear weapons was the terror that it generated. So, if India also had nuclear weapons that would be the greatest deterrent.[98]

Soon after the 1998 tests, the Congress Working Committee, which met on 14 May, lauded the achievement and expressed the party's support for the tests. It reiterated that the party did not view national security in a partisan way.[99] Following Pakistan's nuclear tests the party statement pointed out that the tests "are as expected as they are regrettable. This is a grave development.... At this critical juncture, the Congress stands with the nation united and determined to safeguard the country's independence, security and sovereignty."[100] A later statement, while expressing it's "deep sense of disappointment" that Pakistan went back on its earlier decision not to carry out further nuclear tests, called on the government to build on the initiatives taken by Rajiv Gandhi and P.V.Narasimha Rao for confidence building measures in the region.[101] In its 2004 election manifesto, the Congress party emphasised its commitment to "maintaining a credible nuclear weapons programme," while calling for "demonstrable and verifiable confidence building measures with its nuclear neighbours."[102] The party repeatedly stressed the threat posed by Pakistan's nuclear programme. Debates in parliament by Congress party members have witnessed the stress on the clandestine nature of Pakistan's nuclear programme and the dubious antecedents of Abdul Qadeer Khan.[103] In July 2005 Congress Prime Minister Manmohan Singh voiced serious concern over the security of Pakistan's nuclear assets, stating that there had been 'reckless proliferation' and there was a 'danger' of extremists seizing power and taking control of these weapons.[104]

The BJP (or its precursor, the Bharathiya Jana Sangh) is the only political party, which officially stated that it wanted India to be a nuclear weapons power, a position it has consistently reiterated since 1951, well before there was any issue of Pakistani or Chinese bombs. As early as 1962, the BJS urged India's acquisition of nuclear arms and criticised the government for raising the false issue of economic costs in weapons production. In later years, the nuclear threat from Pakistan and China came to be emphasised in advocating a posture of nuclear deterrence. It has been pointed out that "the 'politics' of Hindutva not only justifies the launching of India's nuclear programme but also serves to mobilise it as a 'Hindu' defence strategy to protect India from Pakistan."[105] The BJP National Council resolution of 1981 read: "Pakistan's nuclear aspirations carry within them dangerous portents for a serious destabilisation of the strategic balance in the subcontinent."[106] Similarly in 1985, responding to news of Pakistan's successful testing of the non-nuclear triggering package for a nuclear weapon, the National Executive resolution stated that the BJP viewed with concern the fact of Pakistan continuing to proceed with its nuclear programme of manufacturing a nuclear bomb. It added that the BJP was firmly of the view that it was much too grave a matter to be taken in such a cavalier and casual manner in which the Prime Minister appeared to be doing. Citing reports from Pakistan it indicated that the threat of a Pakistani nuclear bomb was real and an immediate response to this was necessary. The BJP, therefore called upon the Government to take immediate steps to develop its own nuclear bomb.[107]

Similar responses were evident to most other reported developments in Pakistan's nuclear programme, as for example, A.Q.Khan's disclosures in 1991 and Shahryar Khan's statements in 1992.[108] The BJP manifesto for the 1998 elections stated that if voted to power, the party would "re-evaluate the country's nuclear policy and exercise the option to induct nuclear weapons."[109] According to N.Ram, the 17 May 1998 issue of *Organiser,* "thinly disguised as a Pokhran-I anniversary special was actually released in advance to coincide with Pokhran-II. The collection of hawkish and virulently anti-China and anti-Pakistan articles reiterated the well-worn RSS line that the bomb had to be made to 'tame Pakistan' and teach China a lesson for occupying Indian territory."[110] The BJP government's reactions to Pakistan's nuclear tests of 1998 have been mentioned in the earlier section, the main thrust being that Pakistan's tests vindicated its own nuclear stance. During the Lok Sabha debate on the issue, L.K.Advani pointed out that it was occasions like this that brought out "patriotism" among the people. In terms of nationalist fervour, India's tests stood in the same class as the struggle for the accession of Hyderabad and the liberation of Goa. Those who did not agree with this perspective were labelled by senior BJP leaders as "pseudo-liberals," "friends of Pakistan" and out of sync with the "national sentiment," and were told to "go and live in Pakistan."[111]

Incidentally, George Fernandes, the Defence Minister of the BJP-led government at the time of the 1998 tests, had earlier been a strong critic of nuclear weapons. His views on the issue in the specific context of South Asia merit consideration. In 1985, he had stated:

When India exploded a nuclear device in the

> Pokhran desert in Rajasthan in May 1974, it should have been obvious even to the totally naive politician in the country that it would only be a matter of time before Pakistan would explode its own little 'nuclear toy'.... Whether Pakistan is actually on the threshold of exploding a nuclear device or not, India should take immediate steps to create the required atmosphere to prevent the subcontinent from getting involved in a nuclear arms race. No two countries will look more grotesque in the comity of nations if India and Pakistan should choose to squander the money denied to their hungry and dying millions into the making of nuclear bombs, their delivery systems and the anti-bomb systems.... Only the mentally deranged could lead India and Pakistan to a nuclear arms race.[112]

The BJP has over the years emphasised the possibility of facing nuclear terrorism/blackmail from Pakistan. In fact, during the Asian Security Summit in Almaty, Kazakhstan in June 2002, Prime Minister A.B.Vajpayee directly accused Pakistan of trying to use nuclear blackmail.[113] Senior Party leader, Murli Manohar Joshi, during a speech on national security on 3 August 2006 reiterated: "Pakistan would soon have a nuclear reactor and India should be ready to face nuclear terrorism."[114]

Both the Communist Party of India (CPI) and the Communist Party of India-Marxist (CPI-M) in their policy statements have opposed an Indian nuclear deterrent and expressed concern at the negative implications this could have for relations with Pakistan.

The CPI's Seventh Congress of 1964 declared that "the making of atomic weapons would not only place crippling burdens on our national economy but would also weaken India's role in the preservation and consolidation of world peace."[115] They, however, rejected the international non-proliferation regime in the wider context of the struggle against imperialism. After the 1974 tests, while all other members of the Lok Sabha jubilantly competed in congratulating the scientists responsible, Indrajit Gupta of the CPI questioned the rationale for the timing of the test. He also added:

> I hope we would also take into consideration the fact that people like Prime Minister Bhutto or some other people in Pakistan who may be perhaps more anti-Indian than Bhutto himself...
>
> They would seize upon an opportunity like this to say that India is now preparing to have some sort of aggressive or militaristic designs in this region, and therefore on that plea Pakistan and their allies should be given some protection in the form of a nuclear umbrella.... Nevertheless, I would just remind the Government that a nuclear arms race of any kind, even in the sphere of what Prof. Samar Guha called tactical nuclear weapons, would in my view be a disaster for us.[116]

During the debate in Parliament following A.Q.Khan's statement in March 1984, Indrajit Gupta questioned the rationale of the government in creating an atmosphere of imminent threat, if India already possessed a military advantage over Pakistan.[117] Similarly, after the Indian nuclear tests of 1998, Indrajit

Gupta questioned the timing of the test and the sudden change in policy, wanting to know what the provocation was. However, he added: "Of course, some provocation may have been there, I do not know from the side of Pakistan, because they suddenly developed this Ghauri missile and said that it has a long range of so many thousands of kilometres. This Ghauri missile may be interpreted as a threat to us."[118] He further added "...we are not condemning the fact that nuclear testing has been done. That by itself, technical or scientific, is a good achievement.[119]

Nevertheless, reacting to Pakistan's nuclear tests, a joint press statement issued by the CPI and CPI (M) on 29 May 1998 stated that they were not a vindication of the policy adopted by the BJP-led government as the Prime Minister had claimed, but an inevitable confirmation of how wrong the reversal was of India's long-standing nuclear policy. The statement said that it had undone the progress in establishing good neighbourly relations with India's neighbours and security and peace in the region. It also added: "The short-sighted step taken by the Vajpayee government and the reaction of the Pakistani government is leading to the step by step escalation in the nuclear arms race in the subcontinent and its attendant tensions."[120] In its 2004 election manifesto the CPI(M) committed itself to reverting to the policy of using nuclear energy for civilian and peaceful purposes and opening talks with Pakistan for a de-nuclearised environment in South Asia.[121] CPI(M) Polit Bureau member and Member of Parliament Sitaram Yechury reiterated in September 2006 that although both India and Pakistan have demonstrated their nuclear weapons capability, the CPI(M) was of the opinion that "both the countries must desist from deploying nuclear weapons. This is the essential prerequisite to defuse escalation of tensions...."[122]

Official pronouncements sometimes glossed over varying views within political parties, be they in the government or in opposition. At various points of time, as for example, the 1965 and 1971 wars or the developments in Pakistan's nuclear programme, members of Parliament cutting across party lines urged the government to opt for nuclear weapons to safeguard the country's security. While there was a consensus on India's nuclear policy during the period up to 1998, the post Pokhran period saw some divergence in perceptions. There was however, consensus among the mainstream political parties in emphasising the threat from Pakistan's nuclear programme and endorsing the Government's determination to meet this threat.

## Perceptions of the Strategic Community

Ashley Tellis uses the term *nuclear strategists* to refer to people "who devote most of their thinking not to the task of how best to de-legitimise and get rid of nuclear weapons but to justifying their possession, operationalising their threat, and, if considered necessary, organising their actual use."[123] Similarly, Peter Lavoy alludes to *myth makers* as key individuals who expound threats to the state's security in order to make the myth of nuclear security or nuclear influence more compelling.[124] Haider K. Nizamani uses the concept of *epistemic communities* in the South Asian context to identify segments of the societies in Pakistan and India that constitute the dominant nuclear discourse,[125] while Ashis Nandy identifies these groups as *the strategic elite.*[126] Bidwai and Vanaik refer to *strategic experts*, most of whom are drawn from the bureaucratic, military and diplomatic services, journalism, think-tanks concerned with security matters, and academic disciplines like International Relations and Area Studies.[127] Similarly, Kanti Bajpai refers to the *strategic community* of those outside the formal corridors of power, including former diplomats and officers from the armed forces, prominent media commentators and columnists, research scholars and academics.[128] It is argued that members of this community shape government thinking as well as represent or communicate that thinking to the larger public and to the international community. It is in this context that the perceptions of the strategic community, which in this study is taken to represent all the above sections reflecting the mainstream nuclear discourse in India, need to be particularly emphasised. No specific distinction is made between the groups identified, although the perceptions within the media will be examined in the following chapter. Itty Abraham however defines a sub category of the Indian military-security complex, particularly the research establishments and production facilities that are responsible for the development of the missile and nuclear programmes in India as the *strategic enclave.*[129] Perkovich uses the term in similar context referring to the "scientists and engineers in India's defence research and atomic energy institutions who for five decades had been pushing India to join the exclusive club of nuclear weapon states."[130] The role of this scientific establishment in driving India's quest for nuclear weapons has been well documented,[131] and its perception of Pakistan's nuclear programme is also surveyed here.

The Atomic Energy Commission (AEC) could possibly have been the most important bomb lobby in India, for it was the carefully timed and worded statements of the AEC's chairmen between 1964 and 1970 which in fact gave life to the arguments for an Indian bomb.[132] In 1964 Bhabha had argued: "...atomic weapons give a State possessing them in adequate numbers a deterrent power against attack from a much stronger state. Indeed the importance of nuclear weapons is that they enable a country possessing them in adequate measure to deter another country also possessing them from using them against it."[133]

A publication by the Department of Atomic Energy (DAE) in 1970 entitled *Nuclear Weapons: A Compilation Prepared by the DAE*, while incorporating policy statements by the government also included several articles stridently calling for exercising the nuclear option or outright weaponisation. At the same time, a number of eminent scientists of the DAE had for years argued that Pakistan with its 'considerably inferior' science and technology base, manpower, and infrastructure, could not possibly match India in mastering an 'advanced' technology such as nuclear energy. It could not have mastered a technology that was 'borrowed' or 'stolen', as opposed to that developed 'indigenously', as in the case of India. This assessment seemed to be based more on the reluctance to concede that Pakistan could have mastered a technology – uranium enrichment by the centrifuge method – where India had failed. These scientists included Raja Ramanna who headed the Bhabha Atomic Research Centre (BARC) at the time of the 1974 test and P.K.Iyengar who headed its Physics division (both of whom later became Chairmen of AEC).[134] Nuclear establishment leaders consistently expressed doubts about Pakistan's nuclear capabilities and its claims in this regard. H.N.Sethna, Chairman, AEC, stated in October 1982 that "Pakistan had neither the industrial infrastructure necessary for producing an atomic bomb nor the resources and capable brains" for the purpose.[135] Perkovich notes:

> The Brahminical contempt for the abilities of Pakistan's scientists and engineers also was intensified by the difficulties India's well-educated scientists had in trying to master large-scale uranium enrichment.... Cognitive dissonance may explain the Indian scientists' perspectives toward their Pakistani counter-parts. The Indians recognised that Pakistan's enrichment program benefited enormously from designs stolen from Europe and assistance provided by China, but many still could not overcome their prejudices about Pakistani abilities.[136]

The aftermath of the 1998 tests saw an outpouring of statements by the scientific community, which will be elaborated on in the following chapter. Stressing the importance of nuclear weapons for national security, there was undisguised pride at India's 'indigenous' scientific achievement, while casting aspersions on the capabilities of Pakistan and its 'clandestine' nuclear programme.[137] These perceptions continued to be articulated over the years, as was evident in their reactions to the revelation in 2003 that A.Q.Khan had been a source of nuclear weapons knowledge for North Korea, Iran and Libya;[138] and the India-US nuclear agreement of July 2005, etc.[139] In the context of the A.Q.Khan disclosures, M.R.Srinivasan, former Chairman of the AEC in his article in *The Hindu* "Pakistani nuclear weapons" (5 April 2003) wrote that although this may have come as a frightening piece of information to most Indians, to those familiar with nuclear matters it was no surprise. He argued that there was "no alternative for India except to maintain an overwhelming superiority in the number of nuclear weapons relative to Pakistan. Equally, India has to ensure it has an adequate number of missiles of appropriate range to ensure that its nuclear deterrence is credible."

Srinivasan also maintained that A.Q.Khan systematically stole the blueprints and specifications for the gas centrifuge process when he worked in the Netherlands, and took them with him when he decided to work for the Pakistan programme. He highlighted Khan's 'visceral hatred of India' and his 'vainglorious attitude'. He argued that Khan could also have engendered a 'jihadi' world view among his colleagues. At the same time, referring to United States sanctions against two Indian engineers who held senior positions in the Nuclear Power Corporation of India Limited for their nuclear proliferation actions, Srinivasan stated that the US actions were 'ludicrous in the extreme'.[140] In another article entitled "New opportunities for nuclear energy" in *The Hindu* on 2 August 2005, Srinivasan complimented Prime Minister Manmohan Singh for negotiating the India-United States nuclear agreement that "can end India's nuclear isolation, without in any way compromising our security.... India can, in due course of time, export nuclear hardware and services to an international nuclear market which is bound to grow."

Taking the case of the strategic community in general, there was no specific group of 'strategic experts' who articulated the importance of the nuclear option for India or emphasised the nuclear threats posed by China or Pakistan until 1964. The establishment of the Institute for Defence Studies and Analyses (IDSA), the oldest strategic and security studies think-tank in India in November 1965 is of particular significance in this context. Members of the institute have written extensively on security strategic issues over the years.[141] K. Subrahmanyam's contribution is one such example and is representative of the mainstream strategic discourse on the nuclear issue in India. Besides having been a former Director of IDSA, he had served as Secretary of Defence Production, Government of India. Subrahmanyam was also Convener of the National Security Advisory Board that presented the draft of India's nuclear doctrine in August 1999 and the Chairman of the four member Kargil Review Committee besides having been a member of various other committees formed by the Government. It is in this context, and the fact that he has consistently been the most prolific writer on nuclear security issues since the 1960s, that Subrahmanyam's work is of particular importance. Subrahmanyam has written extensively on the role of nuclear weapons as the "currency of power" in the contemporary world. The important themes, which appear in Subrahmanyam's writings in the context of the present study, include the arguments that Pakistan's security problems were largely self-inflicted, and the product of its leaders' mistaken choice of the path of development rather than of any external threat.

While western commentators consider South Asia as a possible venue for a future nuclear war, writings by security analysts in India largely view nuclear weapons in the region as guarantors of stability.[142] Kanti Bajpai, who categorised the strategic community into three groups based on their desired nature of India's deterrent capability and approach to the non-proliferation regime, points out that the community is, however, largely in agreement that nuclear weapons are essential for India's security.[143] Even in 1969, K.Subrahmanyam had been a strong advocate of the nuclear weapons option for India,[144] as building a nuclear arsenal would force the United States to revise its "contemptuous" view of India and "enable us to deal with China on an equal basis."[145] According to Subrahmanyam, an India without nuclear weapons would send signals of weakness of the Indian elite having no will power. Subrahmanyam contends that

> deterrence in Indo-Pakistan context is not as unsatisfactory as it is between the two superpowers.... It will not mean nuclear winter, rapid escalation involving use of hundreds of warheads and loss of control over the war. It will be analogous to the situation between the superpowers in the early fifties. That situation will still be preferable to one of India remaining non-nuclear facing the threat of humiliation, defeat and disintegration.... This is a case where deterrence with all its imperfections and risks is likely to work.[146]

Subrahmanyam argued that a nuclear Pakistan in the subcontinent, besides a non-nuclear India, would project an image of power far in excess of India, it would assume leadership in the Islamic world as well as among "segments of Muslim populations in other countries of the subcontinent, including recalcitrant sections of our population." A nuclear Pakistan would be "a convenient safe haven for our extremists."[147]

Prior to the May 1998 explosions, the Indian nuclear programme was portrayed as patently 'civilian' in nature, guided by the vision of Nehru and Bhabha, whereas the Pakistani programme was 'militaristic' from the start.[148] While the Indian nuclear programme is perceived as "a nationalist project representing the political will and scientific zeal of the Indian establishment, the Pakistani programme has more to do with the conspiracy of India's adversaries.... The Pakistani nuclear programme is deemed a danger to India not only in terms of its wider scope but also because of Islamabad's malicious intentions."[149] These ill intentions of Pakistan are seen to be manifest in the clandestine operations of its foreign missions and scientists. Sreedhar of IDSA refers to A.Q.Khan as "the Pak scientist-spy."[150] The supposedly sinister nature of the Pakistani programme is highlighted by criticising its claims of being a reactive policy and emphasising the peculiar traits of the Pakistani leadership and their domestic constraints.[151] It is often emphasised that the Pakistani nuclear programme predated the Indian one. K. Subrahmanyam argues that since Pakistan introduced F-104 aircraft, sophisticated tanks, and staged aggressions against India, it would be perfectly reasonable to assume that Pakistan introduced the nuclear factor in India-Pakistan relations! He also emphasises that Islamabad's nuclear ambition predated the 1974 Pokhran test.[152]

Accusations of Pakistan, having introduced the nuclear factor in the subcontinent often emphasised the role of Zulfikar Ali Bhutto. Bhutto was seen as a man obsessed with acquiring nuclear weapons long before India exploded its nuclear device. To some, Bhutto introduced the nuclear factor because of domestic compulsions. According to Ashok Kapur, Bhutto's ambitions, assessments, policies and motivations were the single most dominant influence which shaped Pakistan's nuclear activities since 1972.[153] Discussing Bhutto's role in Pakistan's nuclear policy, P.L.Bhola writes that Bhutto's motives were geared to his drive for personal power and influence. His ambitions were not confined to becoming Pakistan's national hero, but extended beyond the borders of the country.[154] Subrahmanyam maintains that once in power, Bhutto started on his relentless drive to achieve a nuclear weapons capability.[155] D.K.Palit and P.K.S.Namboodiri (who according to the introduction to their book were intimately associated with the IDSA and K. Subrahmanyam in particular) also argue that Bhutto was thinking of nuclear weapons long before India's peaceful nuclear experiment. India was the immediate excuse, whereas his thinking was conditioned by his overall perception of war and strategy in the nuclear age.[156] According to these accounts, it was Bhutto's personality traits or political expediency that was responsible for introducing the nuclear factor into India-Pakistan relations.

The military coup in Pakistan in 1977 and the subsequent Islamisation programme adopted by General Zia ul-Haq provided a new angle to the nuclear discourse in India. The "Islamic bomb," became the theme of the Indian strategic community to highlight the threat from Pakistan. Pakistan's alleged Islamic nuclear bomb became a security concern of "secular and democratic" India.[157] Palit and Namboodiri throughout their book *Pakistan's Islamic Bomb*, speak of an "Islamic nuclear threat." According to them, with Bhutto's "flamboyant personality and obvious intelligence it would not have been difficult to persuade the Arab nations to support Pakistan in the development of an Islamic bomb."[158] They also highlighted a close collaboration between Arab states and Pakistan and argued that "the bomb will be Islamic but the finger on the trigger will be Pakistani."[159]

Strategic discourse relating to the Pakistani nuclear programme began to project the dangers of an "artificial, theocratic, unstable Pakistan" against a more secular and democratic India. The nuclear ambitions of the Zia regime were seen in terms of Pakistan becoming "the defender of the Gulf area" assuming that "money will pour in from Muslim countries" to fund Pakistan's nuclear programme.[160]

Pakistan's proposals for a Nuclear-Weapon-Free Zone or mutual signing of the Non Proliferation Treaty are projected as pro-West, impractical and anti-Indian. To some analysts like Savita Pande and Subrahmanyam, the Pakistani proposals were seen as "a diplomatic move intended to make its own bomb plan for 1972"[161] or to further the West's interests,[162] while to others, these proposals were aimed at benefiting China at the cost of India.[163] According to P.B.Sinha and R.R.Subramanian (then of IDSA), the Pakistani proposal to make South Asia a Nuclear-Weapon-Free Zone, though "*prima facie* very laudable is insincere.... The sinister part of the Pakistanis proposal is that it knows that a nuclear free zone in this region is inconceivable unless China is also included."[164]

In the aftermath of the 1998 nuclear tests there emerged a strong justification of India's nuclear weapons programme by the strategic community. Threats from China and Pakistan, the need to make the country's deterrent credible, and the failure of the five declared nuclear states to disarm were cited as the primary reasons for conducting the tests. Soon after the tests, IDSA convened a meeting of India's prominent serving and retired defence officials, academics, Foreign Ministry officials, and journalists. According to a *Times of India* report, they underlined the "urgent need for

India to both develop a nuclear doctrine and ensure that the success of the tests is not frittered away as did happen after the 1974 nuclear implosion."[165] Perkovich observes that for years the gathered experts had all debated the adequacy of the 'nuclear option', or 'nonweaponised deterrence', or 'recessed deterrence', or 'minimum deterrence'. None of these doctrines envisioned or required thermonuclear weapons, yet these weapons now had to be reckoned with *post facto.*[166] The 'strategic experts' sought to justify the Indian decision and to explain why the tests were inevitable. As Bidwai and Vanaik pointed out, all the pro-nuclear advocates sought to justify the decision to go nuclear as some kind of inevitable and 'logical' culmination of an evolving Indian nuclear policy. They refused to recognise or accept that the decision to test and go openly nuclear represented a sharp change with India's past policy of ambiguity. All of them claimed that the hypocrisy of existing NWSs in part 'drove' India to act as it did. The pro-nuclearists argued that Indian security had improved or would soon enough do so as a result of this decision. They also claimed that India-Pakistan as well as Sino-Indian relations would improve.[167]

Ashok Kapur argues that the Indian tests of 1998 reflected a considered response to Pakistani, Chinese and American provocations in the strategic sphere. While China supplied nuclear and missile aid to Pakistan in violation of its non-proliferation commitments, the Clinton administration repeatedly refused to accept the evidence of the Central Intelligence Agency (CIA) on these issues.[168] K.Subrahmanyam welcomed Pakistan's nuclear tests in the hope that it would give Pakistan confidence: "Pakistan is now in a position to liberate itself from the obsessive feeling of threat vis-à-vis India."[169] Although China is often projected as the main impetus to India's nuclear programme, the essence of the Indian nuclear discourse is primarily Pakistan-centric. According to Nizamani:

> K. Subrahmanyam unwittingly puts Pakistan at the centre of the Indian nuclear programme by arguing that the Indian nuclear doctrine 'is the appropriate language to communicate to the nuclear warriors who believe in the first use of nuclear weapons'. This doctrine would create uncertainty 'in the minds of would-be nuclear intimidators, aggressors and interventionists that those actions against this country would not be rational options'. [170]

In the context of the Kargil conflict of 1999, various analysts contended that the conflict proved the efficacy of nuclear deterrence. Manpreeth Sethi of the IDSA, argued that the fact that the Kargil conflict ended as it did "reveals an inherent nuclear stability that is in place."[171] P.M.Kamath also maintained that the strength of the Indian nuclear policy brought international support led by the United States during the Kargil crisis, which asked Pakistan to withdraw forces from Kargil.[172] In similar vein, C. Uday Bhaskar, Deputy Director of IDSA argued: "The Kargil war of 1999 had an inadvertent silver lining in that it may be seen as an inoculation for both states."[173] He also elaborated on the imperative need to stabilise the India-Pakistan nuclear equation. The revelations in 2003 that A.Q.Khan played a key role in transferring nuclear technology to Iran, Libya and North Korea set off another round of smug satisfaction and a projection of a threat from Pakistan's nuclear programme among the strategic community. This turned to indignation at the closure of the case against the Pakistan based A.Q.Khan Network in 2006. Rajesh Kumar Mishra, Associate Fellow of IDSA points out that Khan's key role in the nuclear black bazaar suggests that Pakistan still remains a dangerous source of proliferation and nuclear terrorism.[174] Thus the analysis of the Indian strategic community reveals its inherent biases with respect to Pakistan and the nuclear weaponisation of the subcontinent.

## Public Opinion

Ascertaining public opinion is a difficult and problematic issue, particularly when it concerns issues such as nuclear and security policies. Over the years, various public opinion polls regarding nuclear policy have been conducted within the country. One such poll conducted among adult literates of metropolitan cities, in the context of the 1974 nuclear test found that three among four persons felt that the nuclear test would act as a deterrent against possible aggression by Pakistan.[175] In July 1981, the Indian Institute of Public Opinion reported that nearly seventy per cent of survey respondents wanted India to manufacture a nuclear bomb, while only nineteen per cent opposed the proposition. The Institute concluded: "The U.S. decision to rearm Pakistan with sophisticated weaponry seems to have convinced a large segment of the Indian people that exercising India's nuclear option alone would enable it to meet the challenge posed by the perceived change in the strategic balance."[176]

The most detailed public opinion survey conducted on nuclear issues in India was commissioned by the Fourth Freedom Forum and the Joan B. Kroc Institute for International Peace Studies.

It surveyed elite public opinion during the period September – November 1995. The survey found that fifty seven per cent of those polled supported India's policy of keeping the nuclear option open. Thirty-three per cent supported acquisition of nuclear weapon capability, and only eight per cent favoured renunciation of the nuclear option. The study stated that the survey proved that the perceived nuclear threat from Pakistan was the single most important factor motivating Indian elites to consider the nuclear option. The evidence suggested that Indian elites would strongly favour the acquisition of nuclear weapons if Pakistan were to test a nuclear device. According to the survey a majority of nuclear advocates identified the threat from Pakistan as the reason why India should develop nuclear weapons. A majority of official policy supporters and ten percent of nuclear opponents also believed that India would be justified in developing nuclear weapons in the event of a Pakistani nuclear test. Of significance in the present context is the finding of the survey that only thirteen percent of the respondents felt that information on nuclear issues is easily available. A majority of respondents (sixty one percent) believed that obtaining information on nuclear issues is not easy. Of particular significance is the conclusion of the study that few Indians have strong opinions on the nuclear issue, and that the majority could be persuaded by new information or changing circumstances. A wider, more informed, and more critical public debate in India could lead to significant shifts in opinion.[177]

A *Times of India* poll in April 1995 showed that seventy nine per cent of residents of urban areas who were surveyed believed that Pakistan's possession of nuclear weapons posed a "serious security threat to

India."[178] Immediately after the 1998 tests, the widely publicised public opinion poll conducted by the Indian Market Research Bureau, in six metropolitan cities found that, ninety one per cent of those polled approved of the tests and fifty five per cent considered the Ghauri tests by Pakistan to have been the major reason for testing.[179] However, Bidwai and Vanaik point out that most opinion polls, particularly the early ones, were limited to the urban areas, and thus tended to exaggerate the popular support for the tests. "The more systematic broad-sample polls done later suggest that large numbers of rural Indians were not even aware of the tests."[180] V.Krishna Ananth adds that the fact that jingoism did not reflect the popular mood, especially in rural India, was reflected in the results of the elections held later in the year.[181]

The popular support for the country's nuclear option is clearly sustained by a select group of vocal opinion-shapers that dominate the nature and direction of the debate on the nuclear issue in the subcontinent. Hence the internal debate resembles more of a monologue of nuclear hawks where dissent risks being categorised as treasonous.[182] Although people may have different perceptions on the threat and costs associated with the nuclear option, these are largely based on insufficient and manipulated information available. As such, with better and more information people may modify their perceptions, which may or may not be in favour of the nuclear option. A nationwide debate on the issue may enable civil society to make informed and better social decisions.

## Dissenting Narratives

The dissenting voices in the nuclear discourse in India are advocates of nuclear disarmament who reject the concept of deterrence on moral, political, legal and strategic grounds. They perceive nuclear weapons to be unable to provide security. Among them, there were scholars who proposed a policy of nuclear abstinence. But this changed with the May 1998 explosions. On the other hand, there are those who would like India to accept the Pakistani proposal to declare South Asia as a Nuclear-Weapon-Free Zone (NWFZ) or sign the Non-Proliferation Treaty (NPT). This reflects an alternative perception of Indian security and identity.[183]

Columnists Praful Bidwai, Achin Vanaik and Gautam Navalakha have been the most persistent and vociferous dissenting voices on the nuclear issue in India. According to Vanaik, the belief in the permanent efficacy of nuclear deterrence was itself an irrational act of faith. As long as there are nuclear weapons there is always the danger of their actual use. He argues that nuclear weapons deployment and nuclear deterrence neither create nor promote security. In fact they reflect and promote insecurity. This was the main lesson of the Cold War period. It is in fact a prior reduction of political hostility that provides greater security, including nuclear security.[184]

Dissenters consider the arguments of those like K.Subrahmanyam, who believe that nuclear bombs will bring peace between India and Pakistan; and that peace and security presuppose mutual confidence that the weapons will never be used, to be inherently contradictory.[185]

Gautam Navlakha observes that nuclear arms are not ordinary weapons but pose a threat to all living creatures and therefore have no capacity to enhance security. "In fact, it is just the opposite."[186] Others argue that even if India faced a tangible nuclear threat, nuclear weapons are no means of meeting it. Bidwai and Vanaik describe how neither India nor Pakistan possesses the infrastructure, such as an acceptable early warning system for deterrence to work, nor can they afford to build one. They also contend that in comparison to external threat perceptions, India's self-perceptions about its potential political 'destiny' and future regional and global positions played a more important role in nuclear policy-making.[187] Vanaik notes that threat perceptions justifying India's refusal to sign the NPT have varied over time:

> Throughout most of the 1960s and 1970s it was the Chinese threat, potential and actual; since the late 1970s it has been the Pakistani threat. But there has also emerged another factor besides the internal pressures generated by the bomb and defence lobbies. India's status as the dominant regional power has progressively become more pronounced.... This means that issues of prestige and self-perceptions have become more important in determining India's nuclear weapons policies.... By contrast, threat perceptions have not experienced any comparable 'intensification', though Pakistan's efforts to reach the nuclear threshold have been watched closely.[188]

Most dissenters share the perception that the BJP decision to conduct the 1998 tests was guided more by internal dynamics than external security concerns. Nuclear politics are seen in the context of the emergence of Hindu nationalism as a social and political force in the 1990s. The tests were seen to be a result of the construction of a nationalist identity, which is antithetical to Pakistan. Bidwai argues that the nuclear tests were an expression of "the raw power of aggressive nationalism" and that the tests were an expression of Hindu nationalism rather than guided by any strategic logic.[189] Bidwai and Vanaik point out that it was not changes in the 'external security environment' or even changes in threat perceptions that was the main reason behind India's decision to go nuclear. It was changes in elite self-perceptions and the fact that the Sangh was in power, albeit in a coalition government. "Self-perceptions, unlike threat perceptions, are far more susceptible to alteration as a result of significant changes in domestic politics and dominant ideologies. Elite frustrations have risen in tandem with external ambitions and also been fed by the lack of adequate fulfilment of these aspirations."[190]

Similarly, Aijaz Ahmad, Senior Fellow, Nehru Memorial Museum Library, contends that the tests helped the BJP cut across the Hindu/secular divide and reach out to claim the mantle of Indian nationalism. Therefore a connection must be made with its communal agenda, and the fact that such a step was taken purely for the greater glory of the RSS. As such a consensus behind Vajpayee's nuclear policy was seen to amount to a consensus behind Hindutva.[191]

Bidwai and Vanaik point out that the external threats most commonly cited by India's pro-nuclearists to justify the tests have been Pakistan and China, both separately and in unison. Citing the Pakistan threat had the advantage of being highly saleable.[192] Aijaz Ahmad also argued that China had not taken any steps in recent years or even decades that posed any threat to Indian security. Neither had Pakistan carried out any nuclear tests. Its 'conventional' intervention in the domestic affairs of India should be dealt with through 'conventional' and political means. The test could also not be seen as a response to 'Ghauri', as India already had the technology to match it.[193] Similarly, Bidwai pointed out that it was irrelevant to cite Sino-Pakistani nuclear cooperation, which apart from being old hat, was of a limited, non-strategic nature. No state had recently threatened India with nuclear weapons or acted more belligerently than before. The global prospect for nuclear weapons elimination had not remained static or deteriorated. On the contrary, since the end of the cold war, the world has witnessed a weak, uncertain, halting, reversible but nevertheless authentic, new momentum favouring nuclear disarmament.[194] According to Amartya Sen the "nuclear adventures of India and Pakistan cannot be justified on the ground of the unjustness of the world order, since the people whose lives are made insecure as a result of these adventures are primarily the residents of the subcontinent."[195]

Voices of dissent even among the scientific community were evident, particularly after the 1998 tests.[196] In an Open Letter, a number of Indian scientists stressed that the magnitude of the achievement of science and technology should not be blown out of proportion.

> These tests are bound to vitiate the atmosphere in the South Asian region, triggering a nuclear weapon race in the region, exacerbating the tensions that already exist and making even more difficult the achievement of peaceful co-existence and co-operation amongst the peoples and the nations of this region.[197]

T.Jayaraman, a theoretical physicist, working at the Institute of Mathematical Sciences, Chennai, pointed out:

> ... in hailing the 'achievements' of Indian scientists in these tests and claiming that they have delivered 'security' to the people, as scientists like Raja Ramanna are doing, is to take a somewhat short-sighted view. This point has been brought home sharply in the aftermath of the Pakistani tests that followed close on the heels of Pokhran-II. There is little doubt that Indian science and technology go deeper and are more sophisticated and broader in scope than anything that Pakistan can boast of. Nevertheless, Pakistan has clearly demonstrated a nuclear weapons capability. Irrespective of the fact that the level of technical sophistication may not match the Indian tests, irrespective of the fact that Chagai-I does not demonstrate an indigenous scientific capability to the same extent as Pokhran-II, we now have an incipient open nuclear arms race in the sub-continent. The over-blown estimation of the superiority of Indian science and technology appears to have blinded important sections of the ruling establishment to the extent that post-Pokhran II little thought was given to the possibility and consequences of tests by Pakistan.[198]

Jayaraman maintains that the celebration of scientific achievements had more to do with jingoism than any objective evaluation of scientific advancement.[199] In a strong critique of the theory of deterrence, M.V.Ramana, a physicist by training, who at the time was working on nuclear disarmament and peace issues at Princeton University, wrote that nuclear weapons, in fact, "lead to different kinds of insecurity."[200] Ramana points out that Hindutva's answer to the new 'elite insecurity', which emerged as a result of the increasing social and political assertion of marginalised groups and the uncertainties of economic liberalisation, "is a quest for 'international status', through the deployment of symbolic gestures of 'great power status' such as the ability to acquire and test nuclear weapons."[201]

The announcement of the 1998 tests saw a number of rallies and demonstrations held in several parts of the country. Those who registered their protests included the Movement in India for Nuclear Disarmament, Pakistan India Peoples Forum for Peace and Democracy, *Parmanu Bomb Virodhi Andolan,* Medha Patkar and the National Alliance of Peoples Movements,[202] Booker prize novelist Arundhati Roy,[203] and numerous others.

Dissenters see Pakistan's route to the nuclear threshold as 'straightforward' and 'reactive' to Indian developments, guided largely by the notion of safeguarding its national interests. Vanaik points out:

> By the mid nineteen sixties India had built a research reactor and a reprocessing plant, and the nuclear weapons issue had become part of the public debate at home. It is at this relatively late juncture that Pakistan entered the nuclear field.... Arguments that Pakistan's nuclear orientation is not fundamentally conditioned by Indian actions or by perceptions of Indian ambitions, but is independently motivated, are unconvincing. These arguments from the Indian side are also self-serving in that they tend to obscure India's responsibility as the

> key referent in the South Asian nuclear dilemma. This is not to say there are no independent factors such as Pakistan's search for prestige in the Islamic world. But the decisive factor remains India and its actions. The 'Islamic Bomb' notion is a red herring, since Pakistan has proposed non-nuclear parity with India. This kind of parity is, reasonably enough, more important to Pakistan than the grandiose idea of producing a bomb for, and leading, an 'Islamic world' which is not and cannot be united in any meaningful sense of the term.[204]

Bidwai and Vanaik further add that Pakistan's deliberations have been based on a realpolitik approach to threat perceptions. Thus, there is no available evidence to suggest that Pakistan ever seriously considered not moving towards a threshold status once India had achieved it. They argue that the Sino-Pak nuclear relation has been exaggerated so as to justify Indian behaviour. According to them, the fact that there has been such a connection is undeniable. Yet, in the context of its contribution to Pakistan's development of a nuclear capability, "it has been very much a secondary factor in comparison to Islamabad's own clandestine efforts at equipping itself with the necessary hardware and software."[205] Vanaik argues that much of what passes for strategic evaluation of Chinese nuclear relations with India is neither objective nor balanced but speculation motivated by the need to paint a picture of "strategic threats" so as to justify a more hawkish stand on India's part with regard to the nuclear issue.[206] In 1995, an official Indian delegation to China was informed that China was in the business of undertaking commercial transactions and would be willing to supply on Indian request every item they believed China had supplied to Pakistan![207] Vanaik says that the effort to cite an immediate danger of the Pakistan threat falters on Islamabad's willingness to explore avenues of regional denuclearisation, in contrast to India's unwillingness to entertain any such proposals.[208]

However, there is a difference of opinion among the dissenters on whether India should sign the international non-proliferation treaties — NPT, CTBT and FMCT. N.Ram argues that capitulating to the discriminatory global nuclear order through joining the CTBT and committing India to the accession to an FMCT, as envisaged by the United States and other nuclear powers while inducting and deploying nuclear weapons themselves, would be the worst possible option.[209] This perception has been endorsed by the traditional left movements and political parties. Achin Vanaik considers the establishment of a NWFZ in South Asia as "the most important and desirable" policy alternative for India. If India had the political will, the technicalities involved in realising the goal of a NWFZ could be overcome. It is also considered self-contradictory of Indians to doubt the sincerity of Pakistan because the latter has proposed ideas like a NWFZ.[210] Giri Deshingkar suggests that despite the NPT being a discriminatory treaty, India should still relinquish the nuclear weapon option. Since India has learned to live in an unequal world in various realms, there is no point in opposing the NPT.[211] By acknowledging the merits of the Pakistani proposal for a NWFZ or international measures like the NPT, CTBT, or FMCT, these dissenters stand in marked contrast to the dominant discourse. Praful Bidwai had in fact criticised India's Draft Nuclear Doctrine as being the final blow for the cause of nuclear disarmament. He argued that this document drawn up by the National Security Council advisory board "marks a hardening of India's nuclear posture after the nuclear tests in May 1998. It is certain to ignite a nuclear arms race in the region with disastrous consequences. And it marks the final Indian nail in the coffin for the cause of global nuclear disarmament which New Delhi promoted for half a century."[212] However, the extent to which these dissenting voices received public attention is open to question.

Notwithstanding these counter-narratives, the nuclear discourse seems to have been dominated by the strategic community who tend to present a justification of official policy. The manner in which nuclear security/insecurity perceptions are defined within the country appears to have changed according to pragmatic and ideological concerns. However, since the 1970s threats are defined in traditional realist terms, seeking to convince the people of existing external nuclear threats, particularly from Pakistan and the ability of the government to meet the situation and ensure collective protection.

Nuclear discourses of the government, mainstream political parties and the strategic community, have been mutually reinforcing, particularly with regard to Pakistan's nuclear programme, notwithstanding the differences noted. Negative images of Pakistan's nuclear policy are projected in contrast to India's own sanitised one, thus inculcating the need for providing security. In the process, nuclear issues are sought to be securitised, raising them above politics and making them unquestionable. Hence, there is a growing demand for unity and consensus on nuclear issues. Public opinion polls, notwithstanding their inherent limitations, reveal that these nuclear security perceptions seem to be reflected in civil society also, despite the existence of a small but vociferous community of dissenting voices. The precise dimensions of these contradicting perceptions within society can be clearly ascertained through an analysis of the coverage of the issue in the mainstream mass media.

## NOTES AND REFERENCES

1 India, Ministry of External Affairs, *Status of Nuclear Weapons in International Law: Request for Advisory Opinion of the International Court of Justice*, Mimeo (New Delhi, 1995), p.7; also see Praful Bidwai and Achin Vanaik, *South Asia on a Short Fuse: Nuclear Politics and the Future of Global Disarmament* (New Delhi: Oxford University Press, 1999), pp.70-72, 142.

2 See Jawaharlal Nehru, "Foreword," in India, Ministry of Information and Broadcasting, *Nuclear Explosions and their Effects* (New Delhi: Publications Division, 1958), p.vi; also see Jawaharlal Nehru's Speech in UN General Assembly, New York, 10 November 1961; India, Ministry of Information and Broadcasting, *Jawaharlal Nehru's Speeches: September 1957-April 1963*: Vol.4 (New Delhi: Publications Division, 1983), p.436.

3 India, Lok Sabha, *Debates,* 24 July 1957, col.4954, in India, Ministry of Information and Broadcasting, *Jawaharlal Nehru's Speeches: March 1953-August 1957: Vol 2* (New Delhi: Publications Division, 1983), p.518.

4 *Jawaharlal Nehru's Speeches,* n.2, p.436; also see India, Lok Sabha, *Debates,* Vol.15, No.37, 25 March 1963, col. 5919.

5 As far back as 1955, Nehru was instrumental in getting Indian scientists to study the physical and biological effects of nuclear explosions. See *Nuclear Explosions and their Effects,* n.2; also see Speech in the Lok Sabha, 10 May 1954, in *Jawaharlal Nehru's Speeches,* n.3, pp.254-262; Speech in the Lok Sabha, 10 August 1960, in *Jawaharlal Nehru's Speeches,* n.2, pp.435-440; India, Lok Sabha Secretariat, *Development of Nuclear Energy for Peaceful Uses: Policy,*

*Programmes and Achievements* (New Delhi, August 1974), pp.11-16. Praful Bidwai and Achin Vanaik point out that an overwhelming number of references can be cited to support these views of Nehru. However, some analysts see his rejection of nuclear weapons to be less than categorical. See the Kargil Review Committee Report, *From Surprise to Reckoning* (New Delhi: Sage, 2000); Itty Abraham, *The Making of the Indian Atomic Bomb: Science, Secrecy and the Postcolonial State* (New Delhi: Orient Longman, 1999). Bidwai and Vanaik argue that it is illogical to put inordinately heavy interpretation on certain statements to conclude that Nehru was ambivalent about nuclear weapons, when the evidence to the contrary, especially from well-considered and carefully enunciated policy formulations, is massive and persuasive. Nehru's actions, as well as the central thrust of his reflections and pronouncements on the issue, support this premise. Any inference regarding ambivalence can only be the result of interpretation, rather than explicit unambivalent statements. See Bidwai and Vanaik, n.1, pp.74-75.

6 India, Lok Sabha, *Debates*, Vol.35, No.10, 27 November 1964, col.2287.

7 Statement by Prime Minister Indira Gandhi, Lok Sabha, 24 April 1968, in J.P. Jain, *Nuclear India: Vol.2* (New Delhi: Radiant, 1974), pp. 201-202.

8 India, Lok Sabha, *Debates*, Vol.41, No.1, 22 July 1974, p.264.

9 See SIPRI, *Yearbook of World Armaments and Disarmament 1975* (Stockholm: Almqvist and Wikell, 1975), p.16.

10 India, Ministry of External Affairs, *Speech of External Affairs Minister A.B. Vajpayee on 4 October 1977 at the 32nd Session, 18th Plenary Meeting of the United Nations General Assembly, New York*, www.meadev.nic.in.

11 India, Ministry of External Affairs, *Speech of External Affairs Minister A.B. Vajpayee on 10 October 1978 at the 33rd Session, 29th Plenary Meeting of the United Nations General Assembly, New York*, www.meadev.nic.in.

12 Statement by Salman Haidar, Foreign Secretary of India, at the Plenary Meeting of the Conference on Disarmament, Geneva, 21 March 1996. See Praful Bidwai and Achin Vanaik, n.1, pp.70-72.

13 Statement by Foreign Secretary, Conference on Disarmament Plenary on CTBT, 20 June 1996. India, Ministry of External

Affairs, *Foreign Affairs Record*, Vol.42, No. 6, June 1996, p. 101.

14 M. V. Ramana, "South Asian Mode of Weaponisation," *Economic and Political Weekly*, Vol.25, No. 11, 11-17 March 2000, p.897.

15 See Itty Abraham, n.5; Dhirendra Sharma, *India's Nuclear Estate* (New Delhi: Lancers, 1983).

16 For further details, see George Perkovich, *India's Nuclear Bomb: The Impact on Global Proliferation* (New Delhi: Oxford University Press, 2000), pp.190-352.

17 The Kargil Review Committee Report, n.5, pp.199 and 205.

18 Official brochure of the Missile Technology Centre quoted in W.P.S.Sidhu, "India's Security and Nuclear Risk-Reduction Measures," W.P.S.Sidhu, Brian Cloughly, John H.Hawes and Teresita Schaffer, *Nuclear Risk Reduction Measures in Southern Asia* (Washington D.C: The Henry L. Stimson Center, November 1998), p.10.

19 George Perkovich, n.16, p.2.

20 Bharatiya Janata Party, *Election Manifesto 1998*, www.bjp.org.; also see National Democratic Alliance, *For a Proud, Prosperous India: An Agenda*, www.bjp.org.

21 "China a bigger threat than Pak, says George," *The Times of India*, 4 May 1998.

22 India, Ministry of External Affairs, Press Statement issued in New Delhi, 11 May 1998, *Foreign Affairs Record*, Vol.44, No.5, May 1998, pp.36-37.

23 Praful Bidwai and Achin Vanaik, n.1, p.209.

24 Prime Minister Vajpayee's letter to President Clinton after the nuclear tests in May 1998, which was leaked to the press states: "I have been deeply concerned at the deteriorating security environment, specially the nuclear environment, faced by India for some years past. We have an overt nuclear weapon state on our borders, a state which committed armed aggression against India in 1962. Although our relations with that country have improved in the last decade or so, an atmosphere of distrust persists mainly due to the unresolved border problem. To add to the distrust that country has materially helped another neighbour of ours to become a covert nuclear weapons state. At the hands of this bitter neighbour we have suffered three aggressions in the last 50

years. And for the last 10 years we have been the victim of unremitting terrorism and militancy sponsored by it in several parts of the country, specially Punjab and Jammu & Kashmir." See "Text of Vajpayee's letter to Clinton," *The Hindu*, 14 May 1998.

25 Suo Moto Statement by Prime Minister Atal Behari Vajpayee in Parliament, 27 May 1998, *Foreign Affairs Record*, n.22, pp.40-42.

26 India, Ministry of External Affairs, Prime Minister's Statement in Parliament, 15 December 1998, www.meadev.nic.in.

27 Ibid.

28 See *Outlook*, 25 May 1998; also see *India Today*, 25 May 1998.

29 Ministry of External Affairs' Press Release, 15 May 1998, n.22, p.38.

30 For the text of the draft report, see *Draft Report of National Security Advisory Board on Indian Nuclear Doctrine*, 17 August 1999, www.indianembassy.org

31 For the Press Release, see India, Prime Minister's Office, *Cabinet Committee on Security Reviews Progress in Operationalizing India's Nuclear Doctrine*, 4 January 2003 www.rajyasabha.nic.in.

32 India, Ministry of Defence, *Annual Report, 2005-2006*, www.mod.gov.in.

33 "No curb on nuclear facilities: Manmohan," *The Hindu*, 8 March 2006.

34 India, Ministry of Defence, *Annual Report, 2006-2007*, www.mod.gov.in.

35 The mandate of the PAEC was to plan and develop 'peaceful uses of atomic energy with special reference to survey, procurement and disposal of radioactive materials; planning and establishment of Atomic Energy and Nuclear Research Institute, installation of Research and Power Reactors, negotiations with International Atomic Energy bodies, selection and training of personnel, application of radio-isotopes to agriculture, health, industry, etc.' See Nasir Ahmad, "The Atomic Energy Commission," *Pakistan Quarterly*, Vol.7, No.3, Autumn 1957, p.14; also see Ashok Kapur, *Pakistan's Nuclear Development* (London: Croom Helm, 1987), pp.36, 82.

36 US Embassy (Karachi) to Secretary of State, Cable no.462, November 18, 1964, p.2, Nuclear Non-Proliferation Policy FOIA files, Pakistan, *National Security Archives*, Washington D.C., cited in George Perkovich, n.16, p.108.

37 Patrick Keatley, "The brown bomb," *Guardian,* 11 March 1965, p.10. See ibid., p.108.

38 Ashok Kapur, n.35, pp.55-56.

39 Zulfikar Ali Bhutto, *Reshaping Foreign Policy: A Collection of Articles, Statements and Speeches: Politics of the People, Vol.1, 1948-1966* (Rawalpindi:Pakistan Publications, n.d.), p.221.

40 Speech at Larkhana, 29 December 1966, *Zulfikar Ali Bhutto, Awakening the People: A Collection of Articles, Statements and Speeches: Politics of the People, Vol.2, 1966-1969* (Karachi: Public Relations, n.d.), pp.19-21.

41 See Haider K. Nizamani, *The Roots of Rhetoric: Politics of Nuclear Weapons in India and Pakistan* (New Delhi: India Research Press, 2001), pp. 72-74.

42 Zulfikar Ali Bhutto, *The Myth of Independence* (Karachi: Oxford University Press, 1969), p.153.

43 Haider K. Nizamani, n.41, pp.17, 78-79.

44 Address at the Karachi Nuclear Power Plant, 28 November 1972, Pakistan, *Zulfikar Ali Bhutto: Speeches and Statements, 1 October 1972 –31 December 1972* (Karachi: Government of Pakistan, 1973), p.162.

45 The Pakistan Foreign Office stated that it was a development that 'cannot but be viewed with the degree of concern matching its magnitude by the world and more especially by India's neighbours. It assured the public of the measures taken by the government to face such a challenge. These included Bhutto's pleas to Ayub Khan to secure the Karachi Nuclear Power Project (KANUPP), and his direct supervision of the PAEC since assuming power in 1971. See *Dawn,* 19 May 1974; also see Haider K.Nizamani, n.41, p. 85.

46 *New York Times*, 20 May 1974; also see George Perkovich, n.16, p.185.

47 *Dawn,* 20 May 1974.

48 Pakistan, National Assembly, *Debates,* Vol.3, No.7, 6 June 1974, pp.297-306.

49 These included the 1976 Symington Amendment barring U.S. aid to any country that imported uranium enrichment

technology without accepting safeguards determined by the International Atomic Energy Agency (IAEA); the 1977 Glenn Amendment, which required the suspension of US aid to Pakistan in the event of Pakistan receiving or exploding a nuclear device; the 1985 Solarz Amendment barring aid to any non-nuclear weapon country which illegally exported nuclear commodities from the United States for use in a nuclear device and the 1985 Pressler Amendment, which required US assistance to Pakistan to be made dependent upon presidential certification that Pakistan did not possess a nuclear device. See Farzana Shaikh, "Pakistan's Nuclear Bomb: Beyond the Non-Proliferation Regime," *International Affairs*, Vol.78, No.1, January 2002, p.32.

50 Haider K.Nizamani, n.41, pp.90-91.

51 Zulfikar Ali Bhutto, *If I am Assassinated* (New Delhi: Vikas, 1979), pp.137-39.

52 Haider K. Nizamani, n.41, p.17.

53 Samina Ahmed, "The (Nuclear) Testing of Pakistan," *Current History*, Vol.97, No.623, December 1998, p.411.

54 Sajjad Hyder, *Foreign Policy of Pakistan: Reflections of an Ambassador* (Lahore: Progressive, 1987), p.74.

55 See "BJP vows to take back Azad Kashmir," *Dawn*, 26 February 1998; Amit Baruah, "BJP statements worry Pakistan," *The Hindu*, 27 February 1998.

56 "Pak reserves right to take appropriate steps," *The Hindu*, 12 May 1998; "Gohar speaks of 'matching response'," *The Hindu*, 13 May 1998.

57 "Roll back proxy war, Pak told," *The Hindu*, 19 May 1998.

58 Praful Bidwai and Achin Vanaik, n.1, pp.112-114.

59 For text of the statement by Prime Minister Nawaz Sharif at Press Conference, 28 May 1998, see www.pak.gov.pk; also see press briefing by the Foreign Secretary of Pakistan announcing further nuclear tests, 30 May 1998, www.pak.gov.pk.

60 Statement by Ambassador Munir Akram at the Special Session of the Conference on Disarmament on 2 June 1998, www.clw.org; also see Pakistan, Ministry of Foreign Affairs, Foreign Affairs Division, *The Nuclear Challenge*, www.pakistan.gov.pk.

61 Haider K. Nizamani, n.41, pp.111-113.

62 "Address by the Foreign Minister, Khurshid M. Kasuri on 'Challenges Confronting Pakistan's Foreign Policy' at the Lowy Institute, Sydney, Australia on 13 May 2005" in Pakistan, *Foreign Office Yearbook 2004-05*, p.142, www.mofa.gov.pk.

63 "Pak won't accept discrimination in nuclear field: Musharraf," *Pak Tribune*, 19 September 2006, www.paktribune.com.

64 "Musharraf says no compromise on nuclear programme," *Daily Times*, 20 March 2008, www.dailytimes.com.pk.

65 Haider K. Nizamani, n.41, p.27.

66 India, Lok Sabha, *Debates*, Vol.3, No.7, 31 May 1967, col. 2166.

67 India, Lok Sabha, *Debates*, Vol.2, No. 5, 17 March 1972, cols. 130-131.

68 However, the Kargil Review Committee Report of 2000, in its section entitled "The 1971 War, the 'Enterprise' Incident and Pokhran-I," explicitly links these issues, stating that "the 1971 war and the US tilt towards Pakistan together constitute a milestone in the nuclear decision making process in India.... These developments would have been a deciding factor in India's security calculus that led to the peaceful nuclear explosion of 1974.... India's nuclear programme does not owe its origin to the threat emanating from Pakistan but developments there naturally impacted on the direction and pace of the Indian programme." (The Kargil Review Committee Report, n.5, pp.184, 199, 203, 206, 239). Interestingly, the section on India's nuclear policy is placed immediately after that on Pakistan's and is entitled 'Indian Response'.

69 India, Lok Sabha, *Debates*, Vol.42, No.14, 8 August 1974, col.287.

70 "Reassurance on nuclear policy likely soon," *The Statesman*, 17 August 1979.

71 K.Subrahmanyam, "India's Dilemma," in K.Subrahmanyam (ed.), *Nuclear Myths and Realities* (New Delhi: ABC Publishing, 1981), p.i.

72 India, Lok Sabha, *Debates*, Vol.46, No.27, 30 March 1984, col.395.

73 For further details, see George Perkovich, n.16, pp.257-259.

74 Rajiv Gandhi, "Our Foreign Policy," Reply to the debate on the demand for grants of the Ministry of External Affairs,

Lok Sabha, 10 April 1985, in India, Ministry of Information and Broadcasting, *Rajiv Gandhi: Selected Speeches and Writings, Vol.1: 31 October 1984 - 31 December 1985* (New Delhi: Publications Division, 1987), pp.292-301.

75 "India to review nuclear policy, Gandhi says," *The Washington Post*, 5 May 1985. See George Perkovich, n.16, p.264.

76 US Embassy (New Delhi) to Secretary of State, cable no.051134Z June 1985, reporting on Gandhi's predeparture interviews with American media. See George Perkovich, n.16, pp.267-268.

77 India, Lok Sabha, *Debates*, Vol.8, No.13, 8 August 1985, cols.283-290.

78 Ibid.

79 Excerpts from Press Conference at Press Club, New Delhi, 11 October 1985, in *Rajiv Gandhi's Speeches*, n.74, p.441.

80 India, Ministry of Defence, *Annual Report 1987-88* (New Delhi, 1988), p.2.

81 "India announces review of nuclear policy," *Reuters*, 27 April 1987. See George Perkovich, n.16, p.284.

82 Chris Smith, *India's Ad Hoc Arsenal: Direction or Drift in Policy?* (Oxford: SIPRI and Oxford University Press, 1994), p.191.

83 The Kargil Review Committee Report, n.5, p.63.

84 India, Ministry of External Affairs, *Nuclear Non-Proliferation* (Washington D.C: Embassy of India), www.indianembassy.org.

85 The Kargil Review Committee Report, n.5, p.205.

86 India, Ministry of External Affairs, *Statements of the Official Spokesman on Pakistan's Nuclear Tests, 28 May 1998*, (Washington D.C: Embassy of India), www.indianembassy.org.

87 India, Ministry of External Affairs, *Brief of India's Nuclear Tests: Global Disarmament or Equal and Legitimate Security for All* (Washington D.C: Embassy of India), www.indianembassy.org.

88 Press Release regarding reactions of the Security Council to the nuclear tests carried out by Pakistan, 31 May 1998, *Foreign Affairs Record*, n.22, p.44.

89 Kenneth J. Cooper, "India's leaders speak of vindication,

urge calm and unity," *The Washington Post*, 29 May 1998. See George Perkovich, n.16, p. 434.

90 The Kargil Review Committee Report, n.5, p.196.

91 Statement in Jalandhar, 6 February 2000. See Praful Bidwai, "Mushroom Cloud of Unreason," *Economic and Political Weekly*, Vol.35, No.14, 1-7 April 2000, p.1134.

92 See mea.gov.in.

93 See India, Lok Sabha, *Debates*, 27 April 2005, www.mea.gov.in.

94 Address by Pranab Mukherjee on "India's Strategic Perspective," at Harvard University on 25 September 2006, www.indianembassy.org.

95 T.Jayaraman, "Good nukes, bad nukes," The *Hindu*, 28 February 2004.

96 For example, see Balwant A.Desai (ed.), *Atoms for Peace: An Exposition of India's Nuclear Policy* (New Delhi: AICC, 1975).

97 *Development of Nuclear Energy for Peaceful Uses: Policy, Programmes and Achievements*, n.5, p.21.

98 India, Lok Sabha, *Debates*, 8 August 1985, n.77, cols.294-296.

99 "N-Question not partisan: Sonia," *The Hindu*, 15 May 1998; also see, "Tests, a national achievement: Congress," *The Hindu*, 14 May 1998.

100 "A grave development, says Congress-I," *The Hindu*, 29 May 1998.

101 "Cong. concerned over Pak. decision on tests," *The Hindu*, 20 June 1998.

102 K.K.Katyal, "Issues that are no less important," *The Hindu*, 13 April 2004.

103 For example, see India, Lok Sabha, *Debates*, Vol.21, No.3, 6 November 1986, cols.374-375.

104 Anil Razdhan, "Manmohan Showed Proof of Osama's Terror Network in Pakistan," 22 July 2005, www.indiadaily.com.

105 Runa Das, "Broadening the Security Paradigm: A Note on the Tension Between the Realist and Anti Proliferation Lobbies in India," *The Indian Journal of Political Science*, Vol.62, No.2, June 2001, p.257.

106 BJP National Council Meeting, Cochin, 25-27 April 1981, Text of Resolutions Adopted, A.M.Zaidi (ed.), *The Annual*

*Register of Indian Political Parties: Proceedings and Fundamental Texts, 1981* (New Delhi: Indian Institute of Applied Political Research, 1981), pp.528-529.

107 BJP National Executive, 19-21 July 1985, Bhopal, Text of Resolutions Adopted, A.M.Zaidi (ed.), *The Annual Register of Indian Political Parties: Proceedings and Fundamental Texts, 1985* (New Delhi: Indian Institute of Applied Political Research, 1987), pp.431-432.

108 For details, see George Perkovich, n.16, pp.324-326.

109 Bharatiya Janata Party, n.20.

110 *Organiser*, Vol.49, No.42, 17 May 1998. The cover legend reads, "25th Year of Pokhran: Nuclear India," see N. Ram, *Riding the Nuclear Tiger* (New Delhi: Leftword Books, 1999), p.17.

111 "The battlelines in Parliament," *The Hindu*, 31 May 1998.

112 George Fernandes, "No Bombs Please," December 1985, in George Mathew (ed.), *George Fernandes Speaks* (New Delhi: Ajanta, 1991), p.369.

113 "India-Pakistan talking past one another," *Taipei Times*, 5 June 2002, www.taipeitimes.com.

114 "Fight global terrorism: Joshi," *The Hindu*, 4 August 2006.

115 Shyam Bhatia, *India's Nuclear Bomb* (New Delhi: Vikas, 1979), p.80.

116 India, Lok Sabha, *Debates*, 8 August 1974, n.69, cols. 223-224.

117 India, Lok Sabha, *Debates*, Vol.46, No.22, 23 March 1984, col.337.

118 India, Lok Sabha, *Debates*, 27 May 1998, www.alfa.nic.in.

119 Ibid.

120 Joint Press Statement issued by the Communist Party of India (Marxist) and the Communist Party of India on 29 May on the Nuclear Tests conducted by Pakistan, www.proxsa.org; also see "Left for dialogue," *The Hindu*, 30 May 1998; Pak tests reinforce fears: Left leaders," *The Hindu*, 30 May 1998.

121 K.K.Katyal, n.102.

122 Speech at the Fourth International Conference of Asian Political Parties, Seoul, 9 September 2006, *Peoples*

*Democracy*, Vol.30, No.38, 17 September 2006, www.pd.cpim.org.

123 The dominant characteristic of this mindset is its preoccupation with thinking as comprehensively as possible *within* the framework of its accepted assumptions. Among these realist assumptions are a notion of security centred on territorial protection and a state-centric notion of 'national' security and the belief in the efficacy of nuclear deterrence. See Achin Vanaik, "Mindset of the Nuclear Strategist," *Economic and Political Weekly*, Vol.37, No.21, 25 May 2001, p.1994.

124 Lavoy defines a nuclear myth as 'an unverifiable belief about the relationship between a state's nuclear weapons policy and its national security, prestige or power' and explores how India's nuclear policy up to the 1974 explosion demonstrates the presence of such a myth maker – Bhabha. Peter Lavoy, *Learning to Live with the Bomb* (Ithaca: Cornell University Press, 2000). Also see Neil Joeck, "Nuclear Developments in India and Pakistan," *Access Asia Review*, Vol.2, www.nbr.org.

125 See Haider K. Nizamani, n.41, p.15.

126 Ashis Nandy, "The Bomb, the NPT and Indian Elites," *Economic and Political Weekly*, Vol.7, Nos. 31, 32, 33, Special issue, August 1972, p.1533.

127 Praful Bidwai and Achin Vanaik, n.1, p.107.

128 Kanti Bajpai, "India's Nuclear Posture After Pokhran II," *International Studies*, Vol.37, No.4, December 2000, p.277.

129 See Itty Abraham, "India's 'Strategic Enclave': Civilian Scientists and Military Technologies," *Armed Forces and Society*, Vol.18, No.2, Winter 1992, p.233; also see George Perkovich, n. 16, p.519.

130 George Perkovich, n.16, p.1.

131 See ibid.; Itty Abraham, n.5; M.V.Ramana, "La Trahison Des Clercs," in M.V.Ramana and C. Rammanohar Reddy, *Prisoners of the Nuclear Dream* (New Delhi: Orient Longman, 2003); Dhirendra Sharma, n.15.

132 Bhabha's two statements in 1964 that India could explode an atom bomb in 18 months and that a ten kiloton bomb would cost only Rs.17.5 lakhs; and Vikram Sarabhai's proposal for a ten-year nuclear development and space research programme costing Rs.398.1 crores, were utilized

by some politicians and journalists as justifications for weaponisation. See Shyam Bhatia, n.115, pp.83-84.

133 See Homi J. Bhabha's talk on All India Radio, 24 October 1964, reproduced in N. Seshagiri, *The Bomb? Fallout of India's Nuclear Explosion* (New Delhi: Vikas, 1975), p.134.

134 See K.Subrahmanyam, "The Path to Nuclear Capability," pp.188-200; Subramaniam Swamy, "India's Nuclear Strategy in the 1970s" pp.201-219; and George H. Quester, "India Contemplates the Bomb," pp.220-235, all in DAE, *Nuclear Weapons: A Compilation Prepared by the DAE, 1970.*

135 See Bhabani Sen Gupta, *Nuclear Weapons? Policy Option for India* (New Delhi: Sage, 1983), p.49.

136 George Perkovich, n.16, p. 276.

137 See for example, "Weaponisation now complete, say scientists," *The Hindu*, 18 May 1998; "We detonated 3 bombs by pulling one trigger," *The Times of India*, 19 May 1998; "India not dependent on others for nuclear technology," *The Hindu*, 25 June 1998; "AEC chief dismisses west propaganda on N-power," *The Hindu*, 2 June 1998; "Doubts about Pak claims," *The Indian Express*, 30 May 1998.

138 See, M.R.Srinivasan, "Pakistan's nuclear deals," *The Hindu*, 13 January 2004. Srinivasan is a former Chairman of AEC. In this lead article, he provides a detailed history of A.Q.Khan and the 'jihadi' mentality of Pakistan's scientists.

139 See, Srinivas Laxman, "Indian nuke scientists go ballistic," *The Times of India*, 9 February 2006; "Nuke deal: India can do without US help," *Deccan Herald*, 10 February 2006; "Atomic reaction," *The Times of India*, 10 February 2006.

140 M.R.Srinivasan, "Pakistan's nuclear deals," *The Hindu*, 13 January 2004; M.R.Srinivasan, "India-US nuclear ties," *The Hindu*, 7 October 2004.

141 IDSA is a registered society governed by an Executive Council, the President of which is the Defence Minister. The Institute is funded by the Ministries of Defence and External Affairs. According to the official website of IDSA, the Indian Parliamentary Committee on Defence frequently utilises the literature, information and expertise of the Institute. As Defence Minister, George Fernandes stated the Government and the informed public of the country have benefited from the work done at IDSA which has contributed to the national security policy formulation. See www.idsa-india.org.

142 See, for example, K. Subrahmanyam, "Introduction," in Sreedhar (ed.), *Pakistan's Bomb: A Documentary Study* (New Delhi: ABC Publishing, 1987), pp.xxvi, 8-9; Bharat Karnad, "Introduction," in Bharat Karnad (ed.), *Future Imperilled: India's Security in the 1990s and Beyond* (New Delhi: Viking, 1994), p.11; P.M.Kamath, "Indian Security Policy: Minimal Nuclear Deterrence," *Strategic Analysis*, Vol.23, No.8, November 1999, pp.1257-1274.

143 See Kanti Bajpai, "India's Nuclear Posture After Pokhran II," *International Studies*, Vol.37, No.4, December 2000, pp.267-301.

144 See K. Subrahmanyam, "India's Problems of Security:•In Retrospect and Prospect," *South Asian Studies*, Vol.4, No.2, July 1969, pp.43-75.

145 *The Times of India*, 26 April 1981.

146 K. Subrahmanyam, n.142, p.12.

147 Ibid.

148 See P.K.S Namboodiri, "Perceptions and Policies in India and Pakistan," in K. Subrahmanyam (ed.), *India and the Nuclear Challenge* (New Delhi: Lancer, 1986), p.198. Interestingly, in 1981 K.Subrahmanyam wrote that no doubt Gandhiji "expressed himself against the bomb, but that was long before nuclear weapons became the legitimate international currency of power," *The Times of India*, 26 April 1981.

149 Haider K. Nizamani, n.41, p.53.

150 Sreedhar, "Preface," in Sreedhar (ed.), n.142, p.ix.

151 Haider K.Nizamani, n.41, p.55.

152 K. Subrahmanyam, *Indian Security Perspectives* (New Delhi: ABC Publishing, 1982), p.201; also see P.R.Chari, "Foreword," in P.B.Sinha and R.R.Subramanian, *Nuclear Pakistan: Atomic Threat to South Asia* (New Delhi: Vision, 1980), p.iv.

153 Ashok Kapur, n.35, p.146; also see P.B.Sinha and R.R. Subramanian, n.152, p.68; K.K.Pathak, *Nuclear Policy of India: A Third World Perspective* (New Delhi: Githanjali Prakashan, 1980), p.183.

154 P.L.Bhola, *Pakistan's Nuclear Policy* (New Delhi: Sterling, 1993), pp.68-90.

155 K.Subrahmanyam, n.142, p.xxiii.

156 D.K.Palit and P.K.S.Namboodiri, *Pakistan's Islamic Bomb* (New Delhi: Vikas, 1979), p.16.

157 Ibid., pp.48-49.

158 Ibid., p.16.

159 Ibid., p.44.

160 K.Subrahmanyam, n.152, pp. 182-183; also see P.L.Bhola, n.154, p.67.

161 Savita Pande, "Nuclear Weapons-Free Zone in South Asia," *Strategic Analysis,* Vol.22, No.11, pp.1681-1693; also see P.L.Bhola, n.154, p.57.

162 K.Subrahmanyam, n.152, p.167.

163 See K.K.Pathak, n.153.

164 P.B.Sinha and R.R.Subramanian, n.152, p.67.

165 "India now needs a nuclear doctrine," *The Times of India,* 24 May 1998.

166 George Perkovich, n.16, pp.341-342.

167 Praful Bidwai and Achin Vanaik, n.1, p.107. See Amitabh Mattoo, *India's Nuclear Deterrent: Pokhran II and Beyond* (New Delhi: Har Anand, 1999); Jasjit Singh (ed.), *Nuclear India* (New Delhi : Knowledge World, 1998); Jaswant Singh, *Defending India* (London : St. Martin's Press, 1999).

168 See Ashok Kapur, "Pokhran II and After: Consequences of the Indian Nuclear Tests of 1998," in Amita Shastri and A. Jayaratnam Wilson, *The Post-Colonial States of South Asia: Democracy, Identity, Development and Security* (Richmond, Surrey: Curzon, 2001), p.338.

169 K.Subrahmanyam, "Nuclear India in Global Politics," *World Affairs*, Vol.2, No.3, July-Sept 1998, p.31.

170 Haider K. Nizamani, n.41, p.66; also see K. Subrahmanyam, "A credible nuclear deterrent," *The Times of India,* 4 October 1999.

171 Manpreet Sethi, "Dangers from Weapons of Mass Destruction: Any Different in South Asia?," *Strategic Analysis,* Vol.24, No.11, February 2001, p.1989.

172 P.M.Kamath, n.142, p.1260.

173 C.Uday Bhaskar, "Reducing Nuclear Dangers in South Asia," *The Monitor,* Fall 2001, in www.arches.uga.edu.

174 Rajesh Kumar Mishra, "Closure of the Pakistan-based

A.Q.Khan Network Case: A Hasty Burial?" *Strategic Analysis,* Vol.30, No.2, April-June 2006, p.482.

175 Indian Institute of Public Opinion, "Public Opinion on India's Nuclear Device," *Blue Supplement to the Monthly Public Opinion Surveys,* Vol.19, No.9, June 1974, p.ii.

176 Indian Institute of Public Opinion, *Monthly Public Opinion Surveys,* Vol.26, No.10, July 1981, pp.7-8.

177 David Cortright and Amitabh Mattoo, "Indian Public Opinion and Nuclear Weapons Policy," in David Cortright and Amitabh Mattoo (eds.) *India and the Bomb: Public Opinion and Nuclear Options* (Notre Dame: University of Notre Dame Press, 1996), p.17.

178 Balakrishnan and Gouri Chatterjee, "Majority backs stance on NPT," *The Times of India,* 22 April 1995.

179 "Most Indians hail N-tests: opinion poll," *The Hindu,* 13 May 1998; "Overwhelming majority supports N-tests," *The Times of India,* 13 May 1998.

180 Achin Vanaik and Praful Bidwai, n. 1, p.273.

181 V. Krishna Ananth, "The Politics of the Bomb: Some Observations on the Political Discourse in India in the Context of Pokhran II," in M.V.Ramana and C.Rammanohar Reddy (eds.), n.131, p.327.

182 Haider K. Nizamani, n.41, p.146.

183 Ibid., p.121.

184 Achin Vanaik, *India in a Changing World: Problems, Limits and Successes of its Foreign Policy* (New Delhi: Orient Longman, 1995), pp. 71-77.

185 Rohini Hensman, Forging a Nuclear Strategy for the Anti-Nuclear Movement in India and Pakistan, www.mnet.fr.

186 Gautam Navlakha, "Reinforcing Insecurity," *Economic and Political Weekly,* Vol.34, No.39, 25 September 1999, p.2782.

187 Praful Bidwai and Achin Vanaik, n.1, p.221.

188 Achin Vanaik, "Nuclear Insecurity in the Indian Subcontinent: An Uneasy Truce," *Bulletin of Peace Proposals,* Vol.20, No.4, December 1989, pp.390-393.

189 Praful Bidwai, "Dangerous descent: flawed logic of nuclear tests," *The Times of India,* 15 May 1998.

190 Praful Bidwai and Achin Vanaik, n.1, p.97.

191 Aijaz Ahmad, "The Hindutva Weapon," *Frontline,* Vol.15,

No.11, 23 May-5 June 1998; Kalpana Sharma writes in a similar way in 'The Hindu Bomb", *The Bulletin of Atomic Scientists*, Vol.14, No.4, July-August 1998, www.bullatomsci.org.

192 Praful Bidwai and Achin Vanaik, n.1, p.86.

193 Aijaz Ahmad, n.191.

194 Praful Bidwai, "Seeking a Paradigm Shift," *Frontline*, Vol.15, No.8, 11-24 April 1998.

195 Amartya Sen, "India and the Bomb," in M.V.Ramana and C.Rammanohar Reddy (eds.) n.131, p. 186.

196 The formation of the Indian Scientists Against Nuclear Weapons may be seen in this context. For details, see www.isanw.org.

197 "Scientists express dismay over N-tests," *The Hindu*, 19 May 1998.

198 T.Jayaraman, "Of Science and Nuclear Weapons: A Scientist's Perspective (from India)," paper presented at Delhi Convention Against Nuclear Weapons, 9 June 1998, www.mnet.fr.; also see T.Jayaraman, "Beyond the Euphoria," in n.191.

199 See T. Jayaraman, "Indian Science After Pokhran-II," *Seminar*, No.468, August 1998, pp.60-64; also see T.Jayaraman, "Good nukes, bad nukes," *The Hindu*, 28 February 2004.

200 M.V.Ramana, "Do Nuclear Weapons Provide Security?," in ibid. pp.50-54.

201 M.V.Ramana, n.131, p.215.

202 See *National Alliance of Peoples Movements Condemns Nuclear Tests*, 14 May 1998, www.mnet.fr.

203 Arundhati Roy, "The End of Imagination," *Frontline*, Vol.15, No.16, 1-14 August 1998.

204 Achin Vanaik, n.184, pp.80-81.

205 Praful Bidwai and Achin Vanaik, n.1, pp.89, 216-217.

206 Achin Vanaik, "Three Misrepresentations," *Economic and Political Weekly*, Vol.32, No.36, 6 September 1997, p.2235.

207 Praful Bidwai and Achin Vanaik, n.1, p.91.

208 Achin Vanaik, n.188, p.392.

209 N.Ram, n.110, pp.108-109.

210 Achin Vanaik, n.184, p.42.

211 Haider K. Nizamani, "Limits of Dissent: A Comparative Study of Dissident Voices in the Nuclear Discourse of Pakistan and India," *Contemporary South Asia,* Vol.7, No.3, November 1998, pp.331-332.

212 Praful Bidwai, India's Nuclear Doctrine ups the ante," *Asia Times,* www.atimes.com, 20 August 1999.

# 4
# Pakistan's Nuclear Programme and the Indian Press

The nuclear issue has emerged as one of the most significant factors in the India media coverage of Pakistan. An analysis of the nature of this coverage in the mainstream media would therefore provide insights into the processes of securitisation and the politics of nuclearisation in the subcontinent. An overview of the depiction of Pakistan's nuclear programme in the English language Indian press is provided here. Studies have shown that English dailies occupy a significant place in India, not only among the decision-makers, but also as opinion setters among the language dailies, particularly where defence and foreign policy issues are concerned. Differences among the various editions of these newspapers are basically related to local news, which is tailored according to the particular region it serves. Differences in national and international news coverage are marginal. The historical review of the coverage of Pakistan's nuclear programme is interspersed with the approach of the press to the question of nuclear weapons in general, as well as India's nuclear policy over the years. This is essential for an understanding of the issue in perspective. Such a contextualization will provide critical insights into the vicissitudes of the press in the security scenario of the subcontinent.

The first section of this chapter provides a random survey of coverage by English language daily newspapers upto April 1998. The nuclear tests by India and Pakistan in May 1998 marked a turning point in the security scenario of the subcontinent. There emerged an invigorated debate encompassing threat perceptions and nuclear issues in the region. The heightened atmosphere of securitisation and action-reaction spiral was most explicitly evident in the mass media. For a deeper insight into the issues at hand, as well as to enable a systematic quantitative analysis, the second section takes as a case study a content analysis of three English language newspapers – *The Hindu*, *The Indian Express* and *The Times of India* over a three-month period from 1 May to 31 July 1998. The study proceeds to examine basic trends in press coverage during the subsequent years based on a random survey of the English language press. Juxtaposed against the perspectives of the government, political parties and the strategic community, this historical review provides clear indications of the role of the Indian press in the process of securitisation vis-à-vis Pakistan.

## THE EARLY YEARS: A REVIEW OF PRESS COVERAGE

During the early years after independence, the role of the Indian press in the context of issues relating to nuclear weapons was basically confined to reporting government pronouncements. This period essentially saw only a reflection of government statements on nuclear disarmament. In 1954, the testing of hydrogen bombs by the United States, and the subsequent controversy regarding contamination by radioactive fallout led to an outcry in the Indian parliament. Several

Indian newspapers, including *The Statesman* and *The Hindu,* commented on the destructive power of hydrogen bombs and the need for restraint.[1] During 1961, Homi J. Bhabha's calls for investment in nuclear power saw counterarguments in the press. *The Hindustan Times* commented:

> In the current stage of fuel science and technology, thermal power stations are a cheaper source of energy than nuclear power stations.... It is obvious that this is not the right time for this country to commit any large amounts of scarce capital or technical sources to the commercial exploitation of techniques which may become rapidly outmoded.[2]

*The Times of India* also editorialised that the Atomic Energy Commission's (AEC) case for nuclear power, was by no means supported by the economics of nuclear power. Experience elsewhere has shown that "nuclear power has been left behind, giving way to conventional fuels primarily as a result of rapid technological achievement.... Apparently there is no limit to the irrational ambitions of the AEC which is currently persuading New Delhi to sanction a second powerhouse."[3]

On surveying India's five major English language daily newspapers, Shyam Bhatia revealed that until 1964 none of them devoted much attention to the issue of an Indian nuclear weapons programme.[4] During this period, the so-called experts on security issues had not made the nuclear issue their main concern yet. As noted in the previous chapter, the official Indian position on the 1964 Chinese nuclear test revealed a lack of political value for the nuclear bomb. Documenting the reaction to the Chinese tests in leading Indian dailies, G.G Mirchandani did not find the situation much different.[5] The major newspapers editorialised in favour of the government's approach. *The Hindustan Times,* for example, averred that although China's bomb was a grave provocation to India, "nevertheless prudence demands that our response is sober and realistic. Nothing should suit Mao's book better than our being bustled into a nuclear race."[6] Eight days after the Chinese test, Bhabha gave his noted broadcast on All India Radio stating that "atomic weapons give a State possessing them in adequate numbers a deterrent power from attack from a much stronger state."[7] Press accounts of Bhabha's broadcast focused on the low cost of nuclear weapons and repeated his calls to the world powers to remove this new threat. The statement was not interpreted by the media as a call to develop nuclear weapons.[8] *The Times of India* suggested that a nuclear bomb was not feasible and, even if it were, would be entirely inconsistent with the country's interests.[9] Other papers also offered various arguments against the bomb.[10]

The general terms of the debate on nuclear weapons in the Indian media was substantially similar to that within the government. During 1964-68 the debate on the Non Proliferation Treaty in the press largely served to inform Indian public opinion about strategic issues rather than to provide insights for the decision-maker. Ashok Kapur maintains that in this context, one must take into account the assessment of A.D Gorewala, formerly a member of the Indian Civil Service. According to Gorewala, the record of the press regarding India's nuclear defence is another instance of falling down on its responsibility to educate. By and large, the press reported the government perspective in its entirety. It ridiculed the idea of making nuclear weapons in competition with China citing high costs, that other countries would come to India's rescue, if necessary; and that economic growth would be jeopardised.[11]

In November 1964, Prime Minister Shastri, while stating in the Lok Sabha that India could produce a nuclear bomb within two or three years if necessary, reaffirmed the commitment of India's nuclear establishment to peaceful purposes only. However, for the first time, the Prime Minister mentioned that this would entail preparations of peaceful nuclear explosives for purposes such as tunnelling through mountains. Quoting Bhabha, Shastri pointed out that nuclear devices can be used both for destructive and for peaceful purposes.[12] Perkovich argues that neither the press nor parliamentarians seemed to understand that Shastri had opened the door to the bomb. Technically, there was little difference between a rudimentary nuclear weapon and a peaceful nuclear explosive. Yet this seemed lost on the major English language papers and the Lok Sabha. None of the headlines reporting Shastri's speech referred to the first ever prime ministerial endorsement of an Indian nuclear explosives programme.[13] On the contrary, they left the impression that Shastri refused any change in policy. *The Hindustan Times* reported, "PM refuses to budge on Bomb"; *The Times of India* wrote, "PM rejects Bomb demand"; and the *National Herald* announced, "PM: Bhabha against making a Bomb–inconclusive debate on non official resolution."[14] At the same time Shastri's call for speeding up the development of nuclear energy for peaceful purposes gradually gathered support in the press. *The Hindu* editorialized that nobody could seriously question the wisdom of the decision. "We cannot, on moral and economic grounds, start making the atom bombs ourselves at this stage. And the Prime Minister was wise in leaving it at that and not committing the Government into abjuring the nuclear weapon for all time and under all circumstances."[15]

N. Bhaskara Rao in his content analysis of Indian newspapers during the period February 1965 to April 1966 makes no mention of reports on the nuclear factor in the India-Pakistan context.[16] The Indian nuclear test of 1974 was welcomed almost unanimously. It was hailed as a morale booster for the country and a great technological achievement by Indian scientists. Briefed by the government, the press announced the test as signifying the country's entry into the 'Select' Group of 'Technologically Advanced Nations' or the 'Nuclear Club'.[17] *The Hindu* editorial stated:

> No more thrilling news could have come to lift the drooping spirits of the people than the Atomic Energy Commission's announcement yesterday that it had successfully carried out an underground nuclear experiment.... And though it is India's policy not to go in for nuclear weapons, its explosion of a nuclear device adds a new and important dimension to its defence capability. India has crossed the nuclear threshold.[18]

Other newspapers wrote in similar vein. Editorials in *The Indian Express* and *The Hindustan Times* read "Inches taller" (20 May 1974) and "Pride without malice"(19 May 1974). The press generally lavished praise in huge front-page columns and related articles, relegating the previously dominant story of the ongoing nationwide railway strike to the back pages. A number of papers further pleaded, that India should not commit its atomic energy for peaceful purposes only, but should keep its options open.[19] *The Hindu* editorial stated that the government cannot renounce nuclear weapons forever considering that there are other countries armed with such weapons, not all of whom are well disposed towards India. "This makes it necessary for India to keep its options open, even while concentrating on using its new power for peaceful purposes only."[20] In contrast to the general trend, *The Hindustan Times* headline queried, "The nation is thrilled?" while *The Statesman* commented:

> The Government of India's decision to let off an underground nuclear device in Rajasthan seems as indefensible as it is irresponsible. Indeed to rational people it will hardly make sense at all. The Prime Minister may say that the intentions are entirely peaceful, but to others they would hardly seem so, especially viewed against India's repeated statements that she has no desire to join the nuclear arms race; for what else is this conceivably in aid of?[21]

Commander Ravi Kaul's (editor of *Chanakya Defence Journal*) analysis of this press report speaks volumes about the general approach of strategic analysts, as pointed out in the previous chapter. He argued that the above editorial was outstanding in its lack of understanding of the nuclear domain. He added:

> A reliable source has recently alleged that the *Statesman's* editorial was the work of the deputy under the influence of alcohol while the editor was away from Calcutta. The language used backs the allegation.... The freedom of the press in this case being sanctified by the *Statesman* to cover freedom

> in abysmal ignorance for what has often appeared to be the last citadel of the British Empire in India. A wealth of information on the country's nuclear programme is available from Atomic Energy Commission, and the department's budget is published annually. Even my daughter Saloni, as a School Certificate student, had received full details of the programme on request.[22]

Press reactions to the Janata government's (1977-79) nuclear policy also deserve mention. Prime Minister Morarji Desai's critique of nuclear weapons and categorical statement abjuring nuclear tests for peaceful purposes in 1977 was played down by the press. Most editorials respectfully urged the government not to foreclose options to develop nuclear technology.[23]

## Projecting the 'Islamic' Bomb

The first extensive media reports on nuclear issues appeared only since 1978-79. The emphasis in these reports was, however, not on basic questions of nuclear policy but on specific operational issues such as the performance of India's power plants, etc. These were largely based on reports from the West. It was also during this period that there emerged an increasing focus on Pakistan's nuclear policy. In April 1979, when the United States invoked the Symington Amendment and cut off military and economic aid to Pakistan on non-proliferation grounds, the implications were strongly perceived in India. The press highlighted the threat of the "Islamic Bomb." Speculative and often sceptical articles on Pakistan's nuclear programme became common. Headlines read: "Pak may explode H bomb by April" (*The Times of India*, 26 November 1979),

"India will review N-policy if Pindi makes bomb: PM" (*The Indian Express*, 6 August 1979), "Muslim nations must help Pak go nuclear" (*The Hindu*, 9 November 1979), "India to carry out nuclear explosions: nation not to be caught napping" (*The Statesman*, 14 March 1980), "Pak N-blast any time after June: Sethna" (*Hindustan Times*, 6 May 1981), "Pak boasts about bomb" (*The Hindu*, 29 November 1981). Parliament as well as the media clearly demanded stronger government action to deal with the 'growing' Pakistani threat. But there was no examination of the costs and benefits of alternate courses.

Writing in *Dawn* in 1981, Yehia M.Syed pointed out that the statements by British Prime Minister Margaret Thatcher that, like India, Pakistan too had an inherent right to arm in order to defend herself was used by the Indian print and electronic media to whip up frenzy in favour of India manufacturing nuclear bombs. The media made use of the arms controversy to whip up public demand that India should make nuclear weapons. While the media set the stage to use Mrs. Thatcher's defence of Pakistan's right to self defence as a ploy to build a nuclear bomb, India announced that it had decided to reprocess nuclear fuel, which comes from the United States into plutonium. The work was to be carried out at Tarapur.[24] Editorials and columns in major newspapers argued that India had little choice but to end its renunciation of nuclear weapons. A report in *The Sunday Observer* in August 1981 pointed out that an orchestrated campaign was being mounted through influential sections of the Indian press to go in for a nuclear weapons programme.[25]

Over the years, there were contradictory reports in the Indian press, usually originating from the West, about Pakistan's ability to make nuclear weapons, and its political will to do so. In early 1983, a supposedly secret CIA report, which stated that Pakistan would attain the capability to detonate a nuclear device within the next three years, but that it was unlikely to conduct an actual explosion since that would jeopardise the US military and economic aid programme, was leaked to the press. The CIA report also suggested that Pakistan was afraid of the growing threat of a pre-emptive attack from India on its nuclear installation. In January 1983 *The New York Times* published a report prepared by the United States Air Force that Pakistan would develop nuclear weapons by the year 2000. All these reports reverberated in the Indian press. Unconfirmed reports of Chinese help to Pakistan to acquire nuclear weapons, which had been appearing for years, also seemed to acquire greater significance. The impact of such reports was often reflected in Parliament. For instance, during a discussion in the Lok Sabha in 1984 on the reported nuclear collaboration between China and Pakistan, Chintamani Jena pointed out that "in the face of such a situation, we all are concerned about the news items published in several papers and also in foreign newspapers."[26]

The February 1984 interview of Abdul Qadeer Khan in *Nawa-e-Waqt,* praising Pakistan's capacity to enrich uranium created a stir in the Indian press, with calls to respond by openly declaring India's nuclear weapons capabilities. By May 1985, there were calls in the press for a stronger response to Pakistan's nuclear programme.[27] There were also strong reactions to American reports that Pakistan had successfully tested a non-nuclear triggering package for a nuclear weapon. In September 1985 American officials visited both India and Pakistan to promote nuclear restraint and urge both countries to undertake regional initiatives to slow down and hopefully freeze their nuclear competition. However, Indian officials and the media urged the United States to do more to curb the Pakistani nuclear programme. Writing about the "Islamic bomb," *The Hindustan Times* noted, that since there was sufficient evidence that the Pakistani nuclear programme was being financed by Libya and Saudi Arabia, there was every likelihood of Libya gaining access to nuclear bombs made in Pakistan.[28] The usual trajectory of reporting nuclear issues in the India–Pakistan context can be evidenced for instance from the headlines of October to December 1985, which read "Islamic Bomb: How far?" (*The Hindustan Times*, 5 Oct 1985), "Pak Bomb foreign financed: PM" (*The Times of India*, 9 October 1985), "Pak Bomb not an empty threat: PM" (*The Times of India,* 26 October 1985), "PM convinced of Pak Bomb plan" (*The Times of India*, 28 October 1985), "Bomb if we need it: PM" (*The Indian Express* 12 November 1985), "Pak going ahead with N-bomb plan" (*The Times of India,* 13 December 1985).

In 1986, prior to the Indian military exercise - Operation Brasstacks, several Indian and Pakistani leaders made important statements about nuclear policy. On 15 September 1986, *The Times of India* reported A. Q. Khan's claim that Indira Gandhi had been deterred from attacking Pakistan's nuclear facilities in 1984 by Khan's earlier pronouncements that Pakistan 'now is a nuclear power'. An article by Bob Woodward in *The Washington Post* claimed, among other things, that Pakistan had conducted additional explosive tests of the non-nuclear components of a bomb and could assemble a bomb in a week.[29] The Indian press sensationalised the article with headlines such as "Many motives behind Pakistan nuclear programme" (*The Indian Express*, 30 December 1986), "Orientation of Pak nuclear plan confirmed" (*The Indian Express*, 3 March 1987), "None can stop our N-plan, says Pak" (*The Times of India*, 9 March 1987), "India to counter Pak nuclear plan, says PM" (*The Indian Express*, 25 March 1987), "PM says, Pak Bomb will be available to Arabs" (*The Times of India*, 28 March 1987), "Pak N-arms programme highly advanced" (*The Indian Express*, 4 April 1987), "India may be forced to make nuclear weapons" (*The Times of India*, 4 April 1987), "Pak can make 3 nuclear weapons a year" (*The Indian Express*, 26 August 1987), and "Pak threatens to go nuclear" (*The Times of India*, 17 November 1987). During the Lok Sabha debate on the issue, K.P.Singh Deo congratulated "the vigilance press on having brought this very important and crucial subject which concerns not only our national security but also has a bearing on the international situation and is having global and strategic implications."[30] Indrajit Gupta during the same discussion also spoke at length on Pakistan's nuclear programme and commented: "According to reports – I am not an expert on this; we are all going by what we read in the press...."[31]

The response of the press to the 1989 Agni missile test was euphoric; stressing that India had become the sixth country to produce successfully an intermediate range ballistic missile (IRBM) from indigenous technology. This was despite the fact that senior Indian politicians were quick to stress the non-nuclear potential in the development. The launch was reported in terms reminiscent of the Pokhran-I celebrations with the missile scientists and engineers being lauded and the test being represented as a vital theme in the national anti-colonial narrative.[32] *The Times of India* editorialised:

> After Pokhran in 1974, the launch of the Agni to a triumphant splashdown in the Bay of Bengal is the biggest step forward in India's quest for a credible deterrent capability. The real success of such a capability is that it should never have to be used; it has to be achieved nevertheless. India cannot stop with just one testing of Agni. Any new missile system has to be tested repeatedly before any reliance can be placed upon it.[33]

However, critics pointed out that the acclaimed success of Agni appeared to have been exaggerated. What had been tested so far did not quite amount to a prototype: it was only a "technology demonstrator," not a missile that "flies and lands reasonably accurately anywhere."[34] Perkovich points out that although *The Wall Street Journal* had reported that India had imported the Agni's guidance system, its first-stage rocket and its nose cone from West Germany; and the Central Intelligence Agency (CIA) had also reported similarly, such reports were not reflected in the Indian press. According to Perkovich this raises the possibility of self-censorship among the Indian press corps. By the early 1990s, the editorials in Indian newspapers, by and large, reflected a pro-nuclear perspective. Perkovich points out that as the strategic enclave continued to develop nuclear and missile capabilities, and sought to rationalise plans for conducting nuclear operations, the seeds of a more traditional approach to the nuclear doctrine were being sown among the small circle of Indian strategic analysts writing in newspapers. This discourse explicitly reflected the theories of Kenneth Waltz and other proponents of nuclear deterrence.[35]

In December 1991, China reiterated its support to the Pakistani proposal for nuclear non-proliferation in South Asia, and the declaration of South Asia as a nuclear free zone. The two countries also signed a protocol on scientific and technological cooperation and a contract under which China was to export a 3,00,000 kilowatt nuclear power plant to Pakistan, and also supply the nuclear fuel and technology to run it. Premier Li Peng stated that it was totally for peaceful purposes and would promote Pakistan's economic growth and nuclear energy development.[36] In February 1992 two subsidiary contracts relating to this were signed and the newly acquired power plant began to be set up at Chashma. However, *The Times of India* and *The Indian Express*, in their reports built up and reiterated the perception of a threat from a Sino-Pak collusion – a factor which was much highlighted by Indian leaders. Some of these headlines read: "Concern over Chinese N-aid to Pakistan" (*The Times of India*, 1 January 1992), "Pak admits it can assemble N-Bomb" (*The Times of India*, 2 February 1992), "Pak not to forgo nuclear option" (*The Times of India*, 22 February 1992), "Sino Pak pacts on N-power plant signed" (*The Times of India*, 24 February 1992), "Sino-Pak pact on N-Plant" (*The Indian Express*, 1 January 1992), and "Pak China sign N-plant contracts" (*The Indian Express*, 24 January 1992). Most of these reports placed importance on giving detailed inventories of Pakistan's arms purchases and their capability against Indian offensive and defensive systems, thereby exacerbating such notions. More than the reports per se, it was their headlines and prominent display on the front pages, which projected such perceptions.[37]

During the impasse in United States-Pakistan relations in January 1992 – owing to Pakistan's nuclear programme and the resultant American cessation of aid – Senator Larry Pressler paid a visit to Pakistan. The visit coincided with the American government spokesman's statement that the United States was unable to say that Pakistan did not possess a nuclear explosive device. This official statement, together with Pressler's call to Pakistan - to dismantle its nuclear programme was much highlighted by the Indian press. Most reports seemed to over-emphasise the nuclear programme of Pakistan, thereby insinuating a threat to India, while at the same time glossing over, or even completely ignoring India's own programme. Headlines read: "Dismantle N-Bomb, Pressler tells Pak" (*The Hindu,* 14 January 1992), "Pressler tells Pakistan to dismantle N-capability" (*The Indian Express,* 14 January 1992), "Pak refuses to curtail N-plan" (*The Times of India,* 14 January 1992), "We will not accede to US plea: Khan" (*The Hindu,* 9 February 1992) etc. Despite the tremendous importance placed on Pressler's statements calling on Pakistan to dismantle its nuclear bomb, etc., not one of the newspapers cared to report the US State Department spokesman's statement the very next day, that Pressler had visited the subcontinent in his personal capacity and that his views were not those of the US administration. Neither did any paper report on President Bush urging India to accept Pakistan's proposal for a five-nation conference aimed at making South Asia a nuclear free zone. Similarly, the euphemistic statement by the American spokesman that "we are unable to certify that Pakistan does not posses a nuclear explosive device," was stated explicitly, with headlines reading, "Pak has ingredients of a bomb: US" (*The Hindu,* 17 January 1992) and "Pak N-Bomb exists, says US govt." (*The Times of India,* 16 January 1992).

In a January 1992 interview to *The Washington Post*, the Pakistan Foreign Secretary Shahryar Khan was alleged to have acknowledged that Pakistan possessed the technology and know-how to produce at least one nuclear explosive device. He dismissed any idea of nuclear disarmament, contending that Pakistan would continue to maintain atomic equivalence with India. He also repeated Pakistan's position that it would neither explode a nuclear device nor transfer nuclear technologies to other countries, pointing out that it had voluntarily frozen production of enriched uranium fuel. He clarified that a "public perception problem" at home precluded the destruction of existing weapons as demanded by US Congress, unless India agreed to a similar step.[38] However, Radio Pakistan quoted Khan as saying that he had been quoted out of context. The Pakistan Foreign Affairs Ministry spokesman described the interview as "distorted."[39] The front page headlines of the Indian press nevertheless cried: "Pakistan has components to make a N-weapon" (*The Indian Express*, 15 January 1992), "Pak admits it can assemble 1 N-device" (*The Hindu*, 8 February 1992), "US reaction to Pak claim muted" (*The Hindu,* 9 February 1992) and "US refuses to confirm Pak N-arms" (*The Times of India*, 9 February 1992). It should be mentioned that statements by Pakistan denying the nuclear bomb report were also covered by the Indian press.[40] However, there is a stark contrast between these tiny reports hidden in obscure corners of the inner pages, and the front-page headlines, which carried the accusations. The pro-nuclear/defence build-up stances are often reflected, as in the following piece in *The Hindu*.

> With the increasing militarisation of Pakistan and the supply of arms and other

> aid to it by China, West European countries and the US, we have to take note of the realities of the situation and be fully prepared to meet them. The belated admission by Pakistan of its nuclear capability and the possible possession of a few atom bombs further compounds this dangerous situation. We must, therefore, keep our nuclear options open, and not be misguided into regionalising a global question like nuclear disarmament.[41]

In the context of the reported involvement of a Pakistani national in a plutonium smuggling racket discovered by Germany, *The Indian Express* editorialised:

> In keeping with its duplicitous record on the nuclear issue, Pakistan has once again been caught in the act, when the German police unearthed a plutonium smuggling syndicate.... It only proves that the Pakistani nuclear weapons programme continues apace, thanks largely to Pakistan's skill in piracy.... The latest in Pakistan's long list of nefarious activities is, however, a significant departure from the past in that it involves plutonium.[42]

On 23 August 1994, former Pakistan Prime Minister, Nawaz Sharif, stated that Pakistan possessed nuclear weapons. The front page report of *The Indian Express* (26 August 1994) cried, "Pakistani bomb: India to maintain utmost vigilance" and opens thus: "The government will act with 'decisiveness' and 'firmness' in thwarting any danger to national security in the wake of Pakistan's open threat to use nuclear weapons against India for settling its outstanding differences."

Although this was, in fact, the quotation of a statement by the Minister of State for External Affairs, Khurshid Alam Khan, neither the headlines nor the text bear quotation marks to this effect, projecting a reiteration of the government stance. Another report, "West concern at Sharif statement" concluded: "The general perception in the west appears to be that while it would be highly desirable for both India and Pakistan to sign the NPT, the real threat comes from Pakistan."[43] Other front-page headlines in this context read, "Pak confirms buying of Chinese missiles" (*The Indian Express*, 9 September 1994), "Pak killer subs will alter force levels" (*The Indian Express*, 25 September 1994), "F-16s almost bombed Indian reactors" (*The Indian Express*, 2 September 1994).

In April 1995, it was reported that an army unit in Hyderabad, India was created to induct and operate the first batch of Prithvi missiles. The following month, the Parliamentary Standing Committee on Defence recommended early deployment of the Prithvi.[44] *The Indian Express* editorialised that the missile should have been deployed earlier, and blamed the government for caving in to "the Americans, who never approved of a Third World country like India attaining mastery in missile technology."[45] There seemed to be an attempt to advance the Agni programme from a 'technology demonstration' project to a deployable weapon system.

## Nuclear Tests and Selective Reporting

As is the general trend in the reporting of Pakistan's nuclear policy, early 1995 also witnessed numerous reports in the Indian press quoting American sources regarding Pakistan's continued development of nuclear weapons. For instance, the front page headlines in bold type "Pak has 10 assembled n-weapons: CIA" (*The Indian Express*, 8 April 1995) quotes Senator Larry Pressler's revelation of a CIA briefing; "Pak continuing to develop N-weapons" (*The Indian Express*, 21 April 1995), quoted the *Boston Globe*; "China supplied key missile parts to Iran and Pak: CIA" (*The Indian Express*, 23 June 1995), quoted the CIA in *The New York Times*; "China gave Pak M-11 missiles" (*The Indian Express*, 14 July 1995), quoted US officials in *The Washington Post*; and "China helped Pakistan develop N-explosives" (*The Indian Express*, 19 July 1995), quoted a report by the US Arms Control and Disarmament Agency. The front-page article in *The Indian Express*, "There's proof of Chinese missile sales to Pak: US" (30 July 1995), quoted Secretary of State Warren Christopher. However, in contrast to the headline, the text states: "At present, though there is a fairly large body of evidence on that, we do not think there is the evidence there that would justify the imposition of sanctions." In this context, an *Indian Express* editorial concluded instigatingly:

> While it is reassuring that the official spokesman has confirmed that necessary steps are being taken 'to safeguard the nation's security', the Government would do well to remove any doubt in the public mind that it might go slow on its plans about Prithvi and Agni in the light of the latest developments [46]

However, there was a drastic change in December 1995 when western media reports suddenly became taboo for the Indian media. *The New York Times* reported that United States intelligence satellites had detected activity at the Pokhran test site indicating India might be preparing to conduct a nuclear weapon test. Indian newspapers either denied any such move or took on a defiant stance. An *Indian Express* editorial depicted *The New York Times* report on the tests to "be construed as part of the continuing effort to keep India in line on the Comprehensive Test Ban Treaty" and concluded that there "should be no backing down from this position in the face of the renewed pressure.... The people of India must be assured there will be no compromises on matters of security and self-respect."[47] *The Hindustan Times* editorialised that nuclear tests would be widely seen by Indian voters as the act of a brave national hero and urged Prime Minister Narasimha Rao not to be "inhibited" by the United States...." While "Rao does not have to conduct a nuclear test to justify the NYT story," the newspaper suggested that he could argue that "he needs the tests for improving upon India's nuclear technology." If he did so, "he would have most of the nation behind him."[48] As the debate proceeded, opinion became more divided. While some called for conducting tests and others for restraint, all urged defiance of American pressure. *The Asian Age* editorialised that "if India's scientists feel that they need to conduct a second test then they should go ahead with it. Washington may not approve, but Indians will applaud. Not only will [Rao] have stood by our scientists," the paper averred, "he will also have reasserted the fact that India's policies are built on just one foundation – independence."[49] The headlines of an article by M.D. Nalapat in *The Times of India* read, "US testing N-test bogey to help Pakistan, says top official" (18 December 1995). Writing in 1997, Shekar Gupta argued that the US government, non-proliferation NGOs and the media nexus were responsible for the December 1995 leak of the Indian test preparation.[50]

Nizamani points out that a "common method to

ascribe ill intentions to the Pakistani nuclear establishment has been a spy-thriller mode of representing the career of Dr. Abdul Qadeer Khan," with reports about his endeavours being splashed on the front pages. In April 1996, *The Washington Post* reported one such alleged incident that took place in the early 1980s when US officials found the blueprint for a centrifuge in the luggage of A.Q.Khan. The three-column *Indian Express* headline read, "History of Sino-Pak n-collaboration exposed" (3 April 1996), while *The Times of India* (2 April 1996) headline stated, "U.S spies found bomb document in Pakistani scientist's luggage." The story was not only an unconfirmed news item from *The Washington Post,* but it also referred to an alleged incident that took place in the early 1980s. The report said that during an overseas trip in the early 1980s, Pakistan's foremost scientist Abdul Qadeer Khan's luggage was secretly rifled by United States intelligence operatives. They found a drawing of a Hiroshima-sized bomb that they insisted must have been supplied by Beijing.[51]

## The CTBT Debate

In 1996, issues surrounding the Comprehensive Test Ban Treaty (CTBT), formed the crux of the nuclear discourse in the Indian press. According to Praful Bidwai, the lopsided and unbalanced debate on the issue of a CTBT is a good example of the planting of stories and private briefings on issues relating to economic and security policies. Throughout the whole year, when the issue was extensively reported and debated in the Indian press, there were no more than three open press conferences by foreign ministry officials in New Delhi. All the rest of the 'official' information came from selective briefings and 'private' discussions. Consequently, stories were slanted and a consensus against the CTBT was manufactured.[52] A report in *The Hindu* noted:

> In the domestic context, the consensus remains live.... As was evident from the recent debates in Parliament and public statements outside, there is remarkable unanimity in the country, with the non-official opinion, if anything, harder than the government's position. Although some foreign governments may find it odd – because of their inadequate appreciation of the domestic political scene here – the reality is as follows – no government in New Delhi could afford to accept the CTBT text in the present form, and if it does, it collapses. The Delhi – based diplomats, it is hoped, will keep their capitals posted with this reality.[53]

Although there were some lead articles against the grain,[54] a veritable public relations industry emerged to justify India's stand on the CTBT, claiming that such a treaty is 'irrelevant', 'iniquitous', and against India's 'national interest'. The invariable conclusion was to justify a strong linkage with 'time-bound' nuclear disarmament and Indian reservations about sub-critical testing. Virtually the entire media subscribed to the claims that India must not sign the CTBT which it was claimed was utterly flawed as it permitted sub-critical tests and computer simulation and was therefore no restraint on the US but was aimed at restraining India.[55] The Indian press framed the CTBT as a United States imposed treaty that threatened Indian sovereignty. There was little criticism of Russia, China, and United Kingdom who were the proponents of the 'Entry into Force' clause, which New Delhi strongly opposed. The Indian press took a populist anti-

US line, highlighting the issue of sovereignty as well as the existence of a consensus on the issue.[56] An editorial in *The Statesman* argued: "In the light of Sino-Pak nuclear link it is also possible that instead of conducting nuclear tests on its territory, China may opt to carry them out in Pakistan. Such profound discrepancies in the treaty strengthen India's position against becoming a signatory."[57]

Sexual inferences also abounded in this debate in the press. Noting that American 'non-proliferation missionaries' pressed India to sign the CTBT and support a treaty to ban unsafeguarded production of fissile materials, Brahma Chellaney argued that accession to these "self-castration measures" would leave India as a "nuclear eunuch."[58] He also argued that "India cannot allow its nuclear option to be vasectomised at the fissban's (fissile material production ban) sterilization camp even before it has procreated enough fissile material to secure itself."[59] Chellaney compared India's 'nuclear option' to 'chronic impotence', and criticised national leaders for leaving the nation 'naked'.[60] In the context of India's missile programme also, Chellaney had earlier referred to the government as behaving like a wimp.[61]

The distortion of the whole terms of the debate on the CTBT issue encouraged further movement towards testing. Bidwai and Vanaik point out that "such had been the (albeit manipulated) public acclaim and approval for India's stand on the CTBT that any future government deciding to test could, with a great deal of confidence, expect widespread public approval for that decision."[62] The media therefore played a significant role in creating an atmosphere conducive to nuclearisation.

## Setting the Stage: Towards Nuclearisation

Besides the CTBT debate, various aspects of both India's and Pakistan's missile and nuclear programmes received consistent press attention during 1996. *The Hindu* editorial regarding the successful test firing of Prithvi in January concluded: "The Prime Minister, Mr. P.V.Narasimha Rao's assurance that the Prithvi was not the last milestone to be achieved in the Integrated Guided Missile Development Programme (IGMDP) is reassuring in view of the concerted international pressure being mounted against India's missile development programme."[63]

June 1996 witnessed a surge of reports in the context of a report in *The Washington Times* that American intelligence agencies had come to the conclusion that Pakistan had deployed Chinese nuclear capable M-11 missiles.[64] These included the report, "Early deployment of Prithvi, Agni suggested" in *The Hindu* which quoted Defence Ministry sources and Parliamentarians attached to the Standing Committee on Defence. (*The Hindu,* 14 June). *The Hindu* editorial of 18 June takes its cue from the above report:

> A critical task before the defence research establishment is to ensure that the work done so far on the indigenous development of Prithvi, Agni and other missiles is completed for their eventual induction into the armed forces... India should no longer delay the deployment of Prithvi and Agni and the quick completion of the user trials of the other missiles to facilitate their deployment which is what the scientists, technologists and all others who have contributed to their wholly indigenous development richly deserve.... The fact that

> Pakistan could build up its missile armoury for menacing India only with an abject dependence on Chinese supplies highlights the qualitative difference between what the two countries in the subcontinent are capable of.[65]

Similarly, a report on 11 July "N-sub era may dawn only after a decade," quotes Rahul Roy-Chaudhury, a specialist on the navy at the IDSA that India was at least ten to fifteen years away from testing a nuclear submarine. Interestingly, an editorial on the issue again took its cue from the above, noting:

> It is disappointing to know that India may have to wait for as long as 10 to 15 years before it could have its nuclear powered submarine. One therefore hopes that the expectations of the scientists working on the Advanced Technology Vessel, the Indian nuclear submarine project, that they are close to testing an indigenously developed reactor on a land-based test bed materialise quickly.[66]

During a public speech in August 1996 the then Defence Research and Development Organisation (DRDO) head Abdul Kalam urged the government to speed defence research programmes and disregard American pressure. He told journalists that he had submitted a proposal to the government to conduct additional development flights of the Agni missile. This generated much support in the media. While *The Hindustan Times* editorialised in favour of resuming Agni tests,[67] a group of strategic analysts and former officials issued a statement calling for India to declare itself a nuclear weapon state, former Vice Chief of Naval Staff Admiral K.K. Nayyar declared it "essential to conduct a series of nuclear tests," and Raja Mohan argued that India must "cross the physiological barrier."[68] In an editorial introduction to two opinion pieces, *The Times of India* noted that "India has hardly ever been so united internally, or so isolated internationally, as on the issue of the Comprehensive Test Ban Treaty."[69]

A flood of reports emerged in August 1996 in the context of a *Washington Post* report[70] that China was helping Pakistan in secretly setting up a medium range missile plant in Rawalpindi.[71] A front-page headline in *The Hindu* (13 September 1996) proclaimed, "Pak developing long-range missile," but opens "China and Pakistan *could be* (emphasis added) working on a new long range missile capable of striking Indian targets in depth." The security perception of *The Hindu* is evident from its editorial of 31 December 1996 regarding the test firing of Trishul. It states:

> ... it must be made clear that there is still a long way to go before it can be confidently said that the country's security can be effectively preserved. An acceleration of India's missile development programme is among the essential pre-requisites to reach this stage. The objective of the missile development programme is essentially that of deterring a potential aggressor from resorting to invasion.... The uncertainty over Pakistan's nuclear weapons policy has rendered it imperative for India to equip its missiles with nuclear warheads in case these are needed as effective deterrents.... The range as well as the payloads of the missiles, which Pakistan has, almost match those of India. Pakistan's missiles have been

> obtained from China or developed with Chinese rocket technology. The wisdom India has shown in having relied wholly on an indigenous effort to design and develop its missile technology can be seen from its not having to depend on external support which can be wholly unreliable at a time of crisis. This reliance on an indigenous capability should fuel the confidence that India needs for safeguarding its security.[72]

The reported decision of the Ministry of Defence to put the Agni missile project on hold in December 1996 led to another outpour of articles. The headlines of the report in *The Hindu*, "Shelving Agni programme will harm India," bore no quotation marks, but was largely based on remarks of members of the Institute for Defence Studies and Analyses (IDSA) that such a move would affect strategic interests and demoralise the scientific community. The decision is seen as linked to US-led opposition to India's missile programme. According to Uday Bhaskar, Deputy Director of IDSA, "with countries around India having ballistic missiles, which can reach most of our cities, it is not advisable to shelve the Agni missile project...."[73] Thus, as Mike Schuster pointed out in 1997, the Indian press was campaigning for "a harder nuclear India"[74] along the lines set up by the strategic community.

In December 1997, when Abdul Kalam was designated to receive the Bharat Ratna, India's highest civilian honour, the press honoured him with such headlines as "The missile magician – a bouquet for Dr. Abdul Kalam."[75] According to Perkovich, Brahma Chellaney, to whom Kalam had reportedly supplied useful information on the nuclear and missile programmes, gushingly heralded Kalam as one of 'only two great scientific visionaries' in independent India's history, Homi Bhabha being the other. "Chellaney contrasted Kalam's 'vision and courage' with 'a growing number of... upper caste Hindus' (who) have fallen victim to self-doubt and the 'should-we-or-should we-not' syndrome."[76] Perkovich points out that Chellaney thus added caste and communal politics to his earlier efforts to push the Indian government toward a more militant nuclear policy.[77]

The early months of 1998 witnessed a focus on Pakistan's missile programmes by the Indian press. Some of the headlines read "New Pak missile capable of hitting Indian cities ready" (*The Hindustan Times,* 4 January 1998), "India should keep nuclear option open" (*The Hindustan Times,* 23 March 1998), "Ghauri: Is it just politics or is it war?" (*The Times of India,* 12 April 1998), S.K.Singh, "Pakistan's missile flexing" (*The Hindu,* 17 April 1998), "Pak to accelerate missile programme" (*The Hindustan Times,* 18 April 1998), "India ready to face any challenge, says PM" (*The Hindu,* 18 April 1998), and "Make People aware of security threat" (*The Hindustan Times,* 28 April 1998).[78]

The latter half of the 1990s thus reflected a hawkish nuclear/missile build-up perspective in the Indian press, with the coverage of the CTBT debate creating an atmosphere conducive to nuclearisation. The emerging role of the media in legitimising nuclear weapons also indicated the promotion of chauvinistic nationalism in reporting nuclear issues.

## REPORTING THE NUCLEARISATION OF SOUTH ASIA - 1998

The period from May to July 1998 witnessed intense media coverage of nuclear questions as a result of the nuclear tests in the subcontinent. This section is based on a content analysis of three newspapers – *The Hindu* (Thiruvananthapuram edition - hereafter referred to as TH), *The Indian Express* (Kochi edition - referred to as IE) and *The Times of India* (Mumbai edition - referred to as TOI), over a three-month period beginning from 1 May to 31 July 1998.[79]

The selected newspapers are national dailies having countrywide circulation. TOI with six editions, TH with eight and IE with nineteen editions were the largest circulated multi-edition English language dailies in India during the period selected for the content analysis.[80] Differences among the various editions are basically related to local news, which is tailored according to the particular region it serves. Differences in national and international news coverage are marginal, but should be kept in mind. A brief profile of these newspapers would also be in order. TOI is owned by Bennett Coleman and Co. Ltd., which also has considerable business interests. Its influence is largely based on its status as the oldest English language daily in India and its journalistic professionalism, but critics also point out that it has tended to be an establishment paper. TH is a family run newspaper, owned by Kasturi and Sons Ltd. Its influence also is based on its age, identification with Indian nationalism prior to independence, and its wide-ranging in-depth coverage of news. IE is owned by the Express group/Goenka family, which also has varied business interests. It is known for its investigative reporting and anti-Congress perspective.[81] The 1981 study by S.K.Goyal and M.Challapathi Rao identified both Bennett Coleman and Co. as well as Express Newspapers as national monopoly houses.[82]

With Pakistan's nuclear programme being an integral part of the nuclear politics of South Asia, all

**Table 4.1 : Quantitative Analysis of Reports Referring to Pakistan's Nuclear Programme: 1 May to 31 July 1998**

| *Category* | *MAY* | | | *TOTAL* | *JUNE* | | | *TOTAL* | *JULY* | | | *TOTAL* | *TOTAL* | | | *TOTAL* |
|---|---|---|---|---|---|---|---|---|---|---|---|---|---|---|---|---|
| | *TO1* | *IE* | *TH* | | *TOI* | *IE* | *TH* | | *TOI* | *IE* | *TH* | | *TOI* | *IE* | *TH* | |
| Editorials | 4 | 5 | 4 | 13 | 11 | 4 | 2 | 17 | 2 | 2 | 3 | 7 | 17 | 11 | 9 | 37 |
| Opinion Page Articles | 8 | 3 | 7 | 18 | 6 | 12 | 8 | 26 | 4 | 4 | 11 | 19 | 18 | 19 | 26 | 63 |
| News Analyses | 15 | 10 | 39 | 64 | 12 | 13 | 34 | 59 | 5 | 4 | 20 | 29 | 32 | 27 | 93 | 152 |
| News Reports | 72 | 78 | 114 | 264 | 60 | 47 | 84 | 191 | 33 | 33 | 81 | 147 | 165 | 158 | 279 | 602 |
| Interviews | 1 | - | 1 | 2 | 1 | - | - | 1 | - | - | 1 | 1 | 2 | - | 2 | 4 |
| Graphics | 2 | 2 | 1 | 5 | - | - | - | - | - | - | - | - | 2 | 2 | 1 | 5 |
| Photos | 4 | 8 | 7 | 19 | - | 4 | 4 | 8 | - | - | - | - | 4 | 12 | 11 | 27 |
| Cartoons | - | - | 4 | 4 | - | - | - | - | - | - | - | - | - | - | 4 | 4 |
| Total | 106 | 106 | 177 | 389 | 90 | 80 | 132 | 302 | 44 | 43 | 116 | 203 | 240 | 229 | 425 | 894 |

* TOI: *The Times of India* (Mumbai), IE: *The Indian Express* (Kochi), TH: *The Hindu* (Thiruvananthapuram)

**Table 4.2 : Quantitative Analysis of Reports Relating to Nuclear Issues in South Asia: 1 May to 31 July 1998**

| *Category* | *MAY* | | | *TOTAL* | *JUNE* | | | *TOTAL* | *JULY* | | | *TOTAL* | *TOTAL* | | | *TOTAL* |
|---|---|---|---|---|---|---|---|---|---|---|---|---|---|---|---|---|
| | *TO1* | *IE* | *TH* | | *TOI* | *IE* | *TH* | | *TOI* | *IE* | *TH* | | *TOI* | *IE* | *TH* | |
| Editorials | 11 | 15 | 4 | 30 | 4 | 7 | 3 | 14 | 7 | 2 | 4 | 13 | 22 | 24 | 11 | 57 |
| Opinion Page Articles | 12 | 18 | 12 | 42 | 7 | 9 | 14 | 30 | 8 | 4 | 6 | 18 | 27 | 31 | 32 | 90 |
| News Analyses | 54 | 25 | 48 | 127 | 5 | 3 | 16 | 24 | 1 | 5 | 17 | 23 | 60 | 33 | 81 | 174 |
| News Reports | 121 | 130 | 177 | 428 | 53 | 35 | 69 | 157 | 26 | 24 | 62 | 112 | 200 | 189 | 308 | 697 |
| Interviews | 7 | 3 | - | 10 | 2 | 2 | - | 4 | 1 | - | 1 | 2 | 10 | 5 | 1 | 16 |
| Graphics | 2 | 2 | 2 | 6 | - | - | - | - | - | - | - | - | 2 | 2 | 2 | 6 |
| Photographs | 12 | 6 | 12 | 30 | 2 | 2 | 3 | 7 | - | - | - | - | 14 | 8 | 15 | 37 |
| Cartoons | 2 | 1 | 4 | 7 | - | - | - | - | - | - | - | - | 2 | 1 | 4 | 7 |
| Total | 221 | 200 | 259 | 680 | 73 | 58 | 105 | 236 | 43 | 35 | 90 | 168 | 337 | 293 | 454 | 1084 |

* TOI: (a) *The Times of India* (Mumbai), IE: *The Indian Express* (Kochi), TH: *The Hindu* (Thiruvananthapuram)

(b) Figures do not include reports specifically referring to Pakistan's nuclear programme, for which see Table 4.1.

write-ups (excluding letters to the editor) referring to nuclear and missile issues in the region were analysed for the study. A distinction has however been made between those items referring directly to Pakistan and the remaining reports/articles thereby enabling a juxtaposition of coverage. While distinguishing the coverage among newspapers wherever relevant, the trajectory of coverage by each newspaper is also studied. A differentiation is made between the periods before India's nuclear tests, the period leading up to Pakistan's tests and the remaining period under survey. A distinction is also made between news reports, opinion pieces and editorials of each newspaper.

During the three month period selected, a total number of 1978 items were published in the three newspapers together, relating to the nuclear and missile developments in South Asia. Of this 894 (45.19 per cent) items specifically referred to Pakistan. Table 4.1 provides a detailed overview of the number of items relating to Pakistan in each news category during each of the three months. Similar details in respect of the remaining 1084 (54.81 per cent) items on nuclear and missile issues in the subcontinent can be seen in Table 4.2.

In analysing the various reports and analyses, particular emphasis has been placed on editorials, headlines, location, and the sources of news. Although readership of editorials is much lower than that of the news pages, it has been pointed out that opinion leaders and decision-makers often make it a point to read editorials and other opinion articles. Editorials reflect the views and opinions of the editor of the newspaper and as such often reflect the orientation of the paper. Similarly, headlines not only define or summarise an event but also evaluate it. Given the time constraints of today's world, it is often the headlines and front-page block items which are glimpsed through and retained in the subconscious mind. Identifying the sources of news is also essential to understand the role of the media in social representations and power relationships in society. Within a hegemony framework the study of sources has been used to show that public issues are largely defined in the media by representatives for powerful institutions, agencies and interests in society. Alternative voices critical of the status quo are much less likely to gain a platform in the mainstream media. It is therefore important to understand how various sources are used and framed by the media.[83]

In the present study, the Pakistani and Indian sources of news reports relating to Pakistan's nuclear programme have been categorised separately. Within each category, five groups - government, political parties, strategic analysts, strategic enclave and dissenting voices (excluding political parties) have been identified. A separate category of United States government sources has also been made given the fact that the United States has had an important role to play in the nuclear discourse in South Asia. It may be noted that these categories are not mutually exclusive. One report possibly quotes various sources. Out of the total number of 250 reports based on Indian sources in all three newspapers together, 64.8 per cent was that of the government, 23.6 per cent that of political parties, 4.8 per cent that of the strategic community, 4 per cent that of the strategic enclave, while only 2.8 per cent reflected dissenting voices (For a detailed analysis, month-wise and paper-wise, see table 4.3. For similar statistics of Pakistani and US sources, see Table 4.4).

**Table 4.3 : Indian Sources Quoted in News Reports Referring to Pakistan's Nuclear Programme: 1 May to 31 July 1998**

| Category | MAY | | | TOTAL | JUNE | | | TOTAL | JULY | | | TOTAL | TOTAL | | | TOTAL |
|---|---|---|---|---|---|---|---|---|---|---|---|---|---|---|---|---|
| | TO1 | IE | TH | | TOI | IE | TH | | TOI | IE | TH | | TOI | IE | TH | |
| Government | 16 | 20 | 40 | 76 | 16 | 20 | 18 | 54 | 9 | 9 | 14 | 32 | 41 | 49 | 72 | 162 |
| | (59.3) | (60.6) | (62.5) | (61.3) | (69.6) | (77.0) | (54.5) | (65.8) | (75) | (69.2) | (73.7) | (72.7) | (66.1) | (68.0) | (62.1) | (64.8) |
| Political Parties | 4 | 8 | 19 | 31 | 4 | 4 | 8 | 16 | 3 | 4 | 5 | 12 | 11 | 16 | 32 | 59 |
| | (14.8) | (24.2) | (29.6) | (25.0) | (17.4) | (15.4) | (24.2) | (19.5) | (25) | (30.8) | (26.3) | (27.3) | (17.7) | (22.2) | (27.6) | (23.6) |
| Strategic Enclave | 2 | 2 | 3 | 7 | - | 1 | 2 | 3 | - | - | - | - | 2 | 3 | 5 | 10 |
| | (7.4) | (6.1) | (4.7) | (5.6) | | (3.8) | (6.1) | (3.7) | | | | | (3.2) | (4.2) | (4.3) | (4.0) |
| Strategic | 4 | 1 | 1 | 6 | 2 | 1 | 3 | 6 | - | - | - | - | 6 | 2 | 4 | 12 |
| Community | (14.8) | (3.0) | (1.6) | (4.8) | (8.7) | (3.8) | (9.1) | (7.3) | | | | | (9.8) | (2.8) | (3.4) | (4.8) |
| Dissenting Voices | 1 | 2 | 1 | 4 | 1 | - | 2 | 3 | - | - | - | - | 2 | 2 | 3 | 7 |
| | (3.7) | (6.1) | (1.6) | ( 3.3) | (4.3) | | (6.1) | (3.7) | | | | | (3.2) | (2.8) | (2.6) | (2.8) |
| TOTAL | 27 | 33 | 64 | 124 | 23 | 26 | 33 | 82 | 12 | 13 | 19 | 44 | 62 | 72 | 116 | 250 |

* (a) TOI: *The Times of India* (Mumbai), IE: *The Indian Express* (Kochi), TH: *The Hindu* (Thiruvananthapuram)

(b) Figures in brackets indicate percentage of the column-wise total.

**Table 4.4 : Pakistani and US Sources Quoted in News Reports Referring to Pakistan's Nuclear Programme : 1 May to 31 July, 1998**

| *Category* | | *MAY* | | *TOTAL* | | *JUNE* | | *TOTAL* | | *JULY* | | *TOTAL* | | *TOTAL* | | *TOTAL* |
|---|---|---|---|---|---|---|---|---|---|---|---|---|---|---|---|---|
| | *TO1* | *IE* | *TH* | | *TOI* | *IE* | *TH* | | *TOI* | *IE* | *TH* | | *TOI* | *IE* | *TH* | |
| **Pakistan** | | | | | | | | | | | | | | | | |
| Government | 16 (84.2) | 13 (81.2) | 19 (79.2) | 48 (81.4) | 8 (80.0) | 10 (71.4) | 16 (76.2) | 34 (75.6) | 9 (100.0) | 10 (71.4) | 18 (100.0) | 37 (90.2) | 33 (86.8) | 33 (75.0) | 53 (84.1) | 119 (82.1) |
| Political Parties | 2 (10.5) | 3 (18.8) | 4 (16.7) | 9 (15.2) | - | 1 (7.1) | 2 (9.5) | 3 (6.7) | - | - | - | - | 2 (5.3) | 4 (9.1) | 6 (9.5) | 12 (8.3) |
| Strategic Enclave | - | - | 1 (4.1) | 1 (1.7) | 1 (10.0) | 2 (14.4) | 3 (14.3) | 6 (13.3) | - | 1 (7.2) | - | 1 (2.4) | 1 (2.6) | 3 (6.8) | 4 (6.4) | 8 (5.5) |
| Strategic Community | - | - | - | - | - | - | - | - | - | - | - | - | - | - | - | - |
| Dissenting Voices | 1 (5.3) | - | - | 1 (1.7) | 1 (10.0) | 1 (7.1) | - | 2 (4.4) | - | 3 (21.4) | - | 3 (7.4) | 2 (5.3) | 4 (9.1) | - | 6 (4.1) |
| TOTAL | 19 | 16 | 24 | 59 | 10 | 14 | 21 | 45 | 9 | 14 | 18 | 41 | 38 | 44 | 63 | 145 |
| **US** Government | **17** | **11** | **26** | **54** | **12** | **12** | **21** | **45** | **14** | **13** | **21** | **48** | **43** | **36** | **68** | **147** |

* (a) TOI: *The Times of India* (Mumbai), IE: *The Indian Express* (Kochi), TH: *The Hindu* (Thiruvananthapuram)

(b) Figures in brackets indicate percentage of the column-wise total.

## Prelude to the Tests

In early May 1998, prior to the nuclear tests in the subcontinent, the press in India continued to focus on Pakistan's missile programme and its external linkages. This was clearly evident in the three papers under study.[84] These reports were interspersed with that on the consequent Indian need for action and the developments in its missile programme.[85] *The Hindu* reported on the imposition of sanctions by the United States against Khan Research Laboratory and a North Korean Company for the transfer of technology relating to the Ghauri missile. It emphasised that Ghauri was actually a Nodong-I missile developed by North Korea. It also reported that this exploded the myth of Ghauri's indigenous origin and eroded the "credibility of Islamabad as a 'responsible nation'."[86] A clarification by the North Korean ambassador that it did not have a hand in Ghauri's development found mention in a one-column report on page 14.[87] In another front-page report on 8 May, TH speculated whether Pakistan was planning another missile test "after the 'successful' test-firing of the Ghauri.... Acquiring such a missile would enable Pakistan to hit almost any Indian city from a base considerably inside its own territory."[88] The paper had earlier pointed out that "Pakistan's missile threats and possible challenges to India's expanding commercial shipping, future energy supplies and the need for a long-term plan for an advanced surveillance system have reinforced the demand for a National Security Council."[89] The headlines of lead articles on the issue during this period read: "Pakistan perceives India as weak" (TOI, 9 May) and "Responding to Ghauri: eschew perverse restraint" (IE 8 May). Anand K. Sahay strongly advocated missile induction to counter Ghauri. He concluded that whether Ghauri came "pre-packaged or in knocked-down condition or whether it was indigenously made (highly unlikely), the threat it poses to India does not change. The leadership would do well to worry about how best to respond without altering the fact of engagement with Islamabad or Washington, rather than engage in idle speculation."[90]

Some concern was also expressed in reports in IE and TH over Pakistan's nuclear programme. However, at this point of time the issue took the backburner.[91]

## Pokhran – II: International Status for India

The day after India's nuclear tests of 11 May, front page headlines of the three newspapers under study triumphantly declared (some of them in banner headlines) - "India conducts 3 underground N-tests: Hydrogen bomb too tested," "India now joins club of five N-weapon states," "Test aimed at countering N-blackmail," "Three underground nuclear explosions conducted in Pokhran: India makes giant leap in N-capability," "India explodes three nuclear devices at Pokhran: tests include Hydrogen blast," "President congratulates scientists." Headlines in the inner pages read: "Tests prove India's N-capability,"[92] "India has broken no commitments," "Conducting three N-tests is historic, says Pant," "I am proud of our N-achievement says Atomic Energy Chairman," "Nuclear weapons: end to the dithering,"[93] "India has proven capability," "India entitled to conduct tests: IAEA," "A repudiation of nuclear apartheid policy."[94] The few reports against the grain were: "US may impose sanctions,"[95] "US disappointed, sanctions likely," "US threatens sanctions," "Pak reserves right to take appropriate steps."[96]

The days following India's tests witnessed a continued projection of the tests as having tremendously enhanced the international status of the country, giving it a voice in international affairs.[97] While K.Subrahmanyam in a front page report in TOI declared "India now joins club of five N-weapon states" (12 May), in another report on the same day he argued that by "conducting three underground nuclear tests at Pokhran on Monday, India will get an effective say in nuclear disarmament...."[98] However, the day's editorial stated that it was a tragic irony that these tests should have been the first definitive act of the new government. It pointed out that when so many social and economic issues are crying out for desperate attention, it seems a tragic waste that countries such as India should invest so much time, money and political resolve on perfecting techniques of mass destruction.[99] Nevertheless, news reports in the same paper stressed that through the decision to test; Vajpayee had set the nation free from the fear of 'punishment'. It was an assertion of national self respect and sovereignty, and a rejection of the hypocrisy and double standards which mark the conduct of the big powers.[100] Even after Pakistan's tests of 28 May, Pokhran-II was viewed by TOI reports as "a momentous decision."[101] Later, a front page report in TOI declared: "India is all set to tell all concerned that it is prepared to play ball with the world community on its own terms."[102]

On 6 June, in an editorial reversal, which had begun even before Pakistan's tests, TOI stated that the real achievement of India's test was that it gave a powerful leverage to the non-nuclear weaponised states to pressure the five nuclear powers to move towards nuclear disarmament in the next Review Conference of the treaty in the year 2000.[103] A later editorial stated that "there is no doubt the Shakti tests constitute a wake up call to the nuclear hegemons that they will not succeed in freezing the iniquitous status quo and therefore they have to engage India."[104] Similarly, K.Subrahmanyam opined that India underwent a rebirth on 11 May 1998. Since it could not persuade the rest of the world to play the game it recommended, it finally decided to join the game the rest of the international community was playing. The name of the game was nuclearised global order.[105]

Soon after the tests, IE editorialised that the tests "had raised India to the level where it can look upon these nations as its peers, and to see that its point of view gets a decent hearing."[106] Subsequent editorials reinforced this perspective, applauding the Prime Minister at every stage, as is evident from the headlines, "The Vajpayee doctrine: he is right to combine consensus with toughness," (27 May) and "Nuclear wise: a statesman-like performance in the house." (29 May) Another editorial stated that India's nuclear tests "were certainly inspired in part by the security threats to it, the one from Pakistan included. But they were inspired also by its vision of a role for itself in world affairs in which Pakistan and indeed any other single country has no part."[107] S.Gurumurthy in his front-page news analysis in IE stated: "So the world has begun to take India seriously; it now regards India as a player in world affairs and not a helpless witness to the global games as it was for decades."[108] Other reports in IE (22 June) read: "India's N-tests put big five in the dock, expose their hypocrisy," "India seen as a serious nation after N-tests," "India is now in a stronger position to ask others to disarm, says Arundhati Ghose." Manvendra Singh in a lead article noted: "The road from Budha Purnima 1974 to Budha Purnima 1998 is as far travelled as one from say a Baby Hindustan to an Astra."[109]

In this context, TH reporting was more restrained with opinion pages incorporating more divergent perspectives. Nevertheless, former Foreign Secretary Muchkund Dubey in a lead article observed: "India has at long last demonstrated its political will and courage expected of any nation which has a modicum of self-respect and aspires to be a regional player of some significance."[110] Analysing the historical context of the tests, C.Raja Mohan pointed out that Vajpayee, "ran the crucial last lap in the long relay race to make India an overt nuclear power."[111]

The number of dissenting voices on the issue was marginal. Kalpana Sharma and Ayesha Khan pointed out in TH that India and Pakistan had not learnt the lesson that true strength was displayed by attacking poverty and challenging social, political and gender inequalities. The current escalation of tensions would only further prioritise defence.[112] Praful Bidwai argued in TOI that the BJP had bestowed "a questionable acceptability and legitimacy upon quintessential instruments of mass annihilation." The Pokhran tests would signify "not India's maturity or her arrival upon the world as a self confident and vibrant nation, but just the opposite. At their heart is the raw power of an aggressive nationalism."[113] In a scathing critique of the tests in IE, noted architect Laurie Baker, stated that it was ridiculous to think that it would be used only to frighten enemies or that the world would look at us with respect and fear.[114]

## Scientific Achievement

The days immediately after the tests witnessed a deluge of articles in the three newspapers in praise of the Indian scientific achievement.[115] TOI reported that the tests demonstrated "a remarkable degree of sophistication in nuclear explosions,"[116] while TH editorialised:

> There is no question that the stunning mastery of technological sophistication and the demonstration of world class versatility that went into the success of the three nuclear tests conducted in Pokhran on Monday are a matter of national pride. The dedicated group of atomic scientists which has been quietly working for decades towards the objective of creating a 'credible nuclear deterrent' has won the gratitude of an entire nation for a history making achievement that places India in the exclusive league of nuclear weapons powers.[117]

IE editorialised that the tests had proven India's fusion capability, and that the fission devices were far more capable than the 1974 device could be made. It suggested that Prithvi and Agni missiles could be armed with nuclear warheads, and that critical data had been obtained to enable scientists to continue work on refining various types and sizes of nuclear weapons in laboratories.[118] Along similar lines, Gurumurthy's article in IE stated that by this "stunning technological expertise and even more stunning secrecy displayed, at one stroke, the world's view of India changed."[119] Other reports also reflected this open celebration of the 'secrecy' "which made it all possible."[120]

Citations by Indian scientists themselves - particularly evident in TH, but reflected in all papers - reinforced the magnitude of the achievement.[121] Quotations of various scientists, often reflected in the headlines, seemed to exceed their briefs.[122] U.R.Rao, former Chairman, Indian Space Research Organisation (ISRO) was quoted as arguing that the tests should have been conducted at least three years ago.[123] Placid Rodriguez, Director, Indira Gandhi Centre for Atomic Research, admitted that mastering fast breeder technology and running the Fast Breeder Test Reactor at Kalpakkam was "as difficult as a bomb, but the importance of the latter could not be overlooked as it had strategic importance and was directly related to the country's security."[124] The period also witnessed numerous reports in adulation of the scientific community which was responsible for Pokhran–II, particularly, R.Chidambaram and A.P.J.Abdul Kalam.[125]

On the other hand, news reports questioning the value of the tests were sidelined. Very little coverage was given to critical voices including that from the scientific community, both within as well as outside the country.[126] The very formation of the "Indian Scientists Against Nuclear Weapons" immediately after the May tests, as a body of scientists to work against the proliferation of nuclear weapons in the country revealed the existence of a large number of scientists who did not share the dominant perspective as depicted by the media.[127] The few reports, which did incorporate such sources, included that of 19 May in all three papers on the statement by scientists of various institutions of India criticising the tests.[128] M.V.Ramana's study *Bombing Bombay: Effect of Nuclear Weapons and a Case Study of a Hypothetical Explosion* which is very relevant in highlighting the impact of a nuclear explosion in the region was quoted in a two part report by C. Rammanohar Reddy in TH.[129] Criticism of the tests by scientists such as T.Jayaraman

**Table 4.5 : Indian Sources Quoted in News Reports Relating to Nuclear Issues in South Asia: 1 May to 31 July 1998**

| Category | MAY | | | TOTAL | JUNE | | | TOTAL | JULY | | | TOTAL | TOTAL | | | TOTAL |
|---|---|---|---|---|---|---|---|---|---|---|---|---|---|---|---|---|
| | TO1 | IE | TH | | TOI | IE | TH | | TOI | IE | TH | | TOI | IE | TH | |
| Government | 46 (52.3) | 39 (40.2) | 57 (41.6) | 142 (44.1) | 23 (59.0) | 16 (55.2) | 28 (57.2) | 67 (57.2) | 14 (63.6) | 16 (66.7) | 22 (52.4) | 52 (59.1) | 83 (55.7) | 71 (47.3) | 107 (46.9) | 261 (49.5) |
| Political Parties | 19 (21.6) | 30 (30.9) | 48 (35.1) | 97 (30.1) | 7 (17.9) | 7 (24.1) | 9 (18.4) | 23 (19.7) | 3 (13.7) | 3 (12.5) | 9 (21.4) | 15 (17.0) | 29 (19.5) | 40 (26.6) | 66 (28.9) | 135 (25.6) |
| Strategic Enclave | 15 (17.0) | 16 (16.5) | 15 (10.9) | 46 (14.3) | 2 (5.1) | 1 (3.4) | 6 (12.2) | 9 (7.7) | 1 (4.5) | 2 (8.3) | 2 (4.8) | 5 (5.7) | 18 (12.1) | 19 (12.7) | 23 (10.1) | 60 (11.4) |
| Strategic Analysts | 3 (3.4) | 5 (5.2) | 5 (3.6) | 13 (4.0) | 5 (12.9) | 3 (10.3) | 3 (6.1) | 11 (9.4) | 3 (13.7) | 2 (8.3) | 3 (7.1) | 8 (9.1) | 11 (7.3) | 10 (6.7) | 11 (4.9) | 32 (6.1) |
| Dissenting Voices | 5 (5.7) | 7 (7.2) | 12 (8.8) | 24 (7.5) | 2 (5.1) | 2 (7.0) | 3 (6.1) | 7 (6.0) | 1 (4.5) | 1 (4.2) | 6 (14.3) | 8 (9.1) | 8 (5.4) | 10 (6.7) | 21 (9.2) | 39 (7.4) |
| Total | 88 | 97 | 137 | 322 | 39 | 29 | 49 | 117 | 22 | 24 | 42 | 88 | 149 | 150 | 228 | 527 |

* (a) TOI: *The Times of India* (Mumbai), IE: *The Indian Express* (Kochi), TH: *The Hindu* (Thiruvananthapuram)

(b) Figures in brackets indicate percentage of the column-wise total.

(c) Figures do not include reports specifically referring to Pakistan's nuclear programme, for which see Table-4.3 of this chapter.

(Indian Institute of Mathematical Science, Chennai),[130] Surendra Gadekar (editor, *Anumukti*),[131] and R.V.G.Menon[132] was almost invisible.

During the month of May, 14.3 per cent of the Indian sources of reports relating to nuclear issues (excluding those referring specifically to Pakistan) quoted the strategic enclave or scientific establishment. This figure may be compared with the total number of dissenting voices (7.5 per cent), which includes that of scientists also, in the same newspapers during this period. (For a detailed statistical analysis see Table 4.5).

A statement by B.K.Subba Rao, a former Indian navy captain with a Ph.D. in nuclear technology from IIT (Mumbai), questioning the claims of the Department of Atomic Energy (DAE) on the tests, found no repercussions in the media, except in TH. He argued that the Indian thermonuclear device failed completely. Whatever yield was recorded had come from a boosted fission device. According to him, the joint press conference of R.Chidambaram and A.P.J.Abdul Kalam was a damage control exercise – "a major science and technology scam."[133] There were only passing comments in the press that the doubts raised by Subba Rao should be answered by the DAE and that former Prime Minister Deve Gowda had called for the controversy to be resolved by the Prime Minister.[134] However, reports were often quick to deflect or refute any allegations against the tests.[135]

Headlines often reflected a trend of camouflaging criticism against India behind headlines relating to Pakistan. TH (30 May) quoted US administration officials' scepticism in *The Washington Post* as to whether India actually detonated a thermonuclear device. However, the report was entitled "Pakistan planning more tests." Similarly, TOI, quoting a *New York Times* report, stated that Pakistan had attempted to cast some doubts on India's tests, but that these were promptly clarified to TOI.[136] The paper in its report "India's claim of having tested H-bomb credible," (27 July) refers to the cover story on the tests in *The Bulletin of Atomic Scientists*. The original article, in fact, had also pointed out that the debate was clouded by the lack of information about India's progress on nuclear weapons.[137] It may be noted that the very same issue of *The Bulletin of Atomic Scientists* also carried a strong critique of the tests by Kalpana Sharma,[138] which went unreported in the Indian press.

However, the opinion pages of TH, IE and TOI did provide some space for dissent. In the specific context of praise for the scientific endeavour, Ramachandra Guha in a lead article in IE went entirely against the grain, vociferously calling on the need to praise creative rather than destructive science,[139] while Praful Bidwai in a lead article in TOI wrote that the most persistent and powerful group lobbying for India's overt nuclearisation was neither the military nor politicians, but nuclear and defence scientists who claimed science had given India security.[140] Quoting Ashis Nandy that since the Second World War, two new reasons of state – science and development – have been added to the traditional one of national security, Partha S.Ghosh pointed out that it was not only the politicians who were agog congratulating the scientists who made the tests possible, "even the scientists concerned arrogate to themselves the right to make political statements on behalf of the state."[141] B.K.Subba Rao stated:

> The rave media coverage while hailing India's capability 'to vacate nuclear threats', has in fact vacated the boundary between a

> political statement and a scientific statement. A political statement can mean many things but a scientific statement has only one meaning. That is the characteristic of science, which distinguishes it from other human pursuits. Both Dr. Chidambaram and Dr. Kalam appear to have ignored this distinguishing feature of science.[142]

Evidently, the projection of national status and scientific triumph reflected the priorities of the press, ignoring the mass destructive nature of nuclear weapons, the costs of nuclearisation, the lack of command and control systems and its resulting dangers and the impact of the tests on nuclear proliferation.

## Consensus in India

After the Indian nuclear tests, the Government claimed in various forums that there was a national consensus on the issue. Vajpayee also asserted in Parliament that despite political differences, "we should give the message that the country is together."[143] Following the tests, most newspapers sought to highlight a consensus of euphoria within the country, as evident in headlines themselves.[144] Describing the reactions to the tests in Delhi, an IE report on 13 May stated:

> Forgotten were the years of abuse at the hands of international diplomacy, forgotten too was the war that we fight daily over Siachen glacier, and forgotten was the slow and deliberate bleeding by Pakistan in Jammu and Kashmir, that powerlessness which comes from having to fight in your own country. There was then, as someone

> once sang, a momentary lapse of reason; it was just elation, pure unadulterated elation....[145]

The headlines of IE editorial of 16 May declared: "Spread it around: Pokharan is a national, not party achievement." TOI (13 May) quoted a public opinion poll in its front-page report, "Overwhelming majority supports N-tests." TH quoted an Indian Market Research Bureau (IMRB) public opinion poll that "Most Indians hail N-tests – opinion poll" (13 May). Other reports highlighted the 'euphoria' in the country.[146] K.K.Katyal wrote in TH that at the popular level, "the excitement over last week's nuclear tests was overwhelming – it covered all sections, all regions and the people of all persuasions. The tests were seen as a spectacular achievement of the scientific community and as an assertion of national independence in the face of pressures, subtle and crude."[147]

Again, counter-narratives on the issue were marginalised. However, Praful Bidwai argued in TOI: "There is emphatically no *informed* consensus.... The early, flimsy consensus has come apart. The left, the centre, and substantial numbers of Congressmen, now oppose weaponisation. Nuclearisation is polarising India."[148] While the opinion pages did again provide some avenue for the expression of dissent, treatment of the same in the other pages of TH requires some attention. TH (1 June) quoted from K.P.S.Menon's talk at the Swadeshi Science Congress, Thiruvananthapuram, that there had been no immediate threat to security that made the nuclear tests imperative. However, through its choice of headlines "Pokhran test criticism absolute impudence" the report stressed only his comment that it was impudent to criticise the Pokhran test. The statement by the Left parties criticising the government's nuclear policy found mention in a two-column report on page 8 of TH (17 May) entitled "Left Parties criticise government's nuclear policy." Other such reports were often hidden in the inner pages of these papers.[149]

IE on 13 May itself reported: "N-tests: left takes critical view." The following day it quoted the Chief Minister of Kerala, E.K.Nayanar questioning the political, economic and technological grounds for the tests and also the impact of sanctions. However, the headlines of the report merely stated: "CM: decision to conduct N-blast India's right." Another report on the joint statement by the Left parties on page 6, was entitled, "N-tests: left sore at not being consulted" (15 May). In contrast, the report, "Nuclear question a national, not partisan matter: CWC" finds mention in the front page of IE (15 May). A report in the paper, quoting eminent personalities such as Rajni Kothari, Kuldip Nayar and Medha Patkar in criticism of the tests can be found on page 9 in a one-column report.[150] An editorial in IE argued that criticism that the opposition had not been taken into confidence was "unreasonable but understandable."[151]

Similar reporting was found in TOI.[152] Rare exhibitions of dissent were the front page photograph of protestors in Bombay in TOI (27 May), a photo of the Green Peace balloon over the Taj Mahal (TOI, 13 June) and a front page report reading, "N-weapon is a message of death," quoting Jnanpith award winner and Urdu writer, Sardar Ali Jafri. (TOI, 6 June) K.Subrahmanyam in his article in TOI, alluded that dissent was merely due to ignorance. He argued that it "is a telling comment how poorly educated our political class is particularly on national security and foreign policy issues."[153]

Although there were reportedly over thirty demonstrations and meetings in at least eight Indian cities involving scholars, scientists, social scientists, human rights campaigners, feminists, trade unionists and environmentalists besides political activists, these did not receive national coverage in the press.[154] Most available reports depicted the people of Khetolai village (Pokhran) to be in praise of the tests and prepared to sacrifice everything for their country.[155] Referring to complaints of nasal bleeding among residents, Vajpayee was quoted in TH as having said that no radioactivity was found. "Even if there had been any trouble, then we should learn to sacrifice as national security is above all considerations."[156] Ironically, the news report was headlined: "We will pay any price for country's security: PM." None of the papers gave national coverage to the unanimous resolution passed by the Khetolai Grama Sabha calling for the worldwide destruction of nuclear weapons, that decisions on nuclear energy should be taken only after informed consultation with citizens, and that there should be a universal ban on nuclear tests.[157]

## Pokhran-II and Pakistan's Response

India's nuclear tests had generated a number of statements and press briefings by the Government of Pakistan.[158] But it was only TH that gave front page headline coverage to Pakistan's reactions. It cited Foreign Minister Gohar Ayub Khan's statement in the Senate that "Pak reserves right to take appropriate steps,"[159] Nawaz Sharif's statement blaming the West,[160] and Pakistan Foreign Secretary, Shamshad Ahmed's statement that "Pak rules out giving up N-option."[161] The representatives of both India and Pakistan at the Conference on Disarmament at Geneva, Savitri Kunnadi and Munir Akram, had pleaded their cases at the conference and the matter had been reported in IE. However, the headlines of the report (15 May) read: "India defends nuclear tests in conference on disarmament in Geneva." Writing on the same issue, Muchkund Dubey, in a front-page news report (box) in TH stated: "*Pakistan, which opened the debate with a long vituperative statement,* did not give any indication of the counter-measures it was planning to take .... *In contrast, India made a short measured statement giving the bare facts of the tests,* putting on record the two statements issued by India."[162] (emphasis added)

A TOI article (19 May) quoted Benazir Bhutto on the circumstances that led Pakistan to decide to keep open the option of a test by making the necessary preparations two years earlier. However, it was her statement that rogue nations that defy world opinion ought to be taught a lesson, which formed the headlines, "A military strike will teach India a lesson." The same report in TH (19 May) was headlined: "Benazir for pre-emptive strike against India," IE in a scathing editorial critique of Benazir Bhutto's response pointed out:

> when India explodes five nuclear devices in the Rajasthan desert on May 11 and 13, Benazir Bhutto with her sharp political instincts smells sweet opportunity in the air. Suddenly, visions of presiding once again over the destinies of 132 million Pakistanis grip her, fantasies of crowds jostling to shower rose petals over the Empress of Islamabad crowd the airspace. Nawaz Sharif can keep his Ghauri, she, the Daughter of the East, will ride back to power on the Indian nuclear programme. She will rise from the earth as the true defender of

Pakistan's security interests.[163]

In contrast to the unquestioned projection of consensus on India's tests, coverage of reactions of the citizens of Pakistan focused on dissenting perspectives critical of an arms race. On 17 May a TOI headline read, "Arms race will hurt common man, say Pakistanis." The front-page report on Pakistan's tests in TOI stated: "a nomadic shepherd near the site in the Chagai Hills said on Friday that they had been forced to leave their herds three days before the first rounds of nuclear devices were tested on Thursday."[164] IE reported on Nawaz Sharif's sttempts to create a national consensus regarding Pakistan's response to the issue.[165] Referring to the reactions in Pakistan, IE editorialised

> The Indian bomb is not specifically aimed at Pakistan, so the question of retaliation does not really arise. Islamabad, like any other nation, is naturally concerned about any nuclear activity in a neighbouring state, but its response ought to be tempered by reason. India has extensive borders and seaboards and is surrounded by several states. Pakistan is only one of several factors that resulted in a perceived need for the tests.... The bomb is a blanket solution for national security, no matter which point of the compass the problem originates from. It would be all too easy for the Pakistani political and military establishments to reduce the situation to a simplistic Hindu bomb versus Muslim bomb issue....[166]

TOI advocated Pakistan to come into the open with its nuclear bomb. It editorialised: "During the cold war such recognition of mutual deterrence and the consequent acceptance of the futility of initiating a war led to détente and arms control talks between the superpowers."[167] The United States policy towards Pakistan in the context of the Indian tests received considerable coverage in the three newspapers, highlighting an American tilt towards Pakistan and a blinkered approach to its nuclear policy.[168]

## Pakistan's Nuclear Capability

While the Pokhran tests had unleashed a torrent of articles on the triumphant achievements of India's scientific community, there were also a number of references at this point of time to Pakistan's nuclear capabilities, which were in marked contrast. Immediately after India's tests, M.D.Nalapat argued:

> As for Pakistan, that country has long been touted by non-proliferation 'experts' as being on par with India in the development of missile and bomb technology. How these analysts believe that a country incapable of producing a lathe can manufacture strategic equipment is unclear. Unless China gifts a bomb to Pakistan – just as it did two missile systems – there is no way Islamabad can detonate any device that is not essentially a firecracker.... Islamabad is likely to make a virtue of its impotence by demanding goodies to exercise a 'restraint' that its own lack of technology has forced on it.[169]

In a front page report, TOI quoted L.K.Advani that it was "'entirely possible' that Pakistan 'unable to match Indian skills in science' could revert to extending its terrorist activities in the Kashmir Valley and elsewhere."[170] There was an increased focus on Pakistan's missile programme. Citing *Jane's Defence*

*Weekly*, TOI in a front-page analysis reported that North Korea had been a silent but significant partner in Pakistan's growing missile capability.[171]

However, by mid May IE quoted CIA officials and *The New York Times* that tests were imminent.[172] While IE of 24 May pointed out, "Technical snags hold up Pak N-test," the paper began to focus on Pakistan's clandestine nuclear programme. A photograph of A.Q.Khan bears the caption, "Smuggling his way to the top: Abdul Qadeer Khan." The adjoining report entitled, "Abdul Qadeer Khan's circle of deceit," describing the history of Pakistan's nuclear programme began thus: "Abdul Qadeer Khan is the best known and the most decorated of Pakistani smugglers." It concluded that this was "just another link in the long chain of smuggling and subterfuge going back to Abdul Qadeer Khan's stint with the Dutch company." Another report on the same day by Manvendra Singh contended that the two incidents which contributed the most to expose the nature of Pakistan's nuclear weapons programme were the arrest in 1988 of A.Q.Khan by Dutch authorities in Amsterdam for travelling on a forged diplomatic passport and his sentence in absentia in 1984 to a four year prison term by a Dutch court for nuclear espionage. It contended: "the continual smuggling of high precision and dual use technologies is the key to the mushrooming of the Pakistani programme."[173] Referring to the Pakistani refusal to permit an Indian play in Karachi, IE editorial observed: "Unable to go in for retaliatory nuclear testing, Pakistan has settled for an almost equally satisfying bout of retaliatory artist bashing."[174] C.Raja Mohan of TH was inclined to think that Pakistan might not choose to test, since there was no technological reason for it to do so, as it was said to have acquired a tested nuclear weapon design from China in the mid-1980s. Furthermore, testing would push Pakistan down the road to economic ruin due to American sanctions, while not testing would win diplomatic gains and could rebuild political and economic relations with the United States.[175]

TH also stressed Pakistan's clandestine nuclear development. The paper quoted *Der Spiegel* that Germany suspected Pakistan of trying to obtain state-of-the-art technology from German companies for its nuclear weapons programme through front companies set up in the United Arab Emirates and Far East, and that Pakistani diplomatic missions had also been involved in the technology transfer.[176] By late May reports of a possible Pak test began to appear. A front-page report in TH quoted American officials as cited in *The Washington Post* and *The New York Times* that Pakistan's tests could happen at any time. There was then an increased focus on the benefactors of Pakistan's nuclear programme and its clandestine nature. A report by PTI in TH cited *Jane's Defence Weekly* and *Le Monde* that, "Pak N-arsenal based on Chinese design" (TH, 28 May). Quoting from the French daily *Le Monde*, IE stated that France, along with US and China had contributed much towards arming Pakistan, and that Islamabad's nuclear programme "is highly dependent on support from these countries...."[177] As in TH, IE also relied on the PTI report citing *Jane's Defence Weekly*, that Pakistan

> may have foregone a retaliatory atomic test in response to Indian explosions, because it may have a 'nuclear arsenal which works' based on a Chinese design handed over to it in the 80s...But the magazine as well as defence experts doubted whether Pakistan

**Table 4.6 : International Media Sources Quoted in News Reports on Pakistan's Nuclear Programme: 1 May to 31 July 1998**

| *Category* | | *MAY* | | *TOTAL* | | *JUNE* | | *TOTAL* | | *JULY* | | *TOTAL* | | *TOTAL* | | *TOTAL* |
|---|---|---|---|---|---|---|---|---|---|---|---|---|---|---|---|---|
| | *TO1* | *IE* | *TH* | | *TOI* | *IE* | *TH* | | *TOI* | *IE* | *TH* | | *TOI* | *IE* | *TH* | |
| PAKISTAN | 2 | - | 1 | 3 | 1 | - | - | 1 | 3 | 1 | 5 | 9 | 6 | 1 | 6 | 13 |
| US | 8 | 9 | 9 | 26 | 5 | 7 | 14 | 26 | 7 | 6 | 9 | 22 | 20 | 22 | 32 | 74 |
| OTHER | 6 | 2 | - | 8 | 6 | 7 | 4 | 17 | 3 | 3 | 2 | 8 | 15 | 12 | 6 | 33 |
| TOTAL | 16 | 11 | 10 | 37 | 12 | 14 | 18 | 44 | 13 | 10 | 16 | 39 | 41 | 35 | 44 | 120 |

* (a) TOI: *The Times of India* (Mumbai), IE: *The Indian Express* (Kochi), TH: *The Hindu* (Thiruvananthapuram)

> had acquired the capability of producing thermo-nuclear bombs which would give it the capacity of making nuclear warheads for its Ghauri and other surface to surface missiles.... 'By failing to respond to public clamour for retaliatory nuclear test, it can be deduced that Pakistan is still wrestling with trigger devices and that its nuclear programme despite tall claims may still be in exploratory stage', experts said.... in comparison to Pakistan's 'part acquired, part clandestine and part developed nuclear programme', India's nuclear programme was far advanced and largely 'home grown'.[178]

As evident, this period saw a number of reports quoting the international media on Pakistan's 'clandestine' nuclear programme. (For a detailed survey of the international media sources quoted in reports on Pakistan's nuclear programme during the three months under study see Table 4.6).

The lack of an immediate retaliatory test by Pakistan was seen purely in terms of its scientific capability, with no regard at this point of time to other factors, which could have influenced this situation. The provocative reporting by TOI at this stage could possibly be perceived as an incitement to Pakistan to carry out its nuclear tests.

## Pakistan's Nuclear Tests

The days immediately following Pakistan's tests saw the emergence of a number of official documents, statements and interviews from Pakistan explaining its rationale for testing.[179] However, only a few of these were actually quoted in the Indian press. Even in such cases, the framing of headlines is notable. The day after

Pakistan detonated its nuclear devices, some of the front page headlines of IE, TH and TOI declared: "Pakistan's tests vindicate our nuclear policy, says Vajpayee," "Pakistan retaliates with five nuclear tests: Sharif says account with India is even," (all of TOI); "A beleaguered Sharif presses the button: Pakistan explodes five nuclear devices in Chagai range," "Our doubts now confirmed: PM," "Pak will step up proxy war: Advani," (all of IE); "India's stand vindicated: PM," "Pakistan also detonates five nuclear devices," "No surprise, says Narayanan," and "A dangerous escalation" (all of TH). Reports in the inner pages included – "Pak N-test expected: K.R.Narayanan," "Our N-sites under threat from India, cries a hysterical Pak,"[180] However, TH reflected a more responsible reporting in its reports and headlines.[181] IE editorialised that the Pakistani tests were essentially for the people of Pakistan "who are being deluded to think the tests demonstrated strength and invincibility."[182]

## Pakistan's Scientific Acumen

In contrast to the celebration of science and technology after India's tests, there was a strong element of scepticism of Pakistan's scientific acumen. The clandestine basis of its nuclear programme as compared to India's indigenous one was highlighted. With the exaggerated claims surrounding Indian science having been exposed by Pakistan's tests, there was a sharp decline in the citation of Indian scientists. This is evident from the contrast between the total number of 46 reports quoting them in May to that of 9 in June and 5 in July. (A detailed quantitative analysis of each newspaper can be seen in Table 4.5).

Front page reports quoted Defence Minister George Fernandes that Pakistan had conducted only one nuclear test and not five on 28 May, and that "they are nowhere near where we are."[183] It was reiterated by R.Chidamabaram the following day that "the yield of the first round of tests on May 28, contrary to Pakistan's chief nuclear scientist A.Q.Khan's claims, was about 10 to 15 kilotonnes, whereas that of May 30 was about 2 to 4 kilotonnes."[184] Announcing Pakistan's nuclear tests, a TOI report opened thus: "Pakistan, long suspected to have had a clandestine nuclear weapons programme, on Thursday carried out five 'successful' nuclear tests...."[185] The sceptical use of quotation marks is to be noted. A few days later the paper quoted an article from *The New York Times* entitled "Experts say Pakistan test was either small or a failure." American experts were quoted as saying in the news item that the architect of Islamabad's nuclear programme, Abdul Qadeer Khan might be "exaggerating the country's atomic prowess."[186] Quoting Raja Ramanna, TOI also raised doubts regarding Pakistan's claim of having conducted 6 tests.[187] M.D.Nalapat in a face saving lead article (in the context of his earlier article on 13 May[188]) contended that "Unlike the Pakistani bomb – which is a China-created device and whose detonation was intended to help persuade India to retrace its path of technological advancement – the Indian nuclear and missile programme is indigenous."[189] Quoting K.Subrahmanyam at a press conference, TOI wrote:

> as far as the international community was concerned, doubts were expressed about the number of tests conducted by Pakistan. 'Some of the international newspapers and intelligence agencies have reported that there was not enough scientific evidence which validates Pakistan's claim of

> detonating six nuclear devices', he said. However, as far as technology was concerned, India's nuclear programme was far advanced than that of Pakistan, he said.[190]

Two weeks later the paper again quoted *Jane's Intelligence Review* that while India's potential nuclear arsenal was bigger than Britain's and in the same league as France and China, "Pakistan, however, exhausted a significant part of its meagre arsenal in last month's nuclear tests and the poor performance of its weapons revealed the country's strategic nuclear weakness, the respected military magazine said."[191]

Two days after Pakistan's nuclear tests TH published a news report citing *The Washington Post* questioning Pakistan's claims on the nuclear tests. The CIA was quoted that Islamabad might have claimed the five tests just to match India's number. There was no evidence of any explosion of a thermonuclear device. Pakistan's capability to test a device on its own was also questioned.[192] The following day also saw a news report in TH quoting seismological experts that Pakistan had conducted only one successful nuclear explosion on May 28 and not five as claimed. It quoted the experts, who cited American intelligence sources that the explosive power of the Pakistani tests was roughly equivalent to 10,000 tonnes of dynamite, which was less than half the size of the atom bomb the US dropped on Hiroshima. As compared to this the yield of the five Indian tests conducted on 11 and 13 May was claimed to be equivalent to about 60,000 tonnes of dynamite.[193] TH also quoted Indian nuclear scientists that according to seismic data and other parameters, the tests were of low efficiency and of the Hiroshima type and not of the Nagasaki kind which produced more energy: "This puts Pakistan in the category of having developed a first generation warhead or a crude device unlike India that has tested the nuclear devices of all types and of the third generation."[194]

IE, in turn, in a front-page report quoted scientists and experts in United States and New Delhi that Pakistan's claims of having tested five nuclear devices were being received with a certain degree of scepticism. American experts were reported to suggest that "Islamabad is either fibbing about the number of tests or has fudged production of fissile material in the past...."[195] The following day's paper also contained a similar report based on doubts raised by an anonymous Indian scientist. According to him available information suggested that Pakistan had conducted only two tests. American seismic network had picked up only two seismic signals. Seismic signals from the tests also suggested their yield to be about two to five kilotons – much lower than what would be expected from boosted fission bombs. The same laboratory had registered a magnitude of five for India's first test at Pokhran in 1974.[196] It is interesting to note that this report quoting an anonymous scientist received three-column twelve-centimetre space, in contrast to the space given to the various critiques of the Indian scientific achievement at Pokhran-II. In early July, IE quoted three scientific studies that the Pokhran blast was thirteen times more powerful than the Pakistani test and that the latter's device was two generations behind India's.[197] Referring to Pakistan's second round of nuclear tests IE editorialised that it did not say much more than the first one. Apart from the possibility that more tests were required to improve the reliability of its weapons and to compensate for shortfalls in the first series, the message was essentially for the Pakistani people who were being deluded to think that the tests demonstrated strength and invincibility.[198] A piece by Santy in IE contended that "it would be quite fair to say that the Pak *pot pourri* bomb is born more out of 'European convictions' than 'native skills'."[199] In similar vein, S.Gopal in a lead article argued that the credit for bringing Pakistan "to this level of technology must go to the Chinese.... It is difficult to believe that the tests in the Chagai Hills of Pakistan were not facilitated by Chinese assistance."[200]

The reporting on the scientists behind Pakistan's tests was in stark contrast to those behind the Indian tests. This trend which was clear even before Pakistan's tests, was evident in the reports, "Smuggling his way to the top: Abdul Qadeer Khan" (IE, 24 May), "Pakistan's partners in proliferation" (IE, 24 May), "The man from Bhopal who builds bombs" (TH, 1 June), "Pak scientists fight for credit" (TH, 3 June), "Efforts are on to deprive scientist Qadeer of N-credit" (TOI, 3 June), "Pak nuclear scientists defect to West" (TH, 29 June) and "Pakistani 'scientist' disowned by his father" (IE, 9 July).[201]

## Pokhran-II: Rationalisations

In the midst of the general sense of exhilaration in the Indian press after Pokhran-II, analyses of the whys and wherefores had begun to emerge, not only in the editorial pages, but also in the front pages. After the Indian tests, there had emerged an increasing number of opinion page articles and editorials analysing various aspects of both India's and Pakistan's nuclear programmes, beginning with a rationalisation of the Pokhran-II tests. TH editorialised that "these tests were inevitable, as part of the process of sharpening India's strategic and defence capabilities...."[202] A week later it again observed that in a nuclearised world "where no part is beyond the reach of nuclear missiles, countries such as India wishing to retain an independent strength have little choice but to go nuclear."[203] According to C.Raja Mohan, "India's nuclear ambiguity was increasingly becoming untenable. It had to come out of the nuclear closet and test before it was too late."[204] Reinforcing the threat from Pakistan, Former Foreign Secretary, J.N.Dixit argued in the same paper that India was impelled towards these tests, first because Pakistan had started a clandestine nuclear weaponsiation programme about two years before India conducted the 1974 test. "This Pakistani nuclear and missile weaponisation programme has shown a consistent incremental pattern, influencing India's threat perceptions.... Pakistan has clearly articulated nuclear and missile threats to India, backed up by increasing missile capacities, as evidenced in the firing of the Ghauri."[205]

On 14 May, IE, in its editorial stated that the tests were "an assertion that the country is set upon doing all it must to ensure its security...."[206] A few days later it observed that the Government had been emphatic in conveying to the governments of other countries that the reason why it had to go nuclear was its deteriorating security environment. Since the tests, the government had maintained an argument which was morally upright, logically persuasive and diplomatically to India's advantage.[207] Concluding his lead article the day after India's tests, Shekar Gupta, editor of IE argued that the "intention behind the tests can only be to see that India is embraced back on the world's centre stage as a stronger power rather than be consigned to the sidelines as some nuclear 'rogue'."[208]

In a different vein, TOI editorialised immediately

after the tests, that they represented a political statement by New Delhi under the saffron flag. It was not clear how the country's security had been strengthened by the tests, which were bound to cast an ominous shadow over India's frayed relations with its neighbours.[209] However, K.Subrahmanyam, in a front-page news analysis on the same day, argued:

> The Indian behaviour confirms that it is a reluctant nuclear weapon state compelled to join the nuclear club because all its pleas to move towards nuclear disarmament were ignored by the nuclear weapon powers who got nuclear weapons legitimised by the international community through the unconditional and indefinite extension of the non-proliferation treaty. The recent Ghauri missile test by Pakistan, the ongoing nuclear and missile technology cooperation between India's neighbours, China and Pakistan, and the inability of the international regimes to enforce non-proliferation obligations on the nuclear weapon powers made it inevitable for India to join the nuclear weapon club.[210]

Another front-page analysis entitled, "Test aimed at countering N-blackmail" by M.D. Nalapat in TOI, also reiterated that as opined by a cross section of analysts and policy-makers, the tests were a result of international postures, together with that of the Chinese and Pakistani nuclear programme. Interestingly, the thought for the day by David Penhaligon, published on the editorial page of 13 May read: "To adopt nuclear disarmament would be akin to behaving like a virgin in a brothel." In deviation from its earlier stance, TOI editorial of 20 May pointed out: "India, surrounded as it is by missiles of various ranges, need not relate its capabilities to specific country threats. This country must deem nuclear weaponisation as an insurance against the uncertainties of a world refusing to move towards disarmament."[211]

News reports also largely reflected government policy.[212] Reports critical of the basic rationale of testing were hard to come by. The questioning of the rationale of the tests by both the Congress (I) and the left parties found mention only in the inner pages. Similar was the case with the accusation that the tests were a bid to divert people's attention, by Tamil Manila Congress (TMC) President, G.K. Moopanar and other political factions. Mention nevertheless was comparatively found most in TH.[213]

The opinion pages however, did reflect some amount of criticism on the rationale for the tests. In an editorial page article, Subramanian Swamy contended that the tests were intended to secure Vajpayee's tenure, to subdue critics and stave off undercurrent realignment of secular and patriotic forces in Parliament.[214] Similarly, Achin Vanaik argued that the tests had nothing to do with any deterioration in the external environment but were motivated by changed self-perceptions.[215] Praful Bidwai pointed out that the tests were devoid of strategic rationale, had lowered India's stature and had sought to win popularity by drumming up macho notions of nationalism and self-esteem.[216] In another biting critique he pointed out:

> India's nuclearisation has nothing to do with lofty values of peace or with the NPTs indefinite extension, the CTBTs 'discriminatory' nature, and the nuclear states' refusal to commit themselves

> genuinely to disarmament. This is just contrived sophistry that Mandarins and Brahmins have always practised to rationalise whatever the powerful do, however deplorable that might be.[217]

TOI, in a one page feature on 24 May with the banner headlines "The bigger bombs in our backyard" included separate articles on the more pressing problems of society such as unemployment, lack of food and education, pollution, population growth, etc. However, such issues were raised largely in the opinion pages alone.

## Post-Chagai Rationalisations for Pokhran-II

After the Chagai nuclear tests, various statements by the Pakistani government stressed that its hands had been forced by the Indian leadership.[218] However, the Ministry of External Affairs' brief on India's nuclear tests maintained that it was a false impression that as Pakistan's tests followed India's, it was a reaction to the latter.[219] Pakistan's tests were projected as a confirmation of its possession of nuclear weapons and a vindication of India's assessment and policy.

Following Pakistan's nuclear tests, there emerged a nuanced shift in the rationalisations of the Indian press. In contrast to its earlier editorial, TOI's post-Chagai one argued that "it was the Ghauri missile launch and Dr. A.Q.Khan's announcement in early April that Pakistan could test nuclear weapons at short notice that triggered off Pokhran-II."[220] An editorial on 29 June stated that the United States-China joint statement issued in Beijing on 27 June highlighted the core security problem faced by India which made the Shakti tests both imperative and timely. As in 1971, India had to deal with a United States-China-Pakistan axis with possible threats of Chinese hegemonism tacitly backed by the United States.[221] The following day it again observed that since the Pakistani weapon preceded the Indian weapon "the only way to prevent horrible scenarios about nuclear strikes being enacted was to get the Indian deterrent ready and make it overt and credible.... The Chinese–US proliferation to Pakistan from the 80s left India with no choice but to develop its deterrent."[222] Another editorial two weeks later argued that the "unprincipled and opportunistic US policies on proliferation resulted in Pakistan going ahead with its weapons acquisition with Chinese help and forced the Indian tests."[223] The complete turnaround in the editorial perspective of the TOI from one initially being critical of India's tests to then justifying the tests by citing the failure of international disarmament, and later Sino-Pakistan nuclear collaboration is particularly noteworthy.

After Pakistan's tests, the IE editorial stressed the need for India to inform the world that "its testing was significantly prompted by the Chinese nuclear support to Pakistan's nuclear programme."[224] TH, however, in a front-page editorial sceptically argued that if the intention of the Vajpayee administration had been merely to sharpen India's strategic capability and keep alive the credibility of the nuclear deterrent when it authorised the conducting of the South Asian tests, "what was the need for the outburst of jingoistic chauvinism that followed the tests."[225] Writing in the same paper, C.Raja Mohan continued to stress that "India's decision to become a declared nuclear weapon power is rooted in the geopolitical changes that have taken place in Asia since the end of the Cold War and would have a significant effect on their evolution..."[226]

Interestingly, the TOI editorial of 26 May refers

to K.Subrahmanyam's lead article on the same page,[227] with the introduction that the "accompanying article on this page explains the genesis of the Indian nuclear programme initiated by the then Prime Minister Rajiv Gandhi."[228] Together with explaining the rationale of the tests, there were clear-cut justifications of the government decision to test.[229] In justifying the tests, the press also sought to stress continuity in India's nuclear policy by the various governments, as projected by the government.[230]

## The Sino-Pak-US Nuclear Nexus

India's Ministry of External Affairs' brief on the country's nuclear tests had stated that Pakistan's weapons predated India's and was built after years of clandestine acquisition.[231] In the aftermath of Pakistan's tests, there emerged several write-ups in the press on the country's nuclear programme, largely centred around Sino-Pakistan-US relations on nuclear issues, the country's clandestine nuclear programme and references to the 'Islamic bomb'. On 4 June, quoting extensively from *The Washington Times* and CIA reports, Arun Shourie began a three part article in IE on Pakistan's nuclear programme, which he contended was pursued single-mindedly with Chinese help. By way of introduction he states that this "brazen story of Chinese complicity and India's blinkered approach for almost two decades is being recounted..."[232] A number of other reports in the paper focused on the Sino-Pakistan-US nuclear relationship.[233]

Atul Aneja's write-up in TH on Pakistan's nuclear history opened thus: "The demonstration of Pakistan's nuclear weapons capability in the Chagai hills today is the culmination of a clandestine programme which began nearly three decades ago."[234] A clarification by

A.Q.Khan found mention on page13 of the paper entitled, "Nothing stolen for Pak bomb: Qadeer Khan" (1 June). On 4 June, TH in a one-column article tucked into page 12 stated that in the context of reported Sino-Pakistani nexus on the nuclear and missile technology front, China has "quietly" passed new regulations to control export of sensitive nuclear technology to other nations.[235] Taking into account that this information was of crucial importance to the general thrust of news reporting on Pakistan, the importance or lack of it, accorded to the report in the newspaper is of significance. Similarly, the Chinese Ambassador, Zhon Gang, in an interview with K.K.Katyal and C.Raja Mohan made some important clarifications which again appeared only on page 14. He maintained:

> the Chinese side has time and again stated that China is a responsible country, and that we Chinese have not transferred, and will not transfer to any country equipment or technology that can be used for making nuclear weapons.... the nuclear cooperation between China and Pakistan only aims at peaceful utilisation of nuclear energy, and that such cooperation is under the safeguards of IAEA. Therefore there exists no issue of nuclear proliferation. This cooperation between China and Pakistan is not intended to direct against India.[236]

Other reports in TH also reflected this trend.[237] TOI, in a box news in bold print, quoted the BBC:

> Several German companies deceived the authorities and clandestinely exported to Pakistan vital and specialist instruments, required for its nuclear programme, probably making its recent tests possible,

> the British Broadcasting Corporation (BBC) has reported. Tonnes of sensitive material, based on the latest technology and which could be easily used to manufacture nuclear bombs, including hydrogen ones, were sent by these companies to Pakistan through the Frankfurt airport, unchecked by the authorities.... Without such help, Pakistan's nuclear tests may not have been possible, it said.[238]

Another box news report in bold print published a few days later revealed that a former Director of CIA's non-proliferation centre had informed the Senate Foreign Relations Committee that the Clinton administration had blocked intelligence documents and ignored concrete evidence that China had transferred 34 M11 missiles to Pakistan in November 1992.[239] Immediately after Pakistan's tests itself, TOI editorial had observed that the tests "confirmed all the media reports over the past 11 years that Pakistan had assembled nuclear weapons in 1987 with active Chinese help and tacit US connivance."[240] TOI editorial of 19 June contended that India had been a victim of the permissiveness of the US "as is evident from the North Korean missile export and the Sino-Pakistan nuclear nexus."[241] "Dangerous liaisons" another editorial along similar lines, appeared on 29 June. On the other hand, Praful Bidwai pointed out that the Sino-Pakistani arms and technology deals were "hyped up. But as anyone familiar with recent Sino-Indian talks will testify, China offered to sell us the very same nuclear and missile components Pakistan bought."[242] Such pieces were however clearly against the grain.

## Pakistan's Islamic Bomb

During this period there were also several references particularly in IE to the so-called 'Islamic bomb'. Prior to the Indian nuclear tests itself, the paper had reported that unlike India

> ...which has been scrupulous in its nuclear dealings (rather, non-dealings) despite the excellent relations it has with Islamic and Arab nations, Pakistan has used the threat of spilling the nuclear beans to the Islamic world to soften up Washington.... Some experts believe that in the long term, there is a basic conflict between US interests and Pakistan's Islam based nuclear drive.[243]

Another front-page box item (16 May) "Fatwa for N-test" cites a Senior Deputy Chief of a religious group addressing an all party meet, as having issued a *fatwa* (edict) ruling that a nuclear test by Pakistan had now become *farz* (duty) in the present circumstances under the Islamic law. After Pakistan's nuclear tests, S.Gurumurthy, long time Rashtriya Swayam Sevak (RSS) member and National Convenor of Swadeshi Jagran Manch, in a front-page article in IE, pointed out that

> it is not just a nuclear bomb; it is essentially an Islamic bomb. The only countries which Pakistan consulted before the Chagai Hills blast were the fundamentalist Islamic nations – Saudi Arabia and Iran. The character of Pakistan's bomb is defined by the character of Pakistan as an Islamic State. For the authors of Pakistan, India is Dar-ul-harb – a land of infidels who worship idols. So more than a deterrent against war,

> the bomb has a religious significance for Pakistan. The Pakistani bomb is an extension of the official faith of the State of Pakistan.... This is how the Pakistani bomb is an Islamic bomb, targeting infidel India. This is what is implicit in naming the missile 'Ghauri' to setting the time for the blasts.[244]

The same day's editorial reflected this perspective when it stated that "Islamabad can be relied upon to try to win over the Islamic world to its bomb as an answer to India's 'Hindu' bomb, and exploit India's newly 'aggressive' Hinduism to win the sympathy of the rest of the world."[245] In another lead article, Gurumurthy argued that the "irony of the Islamic bomb is that it is aimed at a country with the world's second largest Muslim population where every town or city has a sizeable Muslim population. But this may not deter Pakistan's Punjabi Muslim military elite."[246] A news report citing *The Washington Times* stated that stories of an India-Israel 'nuclear kinship story', being floated by the Pakistani media was gathering momentum in some Arab publications. By raising this spectre, analysts felt that Pakistan was "appealing for Islamic solidarity to face the impending sanctions. There is also the underlying sales pitch for the Islamic bomb."[247]

Along similar lines, TOI had already editorialised on 4 June that Zulfikar Ali Bhutto had asserted that among Islamic countries only Pakistan had the expertise to build the bomb. "On the basis of this he staked Islamabad's claim for the leadership of the Islamic world.... Pakistan has already started giving an anti-Israeli orientation to its nuclear capability so as to get the financial support of Arab oil exporting countries..."[248]

Meanwhile, TH on 1 June warned that playing the 'Islamic card' might not help Pakistan. Another report from Washington stated that the US media was agog with reports of the possibility of Pakistan's contribution to the 'Islamic bomb'.[249] The paper also quoted US Deputy Secretary of State, Strobe Talbott's remarks in a Japanese newspaper that Pakistan, which was facing economic collapse following sanctions imposed "might play the 'Islamic card' by threatening to pass the atom technology to the Muslim world in exchange for aid..."[250]

## On Arms Race, Deterrence and Security

After India's tests, front-page reports of newspapers had included Vajpayee's statement that the tests would not lead to an arms race in South Asia.[251] The Ministry of External Affairs brief on India's nuclear tests stated:

> Global experience is that nuclear weapons minimise the risk of major war. USSR and the US with vast differences in their political systems had successfully kept the nuclear peace for over five decades. There is no reason why we in South Asia cannot do as well. Indeed, we have a tradition of good sense that equip us to do this.[252]

A report in TH quoting Raja Ramanna, nuclear physicist and Union Minister, stated that Indians felt secure after the nuclear tests,[253] while C.Raja Mohan stressed the need to educate public opinion about nuclear weapons, their only function being "to deter the use of these weapons against the nation by others...."[254] Although a news report in TH quoting various political leaders of the Congress-I, CPI and CPI (M) stated, "Parties fear nuclear arms race," it was relegated to a three-column report on page 8 of the paper (31 May). Inder Malhotra writing in TH maintained that the "cries of a nuclear arms race in South Asia are phoney."[255] TH editorialised that there was no reason why there should have been such a frenzied disapproval of the Pokhran testing: "The imaginary danger conjured up by India's testing of its nuclear weapons should recede with the moratorium announced by New Delhi."[256] Immediately after India's tests, TOI had editorialised that the tests were bound to cast an ominous shadow over India's frayed relations with its neighbours. Pakistan, which had not yet openly tested a nuclear device, could be expected to take counter-measures. This could lead to a damaging and futile arms race.[257] However, TOI editorials of 20 and 23 May, even as they called for 'No-first-use' declarations, stressed the importance of nuclear weapons for deterrence.[258] Similarly, IE editorialised that the bomb was "a blanket solution for national security, no matter which point of the compass the problem originates from."[259]

Quoting from George Fernandes' interview to CNN, IE reported that the nuclear tests had improved the possibility of a breakthrough in bilateral relations. Both countries now knew each other's positions in terms of nuclear capabilities and both would want to sit down and talk rather than go in for proxy wars.[260] A front-page report in TH (8 June) read: "N-tests have averted war chances," which was actually a quote by the Sri Lankan Foreign Minister for Development of Ports. In "Nuclear co-existence with Pakistan," in the same paper, Raja Mohan argued that there was no inevitability of an arms race (15 June). On the other hand, "...India's nuclear weapons will help stabilise the Asian balance over the long-term.... Having declared it's a nuclear weapon power, after years of vacillation, and in a position now to influence the security dynamics of Asia, New Delhi must learn the art of speaking in terms of national security and national power."[261] In TOI of 2 June, K.Subrahmanyam was quoted as having stated: "The latest self-gained nuclear status will emanate peace and restraint rather than a 'war'...." (TOI, 2 June). Similarly other reports read, "Have a nuclear bomb to end conflict" (TOI, 7 June), and "It should be easier now for India, Pakistan to talk peace, says Gujral" (TOI, 8 June).

Editorial pages reflected a similar stance. IE editorialised that fears about the nuclear situation in South Asia "are being exaggerated by the Clinton Administration for obvious reasons."[262] M.Guruswamy contended in a lead article that nuclear weapons are not war fighting weapons, but are "weapons of coercive diplomacy to prevent wars."[263] TOI editorial of 29 May observed: "What was so far a situation of implicit mutual deterrence now becomes an overt one. With this both countries are bound to realise that a war between them will be meaningless...."[264] M. K. Rasgotra, former Foreign Secretary, also pointed out that the "single most important lesson of India's history is: defence preparedness is the key to independence, peace and security."[265] K.Subrahmanyam in his lead article practically mirrored the MEA brief when he wrote that if one were to compare the eight years of the India-Pakistan nuclear co-existence with the first eight years of US-USSR, US-China and Sino-USSR nuclear relationship, the former was much more stable. Now that the weapons were out in the open on both sides mutual deterrence was fully established. He argued that it was extremely unlikely that India and Pakistan would have a high-intensity conventional war, let alone a nuclear war.[266] TOI's editorial in the same day's newspaper echoed these views:

> Though India reached deterrent capability eight years ago and Pakistan three years before that, there has been no nuclear race so far. It is unlikely one will start now. Most of the predictions about a disastrous arms race between India and Pakistan are made by western experts extrapolating the US-Soviet arms race experience on the subcontinent. That is a totally inappropriate comparison.... The West raised the bogey of enormous costs to prevent India and Pakistan from developing nuclear deterrent capability. Now they warn us of a ruinous arms race, over-looking the past eight years of history. It is crucial that we think through this vital issue independently without uncritically accepting imported wisdom.[267]

A few days later, TOI again editorialised that India's nuclear weapons capability was a source of stability for the wider region.[268]

However, a few reports and lead articles largely in TH did reflect dissenting views on the subject. Reports quoted Left parties that the Pakistani nuclear tests were a vindication of the stand that an arms race had begun, for which the BJP was to blame.[269] TH also quoted the then Kerala State Planning Board member, B.Ekbal, that nuclear tests could not secure the nation's security.[270] In an analytical piece, C.Rammanohar Reddy elaborated: "No nuclear deterrence ever solved any problem.... Even half a dozen nuclear tests will not address the roots of insurgency in the border states."[271] Similarly, V.R.Raghavan in a lead article in TH pointed out that a nuclear weapons status would bring to India more insecurity than security.[272] Praful Bidwai succinctly pointed out in TOI that the bomb had become a symbol of male chauvinist potency. He argued that the actual meaning of nuclearisation had been revealed by "the explosion of triumphalism, communalism and war-mongering over Kashmir in both countries. Contrary to hawkish projections, nuclearisation will not lead to sober, responsible behaviour on the part of either New Delhi or Islamabad owing to perceived mutual deterrence."[273] After Pakistan's nuclear tests, there was clearly an increased stress on the significance of nuclear weapons for stability in the region, while at the same time refuting allegations of an emerging arms race.

## Threat Perceptions

Ironically, post-Chagai reporting saw a projection in the Indian press of specific threats from Pakistan's nuclear and missile capabilities. A front-page box news in bold type in TOI (3 June) carried the headlines, "Pak may use N-arms first." The text was an entirely speculative report citing *The Washington Times*, which, in turn, quoted US intelligence that while neither India nor Pakistan wanted war, if such a situation arose, Islamabad was more likely to be the first to use nuclear weapons. Another front page report, "China-Pakistan nuclear axis has India worried" quoted the Annual Reports of the Ministries of Defence and External Affairs. Yet another front-page report in TOI, based on an article, which was to appear in *Jane's Defence Weekly* stated that according to a senior Pakistani weapons scientist, Pakistani military commanders had discussed pre-emptive nuclear strikes against India and had drawn up a list of cities and military installations to be targeted. The report added that their "demonic first use plans so shocked the nuclear scientist, that in protest he defected with four colleagues earlier this month...."[274] Another speculative report quoted an innocuous piece from *The Washington Post* that according to a former US marine, the US had conducted a secret military exercise two years earlier, whereby it had incapacitated the computers of the two countries, "preventing a possible nuclear war" between them.[275]

A front page report in IE (29 June) citing the *Sunday Observer* also quoted the Pakistani 'scientist' in its report, "Pak considered nuclear strike against India." Numerous other articles appeared in all the three newspapers focusing on Pakistan's nuclear and missile capabilities and future plans, a large number of them quoting select western sources. Headlines of these reports speak for themselves. Those in TH included, "N-warheads for Ghauri?" (31 May), "Pak set to test fire medium range missile" (2 June), "Pak to begin producing M-11 missiles next year?" (6 June, citing *The Washington Post)*, "Pak missiles tipped with N-warheads" (11 June).[276] Referring to the report by the Parliamentary Standing Committee on Defence with reference to Pakistan's missile programme, TH report stated: "Develop entire range of missiles, Govt. urged" (10 July).

A report in IE referred to the second test flights of both Agni as well as Ghauri. However, the headlines read, "Pakistan readying for second launch of Ghauri" (1 June). Other headlines in IE included: "Delhi could be hit in 4 minutes" (31 May), "Pak set to testfire Shaheen-I" (2 June), "Pak has deployed N-arms on border" (quoting defected Pak nuclear scientist on ABC TV, 2 July), and Ajit Bhattacharjea's, "Pak defector's nuclear 'revelations': A taste of fears to come" (20 July).

TOI headlines included the front-page reports citing *The New York Times*, "Pak readies for another missile launch" (1 June) and citing *The Washington Times* in "Pak may use N-arms first" (3 June). Other reports, some of them on the front pages, included "Pakistan set to test-fire medium range missile" (2 June), "Pak scientists bare N-attack plan on India: 5 arms experts defect in disgust" (29 June, citing *Jane's Defence Weekly*), "China giving missile aid to Pak: US" (15 July), and "Pakistan being helped to develop missiles with N-warheads: report" (21 July, citing the Ministry of Defence Report).

## Reflecting International Reactions

A study of front page reports, particularly the headlines of the various papers, during the first few days after India's tests, finds that criticism of the tests by the international community was well reflected in all papers. Particular emphasis was placed on the reactions of the United States and the counter responses.[277] However, although international criticism by other countries as well as international bodies and individuals were reported, these were downplayed by way of headlines, placement and size. On the other hand supportive reports were found on the front pages with striking headlines.[278] Often, while the text of reports noted the criticism by other countries, the headlines were deceptive. For instance, criticism and protests by Nepal were sidelined in TH headlines, "Narayanan's visit to boost bilateral ties" (TH, 28 May), "Pak N-test expected: KRN" (IE, 29 May) etc, diverting the focus of attention of the reader.

In the aftermath of Pakistan's nuclear tests, the Indian press was again deluged with reports of international reactions to Pakistan's tests.

Interestingly, where a particular report cited criticism of both India and Pakistan by international bodies, the criticism of Pakistan was directly quoted, whereas in the case of India, only the government's response to the criticism was stressed, or sometimes even mentioned, often ignoring the original critique. The front-page headlines of two reports in TH (1 June) read: "Pak told to avoid further tests" and "India 'regrets' Security Council remarks." Both reports, of course, referred to the UN Security Council statements, on the nuclear tests of both countries, but the framing of headlines may be noted. Anti-American belligerence was evident in most reporting with the added insinuation that the tests also reflected a defiance of the unequal global non-proliferation regime. The headlines of IE editorial, "Bill, the selective bully: Pokharan explodes the great American pretence" speaks for itself. The text elaborated that international criticism was

> a display of vacuous morality wrapped in economic punishment. India doesn't deserve this, this vindictive diplomacy of demonisation.... Islamic fundamentalism doesn't deny Saudi Arabia a privileged place in the American parlour. Oh., there are quite a few bastards over there, but listen to the Voice of America – they are 'our own bastards'. This is the moral illusion of the only superpower. This illusion can put India alongside such despicable dictatorships like Iraq and North Korea.[279]

Post-Chagai headlines and reporting revealed a change in the thrust of reports relating to the United States reactions, as was evident in the toned down headlines,[280] and a tendency to deflect criticism against

India to Pakistan. This deflection of criticism had been evident to some extent even before the Chagai tests. The headlines of a news report in TH (18 May) had read: "US warns Pak of serious consequences." However, the text had also quoted US National Security Adviser Sandy Berger that *India's* (emphasis added) testing was one of misguided nationalism and that the BJP government was involved in a deliberate campaign of deception that went beyond policy pronouncements. Similarly, a few days later, a report which included a sharp American critique of Indian tests, an enumeration of its incentives to Pakistan and possible action if Pakistan tested, also quoted Secretary of State Madeline Albright as stating that India's actions reflected a reckless disregard for world opinion and for India's own reputation. The leaders of India were accused of having made a grave historical error! However, the report was headlined, "US keen to respond to Pak concerns."[281] The IE report (1 June) on Kofi Annan's deploration of both the Indian and Pakistani tests bore the headlines, "Annan deplores Pak test." On the other hand TOI editorial considered the UNSC resolution debate condemning the Indian and Pakistani nuclear tests as revealing the extent to which the world was frustrated by the failure of the five permanent members to disarm.[282] The statements by various countries and organisations including Afghanistan, Saudi Arabia and the Arab League, expressing solidarity with Pakistan, and empathising with its rationale for testing found no reflection in the Indian press.[283]

## Options for the Future: Reflections in the Media

During this period there was a general tendency in the press to project India as taking initiatives towards détente, while Pakistan dithered. While there were calls to build a consensus in India on signing the CTBT, Pakistan was projected to be in the process of being coerced into signing the CTBT. In early May, prior to India's nuclear tests, K.Subrahmanyam maintained that Nawaz Sharif's offer of a pact with India for a South Asia free of weapons of mass destruction in the wake of the Ghauri missile test "cannot exactly inspire confidence-building. On the contrary, it creates fresh doubts about his own credibility."[284] In a front page article immediately after the Indian tests, Subrahmanyam opined that "India should immediately declare a no-first-use policy and invite China, Russia and Pakistan to come together in a joint no-first-use declaration...."[285] The following day's editorial in TOI, "The day after," reflected this call for the conclusion of a no-first-use agreement. In a lead article in TOI on 14 May, Subrahmanyam reiterated: "Pokhran-II and after: begin a no-first use campaign." The paper's editorials over the next few days, particularly those of 15, 20 and 23 May seemed to do just that.[286]

Interestingly, on 22 May, TH quoted Brajesh Mishra in the front page report, "India declares moratorium on nuclear testing: offers no first use pact to Pakistan." Similarly, the Congress-I General Secretary, Madhav Rao Scindia, talking to TOI on the nuclear tests proposed that "on the lines suggested by defence expert K.Subrahmanyam, we should call an Asian summit to work out a No-first-use treaty in which India, Russia, China and Pakistan should participate."[287] The entire text of a statement by Roshni Mayur, Director, International Institute for Sustainable Future, Mumbai was published in a two-column fourteen-centimetre report in TH, in which she concluded that India should now "let it be known that it cannot be bullied. India should become the defender of the rights of all the nations of world, including those which cannot have any nuclear weapons or even the basic defence."[288] However, editorials in TH did call for constructive diplomacy "to ensure that the gains from Monday's tests outweigh the costs."[289] "If the Government does not immediately embark on this course of constructive diplomacy, the strategic gains from the nuclear tests might not ultimately be worth the political and diplomatic costs."[290]

Similarly, IE editorialised on 18 May that "in the canon of deterrence, the point of acquiring nuclear weapons capability is to create a situation where it does not have to be used."[291] After Pakistan's nuclear tests, IE editorialised on the need "to convey effectively to Islamabad the importance of entering into no-first-use and other confidence building agreements. The siege mentality in Pakistan is not conducive to such a process."[292] A TOI editorial called on Islamabad to

> realise that with explicit mutual nuclear deterrence having been acknowledged between the two countries, steps towards détente are a must... It would be very helpful if the US, Russia, Germany and China would communicate their own experiences to the Pakistani leadership on how to turn the mutual deterrent situation into one of détente and cooperation.[293]

It is interesting to note the underlying implication of Pakistan's leadership obstructing détente despite the fact that a news report on the same day read, "Pak ready to talk N-stabilisation" and another, two days earlier had read, "Sharif invites Vajpayee for talks."[294] On 2 June, TH report, "Pak ready for talks with India: Sharif" was found on page 13. However, a front-page report in TH on 4 June quoted India's Foreign Office spokesman that "India reiterates offer of talks to defuse tension". Furthermore, on 5 June, the report, "India ready for talks with Pak, says PM" was found on the front page. TH also had the report, "PM seeks stable structure of cooperation with Pak" on the front page, while the report "Sharif ready to discuss N-stabilisation steps," was relegated to page 11 (9 June). IE in a five column front-page report, quoting Prime Minister Vajpayee, stated, "Third party mediation on Kashmir issue ruled out: India for early talks with Pakistan," while a similar statement by Nawaz Sharif in the report "N-stabilisation: Pak ready for talks with India" was relegated to a three column report on page 11.[295] In the context of Pakistan's declaration of moratorium on nuclear testing, IE editorial ironically declared that it was an "unexpected but nevertheless a logical consequence of India's own declaration of a voluntary moratorium on tests a week ago."[296]

IE, citing *Jane's Defence Weekly*, quoted from the letter to Kofi Annan by Pakistan's Ambassador to the United Nations, calling for a Nuclear-Weapon-Free Zone in South Asia, a joint Indo-Pak declaration renouncing the acquisition and manufacture of nuclear weapons, mutual inspections by India and Pakistan of each other's nuclear facilities, a simultaneous adherence to the NPT, simultaneous acceptance of full scope safeguards by the IAEA and a bilateral/regional nuclear test ban treaty. The report stated that this was "the first time that Pakistan has outlined concrete proposals for a bilateral or multilateral dialogue on nuclear issues."[297] However, the headlines did not reflect any such importance. It read "Pak asks UN to appoint special representative for Kashmir." TH, while reporting "Pak agrees to talks on FMCT" (quoting Pakistan's Ambassador to the UN) included a subheading, "US prodded Pak to soften stance," which stated that Pakistan agreed to end opposition to commencement of negotiations on FMCT "after the US signalled that it would not block resumption of talks between Islamabad and the IMF on resuming its economic assistance programme."[298] In July, Subrahmanyam stated in TOI: "While India has offered a mutual no-first-use agreement and there is a considerable body of opinion in this country advocating an uncaveated unilateral declaration of no-first-use, Pakistan has declared its inability to accept that offer."[299]

## Comprehensive Test Ban Treaty (CTBT)

Immediately after India's tests, the Vajpayee government indicated its willingness to adhere to some of the undertakings in CTBT and participate in negotiations on FMCT.[300] C. Raja Mohan in his piece, "Time for Indo-US nuclear dialogue," argued that the tests opened more flexibility in India's approach to the CTBT, FMCT and the non-proliferation regime (TH, 19 May). Mohan also argued that some of India's key objections to the CTBT such as its scope and India's national security considerations had now been met by its own testing of five nuclear devices. The treaty could still be questioned for absence of a strong linkage to disarmament. Mohan points out that it should not be impossible for New Delhi to separate its campaign for disarmament from the signature on the CTBT. Besides, acceding to the CTBT could certainly help limit some of the political and economic costs that India has incurred by the series of nuclear tests it had undertaken.[301] The paper, in its front-page report on the Prime Minister's statement in the Lok Sabha wrote, "India willing to sign no-first-use agreement: PM offers to move towards CTBT" (28 May).

A similar trajectory can be seen in IE, with a front page headline on 13 May reading, "Sign CTBT now and without conditions: US." The paper editorialised on the same day: "Now, at this turning point, the government must act with dispatch to capitalise on the event, or lose the initiative forever.... Now, it should sign the CTBT unconditionally, avoid sanctions and regain the moral high ground, which it may soon be in danger of losing."[302] TOI editorialised that the government "needs to do a lot of homework to persuade the people at large that signing the CTBT now would not be as disadvantageous to India as it was earlier...."[303] After Pakistan's nuclear tests, IE editorialised on the need to formulate a clear Indian position on the CTBT and related arms control issues, none of which "will come about if political parties on both sides allow partisan agendas to blur their vision. The country demands a consensus on nuclear policy and all of them better work hard and honestly at achieving it some time soon."[304] In a revealing analysis in TH, C.Raja Mohan observed that in many ways India's nuclear tests had made it easier to conclude a nuclear understanding with the United States. Without the tests to establish the credibility of its nuclear deterrence, New Delhi would have found it impossible to reconsider its past opposition to the Comprehensive Test Ban Treaty. In short, Mohan argues that by formally declaring itself a nuclear weapon power, India had found a badly needed flexibility in approaching the global non-proliferation regime.[305] Mohan also pointed out that the American decision

> to move first in the proposed deal would remove the current cloud of coercion over the Indo-US dialogue, bring the US in line with the other great powers that have

> refused to impose sanctions, and give enough room for New Delhi to convince the Indian public opinion on the benefits of cooperating with the global non-proliferation regime.[306]

An editorial in TH two days later stated that by its "waiver action, Washington can help the Vajpayee Government to evolve a consensus in favour of the CTBT. The political opposition to the reversal of the Indian position needs to be convinced of the long-term benefits of global cooperation."[307] Justifying this turnabout in India's policy, Muchkund Dubey contended that India had decided not to be a party to the CTBT in 1996 because it thought that it may have to carry out a few nuclear weapon tests in the interest of its security. This principal purpose seemed to have been served with the 1998 tests and the determination of India's scientists. This was all that was needed to develop a minimum nuclear deterrent.[308]

Pakistan's inclination to also sign the CTBT was projected by the press as being the result of pressure by the IMF and western countries. TOI in its report (13 July), "Pakistan ready to negotiate CTBT," referred to Nawaz Sharif's expression of willingness to negotiate on signing the CTBT. It contended that Sharif's comments on the CTBT "came amidst media reports that an International Monetary Fund (IMF) delegation, which was here a few days back, had indirectly told the Pakistani leadership to sign CTBT for the resumption of the US $1.56 billion loan which has been suspended under pressure from the G-8 countries after the nuclear tests."[309] Other reports in TH read, "Pak vulnerable to pressure on CTBT" (TH, 7 July), "Pak preparing ground for signing CTBT" (TH, 9 July), and "Pak offer on CTBT" (TH, 10 July). The press clearly rallied around the government on the question of signing the CTBT.

## Nuclear Build-Up

Some of the headlines after Pokhran-II read, "Weaponisation is next logical step for India" (which, in fact, referred to Pramod Mahajan's references to weaponisation, TOI, 16 May), "India's warfare capability should not be reduced" (which cited an IDSA seminar, TOI, 24 May) and "Despite constraints military preparedness is imperative" (which was again a report on public opinion, TOI, 14 May). J.N.Dixit pointed out in IE: "We should not deal with the tests as an end in themselves but proceed to make the capacity we have attained deployable both in terms of weaponisation and delivery systems. There is no need to be paranoid or defensive."[310] After Pakistan's nuclear tests also, several reports reflected the call for a nuclear build up, some such including, "India will not reverse its nuclear programme: PM" (TH, 13 July), "India should weaponise N-capability: J.N.Dixit," quoting the former Foreign Secretary that India should develop missiles, delivery systems and command and control systems (TH, 29 June). A report in TH quoted Air Commodore Jasjit Singh, the Director of IDSA that

> India should develop a small nuclear arsenal of around three dozen nuclear warheads, induct intermediate range ballistic missiles but should deploy its deterrent capability only if necessary.... The low cost 'recessed deterrence' which involves keeping nuclear arms in a 'non-weaponised' state should be India's interim response to its security threats.... More missiles than warheads were required and should be produced at a

faster pace. Besides, India needed to carry 'significantly greater number of tests in the coming months and years'.[311]

Another report quoted Bharat Karnad, Research Professor, Centre for Policy Research, that India should conduct more nuclear tests (TOI, 15 June). Two weeks later, he was again quoted as stating that an anti-ballistic missile system was a must for India (TOI, 30 June). A lead article in TH by C.Raja Mohan contended that "India needs to proceed rapidly to complete the development of a medium range missile which is the missing link in its proposed minimum nuclear deterrent."[312] A few weeks later, Mohan reiterated that given the fact that China and North Korea had already transferred a wide range of missiles and the capacity to produce them to Pakistan, "there is no way India, that relies on its own capabilities will agree to forgo the testing of its new generation missiles."[313]

M.Guruswamy in a lead article in IE, argued vociferously on how to make India's deterrent credible. He called for "a range of warheads and delivery systems to match all situations and be a convincing deterrent."[314] Similarly, Muchkund Dubey, in a lead article in TOI, wrote: "If the weapons programme is indeed frozen, then it will be a vindication of those who have alleged that the BJP government carried out the tests as a bravado for narrow partisan purposes...."[315] A few weeks later, he again pointed out that the United States must understand that having crossed the Rubicon, no government in power in India could afford not to proceed further and complete the programme that had been undertaken. "The Indian people will regard any hesitation as a betrayal of the trust reposed in the government and as a grave compromise of national security interest."[316] TOI in an editorial observed that India could not accept restrictions on further missile testing, weaponisation and deployment. The production of Agni had to go on, especially in view of Washington's disinclination to delay the continuing nuclear and missile technology cooperation between China and Pakistan in violation of the NPT and missile technology control regime.[317]

In stark contrast, the lead article of the day by Praful Bidwai entitled, "Regaining nuclear sanity: no tests, no bombs, ever" (TOI, 6 June), argued that there must be "no weaponisation and no tests. India must give a no-use-ever assurance. If New Delhi wants to contribute to abolition, it should jointly offer with Pakistan complete suspension of nuclear and missile preparations for, say five years, during which the P-5 agree to reduce their arsenals by one-half or more."[318] TOI in an editorial two days later, however, stated that until the nuclear powers move towards disarmament, "the world will have to live with Indian and Pakistani nuclear weapons and perhaps with the weapons of others as well." [319]

## Of Nuclear Tests and Media-Government Interface

The role of the press during the period of the nuclear tests was most explicitly underlined by Prime Minister Vajpayee himself during a speech in Kozhikode, Kerala on 18 May where he stated that the Indian media, "rising to the occasion, played a very positive and creative role in communicating the idea associated with the tests...."[320] Similarly, when asked by the press whether the tests were intended for the greater glory of the BJP, Brajesh Mishra replied: "If you are not concerned with security you could say that. And from the manner in which the Indian media has reported and 'analysed' the event and its fallout it appears that we are all very concerned with 'national security'."[321] Equally revealing was the statement of the Small and Medium Newspapers Guild of India and Association of Newspapers and Editors hailing the government for the tests, saying that the 'bold and timely' act fulfilled the nation's overdue need for self-defence and security.[322] Ironically IE in its editorial of 20 May, stressed the need for media management to turn the situation to India's advantage:

> Like it or not, in this age of media marketing a decision through it is as important as the decision itself, if it is to have much chance of appreciation or at least understanding. For that to happen, a clinical focus on getting the message across is essential.... The government did not use the international media smartly enough at the outset to explain India's decision to go openly nuclear. But putting Jaswant Singh behind the mike is reason to hope that it now knows what to do.[323]

Prabhu Chawla, then editor of the news magazine *India Today* explained the relationship between the media and the Government in this context.

> Rarely in recent times have scribes covering the PMO and the Ministry of External Affairs been wined and dined in the manner that the movers and shakers of the BJP-led coalition have been doing. The sumptuous meals were accompanied by an overdose of India's nuclear case.... The hidden agenda behind this excessive interaction with the fourth estate: to change Atal Behari Vajpayee's image from that of an indecisive

prime minister to an assertive chief executive....[324]

## Reviewing the Content Analysis of 1998

The content analysis of the three newspapers during this crucial period of the subcontinent's nuclear history, reveals that while opinions reinforcing the dominant discourse were found on the opinion pages, and were well cited in headlines and news reports in the other pages of the newspapers as well, negating stances by way of comparison were visible largely in the opinion pages. Table 4.7 provides a detailed analysis of the orientations of opinion page articles, news reports and news analyses referring to Pakistan's nuclear programme. The glaring hiatus between the number of news reports reinforcing Indian government positions (52.8 per cent) and those negating the same (13.8 per cent) may be particularly noted. In the case of opinion page articles, the reinforcing stance constituted 46 per cent while the negating, 30.2 per cent. (For similar details regarding the orientation of news reports and opinion page articles on nuclear issues in the subcontinent not taken into account here, see Table 4.8).

The formation of "Journalists Against Nuclear Weapons"[325] soon after the nuclear tests and also the writings of journalists like C.Rammanohar Reddy (in the context of these three newspapers) reveal the existence of voices of dissent within the journalistic community itself, reinforced by columnists and writers including Praful Bidwai and Achin Vanaik. But the magnitude of articles by pronounced nuclear hawks such as K.Subrahmanyam, C.Raja Mohan, M.D.Nalapat, Manvendra Singh, K.K.Katyal, S.Gurumurthy, and former Foreign Service officials

**Table 4.7 : Orientation of Opinion Page Articles and News Reports Referring to Pakistan's Nuclear Programme: 1 May to 31 July 1998**

| Category | MAY | | | TOTAL | JUNE | | | TOTAL | JULY | | | TOTAL | TOTAL | | | TOTAL |
|---|---|---|---|---|---|---|---|---|---|---|---|---|---|---|---|---|
| | TO1 | IE | TH | | TOI | IE | TH | | TOI | IE | TH | | TOI | IE | TH | |
| **Opinion Page Articles** | | | | | | | | | | | | | | | | |
| Reinforcing | 6 (75.0) | 2 (66.7) | 3 (42.8) | 11 (61.1) | 4 (66.7) | 5 (41.7) | 2 (25.0) | 11 (42.3) | 2 (50.0) | - | 5 (45.4) | 7 (36.8) | 12 (66.7) | 7 (36.8) | 10 (38.5) | 29 (46.0) |
| Negating | 2 (25.0) | 1 (33.3) | 2 (28.6) | 5 (27.8) | 2 (33.3) | 4 (33.3) | 3 (37.5) | 9 (34.6) | 2 (50.0) | 1 (25.0) | 2 (18.2) | 5 (26.4) | 6 (33.3) | 6 (31.6) | 7 (26.9) | 19 (30.2) |
| Mixed | - | - | 2 (28.6) | 2 (11.1) | - | 3 (25.0) | 3 (37.5) | 6 (23.1) | - | 3 (75.0) | 4 (36.4) | 7 (36.8) | - | 6 (31.6) | 9 (34.6) | 15 (23.8) |
| **TOTAL** | **8** | **3** | **7** | **18** | **6** | **12** | **8** | **26** | **4** | **4** | **11** | **19** | **18** | **19** | **26** | **63** |
| **News Reports and Analyses** | | | | | | | | | | | | | | | | |
| Descriptive | 14 (16.1) | 30 (34.1) | 49 (32.0) | 93 (28.4) | 12 (16.7) | 5 (8.3) | 34 (28.8) | 51 (20.4) | 9 (23.7) | 13 (35.2) | 30 (29.7) | 52 (29.5) | 35 (17.8) | 48 (25.9) | 113 (30.3) | 196 (26.0) |
| Reinforcing | 60 (69.0) | 44 (50.0) | 70 (45.8) | 174 (53.0) | 46 (63.8) | 44 (73.4) | 52 (44.1) | 142 (56.8) | 21 (55.2) | 15 (40.5) | 46 (45.5) | 82 (46.7) | 127 (64.5) | 103 (55.7) | 168 (45.2) | 398 (52.8) |
| Negating | 11 (12.6) | 10 (11.4) | 17 (11.1) | 38 (11.6) | 12 (16.7) | 6 (10.0) | 21 (17.8) | 39 (15.6) | 6 (15.8) | 4 (10.8) | 17 (16.8) | 27 (15.3) | 29 (14.7) | 20 (10.8) | 55 (14.8) | 104 (13.8) |
| Mixed | 2 (2.3) | 4 (4.5) | 17 (11.1) | 23 (7.0) | 2 (2.8) | 5 (8.3) | 11 (9.3) | 18 (7.2) | 2 (5.3) | 5 (13.5) | 8 (8.0) | 15 (8.5) | 6 (3.0) | 14 (7.6) | 36 (9.7) | 56 (7.4) |
| **TOTAL** | **87** | **88** | **153** | **328** | **72** | **60** | **118** | **250** | **38** | **37** | **101** | **176** | **197** | **185** | **372** | **754** |

* (a) TOI: *The Times of India* (Mumbai), IE: *The Indian Express* (Kochi), TH: *The Hindu* (Thiruvananthapuram)

(b) Figures in brackets indicate percentage of the column-wise total.

**Table 4.8 : Orientation of Opinion Page Articles and News Reports Relating to Nuclear Issues in South Asia: 1 May to 31 July 1998**

| *Category* | *MAY* | | | *TOTAL* | *JUNE* | | | *TOTAL* | *JULY* | | | *TOTAL* | *TOTAL* | | | *TOTAL* |
|---|---|---|---|---|---|---|---|---|---|---|---|---|---|---|---|---|
| | *TO1* | *IE* | *TH* | | *TOI* | *IE* | *TH* | | *TOI* | *IE* | *TH* | | *TOI* | *IE* | *TH* | |
| **Opinion Page Articles** | | | | | | | | | | | | | | | | |
| Reinforcing | 5 | 11 | 8 | 24 | 4 | 3 | 5 | 12 | 5 | 3 | 2 | 10 | 14 | 17 | 15 | 46 |
| | (41.7) | (61.1) | (66.6) | (57.1) | (57.1) | (33.3) | (35.7) | (40.0) | (62.5) | (75.0) | (33.3) | (55.5) | (51.9) | (54.9) | (46.8) | (51.1) |
| Negating | 3 | 5 | 2 | 10 | 3 | 4 | 8 | 15 | 2 | - | 1 | 3 | 8 | 9 | 11 | 28 |
| | (25.0) | (27.8) | (16.7) | (23.9) | (42.9) | (44.5) | (57.2) | (50.0) | (25.0) | | (16.7) | (16.7) | (29.6) | (29.0) | (34.4) | (31.1) |
| Mixed | 4 | 2 | 2 | 8 | - | 2 | 1 | 3 | 1 | 1 | 3 | 5 | 5 | 5 | 6 | 16 |
| | (33.3) | (11.1) | (16.7) | (19.0) | | (22.2) | (7.1) | (10.0) | (12.5) | (25.0) | (50.0) | (27.8) | (18.5) | (16.1) | (18.8) | (17.8) |
| **TOTAL** | **12** | **18** | **12** | **42** | **7** | **9** | **14** | **30** | **8** | **4** | **6** | **18** | **27** | **31** | **32** | **90** |
| **News Reports & Analyses** | | | | | | | | | | | | | | | | |
| Descriptive | 19 | 19 | 61 | 99 | 5 | 5 | 12 | 22 | 3 | 6 | 19 | 28 | 27 | 30 | 92 | 149 |
| | (10.8) | (12.3) | (27.1) | (17.8) | (8.6) | (13.2) | (14.1) | (12.2) | (11.1) | (20.7) | (24.1) | (20.7) | (10.4) | (13.5) | (23.6) | (17.1) |
| Reinforcing | 102 | 95 | 105 | 302 | 37 | 24 | 52 | 113 | 19 | 17 | 44 | 80 | 158 | 136 | 201 | 495 |
| | (58.3) | (61.3) | (46.7) | (54.4) | (63.8) | (63.1) | (61.2) | (62.4) | (70.4) | (58.6) | (55.7) | (59.3) | (60.8) | (61.3) | (51.7) | (56.8) |
| Negating | 32 | 28 | 38 | 98 | 12 | 5 | 16 | 33 | 4 | 1 | 11 | 16 | 48 | 34 | 65 | 147 |
| | (18.3) | (18.0) | (16.9) | (17.7) | (20.7) | (13.2) | (18.8) | (18.2) | (14.8) | (3.5) | (13.9) | (11.9) | (18.4) | (15.3) | (16.7) | (16.9) |
| Mixed | 22 | 13 | 21 | 56 | 4 | 4 | 5 | 13 | 1 | 5 | 5 | 11 | 27 | 22 | 31 | 80 |
| | (12.6) | (8.4) | (9.3) | (10.1) | (6.9) | (10.5) | (5.9) | (7.2) | (3.7) | (17.2) | (6.3) | (8.1) | (10.4) | (9.9) | (8.0) | (9.2) |
| **TOTAL** | **175** | **155** | **225** | **555** | **58** | **38** | **85** | **181** | **27** | **29** | **79** | **135** | **260** | **222** | **389** | **871** |

* (a) TOI: *The Times of India* (Mumbai), IE: *The Indian Express* (Kochi), TH: *The Hindu* (Thiruvananthapuram)
(b) Figures in brackets indicate percentage of the column-wise total.
(c) Figures do not include reports specifically referring to Pakistan's nuclear programme, for which see Table 4.7.

such as J.N.Dixit, Muchkund Dubey and M. K. Rasgotra leaves no doubt where the balance lay. Table 4.9 identifies the authors of opinion page articles on issues regarding Pakistan's nuclear policy. It may be seen that articles by the strategic community and professional writers and columnists constituted 57.2 per cent of the total number. The backgrounds of those few writers who could not be identified have been included in the 'other' category. The statistics may be viewed keeping this in mind. It should also be specifically noted that the figures reflect those articles that appeared only in the editorial pages. However, most of those who belong to the strategic community are prolific writers who are also given space in the other pages of the newspapers, weighing down the balance of opinion even further. (Similar details for the other items relating to nuclear issues in the subcontinent not referring to Pakistan may be found in Table 4.10).

Although editorial analyses have been referred to in previous pages, specific mention needs to be made regarding the trajectory of editorials on the issue. Table 4.11 provides a detailed statistical indication of the editorial orientations of the newspapers regarding articles referring to Pakistan's nuclear programme. While 67.6 per cent of the total editorials reinforced Indian government perspectives, only 5.4 per cent negated the same. (Statistics regarding the orientations of the other editorials on nuclearisation of South Asia may be found in Table 4.12).

All three newspapers were unanimous in their praise of India's tests, the exaggeration of a threat of nuclear instability by the West and the need to sign the CTBT. While TH was all praise for India's scientific triumph, justifying the inevitability of the tests for the country's nuclear capability as well as for independence

**Table 4.9 : By-lines of Opinion Page Articles Referring to Pakistan's Nuclear Programme: 1 May to 31 July 1998**

| *Category* | *MAY* | | | *TOTAL* | *JUNE* | | | *TOTAL* | *JULY* | | | *TOTAL* | *TOTAL* | | | *TOTAL* |
|---|---|---|---|---|---|---|---|---|---|---|---|---|---|---|---|---|
| | *TO1* | *IE* | *TH* | | *TOI* | *IE* | *TH* | | *TOI* | *IE* | *TH* | | *TOI* | *IE* | *TH* | |
| Retired Civil Servants and Members of strategic think tanks | 4 (50.0) | - | 3 (42.8) | 7 (38.9) | 2 (33.3) | 2 (16.7) | 1 (12.5) | 5 (19.2) | 1 (25.0) | 1 (25.0) | 1 (9.0) | 3 (15.8) | 7 (38.9) | 3 (15.8) | 5 (19.2) | 15 (23.9) |
| Columnists and Professional Writers | 2 (25.0) | 1 (33.3) | 2 (28.6) | 5 (27.8) | 2 (33.4) | 3 (25.0) | 5 (62.5) | 10 (38.5) | - | 2 (50.0) | 4 (36.4) | 6 (31.6) | 4 (22.2) | 6 (31.6) | 11 (42.3) | 21 (33.3) |
| Academics | - | - | 1 (14.3) | 1 (5.5) | 2 (33.3) | - | - | 2 (7.7) | - | - | 3 (27.3) | 3 (15.8) | 2 (11.1) | - | 4 (15.4) | 6 (9.5) |
| Others | 2 (25.0) | 2 (66.7) | 1 (14.3) | 5 (27.8) | - | 7 (58.3) | 2 (25.0) | 9 (34.6) | 3 (75.0) | 1 (25.0) | 3 (27.3) | 7 (36.8) | 5 (27.8) | 10 (52.6) | 6 (23.1) | 21 (33.3) |
| **TOTAL** | **8** | **3** | **7** | **18** | **6** | **12** | **8** | **26** | **4** | **4** | **11** | **19** | **18** | **19** | **26** | **63** |

* (a) TOI: *The Times of India* (Mumbai), IE: *The Indian Express* (Kochi), TH: *The Hindu* (Thiruvananthapuram)

(b) Figures in brackets indicate percentage of the column-wise total.

**Table 4.10 : By-lines of Opinion Page Articles Relating to Nuclear Issues in South Asia: 1 May to 31 July 1998**

| *Category* | *MAY* | | | *TOTAL* | *JUNE* | | | *TOTAL* | *JULY* | | | *TOTAL* | *TOTAL* | | | *TOTAL* |
|---|---|---|---|---|---|---|---|---|---|---|---|---|---|---|---|---|
| | *TO1* | *IE* | *TH* | | *TOI* | *IE* | *TH* | | *TOI* | *IE* | *TH* | | *TOI* | *IE* | *TH* | |
| Retired Civil Servants and Members of strategic think tanks | 2 (16.7) | 2 (11.1) | 3 (25.0) | 7 (16.7) | 1 (14.3) | 4 (44.5) | 2 (14.3) | 7 (23.3) | 2 (25.0) | 2 (50.0) | 2 (33.3) | 6 (33.3) | 5 (18.5) | 8 (25.8) | 7 (21.9) | 20 (22.2) |
| Columnists and Professional Writers | 3 (25.0) | 8 (44.4) | 5 (41.7) | 16 (38.1) | 3 (42.9) | 2 (22.2) | 5 (35.7) | 10 (33.3) | 1 (12.5) | 2 (50.0) | 1 (16.7) | 4 (22.2) | 7 (25.9) | 12 (38.7) | 11 (34.4) | 30 (33.3) |
| Academics | 1 (8.3) | 1 (5.6) | 1 (8.3) | 3 (7.1) | 1 (14.3) | 2 (22.2) | 6 (42.9) | 9 (30.0) | 2 (25.0) | - | 1 (16.7) | 3 (16.7) | 4 (14.8) | 3 (9.7) | 8 (25.0) | 15 (16.7) |
| Others | 6 (50.0) | 7 (38.9) | 3 (25.0) | 16 (38.1) | 2 (28.5) | 1 (11.1) | 1 (7.1) | 4 (13.4) | 3 (37.5) | - | 2 (33.3) | 5 (27.8) | 11 (40.8) | 8 (25.8) | 6 (18.7) | 25 (27.8) |
| **TOTAL** | **12** | **18** | **12** | **42** | **7** | **9** | **14** | **30** | **8** | **4** | **6** | **18** | **27** | **31** | **32** | **90** |

* (a) TOI: *The Times of India* (Mumbai), IE: *The Indian Express* (Kochi), TH: *The Hindu* (Thiruvananthapuram)

(b) Figures in brackets indicate percentage of the columnwise total.

(c) Figures do not include reports specifically referring to Pakistan's nuclear programme, for which see Table 4.9.

**Table 4.11 : Orientation of Editorials Referring to Pakistan's Nuclear Programme: 1 May to 31 July 1998**

| *Orientation* | *MAY* | | | *TOTAL* | *JUNE* | | | *TOTAL* | *JULY* | | | *TOTAL* | *TOTAL* | | | *TOTAL* |
|---|---|---|---|---|---|---|---|---|---|---|---|---|---|---|---|---|
| | *TO1* | *IE* | *TH* | | *TOI* | *IE* | *TH* | | *TOI* | *IE* | *TH* | | *TOI* | *IE* | *TH* | |
| Reinforcing | 2 | 5 | 1 | 8 | 10 | 4 | - | 14 | 2 | - | 1 | 3 | 14 | 9 | 2 | 25 |
| | (50.0) | (100.0) | (25.0) | (61.5) | (90.9) | (100.0) | | (82.3) | (100.0) | | (33.3) | (42.9) | (82.3) | (81.8) | (22.2) | (67.6) |
| Negating | 1 | - | 1 | 2 | - | - | - | - | - | - | - | - | 1 | - | 1 | 2 |
| | (25.0) | | (25.0) | (15.4) | | | | | | | | | (5.9) | | (11.1) | (5.4) |
| Mixed | 1 | - | 2 | 3 | 1 | - | 2 | 3 | - | 2 | 2 | 4 | 2 | 2 | 6 | 10 |
| | (25.0) | | (50.0) | (23.1) | (9.1) | | (100.0) | (17.6) | | (100.0) | (66.7) | (57.1) | (11.8) | (18.2) | (66.7) | (27.0) |
| **TOTAL** | **4** | **5** | **4** | **13** | **11** | **4** | **2** | **17** | **2** | **2** | **3** | **7** | **17** | **11** | **9** | **37** |

* (a) TOI: *The Times of India* (Mumbai), IE: *The Indian Express* (Kochi), TH: *The Hindu* (Thiruvananthapuram)

(b) Figures in brackets indicate percentage of the column-wise total.

**Table 4.12 : Orientation of Editorials Relating to Nuclear Issues in South Asia: 1 May to 31 July 1998**

| Orientation | MAY | | | TOTAL | JUNE | | | TOTAL | JULY | | | TOTAL | TOTAL | | | TOTAL |
|---|---|---|---|---|---|---|---|---|---|---|---|---|---|---|---|---|
| | *TO1* | *IE* | *TH* | | *TOI* | *IE* | *TH* | | *TOI* | *IE* | *TH* | | *TOI* | *IE* | *TH* | |
| Reinforcing | 6 (54.5) | 15 (100.0) | 3 (75.0) | 24 (80.0) | 2 (50.0) | 5 (71.4) | 1 (33.3) | 8 (57.1) | 7 (100.0) | 1 (50.0) | 2 (50.0) | 10 (76.9) | 15 (68.2) | 21 (87.5) | 6 (54.5) | 42 (73.7) |
| Negating | 1 (9.1) | - | - | 1 (3.3) | - | - | - | - | - | - | 2 (50.0) | 2 (15.4) | 1 (4.5) | - | 2 (18.2) | 3 (5.2) |
| Mixed | 4 (36.4) | - | 1 (25.0) | 5 (16.7) | 2 (50.0) | 2 (28.6) | 2 (66.7) | 6 (42.9) | | 1 (50.0) | - | 1 (7.7) | 6 (27.3) | 3 (12.5) | 3 (27.3) | 12 (21.1) |
| TOTAL | 11 | 15 | 4 | 30 | 4 | 7 | 3 | 14 | 7 | 2 | 4 | 13 | 22 | 24 | 11 | 57 |

* (a) TOI: *The Times of India* (Mumbai), IE: *The Indian Express* (Kochi), TH: *The Hindu* (Thiruvananthapuram)

(b) Figures in brackets indicate percentage of the column-wise total.

(c) Figures do not include reports specifically referring to Pakistan's nuclear programme, for which see Table 4.11.

in a nuclear world, editorials became more restrained and nuanced after Pakistan's nuclear tests. This was also reflected in news reports. It criticised the handling of the fallout of the tests, particularly pointing out that it was the provocative statements of the government that led to Pakistan's nuclear tests. This was in stark contrast to the perspectives of the other two papers. It also called for a constructive engagement with Pakistan and the need to build public opinion on the benefits of signing the CTBT.

The IE on the other hand, was not only all praise for India's tests, but also applauded and encouraged Vajpayee on his every move and statement. News reports reflected this perspective. After India's tests IE projected their rationale to be one of enhanced international status. However, following Pakistan's nuclear tests, Sino-Pakistan nuclear collaboration was highlighted. Editorial opinion was that there was no need for Pakistan to retaliate with its own tests, as India's tests had not been aimed at it.

IE considered Nawaz Sharif to have unnecessarily over-reacted to India's tests. Pakistan's siege mentality was seen to have negative implications for dialogue in the region. After Pakistan's tests, editorials mirrored the Indian government's scepticism of its scientific claims.

In contrast to the other two papers, immediately after India's tests, a TOI editorial critically analysed the tests as having a negative impact on India's relations with its neighbours, and not having strengthened the country's security, in view of the fact that there were more important socio-economic issues to be dealt with. However, later editorials viewed India's nuclear capability as insurance in a world with nuclear weapons, and a source of stability for the region.

Following Pakistan's tests, the paper initially projected the Ghauri missile tests and A.Q.Khan's statements as the rationale for India's tests, while later stressing China's nuclear cooperation with Pakistan and US tacit connivance in the same. The tests were also seen as a continuation of India's nuclear policy and a source of pressure on the nuclear powers to disarm. Pakistan's tests were depicted as symbolising solidarity with India against this nuclear regime, but which also confirmed its clandestine nature and would have a negative impact on the region. In view of possible sanctions, an economically desperate Pakistan could possibly sell technology to the Islamic world, indulge itself in drug trade, as well as increase terrorist activities. While calling for consensus and bilateral talks, the editorials also called on the nuclear powers to guide Pakistan on détente. At the same time, they argued that India could not accept restrictions on missile testing, nuclearisation and deployment. This was a sharp about turn from its original stance. As noted earlier, TOI editorials need to be read in consonance with K.Subrahmanyam's articles in the same paper, which seemed to provide the cue.

## TRENDS IN POST-1998 COVERAGE

The reporting of nuclear issues by the Indian press in the post-1998 years revealed certain changes from the preceding years with regard to the coverage of nuclear issues in general as well as India's nuclear policy. Yet the basic trends in the coverage of Pakistan's nuclear policy in the earlier years continued unwaveringly. This needs to be seen in consonance with the changes in the 'spectrum of debate' in the dominant discourse. With regard to India's nuclear policy, the left parties in particular had taken up an openly critical stance against the nuclear weapons build up in the subcontinent. In contrast to earlier reporting/editorialising, *The Hindu* in the post 1998 period took up the cudgels against building up nuclear weapons capability. Editorialising on India's nuclear doctrine and the first meeting of the Nuclear Command Authority, which decided to develop India's weapons programme further, *The Hindu* warned that this would take the country another step down the dangerous path of acquiring and assembling weapons of mass destruction that will bring greater insecurity, rather than peace to South Asia. It pointed out:

> In the more than five years since India and then Pakistan, in that order, declared themselves nuclear weapon states, there has been no evidence that the acquisition of nuclear arms has strengthened security in South Asia. On the contrary, in the nuclear weapons era the two countries have fought, undeclared war (Kargil in 1999) and have come close to war on two subsequent occasions, in December 2001 (following the terrorist attack on Parliament) and in May 2002 (after the killings in an army camp near Jammu). On each occasion there was a heated exchange of words on the use of nuclear weapons. This game of brinkmanship could have spiralled into a nuclear holocaust in South Asia. India and Pakistan have provided proof, if it were needed that the so called theory of nuclear deterrence does not contribute to peace between countries.[326]

In June 2004, the paper again reiterated that "nuclear weapons in the hands of India and Pakistan have made the region a much more dangerous place," that only advocates of the discredited doctrine of deterrence will bother to contest.[327]

Similarly when India and the United States signed the civilian nuclear agreement, the stance of the press reflected the tendency to depict issues according to the 'spectrum of debate' in the dominant discourse.[328] The editorials of *The Hindu* prove to be a case in point. In its editorial "Starting all over" (6 March 2006), *The Hindu* argued: "Besides being rid of a crippling embargo on its nuclear power programme, India has been implicitly recognized as a nuclear weapons state by the US, a handsome achievement by any country." When the text of the civil nuclear cooperation agreement between the two countries was made public on 3 August 2007 the headlines of *The Hindu* editorial read "A sound and honourable 123" (6 August 2007). The opening lines clearly state:

> A close reading of the text of the civil nuclear cooperation agreement between the US and India, which was made public on August 3, confirms this newspaper's editorial endorsement of the deal. It is a sound and honourable agreement and the assurances provided to parliament by Prime Minister Manmohan Singh in 2006 have been fulfilled virtually in their entirety.

On 20 August 2007, Prakash Karat, General Secretary of the CPI(M) elaborated his arguments against the nuclear deal in his lead article in *The Hindu* entitled "Why the CPI(M) and the Left oppose the nuclear deal." The paper's editorial of the same day in its very headlines itself called out "Put the nuclear deal on hold." The editorial states that "the CPI(M) has made it clear that it has serious problems with some of the specifics of the 123 agreement read along with the Hyde

Act and has asked the government not to go ahead even with the next step towards operationalisation." The editorial proceeds to call on the government to heed this call pointing out: "Heavens will not fall if the 123 agreement is put on hold and all the issues opened up for discussion." Media perspectives clearly reflected the perspectives of the dominant discourse, with divergences in opinion within the dominant discourse being reflected in the mass media.

Media - government linkages on the nuclear issue were revealed in the most astounding statement by C.Raja Mohan, Strategic Affairs editor of *The Hindu,* in his book, *Crossing the Rubicon: The Shaping of India's New Foreign Policy.* Mohan wrote that his interviews with Jaswant Singh and Strobe Talbott were a carefully orchestrated effort by New Delhi and Washington to put out public signals of an accommodation on the CTBT and the lifting of sanctions. The Indian government had attempted to rally the possible signing of the CTBT.[329]

As far as the coverage of Pakistan's nuclear programme was concerned, the 'good nukes, bad nukes' frame of reporting continued unabated. The years 2002-2003 witnessed an international uproar over revelations that scientists from the Pakistan Atomic Energy Commission in a show of Islamic solidarity visited Osama bin Laden in Afghanistan. The Indian press, exploiting emotions on the 'war on terror', highlighted a possible threat from Pakistan's nuclear weapons falling into the hands of terrorist or fundamentalist groups.[330] Former Director of IDSA, Jasjit Singh cited reports from Washington in the *Financial Express* expressing "increasing concerns about the safety, security and control over Pakistani nuclear weapons .... Pakistan's nuclear weapons would be acquired and used by a terrorist group...."[331] An article in *The Tribune* argued that the close ties between some scientists working for the PAEC and radical Islamic groups were well known, and that there was an awful lot of Al Qaeda sympathy with Pakistan's nuclear programme.[332] Similarly, an article in *The Pioneer* entitled "Raid Pakistan, save the world" argued: "General Musharraf has openly blackmailed India by threatening to use nuclear weapons in a first strike. An effective solution would be the invasion of Pakistan before it uses the nuclear option or before its nuclear arsenal falls into the hands of terrorists."[333] Other such reports were headlined "Pakistan is the nuclear rogue" (*The Hindustan Times*, 21 October 2002), "Pakistan's nuclear bluff" (*The Pioneer*, 1 January 2003), etc. Anil Narendra, in "Pakistan's dirty nuclear secret" in *The Pioneer* (6 February 2004) points out that "what is worrying India is what if a Pakistani general or scientist decides to sell nuclear technology or weapons to Kashmiri terrorists.... With nuclear technology being illegally exported, it is time the West acted decisively against Pakistan."

This period also saw North Korea's admission that it had a secret uranium based nuclear weapons programme. This was seen to be a confirmation of Pakistan's role in the Korean programme. The Indian press seized the opportunity to highlight the North Korea-Pakistan alliance in the stereotypical mode, referring to Pakistan as a black marketeer. Prakash Nanda, quoting the *New York Times* wrote in the *Asian Age:*

> Both North Korea and Pakistan are 'natural allies'. Both happen to be essentially authoritarian states, with the military dominating their polities. Both are not

> reconciled to the existing states of the partitions of their mother countries.... And what is most important, their negotiating styles vis-à-vis the rest of the world are identical. The strategy is to extract maximum concessions and then dishonour your international commitments. Both the countries go on proliferating weapons of mass destruction (in Pakistan's case, also aiding and encouraging Islamic fundamentalists as terrorists) and then demand huge international assistance, monetary and otherwise in return for restraints.... In other words, both Pakistan and North Korea have excelled in blackmailing the rest of the world and demanding international attention, mainly because of their possession of missile power and nuclear expertise.[334]

Similarly, V.K.Grover pointed out in *The Pioneer* that "Pakistan's ties with North Korea have proved once again its perfidy and deceit.... Pakistan will neither stop supporting terrorism nor nuclear proliferation, be it to North Korea, Iran or the Saudis if they want it."[335] In this context *The Hindustan Times* in its editorial "Pakistan is the nuclear rogue" stated:

> Washington took India to task for years over its nuclear weapons programme - despite the largely indigenous nature of the programme and India's near perfect record on nuclear proliferation.... In the longer term, the US needs to recognize that Pakistan's manic search for a means to negate India's greater strength – a quest that has made it a nuclear proliferator, a

> supplicant of China and a terror incubator – has made it the world's ultimate rogue state.[336]

Pakistan was also criticised as being a 'nuclear blackmailer', after newly appointed Pakistan Ambassador to the United Nations Munir Khan allegedly stated that Pakistan would use nuclear weapons even in a conventional war.[337] Similarly C.Raja Mohan's call for 'Countering Pak's nuclear blackmail' (*The Hindu*, 1 January 2003) stated: "The time has come for India to move beyond this tentative exploration of missile defence options to a more robust effort that would involve early acquisition of a substantive national resource and development effort to create indigenous capabilities in missile defence technology." Reports of nine Pakistani nuclear scientists going missing during this period again saw the projection of a possible threat from nuclear weapons falling into the hands of fundamentalists. The 2003 disclosures that Pakistan, or more specifically – A.Q.Khan, was the source of nuclear weapons know-how for North Korea, Libya and Iran saw intense speculation in the Indian press. *The Hindu* editorialised: "Dr. Khan was one among several prominent Pakistanis who propagated the view that the nuclear arsenal had given the country a leading position in the Islamic world and that it was morally obliged to share some of its knowledge."[338]

In early 2004, Islamabad admitted that A.Q. Khan had been running a clandestine proliferation network that supplied countries such as Iran, Libya and North Korea with uranium enrichment ("without the knowledge of the government"). Khan allegedly developed the network through contacts cultivated while obtaining materials and equipment for Pakistan's nuclear programme. In a television appearance on 4

February 2004 A.Q.Khan admitted that during the past two decades he had secretly provided North Korea, Libya and Iran with crucial technology for making nuclear weapons. Khan apologized to the people of Pakistan for what he had done and was soon after pardoned by Musharraf. These developments witnessed an Indian media overdrive on A.Q.Khan.[339] Headlines screamed: "A Khan of Worms: Pakistan's nuclear strategy shaky" (*The Times of India,* 7 February 2004), "Fallout of Pakistan's nuclear proliferation" (*Financial Express*, 9 February 2004), "Pardon us, but Pakistan's slip is showing" (*The Times of India*, 11 February 2004), "Responding to Pakistan's proliferation" (*The Hindu*, 12 February 2004), "Pakistan's Nuclear bazaar" (*The Indian Express*, 19 February 2004), "Pakistan's dirty nuclear secrets" (*The Pioneer*, 6 February 2004), "Pakistan reviving nuclear black markets" (*Financial Express*, 16 March 2005).

These issues however need to be viewed in the larger context of the IAEA Chief's statement that A.Q.Khan was just the tip of an iceberg in a global black market that sold nuclear technology to Libya, Iran and North Korea.[340] Suppliers, scientists and engineers of France, Holland, Switzerland, Germany, etc. also allegedly helped sustain the international black market and supported A.Q.Khan's proliferation efforts to Iran and Libya. Over the years, Indian firms and retired members of the Indian scientific establishment were also accused of having a hand in this issue. For example, a retired Chairman of Nuclear Corporation of India was accused of acting in complicity with A.Q.Khan. In December 2005 the United States imposed sanctions on two Indian firms Sabero Organics Gujarat Limited and Sandhya Organics Limited under the US-Iran Proliferation Act 2000, relating to the transfer of chemicals to Iran. Again in July 2006, the United States imposed sanctions on two more Indian companies – Balaji Amines and Prachi Poly Products, for the same reasons. However the Indian press, with its fixation with the 'good nukes, bad nukes' framing, has always tended to give such issues short shrift while highlighting A.Q.Khan's activities. As T.Jayaraman points out "the tone of media comment in India on these developments has ranged from smug satisfaction to outright gloating at Pakistan's discomfiture."[341]

In 2005, China announced that it wanted to sell Pakistan two nuclear reactors. But the United States objected to this on grounds that it would violate the guidelines of the Nuclear Suppliers Group on the supply of nuclear goods to states that refuse to open all facilities to international inspections. During the period of negotiations between India and United States regarding the civilian nuclear deal, Pakistan also sought a similar agreement with the United States. Its efforts however proved unsuccessful. The Indian press gloated at Pakistan's failure in both issues, while highlighting its search for nuclear cooperation with other countries. Headlines read – "Neighbour's envy! Pak may seek China's help" (*Hindustan Times*, 3 March 2006), "Pak nuclear shopping spree in response to US-India deal?" (*The Times of India*, 4 January 2006), "Interested in buying nuclear reactors: Pak" (*The Times of India*, 6 January 2006), "No nuclear deal for Pakistan cooking says Rice" (*The Economic Times*, 3 March 2006). The press also took the opportunity to again present issues in the 'good nukes, bad nukes' frame, highlighting India as a responsible nuclear power in contrast to Pakistan. The *Financial Express* in its report "Bush rejects Pakistan's demand on nuclear deal" (3 May 2006) stated that "Washington has maintained that India is a responsible nuclear power in contrast to Pakistan's clandestine help in this sphere to some countries highlighted by the actions of its top scientists A.Q. Khan, now under house arrest."

The question of the safety of Pakistan's nuclear arsenal continues to be exploited by the Indian press at every opportunity be it international or national, as for example in the war against terror cited earlier. This was also reflected in the context of Benazir Bhutto's demise in December 2007, with headlines reading: "Dependent Pakistan: Desperate anxiety about Pak nuclear weapons" (Editorial, *The Statesman*, 29 December 2007), "How safe is Pakistan's nuclear arsenal?" (*The Tribune*, 28 January 2008). The basic framework of projecting a threat from a nuclear Pakistan continues unabated. Headlines still reflect the ongoing underlying general trend of reporting Pakistan's nuclear programme in the Indian press.

Thus, the general framework of media debate on the nuclear issue over the last six decades has reflected that of the dominant discourse. Focusing largely on peaceful uses and nuclear disarmament in the 1950s and 1960s, it changed stance since the 1970s towards a gradual justification of keeping the nuclear option open. Since the late 1970s there was an increased focus on Pakistan's nuclear programme and the threat of an 'Islamic' bomb, based particularly on western reports and statements of Pakistani scientists and leaders. These were reproduced and overemphasised in contrast to the sanitised depiction of India's own policy. There was an increased stress on Pakistan's 'clandestine' programme and its nuclear collaboration with China, providing detailed inventories of purchases and capabilities against Indian offensive and defensive systems. More than reports per se, it was their headlines and prominent display on front pages, which projected perceptions of threat. Early 1998 saw a media focus on Pakistan's missile programme with calls to keep the nuclear option open in the context of the Ghauri tests.

It is evident that while prior to Pokhran-II, the threat from Pakistan's missile programme and the need to meet the same was highlighted, the projection of India's nuclear tests in the press reflected government claims of having secured legitimate international status and scientific achievement based on consensus. A similar reflection was seen in the projection of the government's rationale of Sino-Pakistan nuclear interaction and the need to make the country's deterrent credible, besides the readiness to sign the CTBT. The emphasis of government perspectives in news reports also served to reinforce the same. This sanitised depiction of India's nuclear tests was in stark contrast to that of Pakistan's.

While the press emphasised the ridiculing of Pakistan's nuclear capability after Pokhran-II, projecting technological ineptitude as the sole reason for not testing, by late May, this metamorphosed into a focus on its international liaisons and clandestine basis, which could have provided it with proven technology. With the hyperbole surrounding Indian science having been exposed by the Chagai tests, the press turned to reflecting the scepticism of the number, yield and scientific value of these tests in contrast to India's indigenously successful programme. Simultaneously (excluding TH editorials) the perception of the Chagai tests as a vindication of India's assessment and policies were reinforced, albeit in a more subdued and nuanced manner. The tests were viewed as an unnecessary over-reaction or an act of solidarity against the international nuclear regime. The press also revelled in the negative reaction of other countries to Pakistan's nuclear tests, while deflecting that to its own, by way of selective reporting, placements and taking shelter behind innocuous headlines or those referring to Pakistan alone.

While India had constantly argued against the concept of deterrence and the period following India's tests had witnessed a rebuttal of the likelihood of an arms race, post-Chagai analysis in the Indian press reflected a legitimisation of deterrence and the role of nuclear weapons in providing stability, calling for constructive diplomacy to ensure that the gains outweighed the losses. At the same time there were a number of speculative reports based on international media sources projecting threats from Pakistan's nuclear and missile programmes. Although TH displayed more subtlety in reporting and responsibility in editorialising, the newspapers were generally unanimous in the demonisation of Pakistan's nuclear programme, correspondingly justifying India's nuclear policy. The nature of coverage obfuscated issues in their wider context, projecting the dominant realist paradigm of analysis relating to nuclear weapons in the subcontinent. Although press coverage in the post 1998 phase witnessed some divergences corresponding with the variations in the 'spectrum of debate' within the government, press reporting of Pakistan's nuclear policy, has over the years clearly reflected the dominant nuclear discourse, with the editorial columns sometimes taking their cue from the strategic community. It also helped set the stage for the nuances in India's nuclear policy. Although dissenting voices did exist, they were of marginal significance. Security perceptions of the press in the nuclear context of South

Asia have essentially been that of the dominant discourse.

## NOTES AND REFERENCES

1 See *The Hindu*, 9 April 1954 and *The Statesman*, 10 April 1954.

2 "What price power," *The Hindustan Times*, 23 August 1961.

3 "Misplaced," *The Times of India*, 29 March 1961.

4 Shyam Bhatia, *India's Nuclear Bomb* (New Delhi: Vikas, 1979), p.115.

5 G.G Mirchandani, *India's Nuclear Dilemma* (New Delhi: Popular, 1968), p.25.

6 *The Hindustan Times*, 19 October 1964.

7 Homi J. Bhabha's Address, All India Radio, 24 October 1964, in J.P. Jain (ed.), *Nuclear India*, Vol.2 (New Delhi: Radiant, 1974), p.159.

8 "A temptation for many – atomic bomb will cost only 17 lakhs: Bhabha," *The Hindustan Times*, 25 October 1964; "Low cost of nuclear weapons– 'temptations' to other nations," *The Hindu*, 27 October 1964; see George Perkovich, *India's Nuclear Bomb: The Impact on Global Proliferation* (New Delhi: Oxford University Press, 2000), p. 68.

9 'An Indian bomb," *The Times of India*, 10 November 1964.

10 See "A nuclear testing zone in India," *The Statesman*, 11 November 1964; "The Bomb," *The Hindu*, 10 November 1964; "That Bomb," *The Indian Express*, 10 November 1964; "India and the Bomb," *The Statesman*, 24 August 1964.

11 Ashok Kapur, *India's Nuclear Option: Atomic Diplomacy and Decision Making* (New York: Praeger, 1976), p. 175.

12 India, Lok Sabha, *Debates*, Vol.35, No.10, 27 November 1964, cols.2287-88.

13 "Nuclear race will ruin country's economy – Shastri's firm stand: many MPs. plead for change in policy," *The Hindu*, 28 November 1964.

14 George Perkovich, n.8, p.83. Each of these headlines appeared in the 28 November 1964 editions.

15 Editorial, "The bomb and all that," *The Hindu*, 11 January 1965; also see editorial, "The bomb again," *The Statesman*,

8 January 1965; and George Perkovich, n.8, p.90.

16 See N. Bhaskara Rao, *Indo-Pak Conflict: Controlled Mass Communication in Inter State Relations* (New Delhi: S.Chand, 1971).

17 Praful Bidwai and Achin Vanaik, *South Asia on a Short Fuse: Nuclear Politics and the Future of Global Disarmament* (New Delhi: Oxford University Press, 1999), p.69.

18 Editorial, "India's nuclear achievement," *The Hindu*, 19 May 1974.

19 See "Blast is topic of the day," *The Times of India*, 20 May 1974; V.Venkateswaran, "India's place on the nuclear map," *The Hindu*, 22 May 1974; also see India, Lok Sabha Secretariat, *Development of Nuclear Energy for Peaceful Uses: Policy, Programme and Achievement* (New Delhi, August 1974).

20 See editorial, "Nuclear fallout," *The Hindu*, 22 May 1974.

21 Editorial, "Total irresponsibility," *The Statesman*, 19 May 1974.

22 Ravi Kaul, *India's Nuclear Spin-Off* (Allahabad: Chanakya, 1974), pp.127-128.

23 See George Perkovich, n.8, p.203; also see *The Indian Express*, 15 July 1977; *Patriot*, 15 July 1977.

24 Yehia M.Syed, "Letter from London: Indian media's clamour for nuclear bomb," *Dawn*, 1 June 1981.

25 Yogi Aggarwal, "India makes another bomb," *Sunday Observer*, 31 August 1981.

26 India, Lok Sabha, *Debates*, Vol. 46, No.27, 30 March 1984, col. 401.

27 For example, see K. C. Khanna, *The Times of India*, 28 March 1984; G. K. Reddy, "Nuclear option open if Pak. gets the bomb," *The Hindu*, 5 May 1985; G.K.Reddy, "Containment of Pak bomb threat," *The Hindu*, 11 August 1985.

28 "Islamic Bomb: how far?," *The Hindustan Times*, 5 October 1985; also see "Pak has already got a-bomb: threat is immediate: PM," *The Hindustan Times*, 10 October 1985.

29 Bob Woodward, "Pakistan reported near atom arms production," *The Washington Post*, 4 November 1986.

30 India, Lok Sabha, *Debates*, Vol.21, No.3, 6 November 1986, col. 357-358.

31 Ibid., col.386.

32 George Perkovich, n.8, p.301. See "W. Germany refutes report on Agni," *The Times of India*, 10 July 1989; "CIA says Agni isn't indigenous," *The Times of India*, 2 July 1989.

33 Editorial, "Triumphant splashdown," *The Times of India*, 23 May 1989.

34 See Praful Bidwai, "To Prevent Megadeath, Don't Make Nukes," *Frontline*, 17 June 1998.

35 George Perkovich, n.8, pp.314-315; also see K. Sundarji, "In the nuclear trap: wrong assumptions," *The Hindu*, 11 December 1990; "India must go for N-weapons," *The Times of India*, 4 February 1991.

36 *Asian Recorder*, Vol. 38, No.9, 26 February-3 March 1992, p. 22175; also see "Pakistan and the World," *Pakistan Horizon*, Vol.45, No.1, January 1992, pp.92-93.

37 See, for instance, the three-column front-page report, "Concern over Chinese N-aid to Pakistan," *The Times of India*, 15 December 1991.

38 "Pakistan: A Quantum of Candor," *Time*, Vol. 139, No. 7, 17 February 1992, p.10.

39 *Keesing's Record of World Events: 1992*, Vol. 38, No.2, February 1992, p.38763.

40 See "Pakistan denies N-Bomb reports," *The Indian Express*, 16 January 1992; "N-project not arms oriented, says Pakistan," *The Hindu*, 10 February 1992; "No Pak plan to make N-Bomb," *The Times of India*, 11 February 1992.

41 T.N. Kaul, "Pak needs a second warning," *The Hindu*, 28 February 1992.

42 "Pakistan still at it," *The Indian Express*, 20 August 1994.

43 "West concern at Sharif statement," *The Indian Express*, 26 August 1994; also see "Illegal N-programme: India's call to penalise Pakistan," *The Indian Express*, 24 September 1994; "Concern at Pak Bomb," *The Indian Express*, 11 September 1994; P.R.Chari, "Pakistan's Bomb: A strategy of deterrence crafted on make-believe," *The Indian Express*, 28 August 1994.

44 "Parliament panel favours 'Prithvi' deployment," *The Times of India*, 5 May 1995.

45 *The Indian Express*, 5 May 1995; *The Indian Express*, 8 May 1995; also see Raja Mohan, "Prithvi induction as per security

needs," *The Hindu*, 24 May 1995; "Pakistan has 84 M-11 missiles which can hit Delhi, Bombay," *The Times of India*, 11 July 1995.

46 "Missile next door," *The Indian Express*, 17 July 1995.

47 "India must stand firm," *The Indian Express*, 18 December 1995; also see "Govt. says US report speculative," *The Hindu*, 16 December 1995; "NYT report on N-test a big lie: Ramanna," *The Times of India*, 17 December 1995; also see "Preserving India's sovereignty," *The Hindu*, 18 December 1995; "US media misread military manoeuvres," *The Indian Express*, 21 December 1995; "N-test reports a trap by cold war warriors," *The Indian Express*, 30 December 1995.

48 "A test balloon," *The Hindustan Times*, 18 December 1995.

49 *Asian Age*, 18 December 1995.

50 Shekar Gupta, "Lessons of the missile 'leak' – pity the soft state," *The Indian Express*, 9 June 1997.

51 Haider K. Nizamani, *The Roots of Rhetoric: Politics of Nuclear Weapons in India and Pakistan* (New Delhi: India Research Press, 2001), p.54.

52 Praful Bidwai, "Whose Truth: Indian Media in the Global Village," *Humanscape*, December 1996, www.indiawatch.org.

53 "CTBT: Guarantees do not meet India's concerns," *The Hindu*, 13 August 1996.

54 See, for example, Kanti Bajpai, "India should give up the N-option," *The Times of India*, 24 January 1996; Praful Bidwai, "CTBT: India's veto is futile," *The Times of India*, 11 September 1996; Praful Bidwai, "The CTBT issue-II: Accept treaty and move on," *The Times of India*, 7 February 1996.

55 Praful Bidwai and Achin Vanaik, n.17, p. 100; also see Praful Bidwai and Achin Vanaik, *Testing Times: The Global Stake in a Nuclear Test Ban* (Uppasala: Dag Hammarskjold Foundation, 1996), p.62.

56 See "US warns India others against conducting N tests," *The Times of India*, 12 September 1996; "India will not bow to N-bomb: PM," *Statesman*, 1 June 1997; Brahma Chellaney, "Domineering US: Deferential India," *Pioneer*, 24 September 1997; Editorial, "Welcome a showdown," *The Indian Express*, 20 June 1996; Editorial, "Majestic veto," *The Indian Express*, 17 August 1996; Editorial, "Preserve India's options," *The Hindu*, 15 June 1996; Editorial, "Not now, not later," *The*

*Hindustan Times,* 9 September 1996.

57 "Keep options open," *The Statesman,* 18 June 1996.

58 Brahma Chellaney, *Pioneer,* 31 January 1997.

59 Brahma Chellaney, *Pioneer,* 21 May 1997.

60 Brahma Chellaney, *The Hindustan Times,* 18 May 1997.

61 See Brahma Chellaney, "India's missile programme: behaving like a wimp," *The Indian Express,* 12 October 1995.

62 Praful Bidwai and Achin Vanaik, n.17, p. 100. In this context see the article by K.Subrahmanyam, "India and CTBT: Deterrence requires testing option," *The Times of India,* 21 February 1996.

63 Editorial, "Progress of the missile programme," *The Hindu,* 2 February 1996.

64 See "US 'unaware of M-11 deployment'," *The Hindu,* 14 June 1996; "Media reports on M-11 have no substance: US," *The Hindu,* 15 June 1996; "M-11 issue, tension multiplier in South Asia," ibid.; "Preserve India's options," ibid.

65 Editorial, "Prithvi and Agni," *The Hindu,* 18 June 1996.

66 "The nuclear submarine," *The Hindu,* 15 July 1996.

67 *The Hindustan Times,* 10 August 1996.

68 "India must declare itself nuclear state," *The Times of India,* 10 August 1996.

69 Editor's introduction to the opinion pieces by Praful Bidwai and M.D. Nalapat, *The Times of India,* 11 September 1996.

70 "China linked to Pakistani plant," *The Washington Post,* 25 August 1996.

71 See "US, China discussing Pak missile plant issue," *The Hindu,* 27 August 1996; "US may harp on clinching evidence," *The Hindu,* 27 August 1996; "US evasive on Pak missile factory," *The Hindu,* 28 August 1996.

72 Editorial, "India's missile programme," *The Hindu,* 31 December 1996.

73 Editorial, "Shelving' Agni programme will harm India," *The Hindu,* 3 January 1997.

74 Mike Schuster, "All Things Considered," in *National Public Radio Series on South Asia's Nuclear Equation,* 27 August 1997, www.stimson.org.

75 *The Hindustan Times,* 1 December 1997.

76 George Perkovich, n.8, p.401.

77 Ibid.; also see Brahma Chellaney, "A national icon, a nation adrift," *Pioneer,* 3 December 1997.

78 "Ghauri: A "Chinese Missile' in Pak-colour," *The Hindustan Times,* 5 January 1998; "India to take resolute steps on Pak missile," *The Hindustan Times,* 8 April 1998; "US 'regrets' Pakistan's missile test," *The Hindustan Times,* 8 April 1998; Raja Mohan, "Ghauri missile: India in denial," *The Hindu,* 9 April 1998; "Ghauri technology N.Korean," *The Hindustan Times,* 12 April 1998; and "Russian missiles may find their way to Pak from China," *The Hindustan Times,* 28 April 1998.

79 Unless otherwise specified, all dates cited in this section refer to 1998.

80 Audit Bureau of Circulations, *ABC Certificates: Audit Period 1 July to 31 December 1998, Serial No.100* (Mumbai: Audit Bureau of Circulations, 1998); India, Ministry of Information and Broadcasting, *India 2000: A Reference Manual* (New Delhi: Publications Division, 2000).

81 See Partha Pratim Basu, *The Press and Foreign Policy in India* (New Delhi: Lancers' Books, 2003), pp.29-31; Nireekshak, "The Fourth Estate: Keeping up with the Media," *Economic and Political Weekly,* 5 August 2000, www.epw.org.

82 S.K. Goyal and M.Challapathi Rao, *Ownership and Control Structure of the Indian Press* (New Delhi: Indian Institute of Public Administration, 1981).

83 Anders Hansen, Simon Cottle, Ralph Negrine and Chris Newbold (eds.), *Mass Communication Research Methods* (Basingstoke: Macmillan, 1998), p.108.

84 "Pak's missile plan," TOI, 1 May; "New nuclear test policy: US firm helping Pak," IE, 1 May; "Pak claims on Ghauri dashed," TH, 5 May; "India to take up issue of US firm helping Pak," IE, 6 May; "Pak firm on missile scheme," IE, 6 May; "N.Korea denies US charge on Ghauri," TH, 6 May; and "Pak planning another missile test," TH, 8 May.

85 "We will give fitting reply if attacked: Air Chief," TH, 2 May; "Need for an alert sentinel," TH, 3 May; "Go ahead for Agni second phase?," TH, 4 May; "India revives Agni programme," IE, 4 May; "Government revives Agni programme," TOI, 4 May; "Agni likely to be made battle ready," TH, 5 May; "Agni project was never capped," TH, 11 May.

86 "Pak claims on Ghauri dashed," TH, 5 May; also see "India hails US sanctions," IE, 6 May.

87 See "N.Korea denies US charge on Ghauri," TH, 6 May.

88 "Pak planning another missile test?," TH, 8 May.

89 "Need for an alert sentinel," TH, 3 May.

90 Anand K.Sahay, "Responding to Ghauri: eschew perverse restraint," IE, 6 May.

91 See "Concern over Pak's nuclear plans: US acknowledges Indian stand," IE, 4 May; Manvendra Singh, "New nuclear test policy: US firm helping Pakistan," IE, 1 May; "India to take up issue of US firm helping Pak," IE, 2 May; "Concern over US firm's role in Pak nuclear programme," TH, 2 May.

92 IE, 12 May.

93 All of TOI, 12 May.

94 All of TH, 12 May.

95 TOI, 12 May.

96 See TH, 12 May.

97 Front page headlines read, "India enters big league with 2 more N-tests: nation is geared to meet fallout: declares PM," TOI, 14 May; "Accept India as nuclear power," TOI, 24 May; "India packs big punch in small bomb," IE, 14 May; "PMs stock is up after N-blast," TOI, 14 May; "Vajpayee set the nation free from fear of punishment," TOI, 17 May; Rajat Sharma, "Vajpayee shows who's the boss," IE, 24 May.

98 K.Subrahmanyam, "India has broken no commitments," TOI, 12 May.

99 Editorial, "Ground zero," TOI, 12 May.

100 "Vajpayee set the nation free of fear from punishment," TOI, 17 May.

101 C. Rajinder Puri, "After the bomb: lets learn the power of silence," TOI, 3 June.

102 "Ease curbs on hi-tech transfer, then we will sign CTBT: India," TOI, 6 July.

103 Editorial, "Advice and consent," TOI, 6 June.

104 Editorial, "Outdated mindset," TOI, 18 July.

105 K.Subrahmanyam, "India interactive: talking terms with the U.S.," TOI, 20 July.

106 Editorial, "Seize the day: forget national ego, move on to

CTBT," IE, 13 May.

107 Editorial, "Ignore this Jihad: time for India to play on the world stage," IE, 30 May.

108 S.Gurumurthy, "The national balance sheet after Pokharan," IE, 23 May. (IE has interchangeably used the spellings 'Pokhran' and 'Pokharan').

109 Manvendra Singh, "Ignorant and sanctimonious: a coalition of wise guys," IE, 25 May; also see Manvendra Singh, "The road to Pokharan," IE, 19 May.

110 Muchkund Dubey, "Exercising the nuclear option," TH, 18 May.

111 C.Raja Mohan, "Playing football with nuclear weapons," TH, 25 May.

112 Kalpana Sharma and Ayesha Khan, "Give peace a chance," TH, 6 June.

113 Praful Bidwai, "Dangerous descent: flawed logic of nuclear tests," TOI, 15 May.

114 Laurie Baker, "The 3 reality tests," IE, 21 May.

115 The day after the tests itself, front-page headlines read: "Three underground nuclear explosions conducted in Pokharan: India makes giant leap in N-capability," IE, 12 May; and "President congratulates scientists," TH, 12 May. Elsewhere, reports read: "India had proven capability," TH, 12 May; "Tests prove India's N-capability," IE, 12 May; "Conducting three N-tests is historic, says K.C.Pant," TOI, 12 May; "I am proud of our N-achievement says Atomic Energy Chairman," TOI, 12 May; "India has mastered thermonuclear technology," TH, 1 June; "Pokharan nuclear test: seismic data confirm India's claim," IE, 28 July.

116 "India conducts 3 underground N-tests," TOI, 12 May.

117 Editorial, "A high stakes gambit," TH, 13 May.

118 Editorial, "Scientific breakthrough: in complete nuclear weaponisation," IE, 19 May. It further stated: "Put together, all this is a remarkable demonstration of the nature, range and quality of scientific and engineering work in the nuclear and missile fields carried on for decades in establishments around the country."

119 S.Gurumurthy, "The national balance sheet after Pokharan," IE, 23 May; also see Manvendra Singh, "Ignorant and sanctimonious: a coalition of wise guys," IE, 25 May.

120 IE stated: "Tests conducted without satellites or spooks getting wind of them," 13 May; "Pak N-test likely next week: CIA," IE, 17 May; Manvendra Singh, "The road to Pokharan 1998," IE, 19 May.

121 "Pioneering work by DAE, DRDO," TH, 18 May (quoting R.Chidambaram and Abdul Kalam); "Weaponisation now complete, say scientists," TH, 18 May (A.P.J.Abdul Kalam, R.Chidambaram, K.Santhanam and Anil Kadodkar in a front page report); "N-tests data sufficient for weapons programme," TH, 17 May (quoting among others M.R.Srinivasan and P.K.Iyengar, former AEC Chairmen); "Pokhran blasts tested new ideas: BARC Chief," TH, 20 May (Anil Kakodkar and R.Chidambaram); "India not dependent on others for N-technology," TH, 25 June (R.Chidambaram); "Tests prove India's nuclear capability," IE, 12 May (P.K.Iyengar); "Operation Shakti' took just 30 days after green signal," IE, 18 May (R.Chidambaram and A.P.J. Abdul Kalam); "Simultaneous blasting fooled surveillance," IE, 18 May (R.Chidambaram and A.P.J.Abdul Kalam); "India can produce 200 kt nuclear bomb, says AEC chief," IE, 23 May (R.Chidambaram); "Nuclear technology will flow from Asia in 2 years," IE, 31 July (R.Chidambaram); "We detonated 3 bombs by pulling one trigger," TOI, 19 May (R.Chidambaram); "H bomb yield was between 43 and 45 kilotons: BARC Chief," TOI, 19 May (Anil Kadodkar).

122 For example, see "No dramatic impact of sanctions likely," TH, 16 May (quoting Ajay Shah, Indira Gandhi Institute of Development Research); "Agni variant to help bridge 'missile gap'," TH, 19 May (A.P.J.Abdul Kalam); "N-arms cheaper than conventional weapons," TH, 19 May (P.K.Iyengar, former AEC Chairman); "BARC scientists criticise the 'bullying attitude' of US," TOI, 13 May; "Today's tests may be for tactical weapons," TOI, 14 May (P.K.Iyengar, Raja Ramanna); "Mission now is to become developed nation," TOI, 25 May (A.P.J. Abdul Kalam); "AEC chief dismisses western propaganda on N-power," TH, 2 June (R.Chidambaram); "Operation shakti' took 30 days," TH, 18 May (A.P.J.Abdul Kalam); "BARC's secret programme to be militarised," TH, 13 June (BARC sources).

123 "Tests must have come 3 years ago," TH, 16 May.

124 "India has mastered thermonuclear technology," TH, 1 June.

125 For instance, see Atul Aneja, "The dreamer and the doer,"

TH, 24 May; "The men behind the big bang," IE, 14 May; "Fathering the big bang: profile - Rajagopala Chidambaram," IE, 17 May; "Security forced on unwilling heroes," IE, 21 May; "The select few who kept it under wraps," TOI, 16 May; Dinesh Kumar, "Our man from Rameswaram," TOI, 17 May; "They piloted nukes and missiles through turbulent global weather," TOI, 17 May; John F. Burns, "'Dream! Convert the dreams into thought, action,'" TOI, 26 May; TOI even quoted a Romanian newspaper *Nation* in praise of Indian scientists in its report, "Indian nuclear scientists praised for achievement," TOI, 5 June.

126 See the one column report buried on page 14 of TH, "Scientists feel device was 'primitive'," which quoted a Leeds University scientist; "India has mastered thermonuclear technology," TH, 1 June; "Pokharan nuclear test: seismic data confirm India's claim," IE, 28 July.

127 For details, see www.isanw.org.

128 "Scientists express dismay over N-tests," TH, 19 May; also see "Scientists flay nuclear tests," IE, 19 May; "75 Indian scientists criticise N-blasts," TOI, 19 May; "Nuclear bomb will give no added security: scientist," TH, 29 May; "Scientists call for no-first-use policy," TH, 31 May; "Scientists plan movement against N-tests," TOI, 27 May.

129 "Scenario of a South Asian holocaust-I: effects of a bomb attack," TH, 24 June; and "Scenario of a South Asian holocaust-II: human casualties of a nuclear bomb," TH, 25 June. See M.V Ramana, *Bombing Bombay: Effects of Nuclear Weapons and a Case Study of a Hypothetical Explosion* (Cambridge, Mass: International Physicians for the Prevention of Nuclear War, 1999). Although this study was published in 1999, it had been presented at the Regional Meeting of the International Physicians for the Prevention of Nuclear War, New Delhi, 21-23 February 1997 and was available on the Internet.

130 See T.Jayaraman, "Of science and nuclear weapons: a scientist's perspective," paper presented at Delhi Convention Against Nuclear Weapons, 9 June; "Beyond the Euphoria," *Frontline*, Vol.15, No.11, 5 June, pp.30-31.

131 See Surendra Gadekar, "Buddha is sick of smiling," *Anumukti*, 12 May.

132 See "Nuclear bomb will give no added security: scientist,"

TH, 29 May.

133 "Scientist questions DAE claim," TH, 20 May.

134 See "Gowda criticises BJP leaders," TH, 23 May; C.V.Gopalakrishnan, "Burrowed and pierced planet," TH, 20 June.

135 "India has mastered thermonuclear technology," TH, 1 June; "Pokharan nuclear test: seismic data confirm India's claim," IE, 28 July; "India tested Hydrogen bomb, says magazine," TH, 27 July; "Pokharan nuclear test: seismic data confirm India's claim," IE, 28 July; also see "Pakistan may have nukes based on Chinese design," IE, 28 May.

136 TOI, 17 May.

137 David Albright, "The shots heard around the world," *Bulletin of Atomic Scientists,* Vol.54, No.4, July/August 1998, www.bullatomsci.org.

138 Kalpana Sharma, "The Hindu Bomb," *Bulletin of Atomic Scientists,* Vol.54 No.4, July/August 1998, www.bullatomsci.org.

139 Ramachandra Guha, "Honour the science of creation too: an incomplete iconography," IE, 1 June.

140 Praful Bidwai, "Our science militarised: The deadly fallout of Pokhran–II," TOI, 1 July 1998.

141 Partha S. Ghosh, "Bomb, science and the state," TH, 9 June.

142 "Scientist questions DAE claim," TH, 20 May.

143 Kenneth J. Cooper, "India's leaders speak of vindication, urge calm and unity," *The Washington Post,* 29 May, p.A33; See A. B. Vajpayee's statement in *India Today,* 15 May, reproduced in www.indianembassy.org; also see press release regarding Presidential statement adopted by the UN Security Council on Indian nuclear tests, 15 May 1998, India, Ministry of External Affairs, *Foreign Affairs Record,* Vol.44, No.5, May 1998, pp.38-39.

144 For example, see "PM for consensus on national security," TH, 18 May; "Consensus is BJPs new mantra," TOI, 21 May; "Pak policy based on consensus: Vajpayee," TH, 25 May; "Pak policy based on consensus: PM," IE, 25 May; "Consensus is key to our Pak policy: PM, 'We want good ties with China to promote peace'" TOI, 25 May; "The Vajpayee doctrine: he is right to combine consensus with toughness," IE, 27 May; Editorial, "No national fission: build up a

consensus on nuclear policy," IE, 1 June; KK Katyal, "Urgency of consensus on post test issues," TH, 8 July; Editorial, "Unity as weapon," TOI, 9 July; "India's security policies rooted in consensus, Gujral," TH, 11 July.

145 Manvendra Singh, "Buddha's smile is infectious for us all," IE, 13 May.

146 "Euphoria permeates PMs Durbar," TH, 15 May; "PM hailed for nuclear tests," TH, 18 May; Other reports read: "They smile with Buddha," IE, 14 May; "Indians back nuke tests on internet," IE, 15 May; and "Kashmiris euphoric," IE, 31 May. Rajat Sharma in his column, "My Verdict", projected the tests as "A reason to smile," being a bold step taken, and an achievement of secrecy and consensus, IE, 17 May; TOI, 13 May. Other reports read, "Calcuttans are happy about N-tests," TOI, 15 May; "N-euphoria drowns voice of critics," TOI, 21 May.

147 K.K.Katyal, "Need for restraint," TH, 19 May.

148 Praful Bidwai, "Regaining nuclear sanity: no tests, no bombs, ever," TOI, 6 June.

149 See for example, "Eminent citizens meet against n-weapons," TH, 10 June, p.14; "Survey shows majority opposes N-arms use," TH, 24 June, p.14; "N-tests deplored," TH, 17 May; "Anti-nuclear movement launched in Delhi," TH, 17 May; "Gandhians decry nuclear tests," TH, 20 May; and "Explain Pokharan tests: Patka," IE, 27 June.

150 "Intellectuals condemn nuclear tests," IE, 17 May.

151 Editorial, "The Vajpayee doctrine: he is right to combine consensus with toughness," IE, 27 May.

152 See "Women's national conference condemns nuclear tests," TOI, 2 June, p.8; "Arundhati Roy assails India's N-tests, calls for protests," TOI, 28 July, p.9.

153 K.Subrahmanyam, "Politics of Shakti: new whine in an old bomb," TOI, 26 May.

154 See Praful Bidwai, "For a Citizens Movement," Frontline, Vol. 15, No. 13, 20 June-3 July 1998, pp.78-79; also see www.mnet.fr. While TOI had a report on 15 May entitled, "Calcuttans are happy about N-tests," protest demonstrations held in the city on 17 and 18 May either went unreported or there was no national coverage. Similarly, statements by such organisations as the Alliance for a

Secular and Democratic South Asia (14 May), South Asia Solidarity Group, Pakistan-India Peoples Forum for Peace and Democracy (18 May), Greenpeace press release (28 May), Joint Statement by retired Pakistani and Indian Armed Forces Personnel (July 1998), etc did not receive national coverage.

155 See "They heard the thunder and felt the earth shake," IE, 13 May; "Earth rocked thrice... It was over in 5 seconds," TOI, 13 May.

156 "We will pay any price for country's security: PM," TH, 21 May.

157 See "The Khetolai Declaration," *Frontline*, Vol.15, No.14, 4-17 July 1998, p.99; also see Jean Dreze, "From Hiroshima to Pokhran," in ibid. pp.98-100.

158 See statement of the Foreign Minister to the Senate, 11 May, 12 May and 13 May, www.clw.org; statement by Ambassador Munir Akram in the Plenary meeting of the Conference on Disarmament, 14 May, www.clw.org; "Press briefing by Pakistan's foreign office spokesman on the Indian nuclear tests," 14 May, www.clw.org.

159 TH, 12 May; TOI's report on the issue found mention in the report, "US may impose sanctions," 12 May.

160 "Sharif blames the West," TH, 13 May.

161 TH, 17 May.

162 Muchkund Dubey, "India urged to sign NPT," TH, 15 May (emphasis added).

163 Editorial, "The Benazir bomb," IE, 20 May.

164 "Defiant Pakistan conducts another nuclear test," TOI, 31 May.

165 See "Pak tells Clinton, Blair to restrain India," IE, 24 May.

166 Editorial, "Defence, not offence," IE, 18 May.

167 Editorial, "Pakistan's turn," TOI, 18 May.

168 See "US keen to respond to Pak concerns," TH, 22 May; "US may 'tilt' even more towards Pak," TH, 23 May; "US ready to offer Pak a package," TH, 26 May, (front page); "US offers Pakistan sops in lieu of – No N-test promise," TOI, 26 May, (front page); "US may offer Pak guarantees of security," IE, 21 May. "Pakistan is on the verge of conducting nuclear test: 'NYT': US offers Sharif a deal to refrain," TOI, 15 May

(front page); "Response to Indian nuclear tests: US fails to 'restrain' Pak," IE, 17 May; "US may offer Pak guarantees of security," IE, 21 May; "Pak analysts term US package flimsy," TH, 27 May (front page); "US offered Pak $5b to forgo N-tests," TH, 27 June.

169 M.D.Nalapat, "India's geopolitical options after the tests," TOI, 13 May. On the previous day Nalapat had quoted a 'high-level' policy maker as saying "Enough is enough. It takes two hands to clap, but only one to molest. Thus far, India's restraint has been met only by increased anti-India activities." See M.D.Nalapat, "Test aimed at countering N-blackmail," TOI, 12 May.

170 "Vajpayee accuses big powers of double standards: Pakistan is unable to match Indian skills in science," TOI, 21 May; also see the front-page report "Advani again warns Pak," IE, 21 May.

171 "Consensus is key to our Pak policy: Islamabad attempts to isolate India on N-tests," TOI, 25 May.

172 "'Pak N-test likely next week' CIA," IE, 17 May; "Pak test: 'a question of when not whether'," IE, 18 May; "Odds favour early Pak N-tests," IE, 20 May.

173 Manvendra Singh, "Pakistan's partners in proliferation," IE, 24 May.

174 Editorial, "Tumhari Shabana: Allow culture to cross the Indo-Pak border," IE, 27 May.

175 C.Raja Mohan, "Pakistan's nuclear dilemma," TH, 15 May.

176 "Pak trying to obtain n-technology from Germany?," TH, 25 May; a front page report in IE on 25 May read, "Pak using front companies to get N-parts: Germany."

177 "France, Pakistan's major arms supplier: Paper," IE, 28 May.

178 "Pakistan may have nukes based on Chinese design," IE, 28 May; also see "Pak may have n-weapons based on Chinese design," TOI, 28 May. Incidentally, the report was again found on page 16 of the same paper with the headlines, "Pakistan may have nukes based on Chinese design."

179 See, for example, statement by Prime Minister Nawaz Sharif at Press Conference, 28 May, www.pak.gov.pk; press briefing by the Foreign Secretary of Pakistan announcing further nuclear tests, 30 May, www.pak.gov.pk; statement by Munir Akram at the Special Session of the Conference on

Disarmament on 2 June, www.pakistan.gov.pk; remarks to BBC by Foreign Minister Gohar Ayub Khan, 31 May, www.clw.org.

180 All of IE.

181 See "Sharif offers to resume dialogue," TH, 29 May; "Security dialogue a possibility, says Gohar," TH, 29 May; "Pak tests another device," TH, 31 May.

182 Editorial, "No national fission: build up a consensus on nuclear policy," IE, 1 June.

183 "Pakistan tested only 1 N-device on May 28: Fernandes," IE, 1 June; also see "N-tests nowhere near ours," TOI, 1 June.

184 "Sub-critical tests 'only if necessary,'" IE, 2 June.

185 "Pakistan retaliates with five nuclear tests: Sharif says account with India is even," TOI, 29 May.

186 "Pakistan readies for another missile launch," TOI, 1 June.

187 "Ramanna deplores 'noise' over N-tests," TOI, 16 June.

188 See M.D.Nalapat, n.169.

189 M.D.Nalapat, "Nuclear neo-racism: ending technological apartheid," TOI, 1 June; also see "Pak n-tests superfluous," TH, 20 June.

190 "Agni will be test-fired in June, says defence expert," TOI, 2 June.

191 "India's potential N-arsenal is bigger than Britain's," TOI, 19 June.

192 "Pakistan planning more tests?," TH, 30 May.

193 "Pak conducted only one successful blast: experts," TH, 31 May.

194 "AEC chief dismisses West propaganda on n-power," TH, 2 June.

195 "Doubts about Pakistan claims," IE, 30 May.

196 "Indian nuclear scientist doubts Pakistan claims," IE, 31 May.

197 "Pokharan blast 13 times more powerful than Pak test," IE, 3 July.

198 Editorial, "No national fission: build up a consensus on nuclear policy," IE, 1 June.

199 Santy, "A Pokharan recipe: sandwiches and desserts," IE, 4 June.

200 S.Gopal, "Nuclear Pakistan is a Chinese creation: Vajpayee's 'maladroit' letter," IE, 24 June.

201 Also see "Pak nuclear scientist surfaces in US," TH, 2 July (front page); "Pak N-scientist ready to spill the beans," IE, 2 July; "US mum on Pak scientist's claim," 3 July (front page); "PAEC denied scientists claim," 3 July, p.14; "Doubts over Pak scientist's claim," TH, 4 July, p.14; "Pak firm disputes Govt. claim," TH, 5 July, p.7; "Defector is willing to divulge details of Pak N-programme," TOI, 2 July (front page); "Pakistani defector is disowned by his father, scientist," TOI, 9 July.

202 Editorial, "Containing the risks," TH, 15 May.

203 Editorial, "Clearing the air," TH, 23 May.

204 C.Raja Mohan, "Playing football with nuclear weapons," TH, 25 May.

205 J.N.Dixit, "P-II: managing the fallout," TH, 23 May.

206 IE, 13 May.

207 Editorial, "Angels fear to tread: polls now would make tests an exercise in cynicism," IE, 18 May.

208 Shekar Gupta, "Burdens of the nuclear state: the morning after," IE, 13 May.

209 Editorial, "Ground zero," TOI, 12 May.

210 K.Subrahmanyam, "India now joins club of five N-weapon states," TOI, 12 May.

211 Editorial, "Bringing up the bomb," TOI, 20 May.

212 See "India will convince nations about its hard options," TOI, 13 May; "Indian N-tests put big 5 in the dock, expose this hypocrisy," TOI, 13 May; "PM asserts N-stand," TOI, 12 June; "Explain background of nuclear tests to people, PM asks Party MPs," TOI, 13 June; "Vajpayee explains rationale of nuclear tests to Hasina," TOI, 17 June; "India needed a nuclear deterrent against China," TOI, 18 June; "PM writes to western leaders on nuclear tests," TH, 13 May; "Nuclear weapons only for self defence, says PM," TH, 16 May; "Tests not against any country," TH, 16 May; "Tests served twin purposes," TH, 28 May; "Advani justifies Pokhran tests," TH, 29 May; "World reacts angrily to Pokharan, Germany freezes aid: India to face reactions if any," IE, 13 May.

213 TH, 14 May; also see "BJP trying to divert attention," quoting Yuv Janata Dal president, TH, 18 May; "N-Tests a gimmick

to cover up problems, SP," quoting Samajwadi Party General Secretary, TH 22 May.

214 Subramanian Swamy, "National security or Government security?," TH, 22 May.

215 Achin Vanaik, "Drawing new lines," TH, 23 May.

216 Praful Bidwai, "Dangerous descent: Flawed logic of nuclear tests," TOI, 15 May.

217 Praful Bidwai, "India has shot itself in the head," TOI, 17 May.

218 Statement by Prime Minister Nawaz Sharif at press conference, 28 May, n.179; press briefing by the Foreign Secretary of Pakistan announcing further nuclear tests, 30 May, n.179; statement by Ambassador Munir Akram at the special session of the Conference on Disarmament on 2 June, n.179.

219 See India, Ministry of External Affairs, Disarmament and International Security Affairs Division, *Brief of India's Nuclear Tests: Global Disarmament or Equal and Legitimate Security for All* (Washington DC.: Embassy of India), www.indianembassy.org; India, Ministry of External Affairs, "One More Nuclear Test Conducted by Pakistan," Press Release, 30 May, n.143, p.44; India, Ministry of External Affairs, "Security Council Reaction to the Nuclear Tests Carried out by Pakistan," Press Release, 31 May, in ibid., pp.44-45.

220 Editorial, "Nuclear crescent," TOI, 4 June.

221 Editorial, "Dangerous liaisons," TOI, 29 June.

222 Editorial, "Stale tale," TOI, 30 June.

223 Editorial, "Reaping the whirlwind," TOI, 14 July.

224 Editorial, "Pots judging kettles: Indian diplomacy must expose the US-China nexus," IE, 4 June.

225 Editorial, "A dangerous escalation," TH, 29 May.

226 C.Raja Mohan, "Nuclear balance in Asia," TH, 11 June.

227 K.Subrahmanyam, "Politics of Shakti: new whine in an old bomb," TOI, 26 May.

228 Editorial, "The nuclear legacy," TOI, 26 May.

229 C.Raja Mohan, "India crosses the nuclear Rubicon," TH, 13 May; J.N.Dixit, "P-II: managing the fallout," TH, 23 May; T.N.Kaul, "Pokhran, China and Pakistan," TH, 30 May;

K.Subrahmanyam, "India now joins club of five N-weapon states," TOI, 12 May; also see K.Subrahmanyam, "Hedging against hegemony: Gandhi's logic in the nuclear age," TOI, 16 June; H.K.Dua, "Ending N-Brahmacharya," TOI, 19 May.

230 See "Nuclear tests continuation of Nehru's policy: PM," TH, 28 May; also see C.Raja Mohan, "Playing football with nuclear weapons," TH, 25 May; V.V.Paranjpe, "Fallout of nuclear tests on Sino-Indian ties," TH, 25 May; J.N.Dixit, "Managing contradictions on N-tests: The enemy is self-doubt," IE, 25 June; T.V.R.Shenoy, "Give some credit to the ministry: why the Buddha smiled," IE, 20 May.

231 See India, Ministry of External Affairs, Disarmament and International Security Affairs Division, n. 219; also see India, Ministry of External Affairs, 30 May 1998, n.219, p.44.

232 Arun Shourie, "The story of the Chagai hills blast-I: Pakistan's bomb is and has been a joint venture," IE, 4 June.

233 "India aware of Chinese help in Pak N-programme," IE, 5 June; "Nuclear Pakistan is a Chinese creation: Vajpayee's 'maladroit letter,'" IE, 24 June; "China-Pak nexus prompted N-tests: Defence Ministry," IE, 27 June; "US cannot stop Chinese arms supply to Pak," IE, 8 July; "India aware of China-Pak defence cooperation," IE, 17 July.

234 Atul Aneja, "The Pak nuclear programme," TH, 29 May.

235 "China regulates n-technology exports," TH, 4 June (emphasis added).

236 "China for productive dealings with India," TH, 10 July.

237 Related reports in TH read, "China had helped Pak with missile technology: US," TH, 15 July; "German jailed for N-exports to Pak," TH, 22 July; "German also gave Pak conventional arms material," TH, 23 July.

238 "Pak nuclear know-how came from Germany," TOI, 8 June.

239 "US ignored evidence on Chinese M-11 sales," TOI, 13 June.

240 Editorial, "Ironic solidarity," TOI, 29 May.

241 Editorial, "Licence, not law," TOI, 19 June.

242 Praful Bidwai, "Regaining nuclear sanity: no tests, no bombs, ever," TOI, 6 June.

243 Chidananand Rajghatta, "IAEA probing Qadeer Khan's offer to Iraq," IE, 6 May.

244 S.Gurumurthy, "The two nations, their bombs, and their goals," IE, 30 May.

245 Editorial, "Ignore this Jehad: time for India to play on the world stage," IE, 30 May.

246 S.Gurumurthy, "The new meaning of nuclear ambiguity: now work on real deterrence," IE, 5 June.

247 "'Islamic bomb' swells on rumours of Indo-Israel ties," IE, 3 June.

248 Editorial, "Nuclear crescent," TOI, 4 June.

249 Sridhar Krishnamurthy, "Fears in US over Pak bomb," TH, 21 June.

250 "US worried Pak might pass on nuclear technology," TH, 24 June.

251 See, for example, "India will face down sanctions," TH, 14 May.

252 India, Ministry of External Affairs, Disarmament and International Security Affairs Division, n.219.

253 TH, 16 May.

254 C.Raja Mohan, "India's nuclear policy: What next?," TH, 24 May.

255 Inder Malhotra, "The euphoria and after," TH, 13 May.

256 Editorial, "Clearing the air," TH, 23 May.

257 Editorial, "Ground zero," TOI, 12 May.

258 Editorial, "Bringing up the bomb," TOI, 20 May; also see editorial, "Go the extra mile," TOI, 23 May.

259 Editorial, "Defence not offence: Pakistan has nothing to retaliate against," IE, 18 May.

260 "To resolve Kashmir problem with Pakistan: India can't be pushed to external pressure: Fernandes," IE, 7 June.

261 C.Raja Mohan, "Restoring the Asian balance: Nuclear diplomacy-III," TH, 17 June; also see C.Raja Mohan, "Nuclear balance in Asia," TH, 11 May; C.Raja Mohan, "The art of the nuclear deal," TH, 9 July.

262 Editorial, "The Pak coolant: Does the South Asian thaw require an overseer?," IE, 13 June.

263 M.Guruswamy, "The new meaning of nuclear ambiguity: Now work on real deterrence," IE, 5 June.

264 Editorial, "Ironic solidarity," TOI, 29 May.

265 Mohanakrishna Rasgotra, "Nuclear India must engage the US," in ibid.

266 K.Subrahmanyam, "Arms race myth: fallout of over-active minds," TOI, 30 May.

267 Editorial, "Test to match," TOI, 30 May.

268 Editorial, "Nuclear crescent," TOI, 4 June.

269 "Latest Pakistan N test is proof of arms race: Left parties," TOI, 2 June.

270 "N-tests weakened India's position: Anand," TH, 20 July; also see "N-tests cannot ensure nation's security: Ekbal," TH, 20 July; Anand Patwardhan, "How we learned to love the bomb," TH, 7 June.

271 C.Rammanohar Reddy, "Of bombs, bread and water," TH, 24 May.

272 V.R.Raghavan, "India's nuclear dilemma," TH, 9 June.

273 Praful Bidwai, "Regaining nuclear sanity: no tests, no bombs, ever," TOI, 6 June.

274 "Pak scientists bare N-attack plan on India: 5 arms experts defect in disgust," TOI, 29 June.

275 "Indo-Pak nuclear war prevented two years ago, says US General," TOI, 10 July.

276 Also see "M11 missiles deployed," 13 June (front page); "Pak building new boat for Chinese missile," 22 June, citing *Janes Defence Weekly*, "Nag' missile test fired," 8 July (front page).

277 For instance, see "US disappointed, sanctions likely," TH, 12 May; editorial, "Bill, the selective bully: Pokharan explodes the great American pretence," IE, 15 May; "Sign CTBT or else... US: World reacts angrily: Sanctions on the cards," TOI, 13 May; "US officials are spreading 'sheer lies' says India," TOI, 19 May; "Vajpayee accuses big powers of double standards: 'India waited 50 years before responding,'" TOI, 21 May (front page); "World reacts angrily to Pokharan," "Germany freezes aid: India to face reactions if any," IE, 13 May (front page); "Clinton stops economic aid," IE, 14 May (front page).

278 TOI: "Dalai Lama hurt by Indian move on nuclear tests," 16 May, p.7; "Newt Gingrich defends Indian nuclear blasts," 19 May (front page); "I applaud your PM on N-tests: Gere," 23 May (front page); "Accept India as a nuclear power," 24 May (front page, quoting Edward Teller, father of the hydrogen bomb). "IAEA endorses India's views on disarmament," 15 June; "Vajpayee explains rationale of nuclear tests to

Hasina," 17 June (front page); "US senator defends Indian tests," 17 June (front page); "India lashes out at Philippines for circulating nuclear test document," 27 June; M.D.Nalapat, "ARF refuses to condemn India," 28 June (front page); "India scores a key victory as ASEAN is mild on N-tests," 26 July (front page).

IE: "Australia suspends bilateral defence," 15 May, p.11; "Tibetans see the bright side of Pokharan," 15 May, p.9; "Lanka denounces sanctions, backs India," 16 May; "China's charges baseless: India," 17 May (front page); "India still not 'nuclear weapons state': Sharp US reaction to Vajpayee's claim," 17 May (front page); "G-8 fails to take joint stand against India," 17 May (front page); "India has forfeited claim to permanent seat: Canada," 28 May, p.17; "Nuclear tests: Diplomatic victory for New Delhi as IAEA endorses India's stand," 15 June (front page).

TH: "China rejects PMs statement on N-tests," 9 June, p.11; "G-8 told not to make coercive suggestions," 11 June (front page); "Hasina appreciated India's security concerns," 16 June (front page); "Nuclear India will help stability: Hanoi," 20 June; A major clarification by the Chinese Prime Minister finds mention in a three column report on page 14, "India faces no threat from China: Zhu Rongji," 27 June; "ASEAN targets the big powers too," 26 July (front page).

279 Editorial, "Bill, The selective bully: Pokharan explodes the great American pretence," IE, 15 May.

280 See "US now understands N-test rationale," TOI, 14 June; "After talks with Deputy Secretary of State, Talbott: US grasps rationale of tests: Jaswant," IE, 14 June; "US 'punishes' Chidambaram for N-tests," IE, 16 July; editorial, "Learning to Tango: stay engaged, but grit is key in talking to the US," IE, 22 July; "Indo-US talks on 'right track,'" TH, 21 July; "No rolling back N-weapons programme, India tells US," IE, 21 July (front page); "India tells US it will not roll back its nuclear weapons project," TOI, 21 July (front page); "US may accept our N-status: Fernandes," TH, 26 July (front page).

281 "US keen to respond to Pak concerns," TH, 22 May. Other reports in this context read, "Clinton deplores tests," TH, 29 May, front page; "Pak test: China blames India, Japan to suspend aid," TH, 29 May; "Russia criticises test," TH, 29 May; "Pak will have to pay heavy price: US," TH, 30 May; "Japan slaps sanctions on Pakistan," TH, 30 May; "Sri Lanka

makes no formal comment," TH, 30 May; "Russia, NATO concern over Pak tests," TH, 30 May; "US condemns test," TH, 31 May; "China, Japan express regret," TH, 31 May; "Russia condemns Pak test," TH, 31 May; "Photo of protest against Pakistan tests in South Korea," TH, 2 June; "Arafat supports Pak nuclear programme," TH, 14 July.

282 Editorial, "Disarmament the key," TOI, 8 June.

283 For details see "Pakistan and the world: Chronology – April-June 1998," in *Pakistan Horizon*, Vol.51 No.3, July 1998, pp.96-110.

284 K.Subrahmanyam, "Crisis of confidence: no winners in an Indo-Pak war," TOI, 4 May.

285 K.Subrahmanyam, "India now joins club of five N-weapon states," TOI, 12 May.

286 Editorial, "Riding the storm," TOI, 15 May; editorial, "Bringing up the bomb," TOI, 20 May; editorial, "Go the extra mile," TOI, 23 May.

287 "Vajpayee must convene an Asian summit for N-treaty, says Scindia," TOI, 25 May.

288 "Hypocrisy of US, and vested interests," TH, 16 May.

289 Editorial, "A high stakes gambit," TH, 13 May; also see editorial, "Stepping back from the brink," TH, 6 June.

290 Editorial, "Containing the risks," TH, 15 May.

291 Editorial, "Defence not offence: Pakistan has nothing to retaliate against," IE, 18 May; also see editorial, "Reason after rhetoric," IE, 23 May.

292 Editorial, "No national fission: build up a consensus on nuclear policy," IE, 1 June.

293 Editorial, "Time to talk," TOI, 9 June.

294 See TOI, 7 June.

295 See IE, 9 June.

296 Editorial, "The Pak coolant: does the South Asian thaw require an overseer?," IE, 13 June.

297 "Pak asks UN to appoint special representative for Kashmir," IE, 16 July.

298 "Pak agrees to talks on FMCT," TH, 31 July.

299 K. Subrahmanyam, "Nuclear risk reduction key issue for talks," TOI, 27 July.

300 See press statement regarding three underground nuclear tests, 11 May 1998, *Foreign Affairs Record*, n.143, pp.36-37.

301 C.Raja Mohan, "India's nuclear policy: What next?," TH, 24 May; also see C.Raja Mohan, "Nuclear deal: Focus on reciprocal steps," TH, 20 July.

302 Editorial, "Seize the day: Forget national ego, move on to CTBT," IE, 13 May.

303 Editorial, "Speak up, Mr. Vajpayee," TOI, 28 May.

304 Editorial, "No national fission: Build up a consensus on nuclear policy," IE, 1 June.

305 C.Raja Mohan, "Finessing a nuclear deal," TH, 7 July; also see C.Raja Mohan, "Rethinking CTBT and FMCT," TH, 16 June.

306 C.Raja Mohan, "Nuclear deal: Focus on reciprocal steps," TH, 20 July.

307 Editorial, "Over to Washington," TH, 23 July.

308 Muchkund Dubey, "A possible Indian stance," TH, 20 July.

309 "Pakistan ready to negotiate CTBT," TOI, 13 July.

310 J.N.Dixit, "The way beyond Pokharan: Grit with conciliation," IE, 28 May.

311 See TH, 20 July.

312 C.Raja Mohan, "Nuclear balance in Asia," TH, 11 June; also see C.Raja Mohan, "India's nuclear policy: What next?," TH, 24 May.

313 C.Raja Mohan, "Indo-US relations-II: finessing a nuclear deal," TH, 7 July; also see C.Raja Mohan, "The art of the nuclear deal," TH, 9 July.

314 M. Guruswamy, "The new meaning of nuclear ambiguity: Now work on real deterrence," IE, 5 June.

315 Muchkund Dubey, "Opposition's obstacles: National disunity on nuclear issue," TOI, 2 July.

316 Muchkund Dubey, "A possible Indian stance," TH, 20 July.

317 Editorial, "Advice and consent," TOI, 6 June.

318 Also see Praful Bidwai, "Sign the test ban treaty: But say no to N-deterrence," TOI, 14 July; also see N.Ram, "Centre should roll back nuclear programme," TH, 3 July.

319 See TOI, 8 June.

320 "N-tests strengthened national unity: PM," TH, 18 May.

321 S.Anand, "The spiral of silence," IE, 16 May.

322 "Newspaper bodies hail nuclear tests," IE, 17 May.

323 Editorial, "Charming the media: Communication counts no less than decisiveness," IE, 20 May.

324 Prabhu Chawla, "Vajpayee's blitzkrieg spin doctors work overtime to give the PM a facelift," *India Today*, 1 June 1998.

325 For details, see www.pppindia.com; also see Journalists Against Nuclear Weapons, *Media Bomb* (1998), www.pppindia.com.

326 "Nuclear escalation," *The Hindu*, 4 September 2003; also see editorial, "Reduce nuclear risk reduction with Pakistan," *The Hindu*, 19 June 2004.

327 "Reduce nuclear risk with Pakistan," *The Hindu*, 19 June 2004; also see, editorial, "Significance of Shaheen-II," *The Hindu*, 12 March 2004.

328 See B. Muralidhar Reddy, "Pakistan open stocks with nuclear suppliers groups," *The Hindu*, 12 April 2005; C. Raja Mohan, "Pakistan tailgates India to seek nuclear reactors from France," *The Indian Express*, 19 May 2005.

329 C.Raja Mohan, *Crossing the Rubicon: The Shaping of India's New Foreign Policy* (New Delhi: Penguin Books India, 2003), p.284; also see C.Raja Mohan, "Jaswant Singh for consensus on the CTBT," *The Hindu*, 29 November 1999; C.Raja Mohan, "Early solutions to nuclear issues will help," *The Hindu*, 14 January 2000.

330 See for example, "In dubious hands," *The Pioneer*, 24 October 2002; G.Parthasarathy, "Pervez the proliferator," *The Pioneer*, 24 October 2002.

331 Jasjit Singh, "Future of Pakistan's nuclear weapons: and the consequences of the war against terrorism," *Financial Express*, 27 October 2001.

332 Amar Chandel, "USA knew about Pak N-help to North Korea," *The Tribune*, 23 January 2003.

333 *The Pioneer*, 24 June 2002.

334 Prakash Nanda, "Natural allies in a nuclear world," *The Asian Age*, 21 October 2002.

335 V.K.Grover, "Trading secrets," *The Pioneer*, 21 November 2002.

336 *The Hindustan Times*, 21 October 2002.

337 See "Now n-terrorism," *The Tribune*, 30 May 2002; "Declare Pakistan a terrorist state," *The Pioneer*, 29 May 2002; "Nuclear blackmail," *The Tribune*, 11 June 2002.

338 Editorial, "To curb proliferation," *The Hindu*, 13 Janurary 2004; also see editorial, "Pardoning a proliferator," *The Hindu*, 10 February 2004; "Iran nuclear programme tied to Pakistan: Report," *The Hindu*, 22 December 2003; "Pakistan in a spot over nuclear technology transfers," *The Hindu*, 23 December 2003; "Khan being debriefed," *The Hindu*, 23 December 2003.

339 See M.R.Srinivasan, "Pakistan's nuclear deals," *The Hindu*, 13 January 2004; Rajeev Sharma, "Pakistan under a cloud," *The Tribune*, 25 January 2004; Anil Narendra, "Pakistan's dirty nuclear secrets," *The Pioneer*, 6 February 2004; editorial, "A Khan of Worms: Pakistan's nuclear strategy shaky," *The Times of India*, 7 February 2004; G. Balachandran, "Fallout of Pakistan's nuclear proliferation," *Financial Express*, 9 February 2004; Amit Baruah, "Israel concerned over nuclear proliferation by Pakistan," *The Hindu*, 11 February 2004; Sidharth Varadarajan, "Pardon us, but Pakistan's slip is showing," *The Times of India*, 11 February 2004; C. Raja Mohan, "Responding to Pakistan's proliferation," *The Hindu*, 12 February 2004; Jasjit Singh, "Pakistan's Nuclear bazaar," *The Indian Express*, 19 February 2004.

340 T.Jayaraman, "Good nukes, bad nukes," *The Hindu*, 28 February 2004.

341 Ibid.

# 5
# Conclusion

The mass media, that most ubiquitous of structures of political communication, have come of age. The manner in which information is framed and disseminated by the media has a bearing on the perceptions of people and as such play a crucial role in moulding public opinion. However, the performance of the media in moulding perceptions of threat and security in particular has several serious implications. Though the media often perform the role of the watchdog of democracy in the domestic setting, this is not always the case in the realm of foreign and defence policies. In view of the emerging perspective that security can no longer be viewed only from the traditional perspective of the state and its territorial concerns, the way in which the media engage with issues of security or the shaping of security perceptions has a profound impact on state and society.

The foregoing chapters sought to examine how the mass media help define the parameters of security and perceptions of threat. The increasingly market-driven mainstream media often tend to ignore alternative perspectives and voices of dissent, and to favour the mainstream realist paradigm of foreign policy and security. It is only in cases where consensus in the dominant discourse begins to disappear that the media is forced to take a different course and reflect public debate. The media tend to promote rather than contest the policies of governments in the external sphere. This is often the case if events are placed in the 'national security' frame by the political elite. Divergence in coverage occurs only when there are differences in the 'spectrum of debate' in the dominant discourse. Through the very process of selection and presentation of news, the use of sources, framing of threat/insecurity, etc., the mainstream media reflect the dominant security discourse in society. The media thus play a crucial role in the process of securitisation.

In the case of South Asia, threat perceptions of the dominant discourse in the region continue to be based on a realist state-centric paradigm. Competing notions of national identity are interlinked to perceptions of security in the region. Evidently, the circumstances and process of Partition and the problems emanating from it continue to define the security/insecurity narrative in South Asia. Even after six decades, the perceptions and policies of both India and Pakistan have the same trajectory of 'threat' vis-à-vis each other.

According to the dominant security discourse in India, the main source of threat to the country arises from external forces which also foment trouble within. Indian perceptions are also linked to the extent of international support Pakistan can obtain at any point of time. In keeping with the realist approach, both countries have sought an arms build up to ensure their security. While India continues to maintain its military dominance in the region, Pakistan seeks to reduce this preponderance. Clearly, the approach to security in both countries continues to be based on a state-centric paradigm focusing on military security against external or internal threats. Threat perceptions relating to military balances and imbalances, and territorial concerns are given highest priority. The language of security is one of exclusion, reinforcing boundary distinctions between 'self' and 'other'. In the process, negative qualities are attributed to the 'other'. Issues of security are often sought to be placed above politics so that they cannot be questioned. Dissent to this dominant security discourse in the region however, does exist, albeit in a limited way. Dissenting voices perceive threats to be primarily at the internal level. Threats are perceived to be related to questions of unresolved identity, social, political and economic inequalities, mismanagement and alienation, which have been exacerbated by external factors, and the failure to integrate diverse social groups into the political processes. The counter-narratives in both countries seek reductions in defence spending and an improvement of relations, rather than the projection of an 'evil' 'other'. However, it is the realist security approach that tends to be projected by the mass media.

The analysis of the performance of the mainstream press in India has revealed that it largely emphasises news framed in the realist, state-centric, territorial paradigm of security, thereby marginalising voices of dissent. There is often a reductionist construction of conflict as territorial disputes or ethnic conflicts. This ignores the larger socio-economic and political dimensions of the issues concerned. Defence and foreign affairs being generally considered sacrosanct, there is a distortion of the priorities of security and a reflection of government perspectives regarding security and national interest. In this process, the media tend to willingly participate in the demonisation of Pakistan. Pakistan is usually framed in the press in the context of the danger that it poses. The mainstream Indian press has evidently internalised the national security perceptions of the dominant discourse, reinforcing images of Pakistan as a major source of threat to the country. This becomes explicit even in such circumstances as the reporting of cricket matches between the two countries and the nature of reporting on Kashmir. In reporting Pakistan's defence and foreign policies, the Indian press is largely preoccupied with its relations with other countries, its arms acquisitions, and developments in the nuclear field. All such issues are usually framed so as to enhance threat perceptions. There are often simultaneous calls for increased defence budgets and arms build-up. More importantly, there is a projection of government statements on the threat from Pakistan, as well as its ability to cope with the threat. Negative qualities of aggression, threat and danger are attributed to the 'other'/Pakistan. There is often a demonisation of Pakistan. It is projected as being responsive only to the threat or use of force. There is a stress on the detrimental aspects of Pakistani politics and society, sensationalising human rights violations, separatist movements, voices of dissent, etc. News which depict Pakistan in negative light, tend to appear on the front pages whereas that in positive, if any, are sidelined. In other words, reports reinforcing old stereotypes are highlighted while others ignored. Situated as it is within the historical circumstances of South Asia, news in the region is constructed, with political, economic and socio-cultural interests exerting pressure on the selection and presentation of news. As such there have also been positive changes in the nature of coverage which are in keeping with the changes in the overall political atmosphere in the subcontinent. In times of peace building there is often an overwhelming euphoria in the press. Yet even then, India is projected as the country that took the initiative. An underlying sense of distrust in India-Pakistan relations is reflected in the continuing process of the framing of news relating to Pakistan. Threat perceptions in the South Asian scenario are clearly sustained by various factors, not least being the mass media.

In the context of Pakistan's nuclear programme, the dominant discourse in India has again tended to project adversarial images. The identification of Pakistan as the 'other' in India's security discourse was reflected in discourses on nuclear issues, especially since the 1970s. This was evident in pronouncements by the government, political parties and the strategic community. Governments over the years have stressed the grave consequences that Pakistan's nuclear development would have for India, while at the same time emphasising their ability to cope with any such situation. Concern has also been expressed at China's missile and nuclear cooperation with Pakistan, together with perceptions of a tacit United States-Pakistan relationship in the nuclear field. Immediately following the 1998 Pokhran tests, the government stressed the threat from Pakistan and China, and argued that Pakistan's Chagai tests vindicated its actions. Pakistan's nuclear policy was seen to have predated India's as well as been based on technology obtained through clandestine methods. There has been an increasingly vociferous articulation of threats from Pakistan and the capability of the government to protect the country. There has been near unanimity among the political parties of India also with regard to Pakistan's nuclear programme. Debates in parliament often witnessed emphatic criticism of developments in Pakistan's nuclear policy, underscoring the threat from that country. Efforts to securitise the issue were evident in the parliamentary debates relating to the 1998 tests, where the need for unanimity was stressed. The response to certain criticism was to tell the critic to 'go and live in Pakistan'. One's perceptions of the tests were reckoned to be an indication of patriotism. The strategic community has been the most consistent and vociferous on Pakistan's nuclear policy. While advocating nuclear weapons for varying reasons, including power, prestige, deterrence and stability, it depicted India's policy (until 1998) to be 'peaceful' in contrast to that of Pakistan's 'sinister' and 'militaristic' one. This is sought to be proved by discarding claims of it being reactive to India's policies as well as by emphasising the role of the personality and domestic constraints of Pakistan's leaders. The 1998 Pokhran tests found its strongest supporters among this strategic community which justified the tests based on threats from Pakistan and China, the need to make India's deterrent credible, and the failure of the nuclear weapons countries to take any efforts towards disarmament. Concern has been evinced among the strategic community regarding the implications of an 'Islamic bomb' for secular and democratic India. So also, the various peace proposals put forth by Pakistan are depicted as 'unfeasible', 'impractical', 'anti-India', 'pro-west', etc.

Pronouncements of the government, political parties and the strategic community have therefore been mutually reinforcing with regard to Pakistan's nuclear programme, notwithstanding the differences noted, and have constituted the dominant discourse on the issue. Negative images of Pakistan's nuclear policy are continually projected in contrast to India's own sanitised one, inculcating the need for security. In the process, nuclear issues are also sought to be securitised, raising them above politics and making them unquestionable.

The counter-narrative with regard to the nuclear question in India is based on a negative conception of nuclear weapons. It calls for their rejection on moral, political, economic, legal or strategic grounds. According to the counter-narrative, it is not external threat perceptions, but internal self-perceptions which are important in nuclear decision-making. The counter-narrative perceives the 1998 tests to have been the result of internal factors, specifically the construction of a national identity antithetical to Pakistan in the context of the emergence of Hindu nationalism. In other words, it was not changes in threat perceptions, or the external security environment, but in elite self-perceptions, which led to the tests. The tests were also seen to have granted legitimacy to weapons of mass destruction as well as aggressive nationalism. It is also stressed that there had been no informed consensus on the issue. Dissenting voices consider Pakistan's route to nuclearisation as straightforward and reactive to India, having emerged in the 1960s, after India had built its research reactor and reprocessing plant. Arguments of the dominant discourse that Pakistan's nuclear policy is not conditioned by India's actions, but is independently motivated are considered unconvincing. While the existence of other factors is acknowledged, India is considered to be the decisive factor. The threat projected from Pakistan is seen to falter on it's willingness to explore denuclearisation. So also, the Sino-Pakistan nuclear collaboration is perceived to be exaggerated so as to justify India's policy. Nuclear proliferation is viewed negatively, irrespective of whether it is facilitated by a military regime or a democratic one.

However, notwithstanding the counter-narrative, the nuclear issue is largely framed in the Indian press within the framework of the realist security discourse. This study has clearly shown how the press tends to underscore official perspectives regarding Pakistan's nuclear programme, obfuscating issues in their wider context. The demonisation of Pakistan's nuclear programme is in stark contrast to the sanitised depiction of India's, helping to reinforce and legitimise government perspectives and policies. The mainstream press in the 1950s and 1960s revealed an emphasis on government pronouncements and statements on disarmament and peaceful uses of nuclear energy. The Chinese nuclear explosion of 1964 largely found a reflection of government responses. So also was the case with the later debate surrounding the Non-Proliferation Treaty. India's nuclear explosion in 1974 was almost unanimously welcomed in the Indian press as a morale booster, and a major technological achievement, signifying India's entry into the nuclear club. There were also calls to keep the nuclear option open. Later years found an increased focus on Pakistan's nuclear policy stressing the threat from an Islamic bomb.

Over the years, frequent speculative reports regarding Pakistan's capability and political will to produce nuclear weapons appeared in the Indian press. Largely emanating from the West, particularly from official and non-official sources in the United States and the American media, these write-ups usually focused on unconfirmed reports of Sino-Pak nuclear and missile cooperation, and Pakistan's clandestine efforts at developing its nuclear technology. These reports strongly reverberated in the Indian press. The close attention paid to western media sources on such issues should be seen in contrast to the defensive nature of reports referring to western media criticism of any aspect of India's nuclear or missile programme. The selective manner in which western news was reproduced was also evident in the defensive framing of news regarding developments which were not endorsed by the government.

The 1990s by and large witnessed an explicit pro-nuclear stance by the Indian press, which strongly emphasised the Sino-Pak nuclear cooperation. There was now an increased stress on detailed inventories of Pakistan's arms purchases and capabilities against India, thereby enhancing perceptions of threat. This was particularly evident in headlines more than the text per se. Press coverage of the Comprehensive Test Ban Treaty (CTBT) debate prior to the 1998 tests was reflective of the general trend in reporting nuclear issues, and facilitated a consensus on the debate. Taking a populist, anti-United States approach, issues of state sovereignty were highlighted. The nature of the coverage of the CTBT debate, as well as calls for acceleration of India's missile programme, the manner in which news regarding A.P.J.Abdul Kalam's designation to receive the Bharat Ratna was framed, the strong emphasis on Pakistan's Ghauri missile tests and its capability to hit Indian cities, all served to create an atmosphere conducive to testing nuclear weapons.

The content analysis of the three selected newspapers during the months of May, June and July 1998 is very revealing, reflecting as it did the precise nature of press coverage and information dissemination. In early May 1998, prior to India's Pokhran-II tests, there was a focus on Pakistan's missile programme and its international linkages and consequent threat to India. The projection of India's tests in the Indian press reflected government claims of having secured legitimate international status and scientific achievement based on consensus. A similar reflection of government concerns was seen in the rationale of Sino-Pakistan nuclear interaction, the need to make the country's deterrent credible, and the readiness to sign the CTBT. The strong emphasis on government perspectives in news reports served to reinforce the same. Press reporting also amounted to ridiculing Pakistan's nuclear capability after Pokhran-II, projecting technological ineptitude as its sole reason for not testing. By mid-May, however, reports of an imminent test by western sources saw an increased focus on the 'clandestine' basis of Pakistan's nuclear programme and its supposed benefactors (particularly North Korea and China).

Pakistan's Chagai tests on 28 May 1998 were reflected in the Indian press as a vindication of India's nuclear policy, with a strong emphasis on the reactions of Indian political leaders. *The Hindu,* however, showed more restraint in reporting and provided more space to the reactions and statements from Pakistan. As against the celebration of science and technology after Pokhran-II, all the newspapers displayed a strong scepticism of Pakistan's scientific acumen, questioning the number, size, yield and success of Pakistan's tests as well as highlighting its clandestine basis and Chinese help, in contrast to India's indigenous programme. Reports during the immediate post test period saw an increased focus on Sino-Pakistan cooperation, tacit connivance of the United States, Pakistan's clandestine nuclear programme, explicit references to an 'Islamic bomb,' and the possibility of Pakistan transferring nuclear technology to North Korea or the Islamic world. Analyses in the Indian press during this period reflected a legitimisation of deterrence and the role of nuclear weapons in providing stability, calling for constructive diplomacy to ensure that the gains outweighed the losses. At the same time, there were a number of speculative reports based on international media sources projecting threats from Pakistan's nuclear and missile programmes.

The press also revelled in the negative reaction of other countries to Pakistan's nuclear tests, while deflecting that from India's own tests, by way of selective reporting, placement of reports and taking shelter behind innocuous headlines or those referring to Pakistan alone. The press also projected Pakistan as the main obstacle to détente in the subcontinent. While India's offers for a dialogue got much prominence, those of Pakistan were downplayed. Any positive effort by Pakistan was seen to be a logical consequence of India's own efforts or of international coercion. With regard to the CTBT, the complete turnaround by all the newspapers on the issue of India signing the treaty is of significance. In fact, prior to the tests there had been the most vociferous rejection of the treaty by the press. But the period under study found a unanimous approach to signing the CTBT together with the perspective in the press on the need to create a consensus on the issue. The implications of this need no emphasis. The study of the coverage of the 1998 tests clearly reveals the role of the mainstream Indian press in the process of securitisation. It shows how the press largely served to reinforce threat perceptions in the region. It helped in the process of securitisation of Pakistan and its nuclear policy, simultaneously helping to legitimise India's own policy.

Post-1998 coverage has witnessed certain changes reflecting the 'spectrum of debate' on the issue in the dominant discourse. Divergences of opinion in the dominant discourse were reflected in the mass media. Yet the general trend of highlighting threats from Pakistan continues unabated. Despite the existence of voices of dissent in India, these are very much marginalised in the mainstream press. While opinions reinforcing government perspectives are found in the opinion pages and are well cited in headlines and news reports in the other pages of the newspapers, negating stances by way of comparison are more visible in the opinion pages. The magnitude of articles by pronounced nuclear hawks and former Foreign Service officials leaves no doubt as to which side the balance tilts. More importantly, those in the latter group are also provided space for analysis in the other pages of the newspapers too, and are also often the sources of news reports, thereby weighing down the balance of opinion even further. The selection and presentation of news including the nature of headlines, location and sources of news, all reflect the orientation of the press. Although there are differences among newspapers in their subtlety of reporting and responsibility in editing, there is a general unanimity in the demonisation of Pakistan's nuclear programme, correspondingly justifying India's nuclear policy. While there have been exceptions, press reporting of Pakistan's nuclear policy, over the years, has very clearly reflected the dominant discourse on threat perceptions, with editorials often taking their cue from the strategic community and helping to set the stage for, or sustain the various nuances in official policy.

In keeping with the overall political atmosphere in the subcontinent there have been intermittent changes in the depiction of Pakistan by the Indian press. These changes were largely a reflection of changes in the dominant discourse. However, an essential hostility in India-Pakistan relations is reflected in the continuing process of the framing of news relating to Pakistan.

The role of the media in the process of securitisation and in sustaining the realist paradigm in security matters has been particularly evident in South Asia. This was again reflected in the coverage of the civilian nuclear agreement with the United States where the issue was generally framed in the realist military strategic perspective rather than in a human security or energy security framework. In mediating perceptions of threat, the press has facilitated the inculcation of the values of militarism. The increasing importance of non-military threats and socio-economic insecurities serve as a context for challenging the basic underlying assumptions of the existing security paradigm in South Asia. Security needs to be viewed from a holistic perspective rather than as privileging the state and its military power. There is evidently a necessity to widen security perspectives, a need to reformulate security in less exclusionary terms, emerging from a concern for societal security. The most important prerequisite in changing the national security agenda of both India and Pakistan is a change in the perceptions and mindsets of the people as well as the policy-makers. The significance of the mass media in this process of rearticulating and reshaping security concerns cannot be sidelined. Questions of media ownership and management are often raised in addressing such concerns. An array of media centric recommendations, such as, the judicious use of sources, objective reporting and framing of news and headlines, improvement of cross-border communication, etc. could all make a difference in facilitating changes in mindsets. Yet, in the very specific context of South Asia, the crux of the issue is largely the question of perceptions and the internalisation of images that have taken place over the years. The mass media of the region has the potential and capability to play a positive role in reorienting perceptions of threat and security. This would necessitate a delinking of news frames from its preoccupation with the dominant traditional state security perspective. Media sensitivity to wider notions of security is imperative, given its possible implications for informed debate and policy-making in the region.

# Bibliography

## PRIMARY SOURCES

### Government Documents

India, Department of Atomic Energy, *10 Years of Atomic Energy in India: 1954-1964* (Bombay, 1967).

————, "Two Decades of the Atom in India," *Nuclear India*, Vol.6, No. 12, August 1968.

————, *Nuclear Weapons: A Compilation Prepared by the DAE* (Bombay, 1970).

India, Lok Sabha, *Debates*, 1954 to 2007.

India, Lok Sabha Secretariat, *Development of Nuclear Energy for Peaceful Uses: Policy, Programmes and Achievements* (New Delhi, August 1974).

India, Ministry of Defence, *Annual Report, 1963-64* to 2006-07 (New Delhi).

India, Ministry of External Affairs, *Pakistan's War Propaganda Against India: September 1950 - June 1951* (New Delhi, n.d.).

————, *Pakistan's War Propaganda Against India: 1 July 1951-15 August 1951* (New Delhi, n.d).

————, *Annual Report, 1963-64* to *2006-07* (New Delhi).

————, *Foreign Affairs Record,* 1964 to 2001 (New Delhi).

————, *Disarmament: India's Initiatives* (New Delhi: Publications Division, 1988).

————, *Status of Nuclear Weapons in International Law: Request for Advisory Opinion of the International Court of Justice*, Mimeo (New Delhi, 1995).

————, *Draft Report of National Security Advisory Board on Indian Nuclear Doctrine, 17 August 1999* (Washington DC: Embassy of India), www.indianembassy.org.

————, *Brief of India's Nuclear Tests: Global Disarmament or Equal and Legitimate Security for All* (Washington DC: Embassy of India), www.indianembassy.org.

————, *Nuclear Non-Proliferation* (Washington DC: Embassy of India), www.indianembassy.org.

India, Ministry of Home Affairs, *Annual Reports, 2001-02 to 2006-07* (New Delhi), www.mha.nic.in.

India, Ministry of Information and Broadcasting, *Nuclear Explosions and their Effects* (New Delhi: Publications Division, 1958).

————, *Report of the Fact Finding Committee on Newspaper Economics* (New Delhi, 1975).

India, Rajya Sabha, *Debates*, 1954 to 2007.

India, *Report of the Press Commission: Part I* (New Delhi: Government of India Press, 1954).

India, *Report of the Second Press Commission*, Vol.I (New Delhi: Government of India Press, 1982).

Pakistan, *Foreign Affairs Pakistan*, 1972 to 1980.

Pakistan, Ministry of Foreign Affairs, Foreign Affairs Division, *The Nuclear Challenge*, www.pakistan.gov.pk.

Pakistan, National Assembly, *Debates*, 1957 to 1976.

*Statement by Ambassador Munir Akram at the Special Session of the Conference on Disarmament*, 2 June

1998, www.pakistan.gov.pk.

*Text of the Press Briefing by the Foreign Secretary of Pakistan Announcing further Nuclear Tests*, 30 May 1998, www.clw.org.

*Text of the statement by Prime Minister Nawaz Sharif at Press Conference*, 28 May 1998, www.acronym.org.

Canada, *Human Security: Safety for People in a Changing World* (Ottawa: Department of Foreign Affairs and International Trends, 1999), www.yorku.ca.

## Memoirs, Speeches, etc.

Bhutto, Zulfikar Ali, *Reshaping Foreign Policy: A Collection of Articles, Statements and Speeches: Politics of the People, Vol.1, 1948-1966* (Rawalpindi: Pakistan Publications, n.d.).

————, *Foreign Policy of Pakistan: A Compendium of Speeches made in the National Assembly of Pakistan, 1962-64* (Karachi: Pakistan Institute of International Affairs, 1964).

————, *The Quest for Peace: Selections from Speeches and Writings 1963-65* (Karachi: Pakistan Institute of International Affairs, 1966).

————, *Awakening the People: A Collection of Articles, Statements and Speeches: Politics of the People, Vol.2, 1966-1969* (Karachi: Public Relations, n.d.).

————, *The Myth of Independence* (Karachi: Oxford University Press, 1969).

————, *If I am Assassinated* (New Delhi: Vikas, 1979).

Gopal, S. (ed.), *Selected Works of Jawaharlal Nehru*, Second Series - Volume 11 (New Delhi:

Jawaharlal Nehru Memorial Fund, 1992).

Hyder, Sajjad, *Foreign Policy of Pakistan: Reflections of an Ambassador* (Lahore: Progressive, 1987).

India, Ministry of Information and Broadcasting, *Selected Speeches of Lal Bahadur Shastri: 11 June 1964 to 10 January 1966* (New Delhi: Publications Division, 1974).

————, *For a United India: Speeches of Sardar Patel: 1947-1950* (New Delhi: Publications Division, 1982).

————, *Jawaharlal Nehru's Speeches: August 1949 - February 1953,* Vol.2 (New Delhi: Publications Division, 1983).

————, *Jawaharlal Nehru's Speeches: March 1953 - August 1957,* Vol.3 (New Delhi: Publications Division, 1983).

————, *Jawaharlal Nehru's Speeches: September 1957- April 1963,* Vol.4 (New Delhi: Publications Division, 1983).

————, *Rajiv Gandhi: Selected Speeches and Writings: 31 October 1984 to 31 December 1985,* Vol.I (New Delhi: Publications Division, 1987).

————, *V.P.Singh, Selected Speeches and Writings, 1989-1990* (New Delhi: Publications Division, 1993).

Khan, Liaquat Ali, *Pakistan: The Heart of Asia: Speeches in the United States and Canada, May and June 1950, by the Prime Minister of Pakistan* (Karachi: National Book Foundation, 1976).

Khan, Mohammad Ayub, *Friends, Not Masters: A Political Autobiography* (London: Oxford University Press, 1967).

Mathew, George (ed.), *George Fernandes Speaks* (New

Delhi: Ajanta, 1991).

Pakistan, *Mohammad Ayub Khan, Pakistan Perspective: A Collection of Important Articles and Excerpts from Major Addresses* (Washington DC: Embassy of Pakistan, n.d.).

Pakistan, *Zulfikar Ali Bhutto: Speeches and Statements, 1 October 1972–31 December 1972* (Karachi: Government of Pakistan, 1973).

*Speeches and Statements by Field Marshal Ayub Khan, Vol.IV, July 1961-June 1962* (Karachi: Pakistan Publications, n.d.).

*Speeches and Statements by Field Marshal Ayub Khan, Vol.V, July 1962-June 1963* (Karachi: Pakistan Publications, n.d.).

*Speeches and Statements by Field Marshal Ayub Khan, Vol.VI, July 1963-June 1964* (Karachi: Pakistan Publications, n.d.).

## Reports, Resolutions, etc.

Audit Bureau of Circulations, *ABC Certificates: Audit Period 1 July to 31 December 1998, Serial No.100* (Mumbai: Audit Bureau of Circulations, 1998).

Bharatiya Jana Sangh, *Party Documents: Vol.3: Resolutions on Defence and External Affairs* (New Delhi: Bharatiya Jana Sangh, 1973).

Bharatiya Janata Party, *Election Manifesto 1998*, www.bjp.org.

Desai, Balwant A. (ed.), *Atoms for Peace: An Exposition of India's Nuclear Policy* (New Delhi: AICC, 1975).

Goyal, S.K. and M.Challapathi Rao, *Ownership and Control Structure of the Indian Press* (New Delhi: Indian Institute of Public Administration, 1981).

Haq, Mahbub ul, *Human Development in South Asia, 1997* (New Delhi: Oxford University Press, 1997).

Indian Institute of Mass Communication, *The Media and Kargil: Information War: Media a Victim or a Tool* (1999), www.thehoot.org.

International Commission for the Study of Communication Problems, *Many Voices, One World: Towards a New More Just and More Efficient World Information and Communication Order* (New Delhi: Oxford and IBH, 1982).

Joint Press Statement issued by the Communist Party of India (Marxist) and the Communist Party of India on 29th May on the Nuclear Tests conducted by Pakistan, www.proxsa.org.

Malhan, P.N., *Communication Media: Yesterday, Today and Tomorrow* (New Delhi: Ministry of Information and Broadcasting, 1985).

NAMEDIA, *Media Conference of the Non-Aligned Movement, New Delhi: 9-12 December 1983: Final Report and Documents* (New Delhi: NAMEDIA, 1984).

National Democratic Alliance, *For a Proud, Prosperous India: An Agenda*, www.bjp.org.

Report of the Commission on Global Governance, *Our Global Neighbourhood* (Oxford: Oxford University Press, 1995).

Report of the Independent Commission on Disarmament and Security Issues, *Common Security: A Programme for Disarmament* (London: Pan Books, 1982).

Report of the Independent Commission on International Development Issues, *North-South: A Programme for Survival* (London: Pan Books, 1980).

SIPRI, *Yearbook of World Armaments and Disarmament 1975* (Stockholm: Almqvist and Wikell, 1975).

The Brandt Commission, *Common Crisis: North-South: Cooperation for World Recovery* (London: Pan Books, 1983).

The Kargil Review Committee Report, *From Surprise to Reckoning* (New Delhi: Sage, 2000).

The Report of the South Commission, *The Challenge to the South* (Oxford: Oxford University Press, 1990).

United Nations Development Programme, *Human Development Report: New Dimensions of Human Security* (Oxford: Oxford University Press, 1994).

————, *Human Development in South Asia, 1997: The Challenge of Human Development* (New Delhi: Oxford University Press, 1997).

————, *Human Development in South Asia, 1999: The Crisis of Governance* (Oxford: Oxford University Press, 1999).

UNESCO, *New Communication Order-9: Historical Background of the Mass Media Declaration* (Paris: UNESCO, 1978).

————, *Transnational Communication and Cultural Industries* (Paris: UNESCO, 1982).

————, *Communication and Society-19: A Documentary History of a New World Information and Communication Order Seen as an Evolving and Continuous Process 1975-1986* (Paris: UNESCO, 1988).

World Bank, *Staff Appraisal Report: Islamic Republic of Pakistan: Social Action Program Project* (Washington D.C: World Bank, 8 March 1994).

————, *World Development Report 2000-01: Attacking Poverty* (Oxford: Oxford University Press, 2001).

World Commission on Environment and Development,

*Our Common Future* (Oxford: Oxford University Press, 1987).

Zaidi, A.M. (ed.), *The Annual Register of Indian Political Parties: Proceedings and Fundamental Texts, 1981* (New Delhi: Indian Institute of Applied Political Research, 1981).

————, *The Annual Register of Indian Political Parties: Proceedings and Fundamental Texts, 1985* (New Delhi: Indian Institute of Applied Political Research, 1987).

## SECONDARY SOURCES

### Books

Abraham, Itty, *The Making of the Indian Atomic Bomb: Science, Secrecy and the Post-Colonial State* (New Delhi: Orient Longman, 1999).

Aggarwal, S. K., *Press at the Crossroads in India* (New Delhi: UDH Publishing House, 1988).

Arno, Andrew and Wimal Dissanayake (eds.), *The News Media in National and International Conflict* (Boulder: Westview, 1984).

Ayoob, Mohammed (ed.), *Conflict and Intervention in the Third World* (London: Croom Helm, 1980).

Babbage, Ross and Sandy Gordon (eds.), *India's Strategic Future: Regional State or Global Power?* (Delhi: Oxford University Press, 1992).

Bajpai, Kanti P., P.R Chari, Pervaiz Iqbal Cheema, Stephen P.Cohen and Sumit Ganguly, *Brasstacks and Beyond: Perception and Management of Crisis* (New Delhi: Manohar, 1995).

Banerjee, Sumanta, *India's Monopoly Press: A Mirror of Distortion* (New Delhi: Indian Federation of Working Journalists, 1973).

Barnds, William J., *India, Pakistan, and the Great Powers* (London: Pall Mall, 1972).

Basu, Partha Pratim, *The Press and Foreign Policy in India* (New Delhi: Lancer's Books, 2003).

Bhatia, Shyam, *India's Nuclear Bomb* (New Delhi: Vikas, 1979).

Bhola, P.L., *Pakistan's Nuclear Policy* (New Delhi: Sterling, 1993).

Bidwai, Praful and Achin Vanaik, *Testing Times: The Global Stake in a Nuclear Test Ban* (Uppasala: Dag Hammarskjold Foundation, 1996).

————, *South Asia on a Short Fuse: Nuclear Politics and the Future of Global Disarmament* (New Delhi: Oxford University Press, 1999).

Booth, Ken and Steve Smith (eds.), *International Relations Theory Today* (University Park: The Pennsylvania State University Press, 1995).

Bose, Sumantra, *The Challenge in Kashmir: Democracy, Self-determination and a Just Peace* (New Delhi: Sage, 1997).

Boyd–Barrett, Oliver and Chris Newbold (eds.), *Approaches to Media: A Reader* (London: Arnold, 1995).

Brandt, Willy, *World Armament and World Hunger: A Call for Action* (London: Victor Gollancz, 1986).

Brines, Russell, *India-Pakistan Conflict* (London: Pall Mall Press, 1968).

Buzan, Barry, *People, States and Fear: The National Security Problem in International Relations* (New Delhi: Transasia, 1987).

Buzan, Barry, Charles Jones and Richard Little, *The Logic of Anarchy: Neorealism to Structural Realism* (New York: Columbia University Press, 1993).

Buzan, Barry and Ole Waever, *Regions and Powers: The Structure of International Security* (Cambridge: Cambridge University Press, 2003).

Campbell, David, *Writing Security: United States Foreign Policy and the Politics of Identity* (Minneapolis: University of Minnesota Press, 1992).

Carey, Roger, and Trevor C. Salmon (eds.), *International Security in the Modern World* (Basingstoke: Macmillan, 1996).

Cheema, Pervaiz Iqbal, *Pakistan's Defence Policy, 1947-1958* (Houndmills: Macmillan, 1990).

Cohen, Bernard C., *The Press and Foreign Policy* (Princeton: Princeton University Press, 1963).

Cortright, David and Amitabh Matoo (eds.), *India and the Bomb: Public Opinion and Nuclear Options* (Notre Dame: University of Notre Dame Press, 1996).

Dillon, Michael, *Politics of Security: Towards a Political Philosophy of Continental Thought* (London: Routledge, 1996).

Grover, Verinder (ed.), *Political System in India,* Vol.V (New Delhi: Deep and Deep, 1989).

Gunther, Richard and Anthony Mughan (eds.), *Democracy and the Media: A Comparative Perspective* (Cambridge: Cambridge University Press, 2000).

Gupta, Sisir, *Kashmir: A Study in India-Pakistan Relations* (New Delhi: Asia Publishing House, 1966).

Hansen, Anders, Simon Cottle, Ralph Negrine and Chris Newbold (eds.), *Mass Communication Research Methods* (Basingstoke: Macmillan, 1998).

Harshe, Rajen and K.M. Seethi (eds.), *Engaging with the World: Critical Reflections on India's Foreign Policy* (New Delhi: Orient Longman, 2005).

Herman, Edward S. and Noam Chomsky, *Manufacturing Consent: The Political Economy of the Mass Media* (New York: Pantheon, 1988).

Jain, J.P., *Nuclear India:* Vol.2 (New Delhi: Radiant, 1974).

Jeffrey, Robin, *India's Newspaper Revolution* (New Delhi: Oxford University Press, 1999).

Jervis, Robert, *Perception and Misperception in International Politics* (Princeton: Princeton University Press, 1976).

————, *The Logic of Images in International Relations* (New York: Columbia University Press, 1989).

Joseph, Teresa, *Perceptions of Pakistan in India: A Study of the Coverage of Pakistan in the Indian Press* (Unpublished M.Phil dissertation submitted to the Mahatma Gandhi University, Kottayam, 1993).

Kapur, Ashok, *India's Nuclear Option: Atomic Diplomacy and Decision Making* (New York: Praeger, 1976).

————, *Pakistan's Nuclear Development* (London: Croom Helm, 1987).

Karnad, Bharat (ed.), *Future Imperilled: India's Security in the 1990s and Beyond* (New Delhi: Viking, 1994).

————, *Nuclear Weapons and Indian Security: The Realist Foundations of Strategy* [New Delhi: Macmillan, 2002].

Kaul, Ravi, *India's Nuclear Spin-Off* (Allahabad: Chanakya, 1974).

Kavic, Lorne J., *India's Quest for Security: Defence Policies 1947-1965* (Berkeley: University of

California Press, 1967).

Keohane, Robert (ed.), *Neorealism and its Critics* (New York: Columbia University Press, 1986).

Kharkanis, Sharad, *Indian Politics and the Role of the Press* (New Delhi: Vikas, 1981).

Klapper, Joseph T., *The Effects of Mass Communication* (New York: Free Press, 1960).

Klare, Michael T. and Yogesh Chandrani (eds.), *World Security: Challenges for a New Century* (New York: St Martin's, 1998).

Koithara, Varghese, *Society and State: The Indian Experience* (New Delhi: Sage, 1999).

Kothari, Rajni, *State Against Democracy: In Search of Humane Governance* (New Delhi: Ajanta, 1988).

Krause, Keith and Michael C. Williams (eds.), *Critical Security Studies: Concepts and Cases* (London: UCL Press, 1997).

Krepon, Michael, Khurshid Khoja, Michael Newbill and Jenny S.Drezin (ed.), *A Handbook of Confidence-Building Measures for Regional Security* (Washington D.C.: The Henry L. Stimson Center, 1998).

Lavoy, Peter, *Learning to Live with the Bomb* (Ithaca: Cornell University Press, 2000).

Lee, M.A., *Unreliable Sources: A Guide to Detecting Bias in Mass Media* (New York: Carol Publishing Group, 1990).

Lipschutz, Ronnie (ed.), *On Security* (New York: Columbia University Press, 1995).

Mahmud, Khalid, *Indian Political Scene, 1989: Main Contenders for Power* (Islamabad: Institute of Regional Studies, 1989).

Mattoo, Amitabh, *India's Nuclear Deterrent: Pokhran II and Beyond* (New Delhi: Har Anand, 1999).

McSweeney, Bill, *Security, Identity and Interests: A Sociology of International Relations* (Cambridge: Cambridge University Press, 1999).

Mermin, Jonathan, *Debating War and Peace: Media Coverage of US Intervention in the Post-Vietnam Era* (Princeton: Princeton University Press, 1999).

Mirchandani, G.G, *India's Nuclear Dilemma* (New Delhi: Popular, 1968).

Mohan, C.Raja, *Crossing the Rubicon: The Shaping of India's New Foreign Policy* (New Delhi: Penguin Books India, 2003).

Nizamani, Haider K., *The Roots of Rhetoric: Politics of Nuclear Weapons in India and Pakistan* (New Delhi: India Research Press, 2001).

Palit, D.K., and P.K.S.Namboodiri, *Pakistan's Islamic Bomb* (New Delhi: Vikas, 1979).

Pathak, K.K., *Nuclear Policy of India: A Third World Perspective* (New Delhi: Githanjali Prakashan, 1980).

Perkovich, George, *India's Nuclear Bomb: The Impact on Global Proliferation* (New Delhi: Oxford University Press, 2000).

Pillai, K.Raman, *India's Foreign Policy* (Meerut: Meenakshi Prakasan, 1969).

Ram, N., *Riding the Nuclear Tiger* (New Delhi: Leftword Books, 1999).

Ramana, M.V., *Bombing Bombay: Effects of Nuclear Weapons and a Case Study of a Hypothetical Explosion* (Cambridge, Mass: International Physicians for the Prevention of Nuclear War, 1999).

Ramana, M.V., and C. Rammanohar Reddy, *Prisoners of the Nuclear Dream* (New Delhi: Orient Longman, 2003).

Rao, N. Bhaskara, *Indo-Pak Conflict: Controlled Mass Communication in Inter-State Relations* (New Delhi: S.Chand, 1971).

Rojecki, Andrew, *Silencing the Opposition: Antinuclear Movements and the Media in the Cold War* (Urbana: University of Illinois Press, 1999).

Said, Edward, *Covering Islam: How the Media and the Experts Determine How We See the Rest of the World* (London: Routledge and Kegan Paul, 1981).

Sainath, P., *Everybody Loves A Good Drought* (New Delhi: Penguin, 1996).

Scott, Andrew and Raymond Dawson (eds.), *Readings on the Making of American Foreign Policy* (New York: Macmillan, 1966).

Sen Gupta, Bhabani, *Nuclear Weapons? Policy Option for India* (New Delhi: Sage, 1983).

———— (ed.), *Regional Co-operation and Development in South Asia:* Vol.1 (New Delhi: South Asian Publishers, 1986).

Seshagiri, N., *The Bomb? Fallout of India's Nuclear Explosion* (New Delhi: Vikas, 1975).

Sharma, Dhirendra, *India's Nuclear Estate* (New Delhi: Lancers, 1983).

———— (ed.), *The Indian Atom: Power and Proliferation* (New Delhi: Philosophy and Social Action, 1986).

Shastri, Amita and A. Jayaratnam Wilson, *The Post-Colonial States of South Asia: Democracy, Identity, Development and Security* (Richmond, Surrey: Curzon, 2001).

Sidhu, W.P.S., Brian Cloughly, John H.Hawes and Teresita Schaffer, *Nuclear Risk Reduction Measures in Southern Asia* (Washington D.C: The Henry L. Stimson Center, November 1998).

Singh, Jasjit (ed.), *Nuclear India* (London: Knowledge World, 1998).

Singh, Jaswant, *Defending India* (St. Martin's Press: London, 1999).

Singh, Tavleen, *Kashmir: A Tragedy of Errors* (New Delhi: Penguin Books, 1996).

Sinha, P.B. and R.R.Subramanian, *Nuclear Pakistan: Atomic Threat to South Asia* (New Delhi: Vision, 1980).

Smith, Anthony, *The Geopolitics of Information: How Western Culture Dominates the World* (London: Faber and Faber, 1980).

Smith, Chris, *India's Ad Hoc Arsenal: Direction or Drift in Policy?* (Oxford: SIPRI and Oxford University Press, 1994).

Smith, Steve, Ken Booth and Marysia Zalewski (eds.), *International Theory: Positivism and Beyond* (Cambridge: Cambridge University Press, 1996).

Sreedhar (ed.), *Pakistan's Bomb: A Documentary Study* (New Delhi: ABC Publishing, 1987).

Subrahmanyam, K., (ed.), *Nuclear Myths and Realities* (New Delhi: ABC Publishing, 1981).

——————, *Indian Security Perspectives* (New Delhi: ABC Publishing, 1982).

—————— (ed.), *India and the Nuclear Challenge* (New Delhi: Lancer, 1986).

Taylor, Philip M., *Global Communications, International Affairs and Media Since 1945* (London: Routledge, 1997).

Thomas, Raju G.C., *The Defence of India: A Budgetary Perspective of Strategy and Politics* (Delhi: Macmillan, 1978).

Thussu, Daya Kishan and Des Freedman (eds.), *War and the Media: Reporting Conflict 24/7* ((New Delhi: Vistaar Publications, 2003).

Vanaik, Achin, *India in a Changing World: Problems, Limits and Successes of its Foreign Policy* (New Delhi: Orient Longman, 1995).

Vilanilam, J.V., *Reporting A Revolution: The Iranian Revolution and the NIICO Debate* (New Delhi: Sage, 1989).

Walker, R.B.J., *One World, Many Worlds: Struggles for a Just World Peace* (Boulder: Lynne Reinner, 1988).

————, *Inside/Outside: International Relations as Political Theory* (New York: Cambridge University Press, 1993).

Waltz, Kenneth. N., *Man, the State and War* (New York: Columbia University Press, 1959).

————, *Theory of International Politics* (Reading, Mass.: Addison-Wesley, 1979).

Wolfers, Arnold, *Discord and Collaboration* (Baltimore: Johns Hopkins University Press, 1962).

## Articles

Abraham, Itty, "India's 'Strategic Enclave': Civilian Scientists and Military Technologies," *Armed Forces and Society*, Vol.18, No.2, Winter 1992, pp.231-252.

Abrahamsen, Rita, "Blair's Africa: The Politics of Securitisation and Fear," *Alternatives*, Vol.30, No.1, January-March 2005, pp.59-70.

Ahmad, Aijaz, "The Hindutva Weapon," *Frontline*, Vol.15, No.11, 23 May-5 June 1998.

Ahmad, Irfan, "India-Pakistan: Friendship as Enmity," *Economic and Political Weekly*, Vol.38, No.31, 2 August 2003, pp.3231-3233.

Ahmad, Nasir, "The Atomic Energy Commission," *Pakistan Quarterly*, Vol.7, No.3, Autumn 1957.

Ahmed, Samina, "The (Nuclear) Testing of Pakistan," *Current History*, Vol.97, No.623, December 1998, pp.407-411.

Aiyar, Mani Shankar, "Censorship, Information and Understanding," *Himal South Asian*, June 2002, www.himalmag.com.

Ananth, V. Krishna, "The Politics of the Bomb: Some Observations on the Political Discourse in India in the Context of Pokhran II," in M.V.Ramana and C.Rammanohar Reddy (eds.), *Prisoners of the Nuclear Dream* (New Delhi: Orient Longman, 2003), pp.315-332.

Ayoob, Mohammed, "The Security Problematic of the Third World," *World Politics*, Vol. 43, No.2, January 1991, pp.257-283.

Bajpai, Kanti, "India's Nuclear Posture After Pokhran II," *International Studies*, Vol.37, No.4, December 2000, pp.267-301.

Banerjee, Sumanta, "Mid-Summer Madness over Human Rights," *Economic and Political Weekly*, Vol.25, No.22, 2 June 1990, pp.1193-1195.

Benegal, Som, "The Media in India," in NAMEDIA: *Media Conference of the Non-Aligned Movement, New Delhi: 9-12 December 1983: Final Report and Documents* (New Delhi: NAMEDIA, 1984), pp.117-122.

Bhatia, Michael V., "Fighting Words: Naming Terrorists, Bandits, Rebels and other Violent Actors," *Third World Quarterly,* Vol.26, No.1, 2006. pp.5-22.

Bidwai, Praful, "Whose Truth: Indian Media in the Global Village," *Humanscape,* December 1996, www.indiawatch.org.

————, "Seeking a Paradigm Shift," *Frontline,* Vol.15, No.8, 11-24 April 1998.

————, "For a Citizen's Movement," *Frontline,* Vol.15, No.13, 20 June – 3 July 1998, pp.77-80.

————, "Mushroom Cloud of Unreason," *Economic and Political Weekly,* Vol.35, No.14, 1-7 April 2000, pp.1134-1136.

Boaz, Cynthia, "War and Foreign Policy Framing in International Media," *Peace Review,* Vol.17, No.4, October-December 2005, pp.349-356.

Booth, Ken, "Security and Self: Reflections of a Fallen Realist," in Keith Krause and Michael C. Williams (eds.), *Critical Security Studies: Concepts and Cases* (London: UCL Press, 1997).

Bracken, Paul, "Asia's Militaries and the New Nuclear Age," *Current History,* Vol.98, No.632, December 1999, pp.415-421.

Brown, Seyom, "World Interests and the Changing Dimensions of Security," in Michael T. Klare and Yogesh Chandrani (eds.), *World Security: Challenges for a New Century* (New York: St Martin's, 1998), pp.1-17.

Buzan, Barry, "New Patterns of Global Security in the Twenty First Century," *International Affairs,* Vol.67, No.3, July 1991, pp. 431-452.

————, "The Timeless Wisdom of Realism," in Steve Smith, Ken Booth and Marysia Zalewski (eds.),

*International Theory: Positivism and Beyond* (Cambridge: Cambridge University Press, 1996), pp.47-65.

————, "South Asia Moving Towards Transformation: Emergence of India as a Great Power," *International Studies,* Vol. 39. No.1, January-March 2002, pp.1-24.

Chenoy, Anuradha M., "Bringing Gender into National Security and International Relations," *International Studies,* Vol.37, No.1, January-March 2000, pp.17-29.

Cohen, Bernard C., "Foreign Policy-Makers and the Press," in Andrew Scott and Raymond Dawson (eds.), *Readings on the Making of American Foreign Policy* (New York: Macmillan, 1966).

Cortright, David and Amitabh Mattoo, "Indian Public Opinion and Nuclear Weapons Policy," in David Cortright and Amitabh Mattoo (eds.), *India and the Bomb: Public Opinion and Nuclear Options* (Notre Dame: University of Notre Dame Press, 1996), pp.1-22.

Dalby, Simon, "Security, Modernity, Ecology: The Dilemmas of Post-Cold War Security Discourse," *Alternatives,* Vol.17, No.1, Winter 1992, pp. 95-134.

Das, Runa, "Broadening the Security Paradigm: A Note on the Tension between the Realist and Anti-Proliferation Lobbies in India," *The Indian Journal of Political Science, Vol.62,* No.2, June 2001, pp.253-263.

Diene, Doudou, "UNESCO and Communications in the Modern World," *Journal of International Affairs,* Vol.35, No.1, Spring/Summer 1981, pp.217-224.

Dreze, Jean, "Militarism, Development and

Democracy," *Economic and Political Weekly*, Vol.35, No.14, 1 April 2000, pp.1171-1183.

———— , "Hunger, Malnutrition and the Media," Interview in www.thehoot.org.

Dutt, Bharka, "Media as a Tool of the Nation State," paper presented at the South Asian Media Conference, Islamabad, 1-2 July 2000, www.jang-group.com.

Fernandes, George, "National Security and the Role of the Media," *Mainstream*, Vol.36, No.36, 29 August 1998, pp.11-15.

Gadekar, Surendra, "Buddha is Sick of Smiling," *Anumukti*, 12 May 1998.

Gan, Barry L., "Pressed into War," *Peace Review*, Vol.17, No.4, 2005, pp.341-348.

Ghosh-Dastidar, P., "Pakistani Reporting on India," *Foreign Affairs Reports*, Vol.12, No.11, November 1963, pp.93-100.

Hagerty, Devin T., "India's Regional Security Doctrine," *Asian Survey*, Vol.31, No.4, April 1991, pp.352-372.

Halloran, James D., "Mass Communication Research: Asking the Right Questions," in Anders Hansen, Simon Cottle, Ralph Negrine and Chris Newbold (eds.), *Mass Communication Research Methods* (Basingstoke: Macmillan, 1998), pp. 9-34.

Haque, Nadeem ul and Arif Sheikh, "Concerns of Intelligentsia in Pakistan: Content Analysis of Newspapers," *Economic and Political Weekly*, Vol.29, No.24, 11 June 1994, pp.1182-1186.

Hensman, Rohini, *Forging a Nuclear Strategy for the Anti-Nuclear Movement in India and Pakistan*, www.mnet.fr.

Hindel, Keith, "The Influence of the Media on Foreign Policy," *International Relations*, Vol.12, No.4, April 1995, pp.73-84.

Holm, Hans-Henrik, "Failing Failed States: Who Forgets the Forgotten?" *Security Dialogue*, Vol. 33, No.4, December 2002, pp.457-471.

Hoogensen, Gunheild and Svein Vigeland Rotten, "Gender, Identity and the Subject of Security," *Security Dialogue*, Vol. 35, No.2, June 2004, pp. 155-172.

Hurrell, Andrew, "Security in Latin America," *International Affairs*, Vol. 74, No.3, July 1998, pp.529-546.

Huysmans, Jef, "Defining Social Constructivism in Security Studies: The Normative Dilemma of Writing Security," *Alternatives*, Vol.27, No.1, January-March 2002, pp.41- 62.

Indian Institute of Public Opinion, "Public Opinion on India's Nuclear Device," *Blue Supplement to the Monthly Public Opinion Surveys*, Vol.19, No.9, June 1974, p.i-xvi.

————, *Monthly Public Opinion Surveys*, Vol.26, No.10, July 1981, pp.7-8.

Jayaraman, T., "Beyond the Euphoria," *Frontline*, Vol.15, No.11, 23 May-5 June 1998.

————, "Of Science and Nuclear Weapons: A Scientist's Perspective (From India)," paper presented at Delhi Convention Against Nuclear Weapons, 9 June 1998, www.mnet.fr.

————, "Indian Science after Pokhran-II," *Seminar*, No.468, August 1998, pp.60-64.

Joeck, Neil, "Nuclear Developments in India and

Pakistan," *Access Asia Review*, Vol.2, www.nbr.org.

Johansen, Robert C., "Real Security is Democratic Security," *Alternatives*, Vol. 16, No.2, Spring 1991, pp.209-242.

————, "Building World Security: The Need for Strengthened International Institutions," in Michael T.Klare and Yogesh Chandrani (eds.), *World Security: Challenges for a New Century* (New York: St Martin's, 1998), pp.386-407.

Joseph, Teresa, "Kashmir, Human Rights and the Indian Press," *Contemporary South Asia*, Vol.9, No.1, March 2000, pp.41-55.

————, "Hoodbhoy and the Bomb," *Himal South Asian*, Vol.15, No.4, April 2002, pp.54-56.

————, "Mocking the Digital Divide," *Himal South Asian*, Vol.17, No. 1, January 2004, pp.33-35.

————, "Media in the Time of Cricket," *Meantime*, Vol.5, Issue 23, 25 March - 8 April 2004, pp.16-17.

————, "Elite Perceptions in Foreign Policy: Role of Print Media in Influencing India - Pakistan Relations 1989-1999," Review article, *Contemporary South Asia*, Vol.15, No.1, March 2006, pp.105-106.

Kamath, P.M., "Indian Security Policy: Minimal Nuclear Deterrence," *Strategic Analysis*, Vol.23, No.8, November 1999, pp.1257-1274.

Kapur, Ashok, "Pokhran II and After: Consequences of the Indian Nuclear Tests of 1998," in Amita Shastri and A. Jayaratnam Wilson, *The Post-Colonial States of South Asia: Democracy, Identity, Development and Security* (Richmond Surrey:

Curzon, 2001), pp.326-346.

Karnad, Bharat, "Introduction," in Bharat Karnad (ed.), *Future Imperilled: India's Security in the 1990s and Beyond* (New Delhi: Viking, 1994), pp.1-15.

Khan, Feroz Hassan, "Nuclear Command and Control in South Asia During Peace, Crisis and War," *Contemporary South Asia*, Vol.14, No.2, June 2005, pp.163-174.

Khattak, Saba Gul, "Security Discourses and the State in Pakistan," *Alternatives*, Vol.21, No.3, July-September 1996, pp.341-362.

"Khetolai Declaration," *Frontline*, Vol.15, No.14, 4-17 July 1998.

Knudsen, Olav F., "Post-Copenhagen Security Studies: Desecuritizing Securitization," *Security Dialogue*, Vol.32, No.3, September 2001, pp.355-368.

Krause, Keith, "Critical Theory and Security Studies," *YCISS Occasional Paper* 33, 1996.

Kumar, Sushil, "Rethinking Security in South Asia," *International Studies*, Vol.36, No.2, April-June 1999, pp.91-110.

Lal, C.K., "Conformist Minds of India," *Himal South Asian*, July 2001, www.himalmag.com.

Manchanda, Rita, "Media Wages Info War," *Himal South Asian*, January 2000, www.himalmag.com.

————, *Reporting Conflict: A Radical Critique of the Mass Media, SAFHR Paper Series 9*, May 2001, www.safhr.org.

————, "Redefining and Feminising Security," *Economic and Political Weekly*, Vol. 36, No.22, 2 June 2001, pp.1956-1963.

————, "Dialects on Power: New Recipe for Border Security in South Asia," *Economic and Political*

*Weekly*, Vol.36, No.31, 4 August 2001, pp.2981-2983.

————, "Redefining and Feminising Security: Making a Difference in Security Policies," *Economic and Political Weekly*, Vol.36, No.43, 27 October 2001, pp.4100-4107.

————, "Militarised Hindu Nationalism and the Mass Media," SAFHR Paper 11 (Kathmandu: SAFHR, May 2002).

McChesney, Robert W., "Journalism, Democracy, ... and Class Struggle," *Monthly Review*, Vol. 52, No.6, November 2000, pp.1-15.

McSweeny, Bill, "Identity and Security: Buzan and the Copenhagen School," *Review of International Studies*, Vol.22, No.1, 1996.

Mishra, Rajesh Kumar, "Closure of the Pakistan-based A.Q.Khan Network Case: A Hasty Burial?," *Strategic Analysis*, Vol.30, No.2, April-June 2006.

Mughan, Anthony and Richard Gunther, "The Media in Democratic and Nondemocratic Regimes: A Multilevel Perspective," in Richard Gunther and Anthony Mughan (eds.), *Democracy and the Media: A Comparative Perspective* (Cambridge: Cambridge University Press, 2000), pp.1-27.

Mustafa, Zubeida, "Pakistan-India Relations: The Media in Pakistan," *Pakistan Horizon*, Vol.57, No.3, July 2004, pp.55-66.

Namboodiri, P.K.S, "Perceptions and Policies in India and Pakistan," in K. Subhramanyam (ed.), *India and the Nuclear Challenge* (New Delhi: Lancer, 1986).

Nandy, Ashis, "The Bomb, the NPT and Indian Elites," *Economic and Political Weekly*, Vol.7, Nos. 31, 32, 33, Special issue, August 1972, pp.1533-1540.

Navlakha, Gautam, "Reinforcing Insecurity," *Economic and Political Weekly*, Vol.34, No.39, 25 September 1999, pp.2782-2783.

——————, "ISI: The Ubiquitous Enemy," *Economic and Political Weekly,* Vol.34, No. 51, 18 December 1999, pp.3570-3571.

——————, "Downsizing 'National' Security," *Economic and Political Weekly*, Vol.35, No.20, 13 May 2000, pp.1710-1713.

——————, "Whither People's Security," *Economic and Political Weekly*, Vol.36, No.23, 9 June 2001, pp.2038-2043.

——————, "Security Policy: Enemy of Democracy," *Economic and Political Weekly,* 17 August 2002, www.epw.org.

——————, "Securing India: Treating Unlikely as Likely," *Economic and Political Weekly*, 18 September 2004, www.epw.org

——————, "Shrinking Horizon of an Expanding Enemy: India's Military Spending," *Economic and Political Weekly*, 8 April 2006, p.1340, www.epw.org.

Newbill, Michael, "English Media Commentary in India and Pakistan on Confidence-Building Measures, 1990-1997," in Michael Krepon, Khurshid Khoja, Michael Newbill and Jenny S.Drezin (eds.), *A Handbook of Confidence-Building Measures for Regional Security* (Washington DC.: The Henry L. Stimson Center, 1998), pp.151-188.

Nizamani, Haider K., "Limits of Dissent: A Comparative Study of Dissident Voices in the Nuclear Discourse of Pakistan and India," *Contemporary South Asia,* Vol.7, No.3, November 1998, pp.317-337.

Noorani, A.G., "The Media: Politics, Ethics and the Law," *Economic and Political Weekly,* 11 February 2006, www.epw.org.

Ottosen, Rune, "Enemy Images and the Journalistic Process," *Journal of Peace Research,* Vol.32, No.1, 1995, pp. 97-112.

Page, Benjamin I., "The Mass Media as Political Actors," *Political Science and Politics,* March 1996, pp.20-24.

Pande, Savita, "Nuclear Weapons-Free Zone in South Asia," *Strategic Analysis,* Vol.22, No.11, pp.1681-1693.

Paranjpe, Shrikant, "India's Security Policy: An Evaluation After Fifty Years," *International Studies,* Vol.35, No.2, April-June 1998, pp.139-166.

Pasha, Mustapha Kamal, "Security as Hegemony," *Alternatives,* Vol.21, No.3, July-September 1996, pp.283-302.

Peteet, Julie, "Words as Interventions: Naming in the Palestine-Israel Conflict," *Third World Quarterly,* Vol.26, No.1, 2006, pp.153-172.

Pettiford, Lloyd, "Changing Conceptions of Security in the Third World," *Third World Quarterly,* Vol. 17, No.2, June 1996, pp.289-306.

Pillai, K.Raman, "Jana Sangh: A Rightist Opposition," in Verinder Grover (ed.), *Political System in India,* Vol.V (New Delhi: Deep and Deep, 1989), pp.217-233.

Quester, George H., "India Contemplates the Bomb," in DAE, *Nuclear Weapons: A Compilation Prepared by the DAE, 1970,* pp.220-235.

Raju, Sripada K.S., S.K.Jagadeswari and Wimal

Dissanayake, "Treating the Indo-Pakistan Conflict: The Role of Indian Newspapers and Magazines," in Andrew Arno and Wimal Dissanayake (eds.), *The News Media in National and International Conflict* (Boulder: Westview, 1984), pp.101-132.

Ramana, M.V., "Do Nuclear Weapons Provide Security?," *Seminar,* No.468, August 1998, pp.50-54.

————, "South Asian Mode of Weaponisation," *Economic and Political Weekly,* Vol.25, No. 11, 11-17 March 2000, pp.896- 897.

————, "La Trahison Des Clercs," in M.V.Ramana and C. Rammanohar Reddy, *Prisoners of the Nuclear Dream* (New Delhi: Orient Longman, 2003), pp.206-244.

————, "Subverting Education," *The Daily Times,* 14 August 2003.

Rao, N. Bhaskara, "Foreign Participation in Media," *Economic and Political Weekly,* Vol. 37, No.2, 12 January 2002, p.105.

Reddy, B.Muralidhar, "Reporting on the 'Enemy'," www.thehoot.org.

————, "Indian Media: Toeing the Government Line on Pakistan?," www.thehoot.org.

Robinson, Piers, "The Policy-Media Interaction Model: Measuring Media Power During Humanitarian Crisis," *Journal of Peace Research,* Vol.37, No.5, September 2000, pp.613-633.

Roy, Arundhati, "The End of Imagination," *Frontline,* Vol.15, No.16, 1-14 August 1998.

Samaddar, Ranabir, "The Failed Dialectic of Territoriality and Security, and the Imperatives of Dialogue," *International Studies*, Vol.35, No.1, January-March 1998, pp.107-122.

Sehgal, Ikram, "Regional Conflicts and the Media," paper presented at the South Asian Media Conference, Islamabad,1-2 July 2000, www.jang-group.com.

Sen, Amartya, "India and the Bomb," in M.V.Ramana and C.Rammanohar Reddy (eds.), *Prisoners of the Nuclear Dream* (New Delhi: Orient Longman, 2003), pp.167-188.

Seshu, Geeta, "Media and Kargil: Information Blitz with Dummy Missiles," *Economic and Political Weekly*, Vol.34, No.41, 9 October 1999, pp.2917-2919.

Seethi, K.M., "India's CTBT Policy: From 'Text' to 'Testing Times'," in Harshe, Rajen and K.M. Seethi (eds.), *Engaging with the World: Critical Reflections on India's Foreign Policy* (New Delhi: Orient Longman, 2005), pp.102-122.

Sethi, Manpreet, "Dangers from Weapons of Mass Destruction: Any Different in South Asia?," *Strategic Analysis*, Vol.24, No.11, February 2001, pp.1989-1903.

Shaikh, Farzana, "Pakistan's Nuclear Bomb: Beyond the Non-Proliferation Regime," *International Affairs*, Vol.78, No.1, January 2002, pp.29-48.

Sharma, Kalpana, "The Hindu Bomb," *The Bulletin of Atomic Scientists*, Vol.14, No.4, July-August 1998, www.bullatomsci.org.

Singh, Suneet Vir, "A Regional Communication Policy for South Asia," in Bhabani Sen Gupta (ed.), *Regional Cooperation and Development in South Asia*, Vol.1 (New Delhi: South Asian Publishers, 1986) pp.70-102.

Sinha, Dipankar, "Kargil Episode in Bengali Print Media," *Economic and Political Weekly,* Vol. 37, No.27, 6 July 2002, www.epw.org.

Somavia, Juan, "The Transnational Power Structure and International Information: Elements of a Third World Policy for Transnational News Agencies," *Development Dialogue,* No.2, 1976, pp.15-28.

Sorensen, Georg, "Individual Security and National Security: The State Remains the Principal Problem," *Security Dialogue,* Vol.27, No.4, December 1996, pp. 371-386.

Subrahmanyam, K., "India's Problems of Security: In Retrospect and Prospect," *South Asian Studies,* Vol.4, No.2, July 1969, pp.43-75.

————, "The Path to Nuclear Capability," in DAE, *Nuclear Weapons: A Compilation Prepared by the DAE, 1970,* pp.188-200.

————, "Nuclear India in Global Politics," *World Affairs*, Vol.2, No.3, July-Sept 1998, pp.26-39.

Suhrke, Astri, "Human Security and the Interests of States," *Security Dialogue,* Vol.30, No.3, September 1999, pp.265-276.

Swamy, Subramaniam, "India's Nuclear Strategy in the 1970s," in DAE, *Nuclear Weapons: A Compilation Prepared by the DAE, 1970,* pp.201-219.

Swatuk, Larry A. and Peter Vale, "Why Democracy is Not Enough: Southern Africa and Human Security in the Twenty-First Century," *Alternatives,* Vol.24, No. 3, July-September 1999, pp.361-390.

Thomas, Caroline, "Third World Security," in Roger Carey and Trevor C.Salmon (eds.), *International Security in the Modern World* (Basingstoke: Macmillan, 1996), pp.90-114.

————, "Global Governance, Development and Human Security: Exploring the Links," *Third World Quarterly*, Vol.22, No.2, April 2001, pp.159-176.

Thomas, Raju G.C., "The Growth of Indian Military Power: From Sufficient Defence to Nuclear Deterrence," in Ross Babbage and Sandy Gordon (eds.), *India's Strategic Future: Regional State or Global Power?* (Delhi: Oxford University Press, 1992), pp.35-66.

Thompson, John B., "Mass Communication and Modern Culture: Contribution to a Criiical Theory of Ideology," in Oliver Boyd–Barrett and Chris Newbold (eds.), *Approaches to Media: A Reader* (London: Arnold, 1995), pp.54-65.

Timothy, Kristen, "Human Security Discourse at the UN," *Peace Review*, Vol.16,. No.1, March 2004, pp.19-24.

Tickner, J.Ann, "Re-visioning Security," in Ken Booth and Steve Smith (eds.), *International Relations Theory Today* (University Park: The Pennsylvania State University Press, 1995), pp.175-197.

————, "Feminist Responses to International Security Studies," *Peace Review*, Vol.16, No.1, March 2004, pp.43-48.

Vanaik, Achin, "Nuclear Insecurity in the Indian Subcontinent: An Uneasy Truce," *Bulletin of Peace Proposals*, Vol.20, No.4, December 1989, pp.389-398.

————, "Three Misrepresentations," *Economic and Political Weekly*, Vol.32, No.36, 6 September 1997, pp.2234-2236.

————, "Mindset of the Nuclear Strategist,"

*Economic and Political Weekly*, Vol.37, No.21, 25 May 2001, pp.1194-1196.

Vayrynen, Raimo, "Environmental Security and Conflicts: Concepts and Policies," *International Studies*, Vol.35, No.1, January-March 1998, pp.3-21.

Waever, Ole, "Securitization and Desecuritization," in Ronnie Lipschutz, (ed.), *On Security* (New York: Columbia University Press, 1995), pp.46-86.

Walker, R.B.J., "Security, Sovereignty, and the Challenge of World Politics," *Alternatives*, Vol. 15. No.1, Winter 1990, pp.3-28.

Waltz, Kenneth N., "The Spread of Nuclear Weapons: More May be Better," *Adelphi Papers*, No.171, Autumn 1981.

————, "The Origin of War in Neorealist Theory," *Journal of Interdisciplinary History*, 18, 1988, pp. 615-628.

————, "Realist Thought and Neorealist Theory," *Journal of International Affairs*, Vol.44, No.1, 1991, pp.21-37.

Wilkin, Peter, "Global Poverty and Orthodox Security," *Third World Quarterly*, Vol.23, No.4, August 2002, pp.633-645.

## Journals and Newspapers

*Access Asia Review* (Seattle)

*Adelphi Papers* (Oxford)

*Alternatives* (Boulder)

*Anumukti* (Vedchhi)

*Armed Forces and Society* (New Brunswick, New Jersey)

*Arms Control Today* (Washington DC)

*Asian Age* (Mumbai)
*Asian Recorder* (New Delhi)
*Asian Survey* (Berkeley)
*Boston Review* (Cambridge, Mass.)
*Bulletin of Atomic Scientists* (Chicago)
*Bulletin of Peace Proposals* (Oslo)
*Contemporary South Asia* (Abingdon)
*Current History* (Philadelphia)
*Dawn* (Karachi)
*Development Dialogue* (Uppsala)
*Disarmament Diplomacy* (London)
*Economic and Political Weekly* (Mumbai)
*Far Eastern Economic Review* (Hong Kong)
*Frontline* (Chennai)
*Guardian* (London)
*Himal South Asian* (Kathmandu)
*India Today* (New Delhi)
*Indian Defence Review* (New Delhi)
*International Affairs* (Oxford)
*International Organization* (Cambridge, Mass.)
*International Relations* (London)
*International Studies* (New Delhi)
*Journal of Communication* (Cary, North Carolina)
*Journal of Conflict Resolution* (Thousand Oaks)
*Journal of Interdisciplinary History* (Cambridge, Mass.)
*Journal of International Affairs* (New York)
*Journal of Peace Research* (London)
*Keesings Record of World Events* (Cambridge)

*Mainstream* (New Delhi)
*Meantime* (Calicut)
*Media Asia* (Singapore)
*Monthly Review* (New York)
*Nuclear India* (Mumbai)
*Organiser* (New Delhi)
*Outlook* (New Delhi)
*Pakistan Horizon* (Karachi)
*Pakistan Quarterly* (Karachi)
*Patriot* (New Delhi)
*Peace Review* (Philadelphia)
*Political Science and Politics* (Washington DC)
*RCSS Policy Studies* (Colombo)
*Review of International Studies* (Cambridge)
*Security Dialogue* (London)
*Seminar* (New Delhi)
*South Asian Studies* (London)
*Strategic Analysis* (New Delhi)
*Strategic Digest* (New Delhi)
*Sunday Observer* (New Delhi)
*The Daily Times* (Lahore)
*The Hindu* (Thiruvananthapuram)
*The Hindustan Times* (New Delhi)
*The Indian Express* (Kochi)
*The New York Times* (New York)
*The Pioneer* (New Delhi)
*The Statesman* (New Delhi)
*The Telegraph* (Calcutta)

*The Times of India* (Mumbai)

*The Tribune* (Chandigarh)

*The Washington Post* (Washington DC)

*Third World Quarterly* (Abingdon)

*UNESCO Courier* (Paris)

*World Affairs* (New Delhi)

*World Politics* (Baltimore)

*YCISS Occasional Papers* (York)

# Index

## D